SHAKESPEARE'S IMAGINARY CONSTITUTION

Through an examination of six plays by Shakespeare, the author presents an innovative analysis of political developments in the last decade of Elizabethan rule and their representation in poetic drama of the period. The playhouses of London in the 1590s provided a distinctive forum for discourse and dissemination of nascent political ideas. Shakespeare exploited the unique capacity of theatre to humanise contemporary debate concerning the powers of the Crown and the extent to which these were limited by law. The autonomous subject of law is represented in the plays considered here as a sentient political being whose natural rights and liberties found an analogue in the narratives of common law, as recorded in juristic texts and law reports of the early modern era. Each chapter reflects a particular aspect of constitutional development in the late-Elizabethan State. These include abuse of the Royal Prerogative by the Crown and its agents; the emergence of a politicised middle-class citizenry, empowered by the ascendancy of contract law; the limitations imposed by the courts on the lawful extent of divinely ordained kingship; the natural and rational authority of unwritten *lex terrae*; the poetic imagination of the judiciary and its role in shaping the constitution; and the fusion of temporal and spiritual jurisdiction in the person of the monarch. The book advances original insights into the complex and agonistic relationship between theatre, politics and law. The plays discussed offer persuasive images both of the Crown's absolutist tendencies and of alternative polities predicated upon classical and humanist principles of justice, equity and community.

Shakespeare's Imaginary Constitution
Late-Elizabethan Politics and the Theatre of Law

PAUL RAFFIELD

OXFORD AND PORTLAND, OREGON
2010

Published in the United Kingdom by Hart Publishing Ltd
16C Worcester Place, Oxford, OX1 2JW
Telephone: +44 (0)1865 517530
Fax: +44 (0)1865 510710
E-mail: mail@hartpub.co.uk
Website: http://www.hartpub.co.uk

Published in North America (US and Canada) by
Hart Publishing
c/o International Specialized Book Services
920 NE 58th Avenue, Suite 300
Portland, OR 97213-3786
USA
Tel: +1 503 287 3093 or toll-free: (1) 800 944 6190
Fax: +1 503 280 8832
E-mail: orders@isbs.com
Website: http://www.isbs.com

© Paul Raffield 2010

Paul Raffield has asserted his right under the Copyright, Designs and Patents Act 1988,
to be identified as the author of this work.

All rights reserved. No part of this publication may be reproduced, stored in a retrieval system, or transmitted, in any form or by any means, without the prior permission of Hart Publishing, or as expressly permitted by law or under the terms agreed with the appropriate reprographic rights organisation. Enquiries concerning reproduction which may not be covered by the above should be addressed to Hart Publishing Ltd at the address above.

British Library Cataloguing in Publication Data
Data Available

ISBN: 978-1-84113-921-0

Typeset by Hope Services, Abingdon
Printed and bound in Great Britain by
TJ International Ltd, Padstow, Cornwall

To my mother, Vyvyan, with love

PREFACE

When I was a law student I joined one of the Inns of Court, intent upon a career as a barrister. Dining at Gray's Inn, I started to learn about the entangled histories of law and theatre. After graduating, I jumped ship. I trained and earned a living as an actor, and so began my professional association with the plays of Shakespeare. From my first appearance in a Shakespearean production, as the Officer in *The Comedy of Errors* at Nottingham Playhouse (at the first preview I also played a nun, but that's a story for another book), to my current engagement with Shakespearean scholarship, I have been fascinated at the impact his plays have made on the intellect, the emotions and the imagination. For many years, though, I thought that my twin interests in Shakespeare and the law would run parallel to each other, never to converge. Then I returned to the study of law. Things had moved on since my undergraduate days. At Birkbeck I embarked on a doctoral thesis, examining the culture of the legal community at the early modern Inns of Court, and in particular the use of drama to embody emerging ideas and debates surrounding Crown, common law and constitution. Shakespeare was incidental to the project, although as a member of Gray's Inn I could not have overlooked the infamous performance there in December 1594 of *The Comedy of Errors*.

I arrived at Warwick in 2004 and there I have remained. Stratford-upon-Avon is just down the road and what remains of the Forest of Arden is all around. Was this a sign? The law school at Warwick has been renowned since its foundation for the strong emphasis it places on the study of law in context, and I was encouraged to apply my knowledge and experience of law and theatre to the development of interdisciplinary projects, both in research and teaching. In 2007 I co-organised an international conference on Shakespeare and the Law, hosted by Warwick law school. And that was the start. Galvanised by the enthusiastic response of colleagues and scholars from a wide range of academic disciplines, the book developed from a conference paper (on *Titus Andronicus* and the abuse of executive power) to its present form. The undergraduate courses which I teach have contributed significantly to the formulation of ideas for this book. 'Origins, Images and Cultures of English Law' examines the foundations of common law and constitution in the immemorial myths of nationhood, as propounded by the patriarchs of English law: Sir John Fortescue, Sir Edward Coke *et al.* The relevance of 'Shakespeare and the Law' is obvious. Tort may seem a less conspicuous source of inspiration, but the dramatic narratives of its case law incorporate levels of human suffering and political dilemmas that are Shakespearean in their scope. It

Preface

is appropriate, therefore, that my first acknowledgment is to my undergraduate students, past and present. Their intelligence, curiosity and humanity have added immeasurably to my understanding of matters both legal and Shakespearean.

It is difficult to be certain about when the idea for the book was planted, but evenings spent teaching 'Law and Literature' at Birkbeck were seminal. That they were productive and enjoyable is largely due to the other teachers on the course: Costas Douzinas, Adam Gearey and Piyel Haldar. It was at Birkbeck that I got to know Peter Goodrich. Now based on the other side of the Atlantic, Peter remains a valued colleague and friend. I am grateful to him for his scholarship, support and generosity of spirit. At Warwick law school I must thank Gary Watt for his enthusiastic encouragement and for sharing my interest in Law and Literature. Gary and I co-organised the 2007 conference on Shakespeare and the Law. Together we founded and edit the journal *Law and Humanities*. Our teaching interests reflect belief that the study of literature and the arts is a crucial feature of a humane legal education. My thanks are due to Hugh Beale for his comments on chapter two, John Snape for his observations on chapter five, Alan Norrie for reading drafts of chapters one and two, Lee Bridges for his love of theatre, and John McEldowney for our many informal discussions on literature and constitutional history. In the Department of English I am indebted to Carol Rutter for her remarks on chapter one. Carol is a true Shakespearean and an extraordinary teacher. It was her idea that we should jointly teach a course on Shakespeare and the Law, available to English students and Law students . . . so we did. Beyond Warwick, I owe thanks to Andrew Hadfield for his helpful suggestions on chapter five, to Kenji Yoshino for his perceptive insights into Shakespeare and the representation of justice, and to Emily Jackson for her inspiration by example. I must again thank Ian Ward for the keen encouragement he has offered another of my literary ventures. Richard Hart and his team at Hart Publishing have been unstinting in their support throughout this project: I couldn't wish for a more sympathetic publisher. Going further back, I shall always be appreciative of David Conville and the New Shakespeare Company for giving me my break in Shakespeare. Simon Potter, my English teacher at Wimbledon College, awakened generations of students to the genius of Shakespeare. His example has been a constant factor in my career.

I am grateful to The University of Warwick for granting me two consecutive terms of study leave in which to complete this book. The second term of leave was financed by a generous research award from the Arts & Humanities Research Council. Finally, my lasting thanks go to the actors and directors with whom I worked in so many productions. The path I set out on is not the one on which I have ended up, but some of the happiest and most productive times of my life were spent in performance, in rehearsal rooms and backstage in theatres. My career as an actor informs many of the ideas on community, friendship and society which I discuss in this book.

Paul Raffield
Spring 2010

ACKNOWLEDGEMENTS

The introduction and conclusion include brief extracts from an article in 31(4) *Cardozo Law Review* (2010); a version of chapter one was published in P Raffield and G Watt (eds), *Shakespeare and the Law* (Oxford, Hart Publishing, 2008); part of chapter two was published in 3(2) *Law and Humanities* (2009); the final section of chapter two was included in an article in 17(1) *Law & Literature* (2005); a shorter version of chapter five was published in 22(1) *Law & Literature* (2010). I am grateful to the publishers and editors of the above publications for permission to publish here.

I am pleased to acknowledge the generous financial support of the Arts and Humanities Research Council.

SUMMARY CONTENTS

Preface	vii
Acknowledgements	ix
List of illustrations	xv
Introduction	1
1 '*Terras Astraea reliquit*': *Titus Andronicus* and the Flight of Justice	18
2 *The Comedy of Errors* and the Meaning of Contract	51
3 Reflections on the Art of Kingship: *Richard II* and the Subject of Law	82
4 The Poetic Imagination, Antique Fables and the Dream of Law	117
5 The Ancient Constitution, Common Law and the Idyll of Albion: Law and Lawyers in *Henry IV, Parts 1 and 2*	153
6 The Congregation of the Mighty: the Juridical State and the Measure of Justice	182
Conclusion	218
Bibliography	223
Index	245

CONTENTS

Preface vii
Acknowledgements ix
List of Illustrations xv

Introduction 1

1 '*Terras Astraea reliquit*': *Titus Andronicus* and the Flight of Justice 18
    I. Law, Justice and the Exercise of Executive Power 18
    II. Late-Elizabethan Imperial Government and the Common Law 23
    III. Order, Harmony and Musicality 29
    IV. The Depiction of Troynovant 33
    V. Ritual, Religion and the Culture of Signs 37
    VI. Sacrifice, Tradition and Unwritten Law 42

2 *The Comedy of Errors* and the Meaning of Contract 51
    I. Errors and Confusion, Disorder and Tumult 51
    II. The Promise: 'Dictum Meum Pactum'? 55
    III. The Chain: Symbol of Commerce, Love and Law 59
    IV. Consideration, Conscience and the Gray's Inn Revels, 1594 65
    V. Breaking the Bonds of Servitude: Trade, Markets and the Law 73

3 Reflections on the Art of Kingship: *Richard II* and the Subject of Law 82
    I. 'Landlord of England' or 'deputy elected by the Lord'? 82
    II. *The Commentaries or Reports* of Plowden: Land and the Sacred Body of Law 88
    III. Through a Glass, Darkly: Treason, Law and the Discovery of Self 101
    IV. Theatre, Mimesis and the Counterfeiting of Monarchy 112

4 The Poetic Imagination, Antique Fables and the Dream of Law 117
    I. Festival, Subversion and Misrule 117
    II. Satyrs, Fairies and the Oneiric Imagination 126
    III. Violence on the Edge 133
    IV. A Most Rare Vision 145

5 The Ancient Constitution, Common Law and the Idyll of Albion: Law and Lawyers in *Henry IV, Parts 1 and 2* 153

I.	Kill *All* The Lawyers?	153
II.	Common Lawyers and the Pastoral Idyll	159
III.	The Education of a Prince and 'the rusty curb of old Father Antic the law'	173
IV.	Patriarchal Symbolism and the Common Law	178

6 The Congregation of the Mighty: the Juridical State and the Measure of Justice — 182

I.	Prerogative Power and the Impression of Legitimacy	182
II.	The Divine Lawgiver and the Eye of the Law	191
III.	Religion, Conscience and Conflicts of Jurisdiction	204

Conclusion — 218
Bibliography — 223
Index — 245

LIST OF ILLUSTRATIONS

Plate section between pages 110 and 111

1 Richard II presented to the Virgin and Child by his Patron Saint John the Baptist and Saints Edward and Edmund. 'The Wilton Diptych' (c 1395–99). Unknown artist. © The National Gallery, London.
2 Infra-red detail of orb (right interior panel). 'The Wilton Diptych' (c 1395–99). Unknown artist. © The National Gallery, London.
3 Royal arms of England and France Ancient, impaled with the arms of Edward the Confessor, surmounted by helmet with cap of maintenance and lion passant guardant (left exterior panel); white hart lying among branches of rosemary (right exterior panel). 'The Wilton Diptych' (c 1395–99). Unknown artist. © The National Gallery, London.
4 'The Coronation portrait' of Elizabeth I (c 1600, copy of lost original, c 1559). Unknown artist. © National Portrait Gallery, London.
5 Portrait of Richard II, wood panel painting (c 1395). Unknown artist. © Dean and Chapter of Westminster.
6 Anonymous, *Robin Good-Fellow, His Mad Prankes, and merry Iests, Full of honest Mirth, and is a fit Medicine for Melancholy* (London, F Grove, 1628) Title-page. This item is reproduced by permission of the Huntington Library, San Marino, California.
7 Monument to Sir John Fortescue (c 1397–1479), the parish church of St Eadburgha, Ebrington, Gloucestershire.

'Do I dream? Is this new feeling
But a visioned ghost of slumber?
If indeed I am a soul,
A free, a disembodied soul,
Speak again to me.'

Percy Bysshe Shelley, *Queen Mab*

Introduction

> If then the world a Theater present,
> As by the roundnesse it appeares most fit,
> Built with starre-galleries of hye ascent,
> In which *Iehove* doth as spectator sit.[1]

THESE LINES FROM *An Apology for Actors* were written by Thomas Heywood in 1612, some 12 years after Jaques' declaration that

> All the world's a stage,
> And all the men and women merely players . . .[2]

An actor and dramatist, Heywood shared with Shakespeare evident fascination with the idea of theatre as microcosm, an observation instanced in the above extract by his description of the circular shape of the playhouse and proximity of the stage to the heavens.[3] I refer throughout this book to the representational depiction of human existence in Elizabethan England. In particular, I consider the practice of politics and the enactment of government as a type of aesthetics, which in the late-Elizabethan period found a close correlation with the poetic drama of Shakespeare. As Stephen Greenblatt observed of Shakespeare's Prince Hal, the 'poetics of Elizabethan power' was indivisibly linked to 'a poetics of the theatre.'[4] Figurative art speaks directly to the visual sense, but poetry also appeals to the visual imagination by its capacity to conjure pictures into the minds of its audience. Sir Philip Sidney noted in *The Defence of Poesy* that the facility to write verse and rhyme words was not in itself the identifying feature of the poet (any more, he argued, than a long gown was the identifying feature of the advocate); rather 'it is that feigning notable images of virtues, vices or what else, with that delightful teaching, which must be the right describing note to know a poet by'.[5] Above all, the use of appropriate metaphor enables text to speak to the imagination as much

---

[1] T Heywood, *An Apology for Actors* (London, Nicholas Okes, 1612), 'The Author to his Booke'.
[2] *As You Like It* (2.7.140–41). *As You Like It* was entered in the Stationers' Register on 4 August 1600.
[3] The 'starre-galleries' refer not only to the sky but to the 'heavens': a protective cover that extended over the stage of the Elizabethan playhouse, supported by pillars and painted on the underside with stars. On the design of Elizabethan playhouses, see A Gurr, *The Shakespearean Stage, 1574–1642* (Cambridge, Cambridge University Press, 1992) 115–54.
[4] S Greenblatt, 'Invisible bullets: Renaissance authority and its subversion, *Henry IV* and *Henry V*' in J Dollimore and A Sinfield (eds), *Political Shakespeare: Essays in Cultural Materialism* (Manchester, Manchester University Press, 1994) 44.
[5] Sir Philip Sidney, 'The Defence of Poesy' in G Alexander (ed), *Sidney's 'The Defence of Poesy' and Selected Renaissance Literary Criticism* (London, Penguin, 2004) 12.

Introduction

as it does to the intellect. In Sidney's words, poetry is 'a speaking picture—with this end: to teach and delight'.[6]

Figurative art, in the form of royal portraiture, remained a dominant propagandist tool within the exclusive environs of the royal court during the reign of Elizabeth I. Court painters continued to depict members of the Tudor dynasty as the personification of divinely-ordained, imperial kingship.[7] Insofar as the authority of law has been linked to the affective capacity of the image to control and direct the gaze of its audience,[8] the depiction of the monarch as *Imago Dei* remained a potent rhetorical instrument. The royal portrait lent visible, tangible form to the mystical basis of the law's authority.[9] The iconic power of such portraiture notwithstanding, the audience for this particular art form was necessarily limited, restricted as it was to the royal court and its visitors. The themes addressed by the court painters were circumscribed by the conventions of the genre. Artists addressed the public interests of their royal clients and were therefore inevitably concerned with projecting images of irrefutable, providential authority.

Performance art of the early modern period also incorporated visual imagery of a type which eulogised its royal subjects, especially in the court masques of the Elizabethan and Jacobean eras.[10] But in the playhouses of late-Elizabethan

---

[6] *Ibid* at 10.

[7] See, eg, the large portrait of Elizabeth I (241 × 152cm) by Marcus Gheeraerts the Younger (*c* 1592, National Portrait Gallery), in which the Queen floats over a map of England, thunderous skies behind her and bright sunlight in front. Sir John Harington wrote of Elizabeth I: 'When she smiled, it was a pure sun-shine, that every one did chuse to bask in, if they could; but anon came a storm from a sudden gathering of clouds, and the thunder fell in wondrous manner on all alike', quoted in C S Smith, *The National Portrait Gallery* (London, National Portrait Gallery, 2000) 46. See also 'The Coronation portrait' (*c* 1600, copy of lost original, *c* 1559, National Portrait Gallery), ch 3, fig 4, below. On portraits of Elizabeth I, see S Doran, 'Virginity, Divinity and Power: The Portraits of Elizabeth I' in T F Freeman and S Doran (eds), *The Myth of Elizabeth* (London, Palgrave Macmillan, 2003) 171; see also, ch 3, text to nn 128–31, below.

[8] On the capacity of the image to 'capture' the subject of law, see P Goodrich, *Languages of Law: From Logics of Memory to Nomadic Masks* (London, Weidenfeld & Nicolson, 1990) 260–96.

[9] The above sentence is derived from Montaigne's argument that 'laws remain respected not because they are just but because they are laws. That is the mystical basis of their authority', M de Montaigne, 'On Experience' in Michel de Montaigne, *The Complete Essays*, (tr) and (ed) M A Screech (London, Penguin, 2003) 1216. In the original French, the phrase reads '*fondement mystique de l'autorité*'; for a discussion of Montaigne's essay and its relevance to the foundation of the western legal tradition, see J Derrida, 'Force of Law: The "Mystical Foundations of Authority" ', (tr) M Quaintance (1990) 11 *Cardozo Law Review* 919, 937–39. For a discussion of law and the suggestive power of the image in figurative art, see C Douzinas and L Nead (eds), *Law and the Image: The Authority of Art and the Aesthetics of Law* (Chicago, University of Chicago Press, 1999); also, C Douzinas, '*Whistler v Ruskin*: Law's Fear of Images' (1996) 19 *Art History* 353; C Douzinas and R Warrington, *Justice Miscarried: Ethics, Aesthetics and the Law* (London, Harvester Wheatsheaf, 1994) 265–309.

[10] See, eg, the description of Elizabeth I as the goddess Astraea in *Certaine devises and shewes*, written and performed in 1587 by members of Gray's Inn in the presence of the Queen: 'A dame there is whom men Astrea terme, / She that pronounceth oracles of lawes', N Trotte, 'The Introduction' in T Hughes, *Certaine Devises and shewes presented to her Maiestie by the Gentlemen of Grayes-Inne at her Highnesse Court in Greenwich* (London, Robert Robinson, 1587); see also the comparison of James I to Brutus, the legendary founder of Britain, in Anthony Munday's *The Triumphes of re-united Britania*, produced by the Company of Merchant Taylors in 1605: '*Brute* thus having the whole Land in his owne quiet possession, began to build a citty neer to the side of the River *Thamesis*, in the second yeare of his raign, which he named *Troynovant*', A Mundy, *The Triumphes of re-united Britania* (London,

Introduction

London an unprecedented form of performance art was evolving, characterised especially by large public audiences and an unusually eclectic range of subject matter. The substantive theme of this book is poetic drama of the late 16th century and its capacity to embody emergent political ideas through the synthesis of aural and visual imagery. Specifically, I examine six plays of Shakespeare from the last decade of Elizabethan rule, all of which depict the psychological complexities of the autonomous subject of law in the constitutional and political context of the sovereign nation-State. Drama is an inherently discursive medium: its imperative is conflict. The existence of dialogue immediately complicates the depiction of human relationships. Of course, the meaning of any work of figurative art is determined to an extent by the subjective gaze of the viewer; but in the theatre, before its reception by an audience, the meaning of dramatic text is liable first to interpretation by the actor. Dramatic text is therefore intrinsically ambivalent. When an actor utters a line of dialogue, his character invites dispute and debate. Dialogue (or its absence) in drama is one of the means through which characters communicate with the inhabitants of 'the great globe itself',[11] but Shakespeare's poetic drama is concerned not only with the telling of stories through dialogue; it is concerned also with the dialogue of human ideas, of which dramatic text is only a part. As Shelley argued in his essay, *A Defence of Poetry*:

> The drama, so long as it continues to express poetry, is a prismatic and many-sided mirror, which collects the brightest rays of human nature and divides and reproduces them from the simplicity of their elementary forms, and touches them with majesty and beauty, and multiplies all that it reflects, and endows it with the power of propagating its like wherever it may fall.[12]

It is noteworthy that Shelley should emphasise the importance of a poetic presence in order that drama may enable the transformative process of which he speaks, whereby characters and actions become multifaceted and multidimensional. It is to a political and ethical intent that he appeals in asserting the correlation between poetry and drama, as he reveals later in the same essay: '[T]he connection of poetry and social good is more observable in the drama than in whatever other form'.[13] This statement has much in common with the assertion of Sidney, in his own *apologia* for the poetic art, that a poet is not to be recognised by his ability to versify, but rather by his imaginative representation of 'virtues' and 'vices'.[14] Both Sidney and Shelley describe an ideal coalescence of form and content, whereby the

---

W Jaggard, 1605) A3.*v*. On the masques of this period, see D Lindley (ed), *The Court Masque* (Manchester, Manchester University Press, 1984); also, D M Bergeron, *Elizabethan Civic Pageantry, 1558–1642* (London, Edward Arnold, 1971). On Elizabethan and Jacobean masques at the Inns of Court, see P Raffield, *Images and Cultures of Law in Early Modern England: Justice and Political Power, 1558–1660* (Cambridge, Cambridge University Press, 2004) 124–56.

[11] *The Tempest* (4.1.153).
[12] P B Shelley, *A Defence of Poetry* in H A Needham (ed), *Sidney, An Apology For Poetry; Shelley, A Defence of Poetry* (London, Ginn & Co, 1931) 83–84.
[13] *Ibid* at 85.
[14] See text to n 5 above.

ethic is subsumed by the aesthetic and the two become indivisible.[15] It is because of their participation in the eternal and the infinite, and their understanding and expression of humanity, that poets are described by Shelley as 'the institutors of laws, and the founders of civil society'.[16] Much the same claim was made for poets by Martha Nussbaum at the end of the 20th century. With reference to Walt Whitman's 'By Blue Ontario's Shore', Nussbaum cites the 'poet-judge' as the embodiment of equitable justice.[17] This 'equable man' is the personification of equity in law.[18]

The mention of equity in a book on the subject of late-Elizabethan politics and law obviously calls to mind the parallel system of justice administered in Shakespeare's day by the Court of Chancery, which developed and expounded a body of doctrine and rules that came to rival (and in 1616 to supersede) the jurisdictional sovereignty of the common law.[19] Although I consider the development of Equity in the formal context of the English legal institution,[20] in relation to the expression of juristic ideals in the plays of Shakespeare I share Nussbaum's broad interpretation that equity is more to do with the literary imagination than it is with legal norms and judicial reasoning. To write of the equitable principles of common law in medieval and early modern England may seem oxymoronic to lawyers and legal historians, to whom Equity and common law are rival (and at times incompatible) jurisdictions.[21] But the statement is entirely consonant with the claims made for English law by juristic commentators of the period, whose understanding of equity was founded in the Aristotelian tradition of *epieikeia* rather than in the judicial pronouncements of the Court of Chancery. When Whitman wrote of the poet that

> [h]e is no arguer, he is judgment, (Nature accepts him absolutely,)
>
> He judges not as the judge judges but as the sun falling round a helpless thing[22]

he was prolonging the tradition of an earlier generation of jurists who equated English law with natural moral authority, of immemorial provenance. In *De Laudibus Legum Angliae*, Sir John Fortescue stated that English law was 'deduced

---

[15] Writing in the vanguard of the Law and Literature movement, but in the tradition of Sidney and Shelley, Weisberg notes that 'the carefully crafted utterance (in law *and* literature) unites the message with the medium—indeed, is so constituted that the medium of linguistic expression *is* the meaning', R Weisberg, *Poethics: And Other Strategies Of Law And Literature* (New York, Columbia University Press, 1992) 4.

[16] Shelley, above n 12, at 71.

[17] M Nussbaum, *Poetic Justice: the Literary Imagination and Public Life* (Boston, Mass, Beacon Press, 1995) 80.

[18] 'Of these States the poet is the equable man': Walt Whitman, 'By Blue Ontario's Shore' in Walt Whitman, *Leaves of Grass*, (ed) J Loving (Oxford, Oxford University Press, 2009) 269.

[19] See J H Baker, 'The Common Lawyers and The Chancery: 1616' in J H Baker, *The Legal Profession and the Common Law: Historical Essays* (London, Hambledon, 1986) 205; more generally, see M Fortier, *The Culture of Equity in Early Modern England* (Aldershot, Ashgate, 2005).

[20] See ch 6, text to nn 144–67, below.

[21] See ch 1, text to n 11, below.

[22] Whitman, 'By Blue Ontario's Shore' 269.

Introduction

from the *Law of Nature*',[23] while Sir Edward Coke would later argue not only 'that the law of nature is part of the law of England,' but that it was of greater antiquity (and therefore of greater legitimacy) than 'any judicial or municipal law'.[24] It is the fictive rights guaranteed by the unwritten ancient constitution which underpin the works of Fortescue, Coke and the numerous English jurists of the early modern period whom I cite throughout this book. The literary imaginations of these lawyer-poets lent form and substance to an idealised legal system, an equitably governed realm whose subjects were, according to Fortescue, 'rich, abounding in gold and silver and all the necessaries of life'.[25] For common lawyers such as these, for whom the rationality of natural law was the basis of the political, constitutional and moral sovereignty of common law, English law was predicated upon classical ideals of *societas* and *amicitia*. The existence of community was a prerequisite for the creation of justice; conversely, the non-existence of community prefigured the absence of justice.[26] Consequently, for Fortescue and his juristic descendants (and indeed his Bractonian forebears) law was not a codified system of rules: it was the absence of codification that distinguished the common law from the civilian jurisdictions of Continental Europe. English jurisprudence was located firmly in the Anglocentric notion of custom, which had evolved to reflect the best interests of the community.[27] Paradoxically, considering the nationalist zeal with which English jurists lauded the excellence of English law, at the philosophical core of common law ideology was the unmistakable phantasm of the Roman republican maxim, *Salus Populi Suprema Lex Est*.[28] Both in *De Laudibus Legum Angliae* and *Difference Between an Absolute and Limited Monarchy* (written after *De Laudibus* in c 1471, and published in the 19th century as *The Governance of England*), Fortescue describes a benevolent and beneficent English State, whose laws are made and enforced in the best interests of English subjects. The same concern with the health of the common-weal or *res publica* finds its way into judicial reasoning, as recorded in the published law reports of the 16th and early 17th centuries and discussed throughout this book, mainly in relation to *The Commentaries or Reports* of Edmund Plowden and *The Reports* of Sir Edward Coke.

[23] Sir John Fortescue, *De Laudibus Legum Angliae*, (ed) John Selden (London, R Gosling, 1737) 29. For Aristotle's theory of the universal authority of the law of nature, see Aristotle, *The Nicomachean Ethics*, Bk V.VII.1134b18–20.

[24] *Postnati. Calvin's Case*, in Part 7 (1608) of *The Reports of Sir Edward Coke, Knt. In English*, George Wilson (ed), 7 vols (London, Rivington, 1777) 4: 1a, at 12b.

[25] Sir John Fortescue, 'The Governance of England' in Shelley Lockwood (ed), *On the Laws and Governance of England* (Cambridge, Cambridge University Press, 1997) 52.

[26] On the indivisibility of friendship, justice and community, see *The Nicomachean Ethics*, Bk VIII.I.1155a1–32.

[27] Typical is Waterhouse's eulogy on Fortescue's *De Laudibus*: '[T]here is no humane Law within the Circuit of the whole World by infinite degrees, so apt and profitable, for the honourable, peaceable, and prosperous Government of this Kingdom, as these antient and excellent Laws of England be', E Waterhous, *Fortescutus Illustratus, Or A Commentary On That Nervous Treatise De Laudibus Legum Angliae* (London, Thomas Dicas, 1663) 236.

[28] On Roman law and, more generally, classical literature as the principal source of early modern common law, see J W Tubbs, *The Common Law Mind: Medieval and Early Modern Conceptions* (Baltimore, Md, Johns Hopkins University Press, 2000).

Introduction

In his essay on Samuel Taylor Coleridge, John Stuart Mill stressed the importance of poets to a society in search of reform. He claimed that only poets possessed the necessary imaginations to envisage and describe the configuration and structure of the societal ideal. Community is central to Mill's analysis of a society whose citizens are active in the expression of their collective will to create an equitable framework, within which their political aspirations may be achieved: '[A] principle of sympathy, not of hostility; of union, not of separation'.[29] The ideal of community lay at the heart of Aristotle's ideal State, in the imagination of which he placed great stress on the microcosm. The ideal *polis* which he describes in *The Politics* and *The Nicomachean Ethics* is specifically the city-State, comprising an association of friends from which the political community is born.[30] For Aristotle, the household and the village are both precursors and representations of the State. In these societal arrangements, the inherent purpose of their formation is the achievement of 'the good life'.[31] In other words, as he emphasises at the start of *The Politics*, every State is an association or a community.[32] Its purpose is to serve the best interests of its members, each of whom is implicated in the attainment of this end through his status as a political animal (*Zoon Politikon*). Aristotle distinguishes man as a 'political animal' from other members of the animal kingdom on the basis of his power of speech and capacity to make ethical judgements. Speech alone is the facility through which, Aristotle claims, the difference between justice and injustice, and good and evil, may publicly be communicated.[33] As Alasdair Macintyre has observed, the primary means through which the Aristotelian ideal of public communication took place was in 'the telling of stories',[34] and in ancient Athens drama provided a focus and platform for the dissemination of political and philosophical ideas. Macintyre argues that modern western society lacks a 'shared communal mode' for the representation of political conflict that is in any way equivalent to Greek drama.[35] One of my principal arguments throughout this book is that the

---

[29] J S Mill, 'Coleridge' in J S Mill and J Bentham, *Utilitarianism and Other Essays*, (ed) A Ryan (London, Penguin, 2004) 195; Mill's essay is discussed with reference to the plays of Shakespeare in I Ward, *Shakespeare and the Legal Imagination* (London, Butterworths, 1999) 140.
[30] Aristotle, *The Nicomachean Ethics*, Bk VIII.IX.1159b25–1160a30.
[31] Aristotle, *The Politics*, Bk I.II.1252a34–1253a1.
[32] *Ibid*, Bk I.I.1252a1.
[33] *Ibid*, Bk I.II.1253a1–1253a18. Acknowledging his debt to Aristotle, Weisberg devised the neologism 'Poethics', the purpose of which he claims is to 'fill the ethical void in which legal thought and practice now exist', Weisberg, above n 15, at 4.
[34] A Macintyre, *After Virtue: a Study in Moral Theory* (London, Duckworth, 1981) 114. In a seminal essay on Law and Literature, Cover argues that '[i]n this normative world, law and narrative are inseparably related. Every prescription is insistent in its demand to be located in discourse—to be supplied with history and destiny, beginning and end, explanation and purpose', R M Cover, 'The Supreme Court, 1982 Term—Foreword: *Nomos* and Narrative' (1983) 97 *Harvard Law Review* 4, 5.
[35] Macintyre, *After Virtue*, above n 34, at 130. It is not within the scope of this book to challenge Macintyre's assertion, although the success, for example, of the 'political' oeuvre of David Hare (including *Racing Demon*, *The Absence of War*, *Murmuring Judges*, *The Permanent Way*, *Stuff Happens*, *The Vertical Hour*, *Gethsemane*, and *The Power of Yes*) and other playwrights in the mainstream of modern theatre suggests that Macintyre's observation is unduly pessimistic. Hare's plays have provided focus for important public debate about the actions of politicians and the role of institutional politics in western society. Derbyshire and Hodson argue that '[s]ince Ancient Greece, theatre has acted as a

Introduction

public performance of late-Elizabethan poetic drama operated at one level as a political event in which a communal relationship between audience and actors was engendered and participation in a political process of sorts was enabled.

In January 1562, the first full-length poetic drama in the English language was performed by members of the Inner Temple in the presence of Elizabeth I. *Gorboduc*, also known as *The Tragedy of Ferrex and Porrex*, was written by two common lawyers, Thomas Norton and Thomas Sackville. Its overt representation of political themes (including the royal succession, rebellion, regicide and civil war) was unprecedented in the history of English theatrical performance.[36] Daring though its themes were for the time and occasion, its audience was limited to the monarch and members of the royal court and their guests. The building of the first public playhouses in the late 16th century heralded a revolution in English theatre: on a daily basis thousands of people watched the companies of players perform the works of dramatic poets, of whom Shakespeare was soon to prove the most prolific. The new playhouses included The Rose, which stood on the south bank of the Thames in Southwark and operated under the management of Philip Henslowe; The Swan, in Paris Garden, Southwark; The Theatre, in Shoreditch, north of the City of London; The Curtain, under the auspices of the Lord Chamberlain's Men; and The Globe, on Bankside, which opened in 1599.[37] The presence of lawyers in the audience was an observation made by several commentators: Thomas Nashe remarked in 1592 that the 'afternoon's men' at the playhouses comprised 'Gentlemen of the Court, the Innes of Courte, and the number of Captaines and Souldiers about London'.[38] Thomas Dekker also noted the attendance of lawyers—'the Templer'—who made the short journey downstream and across the river to Southwark's Bankside, situated opposite the Inner Temple and the Middle Temple.[39] In *Histrio-Mastix Or, The Player Whipt!*, John Marston's satirical play about the theatre and the legal profession, the author (a member of the Middle Temple) has a character—Vourcher, a lawyer–declare: 'Why this going to a play is now all in the fashion'.[40] Given that the two resident theatre companies of the 1590s, the Lord Chamberlain's Men and the Admiral's Men, were attracting between them approximately 15,000 people per week,[41] it is fair to suggest that the

---

forum in which political and moral issues can be debated and explored, lacking the immediate practical impact of law but surpassing it in range and depth', H Derbyshire and L Hodson, 'Performing Injustice: Human Rights and Verbatim Theatre' (2008) 2 *Law and Humanities* 191, 198. For a range of ideas on the political ambit of drama, see G Holderness (ed), *The Politics of Theatre and Drama* (London, Macmillan, 1992).

[36] See ch 1, text to nn 28–30, below; also, Raffield, *Images and Cultures*, above n 10, at 127–31.
[37] See W J Lawrence, *The Elizabethan Playhouse and Other Studies* (Stratford-upon-Avon, Shakespeare Head Press, 1912); R A Foakes, 'Playhouses and Players' in A R Braunmuller and M Hattaway (eds), *The Cambridge Companion to English Renaissance Drama* (Cambridge, Cambridge University Press, 2003) 1.
[38] Quoted in Gurr, *Shakespearean Stage*, above n 3, at 217.
[39] T Dekker, *The Guls Horne-booke* (London, RS, 1609) 28; see ch 3, text to n 137, below.
[40] J Marston, *Histrio-Mastix Or, The Player Whipt!* (London, T Thorp, 1610) (Act 1) B.v; see ch 4, text to nn 151–59, below; on the performance of Marston's play at the Middle Temple in 1599, see ch 5, n 19, below.
[41] Gurr, *Shakespearean Stage*, above n 3, at 213.

Introduction

audiences for the plays were reasonably representative of London's population. The notable preponderance of lawyers in the audience no doubt encouraged dramatists to include material in their plays which would have been accessible to those schooled in the *arcana* of the English legal profession, but they were writing for a microcosm of English society and the ideas expressed therein, as well as their mode of expression, reflect to an extent the social composition of the audience. That at least two of Shakespeare's plays were performed at the Inns of Court is well-known: *The Comedy of Errors* at Gray's Inn in 1594, and *Twelfth Night* at the Middle Temple in 1602. As I discuss in relation to *The Comedy of Errors* in chapter two, the author's evident fascination with and knowledge of legal procedure is witnessed throughout this play. But I am not primarily concerned here with the debatable status of Shakespeare's technical legal knowledge; nor with how, where or when he acquired it.[42] My overriding interest lies in exploring the unique models of governance represented in the plays of Shakespeare and the importance of the poetic imagination in transforming the political process so that the subject of law is immanently involved, both within the narratives of the plays and in the audiences of the Elizabethan playhouse.

Returning briefly to Mill's essay on Coleridge, the author argued that during the great political events and movements in English history (which Mill cites as 'the Reformation and the Commonwealth, the final victory over Popery and Puritanism, Jacobitism and Republicanism'), political theory and philosophy

> fell mostly into the hands of men of a dry prosaic nature, who had not enough of the materials of human feeling in them to be able to imagine any of its more complex and mysterious manifestations . . .[43]

It is possible to disagree with Mill over the specific argument that those in positions of political influence were possessed of a 'prosaic nature' (in the early modern period alone, the distinctive and highly poetic visions of the utopian State envisaged by Sir Thomas More and Sir Francis Bacon might be seen as contradicting Mill's claim), while acknowledging support for his general observation that the development and governance of the State demanded imagination as well as pragmatism if the ideal of political community was to be attained. Mill was writing of the 'great struggles'[44] in English political history; those iconic and seismic events when power shifted from church to State, from king to parliament, and from monarchy to republic. My interest here is with a struggle less momentous in terms of its immediate political impact, but no less important in its contribution to polit-

---

[42] Shakespeare's links with the Middle Temple are well-documented. His cousin Thomas Greene was a member of the Inn, becoming Treasurer in 1629; William and Thomas Combe, friends of Shakespeare from Stratford, took over chambers in the Middle Temple from their great-uncle, William Combe (also from Stratford), a Bencher of the Middle Temple. The connections between Shakespeare and the Middle Temple are discussed in A Arlidge, *Shakespeare and the Prince of Love: The Feast of Misrule in the Middle Temple* (London, Giles de la Mere, 2000) 40–59; also, J L Hotson, 'Love's Labours Won' in *Shakespeare's Sonnets Dated* (London, R Hart-Davis, 1949) 37.

[43] Mill, 'Coleridge', above n 29, at 202.

[44] *Ibid*.

ical debate and dissent (and eventually to lasting political change). The last decade of Elizabethan rule, which coincided with the emergence of Shakespeare as a successful dramatic poet, was marked in political terms by a notable absolutist trend.[45] The Royal Prerogative was used increasingly to evade the legitimate authority of common law jurisdiction, as a response to which eminent lawyers (notably Coke) asserted the supremacy of the unwritten ancient constitution, guaranteeing to English subjects certain fundamental freedoms in the face of expansive monarchic claims to absolute, imperial authority.[46] I explore the idea that Shakespeare understood and expressed law not as the formal expression of rules but rather as the symbolic representation of *societas*; that English law provided a flexible juridical framework within which the intricacy and vibrancy of society could be expressed and regulated. The plays which I examine here demonstrate that the ideal constitution, envisaged by Shakespeare for the harmonious governance of England, was predicated on the classical principle of the *pactum*: the equitable social contract between magistrate and citizen.[47] This model is founded upon two distinct but related polities. The first is the Aristotelian notion of the *polis*: the classical city-State or political community, whose rationale was government in the best interests of its citizens. The second is the legitimacy and sovereignty of the ancient English constitution, representing the unwritten authority of precedent and immemorial custom. I am not claiming for Shakespeare the political status of anti-monarchist, but I do suggest that the models of good governance, as depicted in his plays, owe more to the theories of mixed polity described, for example, by Fortescue in *De Laudibus Legum Angliae* and *Difference Between an Absolute and Limited Monarchy*, or by Christopher St German in *Doctor and Student*, than they do to the absolutist model of *fin-de-siècle* Elizabethan rule. The plays of Shakespeare can accurately be defined as republican only in the sense that they are all broadly concerned (to a greater or lesser extent) with the representation of *res publica*: good governance in the best interests of the common-weal.

Of course, the plays of Shakespeare are not political tracts. Each play works discretely in its own right as a dramatic narrative, but in all of the works that I consider there are unmistakable parallels between the political ideas expressed therein and the juristic arguments in the wider sphere of the late-Elizabethan legal institution, concerning the direction of the English State.[48] It is a curious fact that

---

[45] See J Guy (ed), *The Reign of Elizabeth I: Court and Culture in the Last Decade* (Cambridge, Cambridge University Press, 1995); also, J Guy, 'Tudor Monarchy and its Critiques' in John Guy (ed), *The Tudor Monarchy* (London, Arnold, 1997) 78.

[46] See, eg, the clash of jurisdictions between the ecclesiastical court of High Commission and the courts of common law, which I discuss in ch 1, text to nn 37–46, below.

[47] Carlyle argues that 'the conception of a contract between king and people was not merely archaeological nor unimportant in the sixteenth century. It was set out with force and clearness by the most sober and dispassionate writers like Hooker and Althusius, and it was clearly founded, first, on the relation of the king to the law', A J Carlyle, 'Political Theory from 1300 to 1600' in R W Carlyle and A J Carlyle, *A History of Mediaeval Political Theory in the West*, 6 vols (Edinburgh, Blackwood, 1903–36) 6: 395.

[48] On political drama of the period, see M Heinemann, 'Political Drama' in Braunmuller and Hattaway, above n 37, at 164.

Introduction

the plays of Shakespeare did not fall foul of official censorship at a time when State monitoring of dramatic works was prevalent. Through the office of Master of the Revels (to whom all dramatic texts intended for performance had to be submitted), the Lord Chamberlain was able to control the substantive content of plays. Given that licences were traditionally granted to companies of players in order that they should rehearse their performances in readiness for a summons to act before the monarch,[49] it is perhaps even more surprising that some of Shakespeare's plays were not subject to government censure. It no doubt helped that direct reference to developments in the Elizabethan State was never made. The setting of plays in distant historical, mythological or quasi-mythical locations served the pragmatic purpose of disguising or blurring overt references to contemporary political events. Imperial Rome, ancient Athens and medieval England may have had their allusive correlations, but they were palpably not the Elizabethan State. The inventive use of allusion, allegory and metaphor notwithstanding, no one seriously doubted, for example, that the treatment of the eponymous king in *The Tragedy of Richard II* reflected aspects of absolutist rule under Elizabeth I, or that the staged deposition of Richard was a daring representation of contemporary thought on the subject of the succession. The parallels were presumably self-evident to the Earl of Essex, whose supporters commissioned a special performance of *Richard II* on the eve of the Essex Rebellion in February 1601.[50]

Theatre lends humanity, specificity and structure to ideas. Onstage, people interact, and those in the audience watch, listen and judge. The rhetorical schemes of law and theatre operate upon their audience through the deployment and manipulation of images. The costume of the law,[51] the architecture of its institutions, the spatial configuration of its buildings,[52] the peculiar technical complexity of its

---

[49] E K Chambers, *The Elizabethan Stage*, 4 vols (Oxford, Clarendon, 1923) 4: 325; also ch 3, text to nn 142–43, below. On censorship in early modern theatre, with especial reference to the works of Ben Jonson, see A Patterson, 'Censorship and Intepretation' in D S Kastan and P Stallybrass (eds), *Staging the Renaissance: Reinterpretations of Elizabethan and Jacobean Drama* (London, Routledge, 1991) 40; more generally, see C S Clegg, *Press Censorship in Elizabethan England* (Cambridge, Cambridge University Press, 1997).

[50] See ch 3, text to nn 16–19, below. There is an uncharacteristic topical reference to the Earl of Essex and the Irish campaign of 1599, in Act 5 of Shakespeare's *The Life of Henry Fifth*: 'Were now the General of our gracious Empress – / As in good time he may – from Ireland coming, / Bringing rebellion broachèd on his sword' (5.0.30–32). The triumphant tone is a clear indication that the play was completed before the failure of the Irish campaign and the return to England, in September 1599, of the disgraced Earl.

[51] In *De Laudibus*, the Chancellor complains to the Prince that judicial robes are insufficiently ornate: 'which sort of Habit, when You come in Power, I could wish Your Highness would make a little more Ornamental, in Honour of the Laws', Fortescue, above n 23, at 120; see J H Baker, 'History of Gowns Worn at the English Bar' (1975) 9 *Costume: The Journal of the Costume Society* 15; also, J Manningham, *The Diary of John Manningham of the Middle Temple* (London, Camden Society, 1885) 45.

[52] On the power of the State and institutional architecture, see M Foucault, *Discipline and Punish: The Birth of the Prison*, (tr) A Sheridan (London, Penguin, 1991) 195–228; on the architecture of the Inns of Court, see D Evans, 'Theatre of Deferral: The Image of the Law and the Architecture of the Inns of Court' (1999) 10 *Law and Critique* 1; also, D Evans, 'The Inns of Court: Speculations on the Body of Law' (1993) 1 *Arch-Text* 5. For a comparison between the institutional buildings of English common law and those of French civil law, see K F Taylor, *In the Theater of Criminal Justice: Palais de Justice in Second Empire Paris* (New Jersey, Princeton University Press, 1993). On the correlation between the

Introduction

language,[53] the arcane rituals of its practitioners,[54] all are figurative devices or emblems which seek to confer divinity, mystery and legitimacy on the mundane business of law. The symbols of divine, immemorial provenance redeem and elevate the law from the quotidian, creating a spiritual bond between the institution and the subject of law. Through its order of signs, law attains a corporeal form through which it can speak to its subjects. The staging of the drama of community and law, as expressed in the plays of Shakespeare, has the effect of both exaggerating and exemplifying the social drama of law. The performances in the Elizabethan playhouses mark the emergence of law from the formal arena of the legal institution into the imagistic and non-reverential sphere of the social and the public. As James Boyd White has noted, law can be interpreted 'as a way of talking about real events and actual people in the world'; it 'operates through speakers located in particular times and places speaking to actual audiences about real people'.[55] White articulates a theory of law as narrative, and lawyer as narrator; of law's stories being told by its actor-poets.[56] The histrionic tradition of the lawyer as actor was firmly established in ancient Rome, in which the courtroom was a form of public theatre: 'When the speaker rises the whole throng will give a sign for silence, then expressions of assent, frequent applause,' and passers-by 'observing from a distance, though quite ignorant of the case in question, will recognise that he is succeeding and that a Roscius is on the stage'.[57]

In his commentary on *De Laudibus Legum Angliae*, Edward Waterhouse confirmed the correlation between law and theatre when he stated that an advocate 'acts divers parts', the first of which is 'that of an Oratour in proper wording it'.[58] That Serjeants at Law were described by the Latin title of *narratores*, while their counterparts in the ecclesiastical courts were known as *advocati*, is suggestive of the narrative form of common law.[59] The system of precedent (*stare decisis*),[60] upon which the legitimate authority of common law judgments rests, is founded in an encyclopaedic collection of narratives to which successive judges add subsequent

---

law courts and theatre in early modern London, see S Mukherji, 'Locations of law: spaces, people, play' in *Law and Representation in Early Modern Drama* (Cambridge, Cambridge University Press, 2006) 174.

[53] More accurately, this should be the three languages of common law: English, Latin, and law-French; see J H Baker, 'The Three Languages of the Common Law' (1998) 43 *McGill Law Journal* 5.

[54] On the dining rites and oral traditions of the early modern legal profession, see Raffield, *Images and Cultures*, above n 10, at 9–42.

[55] J B White, 'Rhetoric and Law: The Arts of Cultural and Communal Life' in *Heracles' Bow: Essays on the Rhetoric and Poetics of the Law* (Madison, University of Wisconsin Press, 1985) 36.

[56] On law as a narrative representation of human behaviour, see B S Jackson, *Law, Fact and Narrative Coherence* (Roby, Deborah Charles, 1988) 91.

[57] Marcus Tullius Cicero, *Cicero's Brutus or History of Famous Orators*, (tr) G L Hendrickson (London, William Heinemann, 1962) 290.

[58] Waterhous, above n 27, at 136.

[59] Sir William Dugdale, *Origines Juridiciales or Historical Memorials of the English Laws* (London, F & T Warren, 1666) 110; see P Brand, *The Origins of the English Legal Profession* (Oxford, Blackwell, 1992) 48, 94; J H Baker, *The Order of Serjeants at Law* (London, Selden Society, 1984).

[60] *Stare decisis et non quieta movere* ('Stand by that which has been decided and do not disturb that which has been settled').

chapters.⁶¹ The English legal system of the early modern period was derived from an oral tradition; its adversarial juridical procedures were predicated on an agonistic model in which competing *narratores* presented contending stories and were judged on the basis of their persuasive skills. The parallels with drama are obvious and compelling. But the judiciary are not legislators, and the poetic imagination of the equable judge is limited, as Nussbaum concedes, by the institutional constraints of the juridical process.⁶² The limitation on the capacity of lawyers to apply their poetic imaginations to the process of lawmaking was recognised by Tacitus, in *Dialogus de Oratoribus*. There the forensic orator, Curatius Maternus, is accused by his friend Aper of neglecting his profession of 'speaker and pleader', choosing instead to

> spend your whole time on plays. The other day it was 'Medea', and now it is 'Thyestes'; and all the while you are being summoned to the forum by the long list of your friends' cases.⁶³

Maternus replies that he wishes to abandon his career as a forensic orator and 'cultivate eloquence in its higher and holier form', by becoming a playwright.⁶⁴ Maternus does not intend to forsake entirely his rhetorical skills, but rather to apply them elsewhere, in an alternative forum where his ideas might affect political opinion. The rhetorical manuals published in England throughout the 16th century demonstrate adherence to the classical ideal that the cultivation of eloquence was a skill useful not only to lawyers (although the particular literary genre was intended principally for consumption by law students). For example, in *The Arte of Rhetorique*, Sir Thomas Wilson asked:

> For if the worthinesse of Eloquence maie move us, what worthier thing can there bee, then with a word to winne Cities and whole Countries?⁶⁵

Unlike Maternus, Shakespeare did not abandon the career of professional pleader for that of playwright; but he did utilise the Elizabethan conventions and techniques of classical rhetoric in the construction of his plays, cultivating eloquence in the form of poetic drama.⁶⁶ As I have indicated, I do not regard the plays of Shakespeare as examples of polemical theatre. Rather, I suggest that their self-referential theatricality invites the critic to consider the presence and purpose of

---

⁶¹ The theory of judges as successive authors of a chain novel, adding to an interpretive tradition, is expounded in R Dworkin, *Law's Empire* (London, Fontana, 1986) 228–32.

⁶² 'The judge cannot be simply a poet, or even simply an Aristotelian equitable man', Nussbaum, above n 17, at 82.

⁶³ Cornelius Tacitus, *Dialogus de Oratoribus*, (tr) W Peterson (Cambridge, Mass, Harvard University Press, 1970) 237. It is noteworthy regarding the art of forensic rhetoric that the Latin word *actor* translates as both 'pleader' and 'performer'. In legal terminology, a plaintiff was also described in Latin as '*actor*'. 'Plaintiff' has linguistic connections with tragic drama, deriving from the Latin word *plangere*, meaning to beat in grief, lament loudly or bewail.

⁶⁴ *Ibid*.

⁶⁵ Sir Thomas Wilson, *The Arte of Rhetorique* (London, George Robinson, 1585) 'The Epistle', A.ii.v.

⁶⁶ On Shakespeare's use of rhetoric, see F Kermode, *Shakespeare's Language* (London, Penguin, 2000); also, P Mack, *Elizabethan Rhetoric: Theory and Practice* (Cambridge, Cambridge University Press, 2002).

Introduction

metadrama in the Shakespearean canon.[67] The drama-within-drama of all the plays that I consider here serves to emphasise the artifice not only of theatre itself, but of the theatre of politics that is represented therein. Throughout this book I refer to the 'artificial reason' of law.[68] The phrase, which is attributed to Sir Edward Coke, succinctly describes the artistic endeavour of common law to create a juridical framework for the recognition of rights and obligations guaranteed by the unwritten English constitution. In comparable fashion, Shakespeare used poetic drama as a framework for the manifestation of philosophical ideas. The formulation of abstractions is a crucial process in the development of any constitution; as Coleridge remarked: '[T]he constitution has real existence, and does not the less exist in reality, because it both *is*, and *exists as*, an IDEA'.[69] At a symbolic level, the plays of Shakespeare exist somewhere between the two states described by Coleridge:

> That which, contemplated *objectively* (*ie* as existing *externally* to the mind), we call a LAW; the same contemplated *subjectively* (ie as existing in a subject or mind), is an idea.[70]

In institutional terms, the plays are demonstrably not law. But their representations of juristic themes appeal to a higher moral authority than that of the courts, Parliament or the Crown, in the same manner that the common law founds its legitimacy in sources other than statute. In the words of Lord Ellesmere:

> [T]he Common Laws of England are grounded upon the Law of God, and extend themselves to the original Law of Nature, and the universal Law of Nations; and that they are not originally *Leges scriptæ*...[71]

It is through the iconic power of the image that the existence of law is manifested, and it is with the images of law in the plays of Shakespeare that I am primarily concerned.

Each chapter is dedicated to the examination of a single play and analysis of its relevance to particular aspects of the late-Elizabethan State. The selection of plays is necessarily subjective, but I have chosen those which collectively reflect a broad range of important constitutional issues and developments in the last decade of Elizabethan rule. The thematic emphasis throughout is on the absolutist tendency of the Crown, its oppressive effect on the freedom of subjects, and the sustained attempt to address and rectify the imbalance of power, both in the institutional

---

[67] See L Abel, *Tragedy and Metatheatre: Essays on Dramatic Form* (New York, Holmes & Meier, 2003); L Abel, *Metatheatre: a New View on Dramatic Form* (New York, Hill & Wang, 1963); J L Calderwood, *Shakespearian Metadrama: the Argument of the Play in 'Titus Andronicus', 'Love's Labours Lost', 'Romeo and Juliet', 'A Midsummer Night's Dream' and 'Richard II'* (Minneapolis, University of Minnesota Press, 1971).

[68] See ch 5, text to nn 52–59, below; the reference to 'artificial reason' is in Coke, *Prohibitions del Roy*, 12 Reports (1655) 7: 64a, at 65a.

[69] S T Coleridge, *On the Constitution of the Church and State* (London, J M Dent, 1972) 9.

[70] *Ibid* at 5.

[71] Quoted in Dugdale, above n 59, at 3; in the same paragraph, Dugdale quotes from Book I of Bracton's *De Legibus et Consuetudinibus* in support of Lord Ellesmere's pronouncement: '*In omnibus aliis regionibus utuntur Legibus & jure scriptis; sola Anglia usa est jure non scripto & consuetudine*', ibid.

Introduction

forum of the courts and in the informal social arena of theatre and literature. I have adopted a chronological approach to the plays (starting with *Titus Andronicus* in 1594 and ending in 1604 with the first of Shakespeare's post-Elizabethan plays, *Measure for Measure*), intending thereby to illuminate parallels between their various narrative themes and the continuous drama of political events. In chapter one I consider *Titus Andronicus* in relation to the complex constitutional relationship between monarch, State and subject at the start of the 1590s. I contend that through its depiction of tyranny, murder and mutilation the play presents a dystopian vision of a dislocated body politic, in which (as Titus reminds his kinsmen) justice has fled the earth. *Titus Andronicus* addresses directly the pragmatic, political relationship between governor and governed, questioning the efficacy of Aristotle's injunction that government should be enacted in the best interests of the commonwealth.[72]

The first recorded performance of *The Comedy of Errors* was by the Lord Chamberlain's Men, at the Gray's Inn Christmas revels of 1594.[73] The history of the play is therefore permanently linked with the legal profession, as it was probably written with an audience of lawyers in mind. The 1594 performance at Gray's Inn is relevant to my examination of *The Comedy of Errors* in chapter two. I consider the play's themes of commercial relations and legal and social obligations in the context of developments in contract law during the second half of the 16th century, culminating in the landmark decision of *Slade's Case*.[74] *The Comedy of Errors* demonstrates a fascination with the nature of commodities and the centrality of the contractual promise to the regulation of human relations. It also illustrates the relevance of the ascendant middle class to the social and political stability

---

[72] Whilst acknowledging the contribution of the collaborative process to the creation of late-Elizabethan theatre, in relation to the plays considered here I believe it is reasonable to describe Shakespeare as their author. On the possible contribution of George Peele to *Titus Andronicus*, see B Vickers, '*Titus Andronicus* with George Peele' in *Shakespeare, Co-Author: A Historical Study of Five Collaborative Plays* (Oxford, Oxford University Press, 2002) 148; also, R F Hill, 'The Composition of *Titus Andronicus*' (1957) 10 *Shakespeare Survey* 60. On the 'author function' and the idea that '[t]he author's name serves to characterise a certain mode of being of discourse', see M Foucault, 'What Is An Author?' in *Aesthetics, Method, and Epistemology*, (tr) R Hurley, (ed) J D Faubion (London, Penguin, 1998) 211. On Shakespeare as a brand, rather than a historical person, see D Lanier, 'Shakespeare: Myth and Biographical Fiction' in R Shaughnessy (ed), *The Cambridge Companion to Shakespeare and Popular Culture* (Cambridge, Cambridge University Press, 2007) 93. On the general question of authorship in Shakespeare's plays, see J Shapiro, *Contested Will: Who Wrote Shakespeare?* (London, Faber & Faber, 2010); also, E Smith, 'The Shakespeare Authorship Debate Revisited' (2008) 5 *Literature Compass* 618. On the collaborative processes of Elizabethan playmaking, see S Orgel, 'What is a Text?' in D S Kastan and P Stallybrass (eds), *Staging the Renaissance: Reinterpretations of Elizabethan and Jacobean Drama* (London, Routledge, 1991) 83; also, E A J Honigmann, *The Stability of Shakespeare's Text* (London, Arnold, 1965).

[73] The record of the 1594 revels was not published until 1688, under the title *Gesta Grayorum*. It is generally assumed that Francis Bacon wrote the speeches of the six counsellors and that Francis Davison wrote *The Masque of Proteus*; other members of Gray's Inn were almost certainly involved in the authorship of the revels, *Gesta Grayorum: Or, The History of the High and mighty Prince, Henry Prince of Purpoole* (London, William Canning, 1688). Barbara Shapiro claims that these revels 'brought [Bacon's] codification proposals directly to a legal audience', B Shapiro, 'Codification of the Laws in Seventeenth Century England' (1974) *Wisconsin Law Review* 428, 436.

[74] Coke, *Slade's Case*, 4 Reports (1604) 2: 91a.

Introduction

of late-Elizabethan England. In this respect, the frenzied plot of *The Comedy of Errors* mirrors the shift from a vertical model of society (determined by immutable social hierarchy) to a horizontal model, in which freedom of contract is the primary determinant of social status.

In chapter three I consider the art of kingship in relation to *Richard II*. The description of the king as a representational image was central to the Tudor enactment of monarchic government as a form of theatre. The patriarchal model of kingship, in which the king is the earthly manifestation of divine will, is depicted to powerful theatrical effect in *Richard II*, Shakespeare's poetic actor-king. It is Richard's tragedy that he fails to allow his conscience to influence his political judgement as king. Conscience dictates that he should govern with fairness and justice, in accordance with the law. Instead, belief in his divine status as God's anointed deputy impels him towards a series of disastrous and unlawful acts, which lead to his eventual deposition and murder. In this chapter I offer an alternative theory of the mystical nature of kingship to that provided by Kantorowicz in *The King's Two Bodies*.[75] The play's peculiar concerns with property law and the lawful possession and ownership of land find a juridical analogue in several cases reported by Plowden.[76] I argue that the decisions in these cases demonstrate the pragmatic determination of the judiciary to enforce conformity with the principle of limited monarchy, rather than to engage in intellectual debate over the metaphysical nature of the king's two bodies.

The relationship between imperial statute and unwritten law is an implicit theme of *A Midsummer Night's Dream*, which provides the subject of chapter four. I suggest that the play is more than a comic paean to youthful love; it reflects contemporary concerns about the dubious legitimacy of unrestricted monarchic rule and its oppressive consequences. The 'sharp Athenian law' (1.1.162), which demands the execution of Hermia if she refuses to marry Demetrius in accordance with her father's will, is eventually overturned by Theseus. In condoning the marriage of Hermia and Lysander, Theseus tacitly acknowledges the existence of a higher moral law, to which the written laws of earthly magistrates must defer. The perfect order of natural and divine law (as described by St Thomas Aquinas in *Summa Theologica*)[77] is represented in *A Midsummer Night's Dream* through the recurrence of ritual. Whether in the form of dances between Oberon and Titania, Bottom being led in procession to Titania's bower, the performance of 'Pyramus and Thisbe', or the formal blessing at the end of the play, the theme of the sacramental (and its inversion in the form of parody) is focal. With acknowledgment to Mikhail Bakhtin, I investigate the antique customs and carnivalesque rituals of folklore, and the role of these in articulating an aspiration to spiritual unity and

---

[75] E H Kantorowicz, *The King's Two Bodies: A Study in Medieval Political Theology* (New Jersey, Princeton University Press, 1957).

[76] See esp, *Case of the Dutchy of Lancaster* in *The Commentaries or Reports of Edmund Plowden*, 2 vols (Dublin, H Watts, 1792) 1: 212; Plowden, *Willion v Berkley*, *Commentaries* 1: 247; Plowden, *Hales v Petit*, *Commentaries* 1: 253; Plowden, *Hill v Grange*, *Commentaries* 1: 164.

[77] On Thomist Providentialism and its influence over early modern jurisprudence, see I Ward, *An Introduction to Critical Legal Theory* (London, Cavendish, 1998) 12–22.

political community.⁷⁸ The rituals of *A Midsummer Night's Dream* recall also the writing of the Elizabethan divine and Master of the Temple, Richard Hooker. Books I–V of *Of the Laws of Ecclesiastical Polity* were published between 1593 and 1597, during which time *A Midsummer Night's Dream* was written.⁷⁹ Hooker argued that the sacraments and ceremonies of the Anglican Church acted upon the human faculties in an iconic manner, directing the subject to an understanding and revelation of the impossible and the infinite. He was conscious of the persuasive power of the image and its utility in expressing the intangible concepts of unwritten law. His belief in the transformative power of ritual and the capacity of the human imagination to envisage the eternal and indiscernible finds its dramatic equivalent in Bottom's epiphany: 'I have had a most rare vision. I have had a dream, past the wit of man to say what dream it was'. (4.1.200–201)

In chapter five I examine Shakespeare's depiction of the legal profession with reference to *Henry IV, Parts 1 and 2*, and especially to the two characters in *Part 2* most clearly associated with the legal institution: the Lord Chief Justice and Justice Shallow. The former of these is the embodiment of order in a disjointed realm. He reminds the audience of the theatricality of English law and its manifestation in symbols, describing himself as '[t]he image of the King whom I presented' (5.2.79). He represents also the resolute but benevolent authority of the Father: at the end of the play the newly-crowned King Henry V confirms that it is as a 'father' that the Lord Chief Justice 'shall have foremost hand' (5.2.140) in the governance of the State. Through analysis of the paternal theme that dominates the play, I explore the idea of law as the expression of a symbolic order, in which the familial tension between father and son is acted and resolved in the public arena. Justice Shallow is the embodiment of nostalgic values expressed by Sir John Fortescue in *De Laudibus Legum Angliae* and *Difference Between an Absolute and Limited Monarchy*. Fortescue's home was in the Gloucestershire village of Ebrington, a few miles to the south of Stratford-upon-Avon. I suggest in this chapter that the location was a possible source of inspiration for the Gloucestershire scenes in *Henry IV, Part 2*. While civil unrest in the realm threatens the stability of Crown and nation, on Justice Shallow's land the servants are 'good varlet[s]' (5.3.14) and the inhabitants '[d]o nothing but eat, and make good cheer' (5.3.17). Shallow's Gloucestershire is an autumnal pastoral, surrounded and occasionally impinged upon by a violent reality. His predilection for nostalgia—the longing for a distant past—reflects belief that the immutable authority of common law is derived from the myth of Albion. In the words of Coke: '[T]he common law of England had been time out of mind of man before the conquest, and was not altered or changed

---

⁷⁸ M Bakhtin, *Rabelais and His World*, (tr) H Iswolsky, (Bloomington, Indiana University Press, 1984).

⁷⁹ *A Midsummer Night's Dream* was written and first performed between 1595 and 1596; see ch 4, n 43, below. Books VI and VIII of *Of the Laws of Ecclesiastical Polity* were not published until 1648; Book VII was published in 1661. I refer to the 1622 edition, which includes Books I–V, plus the Tractates: R Hooker, *Of the Lawes of Ecclesiastical Politie* (London, William Stansbye, 1622); McGrade's edition contains a useful introduction, but includes only Hooker's Preface, and Books I and VIII, A S McGrade (ed), *Of the Laws of Ecclesiastical Polity* (Cambridge, Cambridge University Press, 1989).

Introduction

by the Conqueror'.[80] This chapter provides an analysis of the fiction of common law's antiquity, and the perpetuation of that myth by the patriarchs of common law.

In chapter six I reflect on the immediate post-Elizabethan period and the prospects for the English State following the accession to the throne of James I. An outbreak of plague in London had forced the closure of the playhouses in March 1603, the month of Elizabeth's death. They did not reopen until April 1604. The first new play of Shakespeare to be performed following the death of the Queen was *Measure for Measure*. Its first recorded performance was in the presence of James I at the Banqueting House, on 26 December 1604. An early-Jacobean rather than a late-Elizabethan play, *Measure for Measure* demonstrates the maturation of constitutional and political themes which Shakespeare addressed in his Elizabethan plays. Uncertainty over the succession had heightened speculation over the form of kingship that Elizabeth's successor would embody and the direction in which the State would be guided. The likelihood that she would be succeeded by James prompted investigation into his political principles and how these might impact upon the conduct of his reign. The sources of such information were not difficult to identify, as James had written two books on the subject of kingship, *The Trew Law of Free Monarchies* and *Basilicon Doron*, published respectively in 1598 and 1599 (revised editions of *Basilicon Doron* were published in 1603). In the former of these works, James stated 'that the King is above the law'.[81] I explore this assertion of absolute authority with especial reference to the conduct of the Duke in *Measure for Measure*, whose style of personal rule constitutes a rival jurisdiction to the established institutions of the law. Throughout the reign of James I, the mysterious and sacred authority of the Royal Prerogative was increasingly invoked to justify interference with the jurisdiction of common law. '[T]he old fantastical Duke of dark corners' (4.3.147–48) bears comparison with James I, especially over belief in the unchallengeable legitimacy of his personal dominion. In 1628, during the Parliamentary debates over the Petition of Right, Charles I was to give his royal word that he would govern according to 'his' law. The response of Sir Nathaniel Rich to the King's promise was concise: 'We have nothing thereby but shells and shadows'.[82] In the evasive dealings of the Duke, carried out in disguise and under cover of darkness, *Measure for Measure* depicts a ruler for whom shells and shadows are the currency of government. It was a prophetic portrait of the Jacobean dawn.

---

[80] Coke, 3 *Reports* (1602) 2: Preface, vib–viia.
[81] 'The Trew Law of Free Monarchies' in J P Sommerville (ed), *James VI and I: Political Writings* (Cambridge, Cambridge University Press, 1994) 75.
[82] R C Johnson, M F Keeler, M Jansson Cole and W B Bidwell (eds), *Proceedings in Parliament* 1628, 6 vols (New Haven, Conn, Yale University Press, 1977) 3: 270.

1

'Terras Astraea reliquit': Titus Andronicus and the Flight of Justice

I. Law, Justice and the Exercise of Executive Power

IT IS AN IRONY that would not have been lost on Shakespeare that the theatre at which *The Most Lamentable Roman Tragedy of Titus Andronicus* was originally staged should have been the subject of juridical proceedings between lawmaker and citizen, nearly 400 years after the play's first performance there in January 1594.[1] Subsequent to the discovery in 1989 of the remains of the Elizabethan Rose Playhouse, a trust was formed whose purpose was to save the site of the theatre from development as an office block.[2] The Rose Theatre Trust applied to the Secretary of State for the Environment to have the property listed under the Ancient Monuments and Archaeological Areas Act, 1979 (s 1). Following the refusal of the Secretary of State to list the site, the Trust was granted leave to apply for judicial review of the decision. The application for review was turned down on the grounds of insufficient standing (*locus standi*): the party seeking judicial review of an administrative decision did not have sufficient interest in the subject matter for which review was being sought.[3] The presiding judge (Schiemann J) considered that the mere gathering together of people with a common interest did not in itself constitute standing. The case raised an important constitutional issue concerning the right of aggrieved citizens to obtain a hearing in the courts. The decision appeared at least to raise doubts about the applicability of Dicey's dictum that the rule of law requires that disputes over the legality of government acts should be decided by the courts, acting independently of the executive branch of government.[4]

---

[1] Philip Henslowe, owner of the Rose Playhouse, records the following entry for 1594 in his diary: 'ne—Rd at titus & ondronicus the 23 of Jenewary . . . iijli viijs', R A Foakes (ed), *Henslowe's Diary* (Cambridge, Cambridge University Press, 2002) 21; 'ne' here almost certainly means that the play was 'new' to the repertoire: see *Titus Andronicus*, (ed) J Bate (London, Arden Shakespeare, 1995), Introduction, 70, n 1. All references to the text of the play are from this edition.

[2] The Rose Playhouse was built in 1587 by Philip Henslowe and John Cholmley, and became home to the Admiral's Men. The remains of the Rose are now entombed in the basement of the headquarters of the Health and Safety Executive. On the Rose Playhouse, and the legal struggle to preserve its remains, see C Eccles, *The Rose Theatre* (London, Nick Hern, 1990).

[3] *R v Secretary of State for the Environment, ex p Rose Theatre Trust Ltd* [1990] 1 QB 504.

[4] A V Dicey, *Introduction to the Study of the Law of the Constitution* (London, Macmillan, 1959) 193.

Law, Justice and the Exercise of Executive Power

In the torrent of blood that engulfs the action of *Titus Andronicus*, it is often forgotten (by audiences and critics alike) that the play is concerned to a great extent with the dire effects on the citizenry of absolute government.[5] The play starts with a plebiscite, the purpose of which is to elect a successor to the recently deceased emperor. Titus, the noble and victorious warrior, is the popular candidate, but he implores the Roman citizens to defer to the ancient principle of primogeniture and accept Saturninus, the eldest son of the emperor, as their legitimate ruler (1.1.227–33). The election of Saturninus provides a political backdrop against which the bloody narrative may unfold. A period of unjust imperial rule is subsequently enacted, in which every arbitrary whim of the emperor is accorded paramount legal status.

Titus Andronicus is set in Rome during the 4th century, and the events portrayed in it are fictitious. This fact notwithstanding, those members of the late-Elizabethan audience who were versed in the republican literature of renaissance humanism would have drawn parallels between the imperial régime of Saturninus and the well-established absolutist tendencies of the Tudor monarchy.[6] Thomas Heywood, the actor and playwright (*c* 1570–1641), identified the quintessential *metaphora* of Elizabethan drama when he observed that

> [i]f wee present a forreigne History, the subiect is so intended, that in the lives of *Romans*, *Grecians*, or others, either the vertues of our Country-men are extolled, or their vices reproved . . .[7]

Allegory was an essential rhetorical weapon in the armoury of educated Elizabethans, its purpose understood by all: 'Allegoria, called of Quintilian, Inversio, is a Trope of a sentence, or forme of speech which expresseth one thing in words, and another in sense'.[8] Allegory also provided an important literary device through which to

---

[5] Possibly the first recorded criticism of the play is included in a letter home, written in 1596 by a French tutor in the household of Sir John Harington: 'le monstre a plus valu que le sujet', quoted in R A Foakes, *Shakespeare and Violence* (Cambridge, Cambridge University Press, 2003) 56. Doctor Johnson wrote of *Titus Andronicus*: 'The barbarity of the spectacles, and the general massacre which are here exhibited, can scarcely be conceived tolerable to any audience', *The Plays of William Shakespeare*, (ed) S Johnson, 8 vols (London, J and R Tonson, 1765) 6: 364. Eliot described it as 'one of the stupidest and most uninspired plays ever written', T S Eliot, 'Seneca in Elizabethan translation', in T S Eliot, *Selected Essays 1917–1932* (London, Faber, 1932) 82. Frank Kermode argues that *Titus Andronicus* has 'the sort of appeal we associate with old Sweeney Todd-like melodramas', F Kermode, *Shakespeare's Language* (London, Penguin, 2000) 51.

[6] On renaissance humanism in Tudor England, see A Fox and J Guy, *Reassessing the Henrician Age: Humanism, Politics and Reform, 1500–1550* (Oxford, Blackwell, 1986); I consider the educational influence of Sir Thomas Elyot's *The Book Named the Governor* (first published in 1531) in ch 5, text to nn 109–21, below.

[7] T Heywood, *An Apology for Actors* (London, Nicholas Okes, 1612) F3.*v*.

[8] H Peacham, *The Garden of Eloquence, Conteining the Most Excellent Ornaments, Exornations, Lightes, flowers and formes of speech, commonly called the Figures of Rhetorike* (London, H Iackson, 1593) 25. Other important 16th-century rhetorical manuals include L Cox, *The Arte or Crafte of Rhetoryke* (1529); T Wilson, *The Art of Rhetorique* (1553); G Puttenham, *The Arte of English Poesie* (1589). Puttenham defines *metaphora* as 'a kinde of wresting of a single word from his owne right signification, to another not so naturall, but yet of some affinitie or conveniencie', G Puttenham, *The Arte of English Poesie* (London, Richard Field, 1589) 148.

criticise obliquely the absolutist pretensions of late-Elizabethan government.[9] Heywood's *An Apology for Actors* is notable for the author's continuous insistence on the didactic imperative of poetic drama; for Heywood, the moral purpose of tragedy was to

> perswade men to humanity and good life, to instruct them in civility and good manners, shewing them the fruits of honesty, and the end of villany.[10]

Applying Heywood's thesis on allegory and tragedy to *Titus Andronicus*, it is apparent that the reign of Saturninus reflects the central tenet of Tudor imperial monarchy (following the Acts of Supremacy of 1534 and 1559) that the king is under God but not law, because the king makes the law. The equitable principles of common law, encapsulated by the medieval jurist Henry de Bracton in the phrase *lex facit regem* ('law makes the king'),[11] have been rejected in favour of the civilian maxim of the emperor Justinian, *quod principi placuit legis habet vigorem* ('the will of the prince has the force of law').[12]

The inherent injustice of the civilian code is perhaps best exemplified in the play by the execution of the Clown, at the instruction of the emperor, Saturninus. His only offence had been to deliver a letter from Titus to the emperor (4.4.39–48). Critics have expressed their dissatisfaction at the summary manner in which the Clown is dispatched to the gallows. Foakes interprets the execution of the Clown as an example of the author's desire to shock: a representation of gratuitous violence, which Foakes believes to be a characteristic fault of the play.[13] Francis Barker makes the important observation that before meeting Titus and receiving his petition for justice, which he agrees to deliver to the emperor, the Clown was already on his way to the *tribuni plebis*, in their judicial capacity as magistrates, to adjudicate over a legal dispute, 'betwixt my uncle and one of the emperal's men'. (4.3.91–93)[14] As so

---

[9] On the regulation of plays and playhouses by the State and civic authorities in the 1590s, see Introduction, text to nn 48–50 above.

[10] Heywood, above n 7, F3.*v*.

[11] '*Ipse autem rex non debet esse sub homine sed sub deo et sub lege, quia lex facit regem*' ('The king must not be under man but under God and under the law, because law makes the king'), Henry de Bracton, *De Legibus et Consuetudinibus Angliae* (*c* 1235), (tr) S E Thorne, 4 vols (Cambridge, Mass, Belknap Press, 1968–77) 2: 33; Sir Edward Coke paraphrases Bracton in the preface to Part 4 of *The Reports*: 'the King is under no man, but only God and the law, for the law makes the King', Part 4 (1604) of *The Reports of Sir Edward Coke, Knt. In English*, G Wilson (ed), 7 vols (London, Rivington, 1777) 2: Preface, xixa. The relevance of the following remark by B J Sokol and Mary Sokol is striking when applied to *Titus Andronicus*: 'The law implied in most of Shakespeare's plays, even those with classical, fantastical, or continental settings, is the English law of his time, most often derived from common law', B J Sokol and M Sokol, *Shakespeare's Legal Language: A Dictionary* (London, Athlone, 2000) 3.

[12] Justinian, *The Institutes*, Bk I, Title II, '*De Iure Naturali, Gentium et Civili*'. The quotation continues: '*cum lege regia, quae de imperio eius lata est, populus ei et in eum omne suum imperium et potestatem concessit*' ('for by the royal law which is passed to confer authority on him, the people yield up to him all its authority and power'); see E Lewis, 'King Above Law? "Quod Principi Placuit" in Bracton' (1964) 39 *Speculum* 240.

[13] Foakes, above n 5, 56, 57.

[14] F Barker, *The Culture of Violence: Essays on Tragedy and History* (Manchester, Manchester University Press, 1993) 145. On the Clown as a metonymic embodiment of 'the ghostly people of Rome', see O Arnold, *The Third Citizen: Shakespeare's Theater and the Early Modern House of Commons* (Baltimore, Md, Johns Hopkins University Press, 2007) 134.

often in the play, law and legal procedure are placed in the narrative foreground of a particular scene.[15] Having identified the theme of reasonable access to justice, Barker subsequently finds the decision to hang the Clown 'inexplicable', 'arbitrary' and 'strange'.[16] The action of Saturninus is definitely arbitrary, but it is not inexplicable and strange to those familiar with juridical developments in the 1590s, when the jurisdiction of common law was encroached on by the prerogative courts, notably in the ecclesiastical court of High Commission. In providing no reason for the emperor's pronouncement,[17] the inherent injustice of imperial rule is demonstrated. It is the arbitrariness of the emperor's action that Shakespeare chooses to illustrate, allowing Saturninus not a moment's reflection before sentencing the Clown to death. It would be far-fetched in the extreme to compare the decision taken by the Secretary of State for the Environment, concerning the remains of the Rose Playhouse, with the tyrannical rule of a fictional Roman emperor. The most that may be argued by way of analogy is that in both instances, one of the principles of natural justice was eschewed, as the law did not allow its subjects recourse to independent arbitration by an impartial tribunal. The questionable legitimacy of an omnipotent executive is a theme that weaves its labyrinthine path through *Titus Andronicus*. From a constitutional perspective, the absence of any institutional structure with which to restrain the conduct of Saturninus poses two obvious questions. First, does the person of the emperor embody the law and, if so, are there any lawful limits to his power? Secondly, if he is not the embodiment of law but rather a symbol of nationhood, is there any law extant which can restrain his unlawful acts?

It is the purpose of this chapter to consider the constitutional significance of *Titus Andronicus* in the historical context of the last decade of Elizabethan rule. There are four themes that I consider. The first is the reaction of those writers of the early modern period who, faithful to the common law and the ancient constitution, opposed the increasing autocracy of government during the 1590s, expressing a preference instead for limited monarchy.[18] Act 1 of *Titus Andronicus* is largely concerned with the succession to the imperial throne. It mirrored political concerns in the 1590s, as the heirless Queen approached the end of her life. Jonathan Bate describes *Titus Andronicus* as a 'descent into imperial tyranny',[19] reflecting speculation about an uncertain political future once Elizabeth had died. The descent into juridical tyranny began during the last decade of Elizabethan

---

[15] See, eg, Act 3, scene 1, in which the judges process past Titus, ignoring his pleas to 'reverse the doom of death' on Quintus and Martius (3.1.24).

[16] Barker, above n 14, 168.

[17] Wilson argues that the scene was possibly based on a petition for freedom of religion, drafted by the Catholic Viscount Montague in 1585, and 'thrust into the Queen's hand' as she walked in Greenwich Park. The petitioner was imprisoned and never released. See R Wilson, *Secret Shakespeare: Studies in Theatre, Religion and Resistance* (Manchester, Manchester University Press, 2004) 30.

[18] The first extensive treatise on the benefits to English subjects of limited monarchy was Sir John Fortescue, *Difference Between an Absolute and Limited Monarchy* (*c* 1471), published as *The Governance of England*, (ed) C Plummer (Oxford, Clarendon, 1885); all references to this work are from Sir John Fortescue, 'The Governance of England' in S Lockwood (ed), *On the Laws and Governance of England* (Cambridge, Cambridge University Press, 1997).

[19] Bate (ed), above n 1, Introduction, 21.

imperial rule, as the jurisdiction of the prerogative courts threatened to usurp that of the courts of common law. It is in this allegorical sense that *Titus Andronicus* may be read as a complementary text, transforming and reconfiguring actual political events into a quasi-historical setting. The existence of an unwritten law, superior in authority to imperial edict, is a theme that not only resonates throughout the play but also underscores *The Reports* of Sir Edward Coke, which he started to compile during the 1590s. Coke equated the supreme judicial authority of common law with the divine provenance of natural law, of which (he claimed) common law was the rational, earthly manifestation.[20] The failure of natural law to redress the shortcomings of imperial law is a significant theme of *Titus Andronicus*, and one that I consider here in relation to the Ciceronian maxim (quoted by Coke on the title page to Part I of *The Reports*): '*Lex est certa ratio e mente divina manans*' ('law is unerring reason, adhering to a divine purpose').[21]

I analyse next the motifs of musical harmony and discord, which provide important aural images throughout the play. I relate these metaphors to the Platonic notion of order (*kosmos*) as a symbol of perfection (*areté*), the achievement of which, in the State or in the individual, depends upon the correct ordering of parts and the performance by each part of its allotted function.[22] The correlation between order, justice and harmony is emphasised, and the distinction is drawn between imperial edict (*lex*) on the one hand and unwritten *lex terrae* (*ius*) on the other.

The third major theme that I consider is the symbolic importance of ancient Rome to the development in England of a body of literature that may loosely be termed republican in nature. Livy's *Roman History* and Plutarch's *Lives* were synthesised by Shakespeare in order to depict an archetypal State that was recognisably Roman in its political structure, but not of a specific period in ancient Roman history. The story of the destruction of Troy, its resurrection in Rome (for which Virgil's *Aeneid* provided most of the source material) and its re-emergence in London as *Troynovant* is a literary device that was employed by Elizabethan poets, dramatists and common lawyers, as a means of establishing the ancient credentials of the English State and English common law.

In the final sections of the chapter, I analyse the various dramatic images of the body politic in *Titus Andronicus*. The continual violation and desecration of the human body is a potent metaphor for the sacrilegious destruction of unwritten, divinely-ordained law, the natural jurisdiction of which was claimed by many common lawyers to be of superior authority to the edicts of earthly magistrates. I consider the anatomical image in its peculiar renaissance context as a representa-

---

[20] 'The law of nature is that which God at the time of creation of the nature of man infused into his heart, for his preservation and direction; and this is *lex æterna*, the moral law, called also the law of nature', Coke, *Postnati. Calvin's Case*, 7 *Reports* (1608) 4: 1a, at 12b.

[21] *Ibid*, 1 *Reports* (1602) 1: title page. On Coke, natural law and the influence of classical jurisprudence over the substantive development of English common law in the early 17th century, see P Raffield, 'Contract, Classicism, and the Common-Weal: Coke's *Reports* and the Foundations of the Modern English Constitution' (2005) 17 *Law & Literature* 69.

[22] Plato, *The Republic*, Bk IV.I.427d–434d, Bk IV.III.441c–444e.

tion of the body politic and, with specific reference to the mutilation of the human body in *Titus Andronicus*, as the *antirrhetic*: the inverted representation of the *apologia*.[23] Related to the unwritten nature of the ancient constitution is the issue of religion, honour and tradition, and their representation in sacrificial ritual. The enactment of religious rites is a recurring dramatic motif in *Titus Andronicus*, a theme that is linked to the idea that the unwritten English constitution is predicated upon the primacy of manners and custom, rather than the codification of rights and obligations.[24] At one level the play operates as an archetypal revenge tragedy, but it is at least arguable that the final, redemptive scene of honour and tradition elevates the play from its diminished status as a dramatic blood-bath (accorded it by numerous critics) to a prophetic treatise on the nature of governance and the constitutional status of the subject of law.

II. Late-Elizabethan Imperial Government and the Common Law

Before his petitions for justice are shot into the heavens, in a scene that combines unbearable pathos with grotesque comedy, Titus informs his brother Marcus that Astraea (the goddess of justice) has left the earth:

> *Terras Astraea reliquit*: be you remembered, Marcus,
> She's gone, she's fled. Sirs, take you to your tools.
> You, cousins, shall go sound the ocean
> And cast your nets:
> Happily you may catch her in the sea;
> Yet there's as little justice as at land. (4.3.4–9)[25]

In terms of the political iconography of late-Elizabethan England, the image of the virgin goddess of justice fleeing the wickedness of mankind and ascending to the heavens as the constellation Virgo (drawn from Book 1 of Ovid's *Metamorphoses*)[26] is striking. The myth of Astraea was so thoroughly associated with the person of

---

[23] On *apologia* and *antirrhesis*, see P Goodrich, *Oedipus Lex: Psychoanalysis, History, Law* (Los Angeles, University of California Press, 1995) 45–56.

[24] The definitive study of the original sources of the English constitution and their interpretation by jurists of the early modern period remains J G A Pocock, *The Ancient Constitution and the Feudal Law: A Study of English Historical Thought in the Seventeenth Century* (Cambridge, Cambridge University Press, 1987).

[25] The pathos is heightened by the tragic-comic spectacle of the one-handed Titus distributing arrows to his family members and instructing them to 'loose when I bid'. (4.3.59) Barker, above n 14, at 167, refers accurately to 'nervous and uncomfortable laughter' which the play 'has both engendered and received'.

[26] 'All duty to gods and to men lay vanquished; and Justice the Maiden was last of the heavenly throng to abandon the blood-drenched earth', Ovid, *Metamorphoses*, (tr) D Raeburn (London, Penguin, 2004) 12, Bk I, 148–50. Bate notes that 'Queen Elizabeth was mythologised as the returned Astraea of Virgil's fourth eclogue', Bate (ed), above n 1, Introduction, 28.

Elizabeth I that any suggestion that the goddess of justice had taken flight from the world was potentially disquieting.[27]

Titus Andronicus was by no means the first dramatic work to represent public concerns about the successor to Elizabeth I. As early in her reign as January 1562, the Inner Temple had presented, in the presence of the Queen, *The Tragedy of Gorboduc* (also known as *The Tragedy of Ferrex and Porrex*), written by two common lawyers, Thomas Norton and Thomas Sackville. The play was the first full-length dramatic work to be written in blank verse. Dramatists were awakening to the suggestive power of the poetic form and its capacity to transmit political metaphors to a receptive audience. In *The Defence of Poesy*, Sir Philip Sidney refers to the 'wholesome iambic, who rubs the galled mind in making shame the trumpet of villainy, with bold and open crying out against naughtiness'.[28] Sidney is especially astute in his assessment of tragic drama and its unique capacity to embody jurisprudential ideals such as justice, equity and liberty, and their antitheses: tyranny, inequality and oppression. He employs two popular poetic images, the anatomical and the architectural (both of which were used extensively by Shakespeare in *Titus Andronicus*), arguing that

> tragedy, that openeth the greatest wounds, and showeth forth the ulcers that are covered with tissue; that maketh kings fear to be tyrants, and tyrants manifest their tyrannical humours; that with stirring the affects of admiration and commiseration teacheth the uncertainty of this world, and upon how weak foundations gilden roofs are builded.[29]

Gorboduc depicts the terrible consequences of an injudicious succession, which left 'the land for a long time almost desolate and miserably wasted'.[30]

A debate over the correct form that the succession should take provides much of the dialogue in the opening scene of *Titus Andronicus*, when Saturninus and Bassianus, the two sons of the deceased emperor, both lay claim to the imperial

---

[27] See F A Yates, *Astraea: The Imperial Theme in the Sixteenth Century* (London, Routledge & Kegan Paul, 1975) 75–80.

[28] Sir Philip Sidney, 'The Defence of Poesy', in G Alexander (ed), *Sidney's 'The Defence of Poesy' and Selected Renaissance Literary Criticism* (London, Penguin, 2004) 26; Sidney admired *Gorboduc* for its 'stately speeches and well-sounding phrases, climbing to the height of Seneca's style, and as full of notable morality, which it doth most delightfully teach, and so obtain the very end of poesy', but he criticised the play on structural grounds for disregarding the classical unities of time, place and action, *ibid*, 44–45. It is noteworthy in the political context of *Gorboduc* that Thomas Norton became a notorious persecutor and State-torturer of Catholics; following his appointment in 1581 as official censor of Catholics, he became known as 'Rackmaster' Norton. See M A R Graves, *Thomas Norton: The Parliament Man* (Oxford, Blackwell, 1994). In 1567, Thomas Sackville was created Baron Buckhurst; he succeeded Lord Burghley as Lord High Treasurer in 1599 and was created the first Earl of Dorset in 1604. For the argument that *Gorboduc* 'was probably a source for *Titus Andronicus*', see D Callaghan and C R Kyle, 'The Wilde Side of Justice in Early Modern England and *Titus Andronicus*', in C Jordan and K Cunningham (eds), *The Law in Shakespeare* (Basingstoke, Palgrave Macmillan, 2007) 41.

[29] Sidney, 'The Defence of Poesy', in Alexander (ed), above n 28, at 27–28.

[30] T Norton and T Sackville, 'The argument of the Tragedie' in *The Tragidie of Ferrex and Porrex, set forth without addition or alteration but altogether as the same was shewed on stage before the Queenes Maiestie, about nine years past, vz. the xviii day of Ianuarie. 1561. by the gentlemen of the Inner Temple* (London, Iohn Daye, 1570) A.i.v. The political symbolism of *Ferrex and Porrex* or *Gorboduc* is discussed in P Raffield, *Images and Cultures of Law in Early Modern England: Justice and Political Power, 1558–1660* (Cambridge, Cambridge University Press, 2004) 127–31.

throne. More closely linked to the themes of the play, and to the polity of Elizabethan and post-Elizabethan England, is the issue of the form that governance would take once the issue of the succession had been decided. Associated with the particular form of governance are its effects on the constitutional structure of the State and the lives of individual citizens. The 1534 Act of Supremacy (*26 H.8. cap. 1*) had the immediate effect of severing English jurisdiction from that of Rome, thereby arrogating to the Crown unrestricted imperial power. Henry VIII annexed all the necessary jurisdictions with which to fulfil his imperial claims. The idea that the monarch was under God but not law was axiomatic of Henrician rule. It ran counter to Sir John Fortescue's theory of mixed monarchy, which was predicated upon the existence of *dominium politicum et regale*.[31] As John Guy has noted, the success of Henrician government ensured the enhancement of *regale* at the expense of *politicum*.[32] The imperial theory of kingship was compatible neither with the equitable principles of justice that were espoused by Christopher St German in *Doctor and Student*,[33] nor with the works of humanist writers, such as Thomas Elyot, whose political theories were heavily influenced by Aristotelian ideals of civic republicanism. The *Imperium* of the monarch was implicitly criticised in Elyot's description of the perfect commonwealth, which he characterised as 'disposed by the order of equity and governed by the rule and moderation of reason'.[34]

The 1559 Act of Supremacy (*1 Eliz. cap. 1*) affirmed the divine provenance of Elizabethan supremacy, in relation to which Parliament was to play the subsidiary role of a legislative instrument: the institutional manifestation of the Royal Prerogative.[35] Conscious of the potentially unrestricted political power with which the theory of divine right endowed the monarch, the Elizabethan cleric (and Master of the Temple) Richard Hooker reiterated Bracton's dictum that '[t]he axioms of our regal government are these, *Lex facit Regem*'.[36] Elizabeth had from the start of her reign laid particular emphasis on the extensive powers of the Royal Prerogative. In the 1590s, fear both of invasion from abroad and rebellion from within led to its more expansive employment. The constitutional implications of late-Elizabethan imperial rule became apparent as the Court of High Commission, under the leadership of Bishop Aylmer, supplanted the jurisdiction of the courts of common law in ecclesiastical causes. Notoriously, the *ex officio mero* prosecutions of High Commission had an historical basis in Roman canon law, the jurisdiction of which had been severely limited by the Act of Supremacy of 1534.

---

[31] Fortescue, 'Governance of England', above n 18, 83.

[32] J Guy, *Tudor England* (Oxford, Oxford University Press, 1990) 13.

[33] On St German and the constitutional sovereignty of the common law, see J Guy, 'Thomas More and Christopher St German: The Battle of the Books', in Fox and Guy, above n 6, 100; see also J Guy, *Christopher St German on Chancery and Statute* (London, Selden Society, 1985).

[34] T Elyot, *The Book Named the Governor* (London, J M Dent, 1962) 1.

[35] On Elizabethan Parliaments and the Royal Prerogative, see J Guy, 'The Elizabethan Establishment and the Ecclesiastical Polity', in J Guy (ed) *The Reign of Elizabeth I: Court and Culture in the Last Decade* (Cambridge, Cambridge University Press, 1995) 133–36.

[36] R Hooker, *Of the Laws of Ecclesiastical Polity*, (ed) A S McGrade (Cambridge, Cambridge University Press, 1989) 147, Bk VIII.3.3.

In procedural terms, the Courts of High Commission were inquisitorial, compelling defendants (on oath) to answer questions that were put to them by ecclesiastical adjudicators. The fundamental question, concerning the limits (if any) to the imperial power of the Queen, was raised in *Cawdrey's Case* in 1591. The case concerned the deprivation of a minister's benefice by the Court of High Commission. The exercise of the Royal Prerogative, which authorised the arbitrary powers of High Commission and its civilian officials, was justified on the grounds that 'by the ancient laws of this realm, this kingdom of England is an absolute empire and monarchy'.[37] The 1559 Act of Supremacy conferred upon the Queen, the

> power to assign commissioners to exercise and execute all manner of jurisdiction spiritual, to visit, reform, &c all schism and heresy, &c and enormities, which by any manner of spiritual jurisdiction can, or lawfully may be reformed.[38]

Cawdrey's Case planted the seeds of conflict between the rival jurisdictions of common law and ecclesiastical law, and by extension between the common law and the imperial power of the Crown.

Dissension continued when James I succeeded the throne. In *Nicholas Fuller's Case* (1607), Coke argued that, contrary to the notion of unlimited imperial power,

> the construction of the statute *1. Eliz. cap. 1* [Act of Supremacy 1559] and of the letters patent of high commission in ecclesiastical causes founded upon the said act, belongs to the Judges of the common law; for although that the causes, the cognizance of which belongs to them, are merely spiritual, and the law by which they proceed is merely spiritual, yet their authority and power is given to them by act of Parliament, and letters patent, the construction of which belongs to temporal Judges.[39]

In May 1611, at a meeting of the Privy Council to which 'all the Justices of England were by command of the King assembled', Coke informed James

> that when we the Just. of the Common Pleas see the commission newly reformed, we will, as to that which is of right, seek to satisfy the King's expectation.

The judges then 'departed without any demand of our opinions'.[40]

Coke's intransigent stance on this issue was a principled response to the constitutional implications of the power vested in High Commission.[41] The civil lawyers

---

[37] Coke, *Caudrey's Case. Of the King's Ecclesiastical Law*, 5 Reports (1605) 3: Preface, viiib. The constitutional implications of the case are discussed in Guy, 'The Elizabethan Establishment', above n 35, at 131–32.

[38] Quoted in Coke, *Sir Anthony Roper's Case*, 12 Reports (1655) 7: 46a, at 46b.

[39] *Ibid*, *Nicholas Fuller's Case*, 42a.

[40] *Ibid*, *High Commission*, 85a, at 86a.

[41] In October 1613, Coke was 'promoted' from the office of Chief Justice of the Common Pleas to that of Chief Justice of the King's Bench. The latter post was considered to be less influential and was in receipt of a lower salary than the former. Bacon, who was instrumental in the transfer, argued that this punitive action 'will be thought abroad a kind of discipline to him for opposing himself in the king's causes'; he also believed that Coke might 'think himself near a privy councillor's place, and thereupon turn obsequious', *The Works of Francis Bacon*, (eds) J Spedding, R L Ellis, D D Heath, 14 vols (London, Longmans, 1857–74) 4: 381.

and clerics who administered the affairs of High Commission sought for themselves the exclusive right to decide what constituted an ecclesiastical cause in any particular case. Also, they exercised the power of imprisonment over a range of offences that were of only peripheral ecclesiastical interest; for example, non-payment of tithes or, as in *Sir Anthony Roper's Case*, 'for a pension out of a rectory impropriate, of which Sir Anthony was seised in fee'. The case was concerned with a dispute over temporal issues and as Coke noted, '[s]ubstraction of tithes is injury and no crime, but concerns interest and property: and for this the High Commission cannot meddle with it'.[42] Coke sought to assign to High Commission a limited role of discussion and declaration on spiritual issues, leaving the courts of common law to resolve matters that were traditionally within their jurisdiction; notably, in the area of disputes concerning property, and secular constitutional causes such as imprisonment of subjects. The Archbishop of Canterbury complained to the Privy Council about the use of *Habeas Corpus* by the Court of Common Pleas, where the purpose was to bring prisoners detained by High Commission before the judges of the common law.[43] Coke was adamant that High Commission had no lawful authority to 'confound the jurisdiction of the Ordinary'.[44] In this respect Coke believed that the power exercised by High Commission was arbitrary and irrational. Coke stated 'that it was good for the weal public, that the Judges of the common law should interpret the statutes, and acts of Parliament within this realm'.[45] In other words, the judges of the common law were the supreme constitutional arbiters and interpreters of legislative intent. By drawing attention to the good of the 'common weal', Coke not only tacitly approved the republican principle, *salus populi suprema lex est*[46]; implicit also in the above comments is Coke's belief in the constitutional supremacy of common law and the hegemony within this putative settlement of its judiciary.

The concerns expressed by Coke in relation to the tyrannical implications of imperial rule are echoed by Shakespeare in *Titus Andronicus*. Both writers employed sophisticated rhetorical techniques in order to convey the nature of governance and its relationship to the lives of citizens within the early modern English State.[47] As Allen D Boyer noted in his study of Coke and the Elizabethan era, '[w]hat Shakespeare has been to those who write in English, Sir Edward Coke

---

[42] Coke, *Sir Anthony Roper's Case*, 12 Reports 7: 46b.
[43] Coke, *High Commission*, 12 Reports 7: 85a. The Archbishop referred to *Sir William Chancey's Case*. Chancey was imprisoned indefinitely in Fleet prison, by force of a warrant from High Commission, 'for adultery, and for expelling her [his wife] from his company, and cohabitation with another woman, and without allowing her any competent maintenance', *ibid*, *Sir William Chancey's Case*, 83a; a writ of *Habeas Corpus* was issued by the Court of Common Pleas, which decided that 'the Commissioners had not power to imprison him in this case', *ibid*, 83b.
[44] Coke, *Sir Anthony Roper's Case*, 12 Reports 7: 47a.
[45] Ibid, *High Commission*, 85a–b.
[46] In *Keighley's Case*, Coke explicitly states that 'the reason thereof is *pro bono publico*, for *salus populi* is *suprema lex*', 10 Reports (1614) 5: 139a, at 139b.
[47] On Shakespeare's use of rhetorical techniques in *Titus Andronicus*, see Kermode, above n 5, at 7–11.

has been to the lawyers of the English-speaking world'.[48] Coke was no dramatist, and was less than well-disposed towards the theatre and its practitioners. Following his appointment as Chief Justice of the Court of Common Pleas, Coke gave the following advice to the Grand Jury at the Norwich assizes in 1606:

> The abuse of *Stage players*, wherewith I find the Countrey much troubled, may easily be reformed: They having no Commission to play in any place without leave: And therefore, if by your willingnesse they be not entertained, you may soone be rid of them.[49]

His antipathy towards actors did not dissuade him from using identical imagery to that employed by Shakespeare, in order to represent the social contract that Coke believed to exist between magistrate and subject of law. Using a familiar anatomical metaphor of the renaissance period, in which the workings of the body politic were likened to the interrelated organs of the human body, Coke describes a reciprocal arrangement between king and subject:

> As the ligatures or strings do knit together the joints of all the parts of the body, so doth ligeance join together the Sovereign and all his subjects, *quasi uno ligamine*.[50]

A similar anatomical metaphor is employed by Menenius at the start of *Coriolanus*, in order to describe the particular nature of the Roman body politic to the rebellious citizenry.[51] While Coke's use of the anatomical metaphor emphasises the interdependency of subject and monarch, in which community and consensus are implied, Menenius describes an authoritarian and hierarchic body politic in which the Platonic cosmic order is reflected in the correct ordering of status and function within human societies.[52]

Bate is alert to the legal and historical context in which *Titus Andronicus* situates the common law principle of precedent, noting the use by Titus of 'the language of the law' in the final scene of the play.[53] Through the systematic reporting of the *ratio decidendi* of contemporary cases, and his emphasis on the antiquity of common law and the legitimacy that its immemorial nature conferred on the discretion of its judges, Coke elevated the binding power of precedent to hitherto unknown levels. Kevin Sharpe makes the important observation that the synthesis between past and present gave to history an exalted status in the governance of

---

[48] A D Boyer, *Sir Edward Coke and the Elizabethan Age* (Stanford, Conn, Stanford University Press, 2003) Preface, ix.

[49] Sir Edward Coke, *The Lord Coke His Speech and Charge. With a Discoverie of the Abuses and Corruption of Officers* (London, Christopher Pursett, 1607) H2.r. Coke addressed the jury at the Norwich assizes on 4 August 1606; he was appointed Chief Justice of the Court of Common Pleas on 30 June 1606.

[50] Coke, *Postnati. Calvin's Case*, 7 *Reports* (1608) 4: 4b. For an analysis of Coke's use of anatomical imagery in *Calvin's Case*, see Raffield, above n 21, at 79–82. Examples of 16th-century, illustrated anatomical textbooks include: C Estienne, *De Dissectione partium corporis humani* (Paris, 1545); T Geminus, *Compendiosa totius anatomie delineation* (London, J Herfordie, 1545); A Vesalius, *De humani corporis fabrica librorum epitome* (Basle, 1543); see J Sawday, *The Body Emblazoned: Dissection and the Human Body in Renaissance Culture* (London, Routledge, 1995); D L Hodges, *Renaissance Fictions of Anatomy* (Amherst, University of Massachusetts Press, 1985).

[51] *Coriolanus*, 1.1.94–161.

[52] See ch 4, text to nn 133–35.

[53] Bate (ed), above n 1, Introduction, 28.

early modern English society.[54] If, as Bate suggests, Titus is 'a dramatic antecedent to Sir Edward Coke',[55] his search for justice marks him out also as the dramatic descendant of the Lancastrian Chief Justice and apologist for the constitutional supremacy of common law, Sir John Fortescue. In *Difference Between an Absolute and Limited Monarchy*, Fortescue asserts that under *dominium politicum et regale* (which he claims provides the English constitutional model), a 'king may not rule his people by other laws than such as they assent to'.[56] Alan Cromartie has remarked that Fortescue's office as Chief Justice under Henry VI provided 'unimpeachable authority . . . for a range of near-republican opinions'. As Cromartie also notes, and of particular relevance to the initiation of the plot in *Titus Andronicus*, Fortescue served the House of Lancaster, the lives of whose members depended upon the efficacious claim of King Henry VI to the lawful succession.[57]

III. Order, Harmony and Musicality

Titus claims that justice, in the form of the goddess Astraea, has fled the earth. The Andronici fire their shafts into the heavens. Attached to each arrow is an injunction to the Gods from Titus, enjoining them '[t]o send down Justice' (4.3.52). It is instructive briefly to consider the philosophical and juristic distinction between justice and law, as this distinction characterises the political polarity that engenders the personal animosity between Saturninus and Titus. Saturninus, the imperial lawmaker, appears to be uncomprehending when he reads Titus's divine injunctions, although there is a degree of irony in the question he poses his attendants: 'A goodly humour, is it not, my lords? / As who would say, in Rome no justice were'. (4.4.19–20) The representation of justice can be traced to pre-Roman and, indeed, to pre-Hellenic antiquity. Common to all these depictions of the goddess of justice is her femininity. For the ancient Egyptians, she was known as Ma'at, and was usually portrayed holding a sword and wearing an ostrich feather in her hair. The Roman goddess, Justitia, is probably the most familiar representation, usually portrayed as holding balanced scales in one hand, a sword in the other, and wearing a blindfold.[58] In *The Digest*, Justinian confirms the feminine association, stating that law is the queen of all things divine and human ('*Lex est omnium divinarum & humanarum rerum Regina*').[59] The Greek goddess

---

[54] K Sharpe, *Politics and Ideas in Early Stuart England* (London, Pinter Publishing, 1989) 174–81.
[55] Bate (ed), above n 1, Introduction, 28.
[56] Fortescue, 'Governance of England', above n 18, at 83.
[57] A Cromartie, *The Constitutionalist Revolution: An Essay on the History of England, 1450–1642* (Cambridge, Cambridge University Press, 2006) 21.
[58] On the historical importance of the effigy or statue in legal iconology, see Goodrich, above n 23, 108–15.
[59] Justinian, *The Digest* 1.3.2; Justinian was quoting from the Greek Stoic philosopher, Chryssipus (c 280–207 BC); the translation from Greek into Latin is provided by Sir William Dugdale, *Origines Juridiciales or Historical Memorials of the English Laws* (London, F & T Warren, 1666) 2.

of justice, Themis, represents most clearly the ideals of equity, community and consent, to which the juristic principles of Fortescue, St German and Coke are traceable.[60] Of great relevance to the semiotics of legal iconography, unlike Justitia (her Roman counterpart), Themis was never depicted holding a sword: consent rather than coercion was her preferred form of governance.[61]

For Plato, justice (*dikaiosunê*) was only one of the four cardinal virtues which the ideal State must embody.[62] Plato's concept of justice was not legalistic; as Alasdair Macintyre has argued, *dikaiosunê* was concerned with 'allocating each part of the soul its particular function: sometimes translated as "justice" '.[63] Plato's idea of justice is inextricably linked to the notion of harmonious relations between the State and the individual, and between fellow citizens of the State. Roman *justitia* was concerned with formal, legal relations; whereas Greek *dikaiosunê* implied the ideal good of society, across a wide range of collective existence, not merely in terms of laws and their application. The theme of harmonious relations between governor and governed is central to Plato's depiction of the State. He insists that justice should establish in the minds of all citizens a 'natural relation of control and subordination',[64] and that *dikaiosunê* regulates the functions of the other three virtues, 'keeping all three in tune, like the notes of a scale'.[65] The Greek *nomos* means both 'tune' and 'law', and as Trevor J Saunders notes, Plato employed the pun on *nomos* throughout *The Laws*, for example in his assertion that 'After the prelude [the preliminary analysis of the State] should come the "tune", or more accurately a sketch of a legal and political framework'.[66] The relationship between musical harmony and the making of good laws is a recurring theme in *The Laws*. Writing about the legal regulation of music in the Athenian democracy, Plato describes a

> kind of song too, which they thought of as a separate class, and the name they gave it was this very word that is so often on our lips: 'nomes' ('for the lyre', as they always added).[67]

The association of the lyre with the harmonious governance of society was first recorded in the myth of Orpheus, and remained a central image in the iconography of common law during the early modern period.

---

[60] Emphasising the image of femininity and chastity, John Selden writes that 'the Lady Common Law must ly alone', in *Titles of Honor* (London, Iohn Helme, 1614) a.3.*v.*

[61] On the mythological background of Themis, and her distinction from Dikê (princess of justice), see C Burnett, 'Justice, Myth and Symbol' (1987) 11 *Legal Studies Forum* 79.

[62] Plato, *The Republic*, Bk IV.I.427d–434d. The other Platonic virtues are: *sôphrosunê* (temperance or restraint imposed by reason); *andreia* (courage or fortitude); *sophia* (wisdom)

[63] A Macintyre, *After Virtue: a Study in Moral Theory* (London, Duckworth, 1981) 132. On *dikaiosunê* and the 'sense of justice' in the State, see Aristotle, *The Politics*, (tr) T A Sinclair (London, Penguin, 1992) 61, Bk I.II.1253a29–b1. *Dikaiosunê* is the virtue of justice, while *dikê* is the institutional expression of justice in the legal system; see *ibid*, 61, n 24.

[64] Plato, *The Republic*, (tr) Desmond Lee (London, Penguin, 1987) 162, Bk IV.III.444d.

[65] *Ibid*, 161, Bk IV.III.443d.

[66] Plato, *The Laws*, (tr) T J Saunders (London, Penguin, 2004) 156, Bk V.IX.734e; see also, *ibid*, 513, n 1.

[67] *Ibid*, 107–08, Bk III.V.700b.

Order, Harmony and Musicality

The musical metaphor of the stringed instrument was employed by the Elizabethan divine, Richard Hooker, with reference to the nature of kingship. In *Of the Laws of Ecclesiastical Polity*, Hooker aligns Christian theology with an Aristotelian model of community.[68] The co-existence of Church and State is a central tenet of Hooker's communitarian ethos. In the ideal commonwealth that Hooker describes, the monarch is the unifying figure that links the Church in an indivisible bond with the people. Crucially, the subject of power in Hooker's commonwealth is not the monarch in person but the 'body of the commonwealth'.[69] In such a polity, 'where the King doth guide the state and the law the King, that commonwealth is like an harp or melodious instrument'.[70] Hooker's allusion to the musical harmony of Orpheus's lyre demonstrates the potency of classical mythology and the resonance of its images in the imaginations of early modern writers. As George Hersey has noted, the myth of Orpheus and the lyre 'records the moment when law was first introduced into the society that invented that myth'.[71] The playing of music does not figure greatly in *Titus Andronicus*, but reference to music does. Where music is played, it is confined to flourishes, which usually signal the arrival of important personages in the Roman State, such as the emperor, senators and tribunes. Of the 10 stage directions in the First Quarto (published in 1594) that refer to music, four of them occur in Act 1.[72] The music of Act 1 is of a ceremonial kind, intended to convey the pomp, power and dignity of the Roman State. In the words of Saturninus: 'Proclaim our honours, lords, with trump and drum'. (1.1.279) The use of drums and trumpets, in the form of brief martial flourishes, suggests the imposition of imperial order rather than the natural order of the Platonic cosmos or the equitable political order of the Aristotelian city-State. Still less does the Rome of *Titus Andronicus* resemble the 'melodious instrument' of Hooker's ideal commonwealth.

Beyond the first scene of the play there are only six stage directions in the First Quarto that refer to the inclusion of music, three of which are in Act 5 and signal

---

[68] On the influence of Aristotle over the political theory of Hooker, see T Moore, 'Recycling Aristotle: The Sovereignty Theory of Richard Hooker' (1993) 19 *History of Political Thought* 345.

[69] McGrade (ed), above n 36, 179, Bk VIII.6.1.

[70] *Ibid*, 146, Bk VIII.3.3; on Hooker's subjection of the monarch to the interests of society, see P Lake, *Anglicans and Puritans? Presbyterianism and English Conformist Thought from Whitgift to Hooker* (London, Unwin Hymen, 1988) 109, 201.

[71] G Hersey, *The Lost Meaning of Classical Architecture: Speculations on Ornament from Vitruvius to Venturi* (Cambridge, Mass, MIT Press, 1988) 5. George Puttenham wrote that 'Orpheus assembled the wilde beasts to come in heards to harken to his musicke, and by that meanes made them tame, implying thereby, how by his discreete and wholsome lessons uttered in harmonie and with melodious instruments, he brought the rude and savage people to a more civill and orderly life', Puttenham, *The Arte of English Poesie*, above n 8, at 4. See also, Cicero: 'What the musicians call harmony in song is concord in a State, the strongest and best bond of permanent union in any commonwealth', Marcus Tullius Cicero, *De Re Publica* in *De Re Publica, De Legibus*, (tr) C W Keyes (Cambridge, Mass, Harvard University Press, 2006) 183, Bk II.XLII.69.

[72] *The Most Lamentable Romaine Tragedie of Titus Andronicus* (London, Edward White & Thomas Millington, 1594): 'Enter the Tribunes and Senatours aloft: And then enter Saturninus and his followers at one dore, and Bassianus and his followers, with Drums and Trumpets' A3.*r*; 'Sound Drums and Trumpets, and then enter two of Titus sonnes' A4.*r*; 'Sound Trumpets, and lay the Coffin in the Tombe' B.*v*; 'sound trumpets, manet Moore' C2.*v*.

the imminent arrival of a new imperial order under the rule of Titus's son, Lucius. The only contrast with the ceremonial flourishes of trumpets occurs in Act 2, in which the natural order of the forest is immediately juxtaposed with the artificial order of the Capitol. The First Quarto's stage direction at the start of Act 2 reads: 'Enter Titus Andronicus, and his three sonnes. making a noise with hounds & hornes'. (2.1.0) This is followed a few lines later by: 'Here a crie of Hounds, and wind hornes in a peale' (2.1.10).[73] The natural harmony of the forest is soon to be shattered irrevocably by the murders, mutilations and rape that take place there. In such inharmonious circumstances, the further use of music may be considered extraneous and inappropriate. Instead, the violated body of Lavinia becomes the mute embodiment of a discordant society, in which the intrinsic reason of natural law has been replaced by the irrationality of tyranny. Referring to the appalling act of mutilation and violation, perpetrated upon Lavinia by her barbaric assailants, Marcus Andronicus draws our attention to a central metaphor of the play: the body as the symbol both of the harmonious commonwealth, of the kind envisaged by Hooker, and of the *ordo naturae*.[74] In contemplation of the terrible and pitiful sight of Lavinia, Marcus laments:

> O, had the monster seen those lily hands
> Tremble like aspen leaves upon a lute
> And make the silken strings delight to kiss them,
> He would not then have touched them for his life.
> Or had he heard the heavenly harmony
> Which that sweet tongue hath made,
> He would have dropped his knife and fell asleep,
> As Cerberus at the Thracian poet's feet. (2.3.44–51)[75]

It is especially apt that Shakespeare should refer to Orpheus, the Thracian poet, in the context of the hideous crimes committed against Lavinia. As Marcus tells the audience, she was the personification of natural harmony; but such is the level of barbarity to which the subjects of tyrannical rule have sunk, that they do not hear the melodious charms of Orpheus's lyre. Aurality and orality are recurring metaphors in the play[76]: Lavinia cannot speak of her violation because her tongue

---

[73] *Ibid*, D.r.

[74] On the political symbolism of the rape of Lavinia and the subsequent mutilation of her body, see A Hadfield, *Shakespeare and Renaissance Politics* (London, Arden Shakespeare, 2004) 121.

[75] With reference to the myth of Orpheus, Hersey states that Giambattista Vico, in *La Scienza nuova seconda* (1744), developed tropes of the word *corda*, meaning variously tendons, sinews, lyre strings and musical chords, all of which implied 'the union of the cords and powers of the fathers, whence derived public powers', quoted in Hersey, above n 71, at 5. Fortescue also noted the linguistic and symbolic connection between laws and ligaments: 'The Law, under which the People is incorporated, may be compared to the Nerves or Sinews of the Body Natural; for, as by these the whole Frame is fitly joined together and compacted, so is the Law that Ligament (to go back to the truest Derivation of the Word, *Lex à Ligando*) by which the Body Politic, and all its several Members are bound together and united in one entire Body', Sir John Fortescue, *De Laudibus Legum Angliae*, (ed) J Selden (London, R Gosling, 1737) 22.

[76] On the importance of the aural metaphor in legal discourse, see B J Hibbitts, 'Making Sense of Metaphors: Visuality, Aurality and the Reconfiguration of American legal Discourse' (1994) 16 *Cardozo Law Review* 229.

has been cut out[77]; unlike Cerberus, in the myth of Orpheus, the bestial Chiron and Demetrius are deaf to the sweet music of the lyre; Quintus and Martius, Titus's sons, are denied the right to speak in their defence against the wrongful charge of the murder of Bassianus; and Saturninus and the Roman judiciary refuse to entertain Titus's oral plea for justice on behalf of his sons.

Saturninus prejudges the guilt of Quintus and Martius and denies them even the semblance of a trial: 'Let them not speak a word: the guilt is plain' (2.2.301). The uncaring, unhearing judges process past Titus, on their way to the execution of his two sons. 'Hear me, grave fathers' (3.1.1), he entreats the patriarchs of the law, prostrating himself as they pass; but they are oblivious to his injunction for mercy. Lucius reinforces the metaphor of aurality, telling his father 'The tribunes hear you not' (3.1.28) and reminding him four lines later that 'no tribune hears you speak'. (3.1.32) Titus replies that 'if they did hear, / They would not mark me' (3.1.33–34), observing that 'tribunes with their tongues doom men to death'. (3.1.47) The absence of an impartial trial before an independent tribunal is a flagrant breach of one of the basic principles of natural justice, *audi alteram partem* ('hear the other side'): the right to a fair hearing.[78] In the 1590s, it was the blatant disregard for this right that exercised Coke, in those cases concerning the deprivation of liberty by the Court of High Commission. It is over the issue of speaking and being heard that Shakespeare comes closest to approving the oral tradition of common law, in preference to the civilian predilection for textual exposition of law. The former represents a jurisprudence that is spoken by its patriarchs, the judges, having heard the arguments placed before them by the disputants. It is a flexible system that allows judges to exercise their legal imaginations in the interests of justice, delivering equitable judgments that demonstrate a palpable response to the human complexities of individual cases.[79]

IV. The Depiction of Troynovant

The idea that constitutional theory could be represented through an order of visible signs was central to the development of a political aesthetic during the 16th

---

[77] Marcus Andronicus refers to the Ovidian myth of Philomela, from which the story of Lavinia is derived: 'Fair Philomela, why she but lost her tongue, / And in a tedious sampler sewed her mind' (2.3.38–39). In Ovid's story, the compassionate gods turned Philomela into a nightingale and her sister, Procne, into a swallow (*Metamorphoses*, Bk VI.412–674), although ancient Greek sources have Procne turned into a nightingale and her tongueless sister, Philomela, into a swallow. On the Philomel story as a paradigm of, or precedent for, *Titus*, see J Bate, *Shakespeare and Ovid* (Oxford, Clarendon, 1993) 101–17.

[78] For a reading of *Titus Andronicus* 'as a play which presents political tyranny as the refusal of an open hearing of the evidence', see L Hutson, *The Invention of Suspicion: Law and Mimesis in Shakespeare and Renaissance Drama* (Oxford, Oxford University Press, 2007) 91.

[79] On the poetic imagination of the ideal judge, see M Nussbaum, *Poetic Justice: the Literary Imagination and Public Life* (Boston, Mass, Beacon Press, 1995) 80–82.

century. John Guy notes that '[t]he most spectacular assets of the monarchy were the person and image of the ruler',[80] but he also observes that the iconography of humanist and classical literature linked the Aristotelian notion of *amici principis* ('friends' or counsellors to the ruler) to the principle of limited monarchy in the best interests of the commonwealth.[81] The ideology of the commonwealth is a theme that dominated the writing of humanist authors throughout the Tudor period, from Elyot's *The Book Named the Governor* to Hooker's *Of the Laws of Ecclesiastical Polity*. Sir Thomas Smith had linked the notion of commonwealth with liberty, community and self-determination, defining it as 'a society or common doing of a multitude of free men collected together and united by common accord and covenauntes among themselves'.[82] The theme of the equitable commonwealth became dominant amongst Neoplatonic humanists partly because of the greater availability of the published works of 'communitarian' writers of the classical and medieval periods (notably Plato, Aristotle, Cicero, St Augustine and St Thomas Aquinas), facilitated by the revolutionary improvements in printing technology.[83] The creation by Henry VIII of a sovereign English jurisprudence provided the intellectual impetus for a generation of writers to imagine and describe the ideal State, and the relationship therein between ruler and citizen.

Titus Andronicus was the first of Shakespeare's Roman plays. Throughout his career, he found the political structure and institutions of ancient Rome an illuminating metaphor for the human aspiration to create a nation from the ashes of an earlier civilisation. In *The Roman History*, Livy records the legendary foundation of Rome by Aeneas, after his escape from Troy. As Bate reminds us in his introduction to *Titus Andronicus*, English writers replicated this myth, accrediting the foundation of Britain to another Trojan fugitive, Brutus.[84] *Troia Nova*, the new Troy, or *Troynovant* as it was known to Elizabethan writers, represented an aspiration for a nation that had been reborn in 1534 as a sovereign nation-State. As Edmund Spenser wrote in *The Faerie Queene*: 'For noble *Britons* sprong from *Troians* bold, / And *Troynovant* was built of old Troyes ashes cold'.[85] Elizabeth was depicted not only as Astraea, the goddess of justice, but also as the 'beauteous Queene of second Troy'.[86] The image of a mythical State, governed by a benevolent law-maker, was employed by Coke in *The Reports*. As he sought to invest the

---

[80] J Guy, 'Tudor Monarchy and its Critiques' in J Guy (ed), *The Tudor Monarchy* (London, Arnold, 1997) 78; see also K Sharpe, *Selling the Tudor Monarchy: Authority and Image in 16th-Century England* (New Haven, Conn, Yale University Press, 2009).

[81] Guy, 'Tudor Monarchy and its Critiques', above n 80, at 81.

[82] Sir Thomas Smith, *De Republica Anglorum* (1583), (ed) M Dewar (Cambridge, Cambridge University Press, 1982) 57.

[83] On the socio-political effects of the innovative printing process, see E L Eisenstein, *The Printing Press as an Agent of Change*, 2 vols (Cambridge, Cambridge University Press, 1979).

[84] Bate (ed), above n 1, Introduction, 17.

[85] Edmund Spenser, *The Faerie Queene*, (ed) T P Roche, Jr (London, Penguin, 1987) 515, Bk III. IX.38.

[86] In H James, *Shakespeare's Troy: Drama, Politics and the Translation of Empire* (Cambridge, Cambridge University Press, 1997) 18; see also D M Bergeron, *Elizabethan Civic Pageantry, 1558–1642* (London, Arnold, 1971) 58.

common law with constitutional sovereignty, whose legitimacy was bound up with its antiquity, so the Trojan king, Brutus, became for Coke the prototypical author of the ancient constitution. In *The Reports*, Coke argued that:

> Brutus the first King of this land, as soon as he settled himself in his kingdom, for the safe and peaceable government of his people, wrote a book in the Greek tongue, calling it the Laws of the Britons, and he collected the same out of the laws of the Trojans.[87]

After landing at Totnes in Devon, Brutus had made his way east and founded a new city, Troynovant, on the banks of the Thames.[88] For Fortescue, Coke and other jurists of the early modern period, Brutus was the father of the Britons, the archetype and icon of English nationhood. According to Fortescue, Brutus had founded *dominium politicum et regale*: he was the original personification of constitutional rule.

The influence of Brutus, Troy and the Roman Republic over Coke's perception of his role as a counsellor (and later as a judge) cannot be overstated. He repeatedly invoked the ideal of the 'Publique Weale', or *res publica*, depicting it as the ultimate object of government, law and legislation. Coke described himself to the Grand Jury of the Norwich assizes as an unwilling judge, comparing himself to an unnamed young Roman, who had accepted judicial office only 'to give encouragement unto other Romane Citizens by their good endevors to attain unto like estate & credit in the government of Romes Publique Weale',[89] but whose reluctance stemmed from the necessity of presiding in judgment over 'many Friends, Kinsfolkes, & Allies'.[90] As so often in his career, Coke provided the foundations for modern administrative law[91]: here he invoked the rule against bias (*nemo iudex in causa sua*), stating that '*Cave ne fis Iudex inter Amicos* because *inter Amicos Inditare*, Amongst friends to iudge, is a thing nothing more dangerous'.[92] This was of considerable relevance at the Norwich assizes, as Coke's family connections with the area would have meant that he was known personally to many litigants, defendants, and witnesses.[93] Again, he compared his position to that of the young Roman citizen who was made a judge by the Senate: the reluctant judge was persuaded to accept the post, 'in thy love to Romes Common-wealth'.[94] Coke goes on to describe a dramatic scene, in which the young Roman judge hosts a valedictory banquet, prior to his departure from his friends:

---

[87] Coke, 3 *Reports* (1602) 4: Preface, viiia.
[88] The tale of Brutus, his exile from Italy, his odyssey and eventual arrival in England, was recorded by Geoffrey of Monmouth in 1136: Geoffrey of Monmouth, *The History of the Kings of Britain*, (tr) L Thorpe (London, Penguin, 1966) 53–74.
[89] Coke, above n 49, B.*v*.
[90] *Ibid*, B.ii.*r*.
[91] On Coke and the evolution of judicial review, see J Goldsworthy, *The Sovereignty of Parliament: History and Philosophy* (Oxford, Clarendon, 1999) 111–17.
[92] Coke, above n 49, B.ii.*v*.
[93] Coke was born in 1552, in the village of Mileham, approximately 20 miles from Norwich; as a boy, he attended Norwich Free School.
[94] Coke, above n 49, B.iii.*v*.

> Thus must I depart from you, & yet continue amongst you, for by the love, power & authoritie of the Senate, I am appointed to be a Iudge, and in the seate of Justice, I must forget the remembrance of your former friendships and acquaintance, and onely in the person of a Iudge, with respect to keepe my conscience cleare, I must with equitie & uprightnes, iustly administer iustice unto you all.⁹⁵

It has already been noted that Coke was no friend to the acting profession but, as the above extract amply demonstrates, he understood the potential for dramatic conflict between the public and private life of the judge. The scene that he described finds many echoes in the plays of Shakespeare: a law-maker who has departed from his subjects but is simultaneously amongst them is redolent of the Duke in *Measure for Measure*; and the decision by the young Roman to depart from his friends before returning to administer justice is remindful of Titus's son, Lucius, who must leave Rome and abandon his friends, before returning to restore harmony to a shattered populace: 'To heal Rome's harms and wipe away her woe'. (5.3.147) References to Troy abound in *Titus Andronicus*: only a few lines into the play, Titus compares the loss of his sons in battle to that of King Priam of Troy (1.1.82–84). The mythical heroes and heroines of Homer, Ovid and Virgil—Aeneas, Astraea, Dido, Hecuba, Hector, Philomela—are mentioned. Contemplating his unutterable grief at the ravaged body of Lavinia, Titus refers to 'bright-burning Troy' (3.1.70). Names of characters are reminiscent of Trojan legend: in Virgil's *Aeneid*, Lavinia was given in marriage to Aeneas; in Shakespeare's play, Titus's son, Lucius, has obvious associations with Lucius Junius Brutus, who expelled the Tarquins from Rome. In the play, Lucius makes the explicit connection between himself and his illustrious counterpart. Before leaving Rome to raise an army of Goths, he makes the following promise to his father:

> If Lucius live, he will requite your wrongs
> And make proud Saturnine and his empress
> Beg at the gates like Tarquin and his queen. (3.1.297–99)

Like the mythical founder of Britain, he is a fugitive from his city.

Towards the end of the play, Shakespeare indirectly links Troy and Rome with *Troynovant*, or London, giving the following line not to a member of the imperial family but to a citizen of the State, a Roman Lord: 'Or who hath brought the fatal engine in / That gives our Troy, our Rome, the civil wound'. (5.3.86) The repeated use of 'our' is significant. To the audience at the Rose Playhouse in 1594, as much as to Spenser in *The Faerie Queene*, 'our Troy, our Rome' was England. For Coke and many common lawyers, England's 'civil wound' was the threat posed to ancient liberties by excessive and unlawful use of the Royal Prerogative; liberties that were guaranteed (as Coke continually reminds his readers) in *Magna Carta* but which had existed since time immemorial. Unlike the *Utopia* of Sir Thomas More—translated from the Greek as 'no place'—Troynovant was not a fictional realm. It was recognisably London: the heart of Tudor government. And what was

---

⁹⁵ *Ibid*, B.iiii.r.

'the fatal engine', the Trojan Horse, that caused the civil wound to which the Roman Lord refers in the play? In a constitutional sense, 'the fatal engine' was the introduction of the regal *Imperium* into the English State. Far from enabling a new Troy to spring from the ashes of the old, it facilitated absolutism. By the last decade of the 16th century, the ancient liberties which formed the basis of the unwritten, ancient constitution were under threat from a rival jurisdiction; one that sought to supplant the sovereignty of common law and the equitable principles which underlined its practice. Although Troynovant was recognisably London, at a symbolic level it represented the longing for an imaginary realm, located in a fictional past: the unattained and unattainable state of ideal governance, to which all rational citizens aspired but which none would experience. Returning to Act 4, scene 3, moments before his arrows are shot into the heavens, Titus vows to his brother Marcus:

> Yet wrung with wrongs more than our backs can bear.
> And sith there's no justice in earth nor hell,
> We will solicit heaven and move the gods
> To send down Justice for to wreak our wrongs. (4.3.49–52)

It would be more than 50 years after the first performance of *Titus Andronicus* before justice was finally sent down to 'wreak' the wrongs of the Royal Prerogative and exact retribution in the form of the execution of a king and the abolition of the monarchy. Would a new Troy or, as Milton described it, 'another Rome in the west',[96] arise from the ashes of the old régime? That remained to be seen.

V. Ritual, Religion and the Culture of Signs

Writing in 1610, John Selden conceded that the story of Brutus and the foundation of Troynovant on the banks of the Thames was

> patched up out of Bards Songs and Poetick Fictions taken upon trust, like Talmudical Traditions, on purpose to raise the British name out of the Trojan ashes.

But he at least considered the possibility that Troy existed, twice asking the question: 'what are those Trojan Laws?' His conclusion was that 'Natural Equity' rather than positive law was 'adapted, applied, and fitted to the variety of emergent quarrels'. Although never explicitly denying the existence of Troy, Selden strongly implied that it was the imaginary creation of poets, representing an aspiration of justice in the ideal State. Hence, he argued that the Trojan laws were

> [p]erhaps the same with those, by which *Nephelococcygia*, the City of the Birds in Aristophanes (or, as we use to say, Utopia) is Governed.

---

[96] John Milton, *The Readie & Easie Way To Establish a Free Commonwealth*, 1659 (Thomason Tracts E 1016 [11]) 2.

The only positive Trojan law which Selden claims to identify concerns 'the Prerogative of the eldest Sons, by which they inherited the whole Right and Estate of their deceased Father'.[97] In the context of *Titus Andronicus*, this is significant, as Titus exhorts the populace to 'create our emperor's eldest son, / Lord Saturnine' (1.1.228–29). The appeal to the ancient principle of primogeniture is one of several instances that distinguishes Titus as an embodiment of the common law tradition, initiated by the Trojan king, Brutus. The observation of Marcus Andronicus that Titus 'takes false shadows for true substances' (3.2.81) may be applied to the numerous early modern jurists who stated that the English legal system was founded by Brutus. I refer above to the claim made by Coke that, upon arrival in England, Brutus wrote a book of laws 'in the Greek tongue', which were derived from Trojan laws.[98] The existence of such a book has never been proved, but to engage exclusively with the veracity of the Trojan legend is to overlook its allegorical importance as a symbol of 'Natural Equity'. The idea that English law was coextensive with and indivisible from nature was developed in the early 16th century by Christopher St German, who accorded the 'law of nature of reasonable creatures' (or the law of reason) paramount legal authority: '[A]gainst this law, prescription, statute nor custom may not prevail . . .' Any attempt at law-making which contravened the law of reason was, according to St German, 'void and against justice'.[99] The injunction against irrationality was famously invoked by Coke in his report of *Dr Bonham's Case*, in which he asserted that

> when an act of Parliament is against common right and reason, or repugnant, or impossible to be performed, the common law will controul it, and adjudge such act to be void . . .[100]

One of many images of manifest irrationality in *Titus Andronicus* (and a fundamental breach of the 'law of nature of reasonable creatures') is the violated body of Lavinia. Deep in the forest, the harmony of natural law is shattered by the many acts of violence that are perpetrated there, of which the rape and mutilation of Lavinia is the most shocking. Given the terrible sight of the hand-less, tongue-less and raped Lavinia, it is strange that Marcus should refer to the hideous crimes of violence, perpetrated upon his niece, as 'treason' (4.1.67).[101] The word momentarily distracts the audience from Lavinia's trauma, reminding it of the political symbolism of the human body. Use of anatomical imagery with which to depict the Roman State has been made at the start of the play by Marcus, in his unsuccessful attempt to persuade Titus to accept the imperial crown: 'Be *candidatus* then

---

[97] John Selden, *The Reverse or Back-Face of the English Janus*, (tr) R Westcot (London, Thomas Basset & Richard Chiswell, 1682) 8, 10.

[98] Above, n 87.

[99] C St German, *Dialogues Between a Doctor of Divinity and a Student in the Laws of England*, (ed) W Muchall (Cincinnati, Id, Robert Clarke, 1874) 5.

[100] Coke, *Dr Bonham's Case*, 8 Reports (1611) 4: 107a, at 118a; on the meaning of 'void' in early modern English law and Coke's method of statutory interpretation, see I Williams, '*Dr Bonham's Case* and "void" statutes' (2006) 27 *The Journal of Legal History* 111.

[101] Bellamy notes that Tudor Parliaments passed 68 treason laws, J G Bellamy, *The Tudor Law of Treason: An Introduction* (London, Routledge & Kegan Paul, 1979) 12.

and put it on, / And help to set a head on headless Rome'. (1.1.188–89) Titus refuses to accept the candidature, on the grounds that 'A better head her glorious body fits' (1.1.190). It is difficult to imagine a less appropriate head for the Roman body politic than Saturninus, and we are reminded of the anatomical image of the desecrated and despoiled State when the messenger returns to Titus 'the heads of thy two noble sons' (3.1.237), along with his severed hand. The literal equation of the body politic with the human body was a popular rhetorical device amongst jurists and lawyers in early modern England. On the first page of *The Book Named the Governor*, Sir Thomas Elyot argued that 'a public weal is a body living'[102]; while in the *Case of the Dutchy of Lancaster*, Edmund Plowden delineated the bodies natural and politic of the king, asserting that the body politic is 'constituted for the Direction of the People, and the Management of the public weal'.[103] When William Fulbecke writes of law being trodden under foot by the Godless, the reader is reminded not only of Plato's remark that justice lurks under our feet, but of his use also of the visual image, to depict justice as a corporeal phenomenon, albeit as the quarry of hunters.[104]

The mute presence of Lavinia until her death in the final scene of the play serves as a constant symbol of the appalling injuries that are inflicted on the body politic by an unaccountable and tyrannical lawmaker.[105] Her body is an image of negativity: the antithesis of reason, the opposite of law. At the level of political symbolism, the author has subjugated her humanity and made her instead an image of dehumanisation. In rhetorical terms, she (or rather her mutilated body) is a visual and silent form of *antirrhesis*: the converse of *apologia*. Where *apologia* seeks to defend doctrine, belief or law, so *antirrhesis* rejects authority or opinion for its inherent error or wickedness. In the words of Sir Henry Peacham, *antirrhesis* 'doth specially belong to confutation and is most apt to repell errors and heresies, and to reiect evill counsell and lewd perswasions'.[106]

Tamora performs a similar antirrhetical function: she is the antithesis of civility, the embodiment of barbarism. Barker emphasises the contrast in the play between honour and nobility on the one hand and, on the other, the nether-world, the 'wilderness of tigers' (3.1.54) to which Tamora, a 'ravenous tiger', belongs (5.3.194). He notes the comparisons with Semiramis (1.1.521; 2.2.118), marking Tamora as a 'lustful alien'.[107] Her barbarous and sexually intemperate conduct delineates Tamora as one outside the civility of law. To that extent she is a stereotype of early

---

[102] Elyot, above n 34, at 1.

[103] E Plowden, *Case of the Dutchy of Lancaster, The Commentaries or Reports of Edmund Plowden*, 2 vols (Dublin, H Watts, 1792) 1: 212; I discuss Plowden's *Reports* and this case in particular, in ch 3, text to nn 39–74 below. The organic analogy is found in *The Politics* of Aristotle, Bk V.III.1302b33.

[104] W Fulbecke, *A Direction or Preparative to the Study of the Lawe Wherein is showed, what things ought to be observed and used of them that are addicted to the study of the Law* (London, T Wight, 1600) B.v; Plato, *The Republic*, Bk IV.I.432d.

[105] Foakes argues that Lavinia's 'silent presence' serves as an emblem of the wilderness of tigers which, as Titus observes, Rome has become, Foakes, above n 5, at 55.

[106] Peacham, above n 8, at 89; Goodrich characterises *apologia* and *antirrhesis* as, respectively, defence and denunciation: Goodrich, above n 23, at 44.

[107] Barker, above n 14, at 147.

modern drama: the female as sexual transgressor and bestial avenger, whose negative image affirms the jurisdiction of the commonwealth. In The *Misfortunes of Arthur*, the character of Guinevere is seduced by her stepson, Mordred, and subsequently develops an unnatural sexual obsession with him: 'Desire to joy him still, torments my mynde'.[108] In *Circe and Ulysses*, presented by the Inner Temple in 1615, women are depicted as perversions of nature. Circe is a sorceress, changing men into wild animals: a self-proclaimed enemy of natural law.[109] These 'women' are the idolatrous enemies of reason, while the heroic figures of King Arthur and Ulysses are archetypes and icons of reason, law and justice. Although Aaron describes Tamora as a siren (1.1.522), the Queen of the Goths is distinguished from the conventional feminine stereotypes by her acceptance into the symbolic heart of civility, Rome. Saturninus rejects the hand of the virginal Lavinia, choosing for his bride Tamora, who describes herself as 'incorporate in Rome, / A Roman now adopted happily' (1.1.467–68). So long as Rome is governed by a tyrannical oppressor and his barbarian queen, the body politic will continue to be mutilated; in the words of William Fulbecke, justice and law 'are together trodde under foote by such as neither care for God, nor goodness'.[110]

The correlation between religion, justice and law is a major theme of *Titus Andronicus*, and is of especial interest in the context of the early modern doctrinal dispute, in the Church and the law, concerning the authoritative status of text and sign. Sir Thomas More remarked upon the significant similarity between the threat to the Church posed by the reliance of the reformers on textual as opposed to institutional authority, and the threat to the authority of the law posed by textualisation.[111] It was axiomatic of English law that it was predicated upon the law of God; as Lord Ellesmere said, the laws of England 'are not originally *Leges scriptae*'.[112] The legitimacy of common law was inextricably linked with its divine provenance; it was inscribed upon the memory of man, rather than transcribed upon the printed page. The argument was taken up by Coke, who warned that it was a

> dangerous matter for civilians and canonists (I speak what I know, and not without just cause) to write either of the common laws of England which they profess not, or against them which they know not.[113]

---

[108] T Hughes and N Trotte, 'The Misfortunes of Arthur' in *Certaine Devises and shewes presented to her Maiestie by the Gentlemen of Grayes-Inne at her Highnesse Court in Greenwich* (London, Robert Robinson, 1587) 5.
[109] W Browne, *Circe and Ulysses, The Inner Temple Masque, January 13, 1615*, (ed) G Jones (London, Golden Cockerel, 1954); on the depiction of women in the masques and dramas of the early modern Inns of Court, see Raffield, above n 30, at 148–53.
[110] Fulbecke, above n 104, B.v.
[111] Sir Thomas More, 'The Confutacyon of Tyndale's Answere by Sir Thomas More Knyght Lorde Chancellor of England' in L A Schuster (ed), *The Yale Edition of the Complete Works of St Thomas More*, 15 vols (New Haven, Conn, Yale University Press, 1973) 8: 291.
[112] Quoted in Dugdale, above n 59, at 3.
[113] Coke, 10 *Reports* (1614) 5: Preface, xviia.

Ritual, Religion and the Culture of Signs

Shakespeare demonstrates awareness of the debate in Act 4, scene 1, in which Young Lucius enters with books under his arm, pursued by Lavinia. Among the books is Ovid's *Metamorphoses*, but crucially it is not the text itself that exposes the identity of Lavinia's assailants (although Titus correctly surmises, when Lavinia directs him to the story of Philomela, that she has been raped). The truth is revealed only by looking beyond the text to the sign: 'Give signs, sweet girl' (4.1.61), Titus exhorts his daughter; and it is the invocation to the Gods by Marcus to '[i]nspire me' (4.1.67), that eventually leads to the identification of Chiron and Demetrius as Lavinia's attackers.

Religious ceremony and sacrificial rite, in which the symbolic power of the sign is paramount, provide strong visual motifs throughout the play, and inevitably draw comparisons with the rituals of the Roman Catholic Church. Indeed Aaron makes a perceptive observation about Lucius, whose religious observance is notable for its sacramental predilection:

> Yet for I know thou art religious
> And hast a thing within thee called conscience,
> With twenty popish tricks and ceremonies
> Which I have seen thee careful to observe . . . (5.1.74–77)[114]

It is noteworthy that during the year before the first performance of *Titus Andronicus*, Books I–IV of Richard Hooker's *Of the Laws of Ecclesiastical Polity* were published.[115] Books II and IV especially were concerned respectively with the rites and ceremonies of the Anglican Church, providing a response to the contention that scripture was the only rule of all matters ecclesiastical. Patrick Collinson has noted of sacrament-based Anglicanism, of which Hooker was arguably the founder, that it was not easily distinguishable from the rites of the Roman Catholic Church and 'church papistry'. He goes on to remark that Hooker was unsympathetic to the political shift of the 1590s, away from mixed monarchy and towards imperial rule according to principles of divine right.[116] It is undeniable that Hooker's dedication to the rhetorical power of the sign and its representation through ecclesiastical iconography is suggestive of belief in the superiority of unwritten law to imperial edict or statute. Wisdom, or the knowledge of divine will, was not to be attained through the text alone:

> Some things shee openeth by the sacred Bookes of Scripture; some things by the glorious Workes of nature: with some things she inspired them from above by spirituall influence . . .[117]

---

[114] It is significant in the context of Elizabethan persecution of Catholics that it should be Lucius who asks the mutilated Lavinia 'who hath martyred thee?' (3.1.82)

[115] The Preface and Books I–IV of *Of the Laws* were published in March 1593; Book V was published in 1597.

[116] P Collinson, 'Hooker and the Elizabethan Establishment' in A S McGrade (ed), *Richard Hooker and the Construction of Christian Community* (Binghampton, Medieval & Renaissance Texts & Studies, 1997) 153, 161; Books VII and VIII of *the Laws of Ecclesiastical Polity*, published respectively in 1662 and 1648, demonstrate emphatic opposition to the principle of rule by divine right.

[117] R Hooker, *Of the Lawes of Ecclesiastical Politie* (London, William Stansbye, 1622) 56, Bk II.I.

For Hooker, the text was not the exclusive exponent of truth. The legitimate purpose of the sacraments was to reveal the 'spirituall influence' by which wisdom may be attained. Ceremony and sacrament were not therefore vain and idolatrous forms of papist rhetoric, but rather the licit means through which invisible and intangible truths could be represented.

The gruesome public executions of traitors and the persecution of Catholics in Elizabethan England are relevant to any discussion of *Titus Andronicus*. Given the highly contentious issue of religious worship during the 1590s, the allusions to Catholicism by Shakespeare are, to say the least, daring. For example, concerning the references to Astraea, Frances A Yates noted that many contemporary symbols of the Virgin Queen were also associated with the Virgin Mary, and that Astraea, 'though not the Virgin Mary, was an echo of her'.[118] The references in the play to martyrdom (3.1.82) and the 'ruinous monastery' (5.1.21) clearly allude to events in the religious history of 16th-century England. As Bate suggests, that a Goth should be 'earnestly' gazing upon a ruined monastery defies the stereotype of the barbarian and introduces the theme of reformation into the play. The civility of the Second Goth, reflected in the eloquence with which he expresses himself in Act 5, scene 1, augurs well for the equitable régime of Lucius, who depends for his usurpation of Saturninus not only on the electoral support of the Roman citizenry, but also on the military backing of the Goths.[119]

VI. Sacrifice, Tradition and Unwritten Law

The mutilations and dismemberments in the play, and the depraved enjoyment with which the characters of Aaron, Chiron and Demetrius inflict physical pain, mirror the punishments that were meted out to suspected members of the Jesuit mission to England in the late 16th century. Shakespeare would have found inspiration for scenes of ritualised violence in the public executions of those found guilty of High Treason and in the monstrous forms of torture, which were enthusiastically inflicted by Richard Topcliffe, Thomas Norton and other State torturers upon suspected members of the Society of Jesus.[120] In the public playhouses,

---

[118] Yates, above n 27, at 80.

[119] See Bate (ed), above n 1, Introduction, 19–21; also, S Kliger, *The Goths in England: a Study in Seventeenth and Eighteenth Century Thought* (Cambridge, Mass, Harvard University Press, 1952).

[120] Edmund Campion, the Jesuit missionary, was arrested in July 1581 and tortured while awaiting trial for conspiracy to murder Elizabeth I; he was hanged, drawn and quartered on 1 December 1581. His fellow Jesuit, Robert Southwell, was arrested in 1592 and imprisoned in the Tower for three years before his trial for treason. During his imprisonment he was frequently tortured; he was hanged, drawn and quartered on 21 February 1595. Topcliffe's enthusiasm for torturing his victims was such that he had a torture chamber installed at his home in Bridewell; see Callaghan and Kyle, above n 28, at 38–41. On the Jesuit mission to England, see A Hogge, *God's Secret Agents: Queen Elizabeth's Forbidden Priests and the Hatching of the Gunpowder Plot* (London, Harper Perennial, 2005). A persuasive argument for a recusant Shakespeare is offered in Wilson, above n 17: on the Jesuits especially, see *ibid* at 44–70.

Shakespeare was writing for an audience that was accustomed to witnessing gruesome public executions: the stage is, at the level of ritualised violence, a substitute for the scaffold.[121] But to argue, as Foakes does, that the violence of *Titus Andronicus* is 'disconnected from any moral centre' and is 'designed to shock',[122] is to ignore the fact that much of the violence is of a sacrificial nature and is intended to illustrate the centrality of ceremonial ritual to civilised society. This is not to say that Foakes is oblivious to the symbolic importance of sacrifice in the play: he cites the theory of René Girard, for whom sacrifice represents a primitive judicial system in which the victim acts as a scapegoat, thus diffusing conflict and the potential for retaliation.[123] A jurisprudence that is predicated upon sacrifice may be described as primitive, but it is hardly amoral. In *Titus Andronicus*, sacrifice is clearly distinguished from the acts of bestial violence committed by Chiron and Demetrius, 'the tiger's young ones' (2.2.142): their home is the savage world of the Goths,[124] far beyond the walls of the Roman citadel.

The barbarous conduct of Chiron and Demetrius contrasts starkly with the sacrificial rites enacted by Titus. Of the killings in which Titus participates, only the death of his son Mutius (stabbed by his father as Titus attempts to reunite Lavinia with Saturninus, following their betrothal) is an act of spontaneous violence (1.1.295).[125] And even there, when reminded by Marcus that to be a Roman is to 'be not barbarous' (1.1.383), Titus agrees that Mutius should be interred in the family tomb, enabling him to cross the Styx into the underworld. A sense of honour and respect for precedent guide the decisions made by Titus in the first scene of the play, all of which determine the subsequent action. His first fatal decision, which initiates the vengeful conduct of Tamora and her sons, is to condone the sacrifice of Alarbus, '[t]'appease their groaning shadows that are gone'. (1.1.129) The manner of Alarbus' death—his limbs cut from the living body and his remains

---

[121] Greenblatt refers not only to the public celebration of *Gloriana*, but also to the 'theatrical violence visited upon the enemies of that glory', S Greenblatt, 'Invisible bullets: Renaissance authority and its subversion, *Henry IV* and *Henry V*' in J Dollimore and A Sinfield (eds), *Political Shakespeare: Essays in Cultural Materialism* (Manchester, Manchester University Press, 1994) 44.

[122] Foakes, above n 5, at 57. I incline more to the argument of Nuttall, that 'the play is saved morally by its compassionate psychological reference', A D Nuttall, *Shakespeare the Thinker* (New Haven, Conn, Yale University Press, 2007) 88.

[123] Foakes, above n 5, at 6; R Girard, *Violence and the Sacred*, (tr) P Gregory (Baltimore, Md, Johns Hopkins University Press, 1977).

[124] *Pace* the Second Goth (5.1.20–39).

[125] Like Moses (who disobeyed God in striking the rock to bring forth water, and was therefore not allowed to enter the Promised Land, *Numbers* 20:8–12), Titus is an archetype of flawed humanity and leadership; he does not live to see the liberation of his fellow Romans. His role, like that of Moses, is to lead his people to freedom, but not to experience it himself. It is noteworthy that in the Mosaic legend the only other person who is denied entry to the Promised Land is Moses' brother, Aaron (*Numbers*, 20:12). The characters of Titus and Aaron are distorted images of each other: both are agents of destruction and loyal fathers. Concerning Aaron, Fortier refers to '[n]ihilism and commitment tangled together . . . all round destroyer and desperately protective father at once', M Fortier, 'Shakespeare and Specific Performance' in P Raffield and G Watt (eds), *Shakespeare and the Law* (Oxford, Hart Publishing, 2008) 16. On the mythical hero as an archetype of nationhood, empire and religion, see S Freud, 'Moses and Monotheism' in *The Origins of Religion*, (tr) J Strachey, (ed) A Dickson (London, Penguin, 1990) 246–47.

burnt—marks neither the action nor his killers as barbaric. Both Titus and Lucius emphasise the necessity of religious sacrifice, '*Ad manes fratrum*' (To the Shades of our Brothers) (1.1.101).

The decision to sacrifice Alarbus is the first of many indications that Titus is simultaneously judge and high priest. In medieval England, the combination of the two offices—judge and priest—in one body was a commonplace. Henry II chose his justices from the prelates of the Church: as Dugdale notes, the itinerant justices of the king's courts were 'antiently persons in holy Orders'.[126] But it was not until Sir John Fortescue wrote his influential treatise, *De Laudibus Legum Angliae*, that the religious symbolism of the judge's role was clearly enunciated:

> [W]e, who are the Ministerial Officers, who sit and preside in the Courts of Justice, are therefore not improperly called: Sacerdotes (Priests): The import of the Latin Word (Sacerdos) being one who gives or teaches Holy Things.[127]

In the late 16th century, as apologists for the constitutional sovereignty of common law sought to establish its divine authority, the indivisible roles of judge and priest were associated by many commentators with the ancient, Druidic origins of English law.[128] Coke, Selden and Spelman cite Book VI of Caesar's *De Bello Gallico* as authority for the claim that the institutional correlation between law and religion was founded in the rites and practices of the Druids. Coke argues that 'to the Druides appertained the ordering as well as of matters ecclesiastical, as the administration of the laws and government of the commonwealth'; he agrees with Caesar that 'the Druides in France, was nothing else but a very colony taken out from our British Druides'.[129] For Selden, the Druidical 'Gownmen among the *Gauls* and the *Britons* too, were the Interpreters and Guardians of the Laws'.[130] The polemical argument that the original of all law is British is a characteristic, insular trait of Coke's *Reports* and *Institutes*. Given Selden's dedication to historical accuracy, it should perhaps not be surprising that his analysis of the juristic and ecclesiastical rites of the Druids displays greater anthropological insight than Coke's.[131] The Druids provided a factual link between the poetic fiction of the Trojan kings and the principles and practices of common law in early modern England. Selden implies that the cultural origins of the Druids were (like the Trojans) Hellenic: 'they make use of *Greek letters*'.[132] He suggests also that the

---

[126] Dugdale, above n 59, at 141.
[127] Fortescue, above n 75, at 4–5.
[128] On the Druids and the foundations of English law, see P Goodrich, 'Druids and Common Lawyers: Notes on the Pythagoras Complex and Legal Education' (2007) 1 *Law and Humanities* 1; for a comprehensive history of British Druids, see R Hutton, *Blood and Mistletoe: the History of the Druids in Britain* (New Haven, Conn, Yale University Press, 2009).
[129] Coke, 3 *Reports* (1602) 2: Preface, viiib–ixa.
[130] Selden, above n 97, at 12–16; see also, H Spelman, *Of the Law Terms: A Discourse* (London, Gillyflower, 1684) 12.
[131] Pocock, above n 24, at 56, remarks upon the peculiar insularity of 'Coke's mind', but concedes that there was no reason why a practising common lawyer should have adopted a comparative approach to the study of English law, other than to satisfy intellectual curiosity.
[132] Selden, above n 97, at 13.

Sacrifice, Tradition and Unwritten Law

word 'Druid' is derived from the Greek word for 'Tree' or 'Oak', and reports that 'they performed none of their devotions without oaken leaves'.[133] God, law and nature are inextricably bound: the natural world represents the harmonious order of divine will, while the law is the sacred art whereby divine order is honoured and maintained through the application of artificial reason.

In *Postnati. Calvin's Case*, Coke argued that English law was 'written with the finger of God',[134] and that it was for the judges to extract its meaning by applying their mysterious, ancient art to the facts of individual cases. Those excluded from the priesthood of the common law should 'meddle not with any point or secret of any art or science, especially with the laws of this realm'.[135] Coke believed in common law as custom, in the sense of the acquisition, exposition and application of prior judicial knowledge and experience. Consequently, '[t]he expounding of laws doth ordinarily belong to the reverend Judges and sages of the realm'.[136] It was primarily an oral tradition: law was spoken *ex cathedra* by its guardians and oracles, the judges. Common lawyers shared with their Druidical ancestors an inherent suspicion of the written word. The early 17th-century antiquary, William Jones, argues that 'never would that there [the Druids'] knowledge and learning should be put in writinge'[137]; while Selden claims '[t]hey are said to learn without Book ... Nor do they judge it meet to commit such things to writing'.[138] The resemblance to the oral, inherited and exclusive tradition of common lawyers is striking. For civil lawyers such as the Cambridge scholar John Cowell, it was the exclusive *arcana* of common law, rather than its substantive content, which rendered it a 'darke and melancholy' art.[139] For Coke, Selden and others, the Druids provided an iconic image not only of the antiquity, sanctity and mystery of common law, but also of its indivisible link with nature: unlike its civilian counterpart, common law was made not by man but by God. Hence, the considerable emphasis placed upon the natural environment in which the Druids lived and practised their art. According to Jones, 'they dwelled in rockes and woods and darke places', and were to be found mainly in Anglesey, 'because it was a solitary Iland full of wood, so that it was so darke by reason of that wood, and not inhabited of any but themselves'.[140]

---

[133] *Ibid* at 12.

[134] Coke, *Postnati. Calvin's Case*, 7 *Reports* (1608) 4: 12b.

[135] *Ibid*, 3 *Reports* (1602) 2: Preface, xiiia.

[136] *Ibid*, 4 *Reports* (1604) 2: Preface, v. On Coke's interpretation of custom, see Pocock, above n 24, at 35.

[137] 'Mr Jones his Answeares to Mr Tate's Questions' in T Hearne (ed), *A Collection of Curious Discourses, Written by Eminent Antiquaries Upon several Heads in our English Antiquities* (Oxford, Thomas Hearne, 1720) 213.

[138] Selden, above n 97, at 13. 160 years later, Lord Mansfield made a similar observation in relation to the common law: 'Matters of practice are not to be known from books. What passes at a judge's chambers is matter of tradition: it rests in memory', *R v Wilkes* [1770] 4 Burr 2527, 2566, *per* Lord Mansfield CJ.

[139] J Cowell, 'To the Readers' in *The Interpreter: or Booke containing the signification of words wherein is set foorth the true meaning of all, or the most part of such words and termes, as are mentioned in the law writers* (Cambridge, Iohn Legate, 1607) *3.r.

[140] Jones, above n 137, at 213–14.

Titus Andronicus *and the Flight of Justice*

Tawney suggested that the law of nature provides a useful metaphor for the representation of natural justice in positive law. Drawing on the theory of St Thomas Aquinas, that a man-made law which conflicts with the law of nature is a perversion of law, he argued that the law of nature provides a standard by which to judge whether or not 'particular relations' were equitable.[141] It is in the sense of nature as a metaphor for natural justice that the early modern depiction of lawgivers as integral facets of the natural world should be understood. Coke described the law of nature as

> that which God at the time of creation of the nature of man infused into his heart... and therefore the law of God and nature is one to all.[142]

Such was Coke's devotion to the indivisible trinity of God, nature and law that his life and career were compared to an iconic symbol both of nature and the Druids: the oak tree. In his *Elegy on Sir Edward Coke* (1634), Robert Codrington referred to Coke as 'an Oake spreading faire / And high his boughs'. Alluding to Coke's dismissal as Chief Justice of the King's Bench in 1616, Codrington extended the arboreal metaphor:

> ...when this feareles oake
> That stood the fury of each dreadfull stroke,
> Wrapt in the clowdes, shooke his loose scattring locks,
> And hardly wearied by a thousand shocks
> Forgave the Gods his fall, his leaves did rove
> Ore the sadde circuit of the trembling Grove,
> And falling whispered to the trees more nigh,
> They live unsafe that are exalted high.[143]

The intimation of hubris, precipitating a tragic downfall, and the metamorphosis of Coke into a mighty oak is Ovidian in tone and style.[144] The same tragic sense of a Titanic figure representing natural law, but being destroyed by external events over which he has no control, may be applied to the character of Titus in Shakespeare's play. He has a particular affinity with the natural order, assuring the earth itself, as Quintus and Martius are led away to execution, that

> ...I will befriend thee more with rain
> That shall distil from these two ancient ruins
> Than youthful April shall with all his showers. (3.1.16–18)

---

[141] R H Tawney, *Religion and the Rise of Capitalism* (Harmondsworth, Penguin, 1984) 51–52.

[142] Coke, *Postnati. Calvin's Case*, 7 Reports (1608) 4: 12b. According to Doddridge, '[a] Ground Rule, or Principle of the Law of England is a conclusion either of the Law of Nature, or derived from some generall Custome used within the Realme', Sir John Doddridge, *The Lawyers Light: or, A due direction for the study of the law for methode* (London, Benjamin Fisher, 1629) 6.

[143] Robert Codrington, *Elegy on Sir Edward Coke* (1634), BL Add MS 37484 ff 18*v*–19*r*; on Codrington's *Elegy*, Coke and pastoral myth, see Raffield, above n 21, at 69–70.

[144] See, eg, the tale of Baucis and Philemon, in which Baucis is transformed into a linden tree and Philemon into an oak: Ovid, *Metamorphoses*, Bk VIII.611–724.

Later in the same scene, his pleas for clemency having been ignored by the unspeaking tribunes, he chooses to confide instead in the stones:

> A stone is soft as wax, tribunes more hard than stones;
> A stone is silent and offendeth not,
> And tribunes with their tongues doom men to death. (3.1.45–47)

The persuasive power of the natural order over the actions of Titus is emphasised in the first scene of the play when, having slain Mutius, he is exhorted to give his son an honourable burial. Marcus and Titus's second son appeal to his natural status, respectively as brother and father:

> *Marcus:* Brother, for in that name doth nature plead—
> *2 Son:* Father, and in that name doth nature speak—
>
> (1.1. 375–76)

The order to be found in nature, *ordo naturae*, is not to be confused with the barbarous conduct of Aaron, Tamora and her sons. Their lustful and murderous actions identify them as the unnatural other, and it is ironic that at the end of the play, when the natural order has been restored through the magistracy of Lucius, that Tamora should finally be subject to natural law, her body thrown 'forth to beasts and birds to prey' (5.3.197).

Titus is of course an archetypal revenger. It is a characteristic that he shares with the Druidical founders of English law. Examining the etymology of the word 'Drud' (the singular of 'Drudion'), Jones claims it 'hath many significations, one signification is (*dialror*) that is a revenger, or one that redresseth wronge'.[145] But Titus wants more than revenge, as he makes abundantly clear when Tamora appears at his door, disguised as the character of Revenge. Seeing through her disguise immediately, he is palpably amused at the idea that he should seek only revenge. He jokes when he recognises Chiron and Demetrius, disguised respectively as Rape and Murder, the ministers of Revenge, exclaiming: 'Good Lord, how like the empress' sons they are' (5.2.64). Towards the end of the scene, he bids 'sweet Revenge, farewell' (5.2.148), and it is clear from the elaborate preparations for the deaths of Chiron and Demetrius that he has something more in mind than avenging the appalling suffering that Tamora and her sons have inflicted upon him. The formal prelude to the deaths of Chiron and Demetrius recalls a sacrificial rite, the arcane lore (and law) of an ancient religion. 'I mean to martyr you' (5.2.180), Titus informs his victims, as Lavinia stands by him with a basin with which to collect their blood, the handless handmaiden to the judge and high priest. At this moment in the play, the temporal and the spiritual merge indiscernibly, as Titus enacts another Druidical role, that of

> Justicers as well in religious matters and controversies, as Law matters and controversies for offenses of death and title of Landes: thes did the sacrifices to the heathen Gods, and the sacrifices could not be made without them.[146]

---

[145] Jones, above n 137, at 212.
[146] *Ibid* at 213.

Titus Andronicus *and the Flight of Justice*

Titus passes sentence on the brothers—'But let them hear what fearful words I utter' (5.2.168)—and informs them of their fate. He enacts a version of the Eucharistic rite, echoing the words of the celebrant during the sacrament of Holy Communion—'Receive the blood' (5.2.197)—before slitting their throats. In a further evocation of the Eucharist, the sacrificial victims are eaten at a formal feast.[147] Titus's final act of sacrifice is to kill his daughter, Lavinia. Again, this is no savage murder but rather, according to Titus, an act of love, ending her terrible suffering and 'thy shame' (5.3.45). Of relevance to his symbolic status as an embodiment of common law principle, Titus defends the killing on the basis of 'precedent, and lively warrant' (5.3.43), reminding Saturninus of Livy's narrative of the Centurion, Virginius, who killed his daughter to prevent her rape by Appius Claudius (5.3.36–38). In symbolic terms, the killing of Lavinia was a necessary act: the desecrated body of Rome—mute to the injustices that were perpetrated upon it by its tyrannical ruler—had to perish that a new, benevolent order might arise from the ruins of the old.

Girard has observed that there is hardly any form of violence that cannot be depicted as sacrifice: rhetoric can be an effective veil with which to conceal the squalid realities of life and death.[148] But Shakespeare distinguishes clearly between barbarous acts of violence and the sacrificial rites which are enacted by Titus. In terms both of temporal and divine jurisprudence, the legitimate form of sacrifice became a central tenet in the creation of the English nation-State. To a great extent it was over the meaning of a particular sacrificial rite, the Eucharist, that the religious disputes of the early modern period were triggered. If law derives from God then the issue of His absent presence is always going to be an issue of paramount importance in establishing the legitimacy of law.[149] As Goodrich has noted, the theological concept of presence in the Eucharist translates into secular jurisprudence as a question of the 'spirit of law'.[150] With reference to *Coriolanus*, Stanley Cavell observes that both Christian and pre-Christian sacrifice is concerned with the foundation and preservation of community: individuals are bound together as one body through partaking 'of a common victim'.[151] The Henrician Reformation had the immediate effect of transferring authority from Church to State (even though the Head of State was also head of the nation's Church). Thus, a sacrifice of rival status to the Eucharist was initiated: implicit in the social contract between subject and ruler was the sacrifice of individual freedom in return for the protec-

---

[147] In relation to the establishment of law in *Coriolanus*, Katrin Trüstedt suggests that 'the foundation of a lawful community rests on a common sort of cannibalism that is linked in an uncanny manner to the theatre as a place of rituality', K Trüstedt, 'The Tragedy of Law in Shakespearean Romance' in Raffield and Watt (eds), above n 125, at 106.

[148] Girard, above n 123, at 1; on 'the "foundational violence" of theatre', see also R Girard, *A Theater of Envy: William Shakespeare* (New York, Oxford University Press, 1991) 210.

[149] On the embodiment of presence in the image, and the relationship between law and theology, see L Marin, *Portrait of the King*, (tr) M M Houle (Basingstoke, Macmillan, 1988) 3–15.

[150] P Goodrich, *Languages of Law: From Logics of Memory to Nomadic Masks* (London, Weidenfeld & Nicolson, 1990) 55.

[151] S Cavell, *Disowning Knowledge In Seven Plays of Shakespeare* (Cambridge, Cambridge University Press, 2003) 165.

tion of the commonwealth and its citizens by the State. The presence of sovereign authority was predicated on recognition of the body politic rather than recognition of deity. For early modern common lawyers, the sacrifice was enacted daily in commons: the sacramental rite of dining in the halls of their Inns of Court, at which the presence of God in the common law was celebrated by the consumption of food and drink.[152] A lawful community of the faithful and an order of privileged knowledge were thereby founded and nourished. Common to the rituals of religion, law and the theatre is the pre-eminent authority of the sign. Of course, texts—*leges scriptae*—play their part in disinterring and representing the presence of law, but ultimately their status too is semiotic: signs of an absolute reference.

Returning to *Titus Andronicus*, the triumph of unwritten law or custom over statutory authority is symbolised by the death of Saturninus and the succession of Lucius, whose respect for ceremony, precedent and sacramental ritual marks him as one who can knit '[t]hese broken limbs again into one body'. (5.3.71) There are no guarantees that the rule of Lucius will be more just than that of Saturninus. His first official act as emperor is, after all, to condemn Aaron to a cruel, lingering death: 'Set him breast-deep in earth and famish him; / There let him stand and rave and cry for food'. (5.3.178–79) Indeed, the right of Lucius to claim the imperial throne is questionable, but at least 'the common voice do cry it shall be so'. (5.3.139) The imputation of civic approval is an important distinction from the election of Saturninus. As the English monarchy appeared to slide inexorably towards absolutism,[153] the play offered an alternative polity in which the *pactum* or social contract provides a preferred basis for the constitutional relationship between citizen and magistrate. There is no escaping the violence of *Titus Andronicus*. Whether ritualised and sacrificial or barbarous and visceral, it is there at every turn. Nuttall claims to 'flinch' from the play, finding the contrast between its elegant language and the horror of its narrative 'upsetting'. He seeks to 'avert [his] mind' from the stage direction at the start of Act 2, scene 3: '*Enter the Empress' Sons with LAVINIA, her hands cut off and her tongue cut out, and ravished*'.[154] A strong stomach may be considered a prerequisite for any member of the audience at a performance of the play, but to avert the mind from contemplation and interpretation of the graphic horror in *Titus Andronicus* is to disengage with a moral and political dialectic, in which Shakespeare presents the audience with the most shocking images of a disjointed society. The disjuncture has been caused by the tyranny of unrestrained imperial rule, under which the equitable ideology of unwritten law has been rejected, the commonwealth dismembered and the natural rights of the subject violently suppressed.

---

[152] On the religious significance of the dining rituals at the Inns of Court, see Raffield, above n 30, at 16–20.

[153] An indication of this trend is that the size of the Privy Council gradually shrank from 227 members in the reign of Henry VII to 19 in 1559; by 1597 there were only 11 members; see Guy, above n 32, at 310, 438.

[154] Nuttall, above n 122, at 87–88.

Titus Andronicus *and the Flight of Justice*

On 24 March 1603, England's own Astraea finally abandoned the earth. Was the death of Elizabeth to herald (as the flight of Astraea did in *Metamorphoses*) an Age of Iron, characterised by violence and social discord? Or was there to be a new Golden Age in which subjects were governed not by statute or imperial edict but by a natural propensity for justice? For common lawyers such as Coke, Fulbecke and Selden the answer lay in the immemorial authority of common law. Its divine provenance, allied to the sacerdotal standing of its judges, guaranteed that justice would never depart the earth so long as common law was accorded paramount constitutional status:

> the chiefe end or last marke of ye law aswel as other sciences is God his glory. But ye next and immediate end, which is allotted to it, is to administer Justice to al, & in that sence it maybe called the rule of Justice: For religion, Justice, and law do stand together.[155]

---

[155] Fulbecke, above n 104, B.*v.*

2

The Comedy of Errors and the Meaning of Contract

I. Errors and Confusion, Disorder and Tumult

P HILIP HENSLOWE REPORTED healthy box office receipts for the performances at the Rose Playhouse in January and February 1594 of *Titus Andronicus*, before an outbreak of plague forced the closure of his theatre on 7 February.[1] By the end of the same year, the first recorded performance of *The Comedy of Errors*, Shakespeare's inventive re-imagining of Plautus' *Menaechmi*, had taken place in the Hall of Gray's Inn before a raucous audience of lawyers and their guests. There have been numerous commentaries on 'The Night of Errors' at Gray's Inn, all based upon the anonymous account of one who apparently attended the 'grand Night' of 28 December (Innocents' Day) 1594, and wrote that 'a Comedy of Errors (like to *Plautus* his *Menechmus*) was played by the Players.'[2] This record of the revels was published by William Canning in 1688, nearly 100 years after the event. Whether *The Comedy of Errors* was commissioned for performance at the Gray's Inn revels of 1594 is debatable,[3] although I suggest in this chapter that the subject matter of the play made it uniquely suited to this specific occasion. Given that, by tradition, the Inns of Court revels lasted approximately three weeks, these particular festivities extended over an unusually long

---

[1] Receipts for *Titus Andronicus* in January and February 1594 were as follows: £3 8s (23 January); 40s (28 January); 40s (6 February), R A Foakes (ed), *Henslowe's Diary* (Cambridge, Cambridge University Press, 2002) 21; see also *Titus Andronicus*, (ed) J Bate (London, Arden Shakespeare, 1995) Introduction, 69–70.

[2] D Bland (ed), *Gesta Grayorum, or, the History of the High and Mighty Prince Henry Prince of Purpoole, Anno Domini, 1594* (Liverpool, Liverpool University Press, 1968) 32. References to the 1594 revels are to this edition of *Gesta Grayorum*. On the 1594 Gray's Inn revels, see P Raffield, *Images and Cultures of Law in Early Modern England: Justice and Political Power, 1558–1660* (Cambridge, Cambridge University Press, 2004) 111–23; B Cormack, 'Locating *The Comedy of Errors*: Revels Jurisdiction at the Inns of Court' in J Archer, E Goldring and S Knight (eds), *The Intellectual and Cultural World of the Early Modern Inns of Court* (Manchester, Manchester University Press, Forthcoming).

[3] Foakes concedes that '[t]here is no compelling reason why the play should not have been written for a special occasion—perhaps the Gray's Inn Revels of 1594', but his personal preference is for a date between 1590 and 1593, see *The Comedy of Errors*, (ed) R A Foakes (London, Arden Shakespeare, 1962) Introduction, xxiii; Wells places it in the early 1590s, see *The Comedy of Errors*, (ed) S Wells (Harmondsworth, Penguin, 1972) Introduction, 11; Whitworth supports the view that the play was 'a new composition, purpose-written for the Christmas season, 1594', *The Comedy of Errors*, (ed) C Whitworth (Oxford, Oxford University Press, 2002) Introduction, 4.

period.⁴ The Gray's Inn revels formally commenced on 20 December 1594 with the inauguration of Mr Henry Helmes as the Prince of Purpoole; they ended with a performance of Francis Davison's *The Masque of Proteus*, presented to the Queen at the royal court, on Shrovetide, 11 February 1595.

Despite the fact that the 1594 revels lasted nearly two months, it is understandable that most commentators should concentrate on the spectacular events of 28 December, and the performance that night of *The Comedy of Errors*. In particular, they are drawn to the 'disordered Tumult and Crowd upon the Stage', which preceded the play and precipitated the indignant departure of the offended guest of honour, the Ambassador of the Inner Temple's 'Emperor', *Frederick Templarius*. On the night of 29 December, members of the Inn convened a tribunal, at which the 'Sorcerer or Conjurer that was supposed to be the Cause of that confused Inconvenience' was indicted.⁵ Thus the action of Shakespeare's play is mirrored in the proceedings of the revels: a trial, a conjuror and (above all) confusion are memorable features of the plot in *The Comedy of Errors*. Much academic interest has focused on whether the alleged riot at Gray's Inn was spontaneous or staged, real or fabricated: were the lawyers complicit in exploring Shakespeare's theme of errors and confusion; or, in the words of Nietzsche, had 'the separate art worlds of dreamland and drunkenness' collided, and the 'Apollonian world of pictures' succumbed to 'the mystical cheer of Dionysus'?⁶

Such speculation is not without its uses in attempting to identify the level to which the revels were stage-managed, and the extent to which individual members exercised their autonomy in direct opposition to the rule of the Inn. If it can be proved that the night of 28 December instanced genuine

> Disorders and Misdemeanours, by Hurly-burlies, Crowds, Errors, Confusions, vain Representations and Shews, to the utter Discredit of our State and Policy⁷

then the riotous conduct of members represented a public renunciation of the authority of a highly regulated community, whose governing body legislated for

---

⁴ In the 1630s, a Parliament of the Inner Temple decreed 'that Christmas Commons should continue by the space of three weeks only, and no longer, according to the antient usage and custome of this House', Sir William Dugdale, *Origines Juridiciales or Historical Memorials of the English Laws* (London, F & T Warren, 1666) 149. Bland notes that the holding of a 'grand Christmas' at Gray's Inn was sanctioned by its governing body on the grounds that solemn revels had not been held there for several years prior to 1594, Bland (ed), above n 2, Introduction, xv–xvi.

⁵ Bland (ed), above n 2, 31–32.

⁶ F Nietzsche, *The Birth of Tragedy*, (tr) W A Haussmann (Edinburgh, Foulis, 1909) 22, 68, 121. Zurcher argues that the disorder 'was probably itself staged, and the errors scripted in order to make way for the elaborate restitutions that followed', A Zurcher, 'Consideration, Contract and the End of *The Comedy of Errors*' in P Raffield and G Watt (eds), *Shakespeare and the Law* (Oxford, Hart Publishing, 2008) 33; West suggests an element of self-conscious complicity, and that the vocabulary employed in the account of the 'Tumult' encompasses 'playing and playgoing alike', W N West, ' "But this will be a mere confusion": Real and Represented Confusions on the Elizabethan Stage' (2008) 60 *Theatre Journal* 217, 218; Bland states that '[t]he record leaves no doubt that the disorders were quite unexpected', Bland (ed), above n 2, Introduction, xiii, n 1.

⁷ Bland (ed), above n 2, at 32.

ordered participation in the revels.⁸ There is interest also in the symbolic conjunction of Shakespeare and the law: the fusion of the rites of the legal community with those of the theatre, which the anonymous author of *Gesta Grayorum* is keen to emphasise. But concentration on this single incident distracts attention from the central thematic conceit of both the Gray's Inn revels and Shakespeare's play: the enhanced role of commerce, free trade and the market in late-Elizabethan society, and the elevated status of contract law as the principal means through which societal relations were arranged and controlled.

In this chapter, I investigate the extraordinary advancement of the law of contract in Elizabethan England, and in particular the significance of the promise to the status of binding bilateral agreements. In legal terms, the importance of this phenomenon is inextricably linked to the rise, during the reign of Elizabeth I, of *assumpsit*: an action of trespass on the case for breach of a promise or undertaking. I analyse the promotion of assumpsit at the expense of actions for debt, in the context of a society (and a legal profession) whose mores were heavily influenced by humanist notions of the individual conscience, which simultaneously bound the subject of law into an ethical relationship with his fellow citizens and freed him (at least putatively) from the constraints of immutable, ancient law.⁹

Section II. of this chapter examines the conflict between the Court of Common Pleas and the Court of King's Bench, over whether action for debt or action on the case for assumpsit was the correct means of redress for breached commercial undertakings: a jurisdictional dispute which was only resolved in 1602 with the landmark decision of *Slade's Case*.¹⁰

In section III. I analyse the most symbolically charged property in the play: the gold chain, purchased by Antipholus of Ephesus as a gift for his wife, Adriana. The chain in *The Comedy of Errors* acts partly as the symbol of a society which is bound together only by the market, having abandoned or mislaid the true bonds of friendship and love, through which a just community may be recognised.¹¹ In addition to its obvious commercial connotations, the chain has, at least since *The Laws* of Plato, served as a metaphor for the unifying power of law itself. I consider

---

⁸ The governing body of Gray's Inn is Pension; the Inner Temple and the Middle Temple are governed by their respective Parliaments; Lincoln's Inn by its Council. At a Gray's Inn Pension, 'held there in Michaelmas Term 21.H.8. there was an Order made, that all the Fellows of this House, who should be present ... upon any other day, at Dinner, or Supper, when there are Revells, should not depart out of the Hall, until the said revels were ended, upon the penalty of xiid', Dugdale, above n 4, at 285; at the Inner Temple, '[i]f the Steward, or any of the said Officers named in Trinity Term, refuse or fail, he or they were fined every one, at the discretion of the Bench', *ibid* at 153.

⁹ In the words of Sir Henry Maine: '[T]he movement of the progressive societies has hitherto been a movement from Status to Contract', H Maine, *Ancient Law* (London, Dent, 1917) 100. Bruster notes, regarding *The Comedy of Errors*, that 'urban farce stresses a horizontal obligation', in which relationships are governed by capital, rather than the social abstractions implicit in a vertical hierarchical order, as described for example by Ulysses in *Troilus and Cressida* and Menenius in *Coriolanus*: D Bruster, *Drama and the Market in the Age of Shakespeare* (Cambridge, Cambridge University Press, 1992) 76.

¹⁰ *Slade's Case*, in Part 4 (1604) of *The Reports of Sir Edward Coke, Knt. In English*, (ed) G Wilson, 7 vols (London, Rivington, 1777) 2: 91a, at 92b.

¹¹ See I Ward, *Shakespeare and the Legal Imagination* (London, Butterworths, 1999) 137.

here the capacity of the theatrical property—the prop—to embody classical and Judaeo-Christian juristic ideals, and, in the narrower context of *The Comedy of Errors*, to represent the primacy of commodity in a society which values wealth over the human association that the classical interpretation of contract implies.[12] In the context of the various disputes in the play over who has promised what to whom and when, I examine the archaic juridical procedure known as 'wager of law', whereby the defendant swore that he did not owe money or had not withheld goods, and provided 11 'compurgators' to testify on his behalf.[13] I am particularly interested in exploring here what Baker terms 'the farce' of wager of law,[14] and the obvious potential that this method of 'proof' held for the writer of comic drama. That Shakespeare was familiar with Plowden's *Commentaries or Reports* is well documented[15]; in this section I consider the influence of Plowden over the themes and plot of *The Comedy of Errors*. In particular, I argue that legal discourse on doctrinal matters (such as whether a promise constitutes sufficient consideration to a contract) would have provided Shakespeare not only with dramatic scenarios involving agreements, disagreements, non-agreements and misunderstandings, but also with a moral framework in which to place the action of his play.

Section IV. examines a major substantive theme of the 1594 Gray's Inn revels: the reconciliation of monarchic rule with the imperatives of a commercial society. This theme (like many others in the Gray's Inn revels) is mirrored in *The Comedy of Errors*, in which Shakespeare's Ephesian society appears to be governed by freedom of contract, rather than by the dictates of the supreme magistrate (Solinus), who opens the play by condemning to death a merchant from an enemy State and ends it by reprieving him.

In section V. I address the theme of slavery and emancipation. The bond has numerous meanings in the play. These include the rope that bound Egeon and his family to the shipwrecked mast (as reported by Egeon at the start of the play), the shackles from which Emilia releases her husband at its conclusion, the disputed contractual bond between Antipholus of Ephesus and Angelo over the manufacture, sale and purchase of the gold chain, and the social status of the Dromios as 'bondmen' to the Antipholi twins. My interest here lies in exploring the socio-political nature of the contractual bond and the emergence of a more equitable basis by which such associations were controlled. I refer especially in this section to those commercial cases reported by Coke, regarding the contentious constitutional issue of disputed rights to freedom of trade, in the face of prerogative grants of monopolies by the Crown.

---

[12] See, eg, Cicero: '*omnium divinarum humanarumque rerum cum benevolentia et caritate consensio*' ('a complete accord on all subjects human and divine, joined with mutual goodwill and affection'), M T Cicero, *Laelius De Amicitia*, (ed) St G W J Stock (Oxford, Clarendon, 1930) VI.20.

[13] Wager of law was not abolished until 1833; see J H Baker, *An Introduction to English Legal History* (London, Butterworths, 2002) 5–6.

[14] J H Baker, 'New Light On Slade's Case' in J H Baker, *The Legal Profession and the Common Law: Historical Essays* (London, Hambledon, 1986) 424.

[15] See ch 3, n 40, below; also, ch 6, n 25, below.

II. The Promise: *'Dictum Meum Pactum'*?

The history of contract law in Elizabethan England is as much a history of conflict between rival courts of common law as it is a narrative of doctrinal development. Problems of jurisdictional differences between the Court of Common Pleas and the Court of King's Bench over available remedies for breached commercial relations are founded in medieval definitions of contract. A contract was a transaction, which involved the transference of property and the creation of a debt. The modern idea of contract as either an exchange of promises or a reciprocal agreement finds its closest parallel in the medieval covenant (*conventio*); but the covenant was enforceable in the courts of common law (by the *praecipe* writ of covenant) only if it was evidenced by deed. Obviously, this requirement was a major inconvenience and obstacle for parties to minor commercial transactions, but the courts remained intransigent. For example, in 1321, where a carrier failed to deliver a cartload of hay, as he had covenanted to do, the action failed for want of a deed, the judge insisting that the courts would not 'undo the law for a cartload of hay'.[16]

This did not mean that a debt was enforceable only if it had been sealed under deed. An original transaction, which related to the exchange of property rather than promises, was enforceable through an action for debt, and such an action would not fail merely because no deed had been executed. Informal transactions could be prosecuted by a writ of debt, the plaintiff only having to overcome the evidential burden of proof, against which the defendant was entitled to 'wage his law', a juridical procedure to which I shall return. As Baker has noted, an action for debt was available only for the liquidated sum owed in the original transaction. It offered no remedy for damage suffered as a consequence of the unpaid debt; for example, if the defendant failed to deliver fungible goods to the plaintiff by an agreed date, and the plaintiff's business suffered as a result of fluctuations in the market value of that particular commodity.[17] Actions on the case to recover special damages such as the above were, since the 15th century, dependent on the writ of a*ssumpsit super se* ('took upon himself'); and thus the 'assumption' or undertaking was ushered into English law, a development which took on greater moral and spiritual significance during the 16th century as the undertaking came to be interpreted by the courts as a form of promise.[18]

Conflict between the Court of Common Pleas and the Court of King's Bench arose over three principal issues: whether it was fair for a defendant to be forced

---

[16] Anon (1321), in J H Baker and S F C Milsom, *Sources of English Legal History: Private Law to 1750* (London, Butterworths, 1986) 286.
[17] Baker, 'New Light On Slade's Case', above n 14, at 415–16. In an action for debt, a small amount beyond the original sum owed was available as *damna detencionis*; whereas in assumpsit, damages were assessed by a jury: see D Ibbetson, 'Sixteenth Century Contract Law: *Slade's Case* In Context' (1984) 4 *Oxford Journal of Legal Studies* 295, 309.
[18] On covenant and debt, see Baker, above n 13, at 317–28; on assumpsit, see *ibid* at 329–46.

by the plaintiff into trial by jury in an assumpsit action, thus depriving him of the right to wage his law in an action for debt; whether the undertaking in an assumpsit action was an express or an implied promise; and whether the two separate forms of action—debt and assumpsit—were available to the plaintiff in the same cause. As far as the promise itself was concerned, an element of illusion was involved: might a promise be conjured out of the original transaction which created the debt? The Court of Common Pleas was adamant that the promise had to be expressly conveyed; while in King's Bench, actions were allowable on the basis of an implied 'fictitious promise'.[19] In practical terms, the effect of this difference of judicial opinion was that in King's Bench the implied existence of a promise amounted to a point of pleading: if the plaintiff could prove that the debt existed then a promise would be implied; whereas in Common Pleas, proof of an actual promise was required. These contentious issues were resolved only at the start of the 17th century in *Slade's Case*, in which King's Bench prevailed over Common Pleas at a hearing convoked in 1602 by Sir John Popham, Chief Justice of the King's Bench,

> for the honour of the law, and for the quiet of the subject in the appeasing of such diversity of opinions . . . before all the Justices of England, and Barons of the Exchequer . . .[20]

It was determined that an action for assumpsit could lie even though an existing remedy for debt was available, and, of great importance to the development of modern contract law,

> every contract executory imports in itself an *assumpsit*, for when one agrees to pay money, or to deliver any thing, thereby he assumes or promises to pay, or deliver it . . .[21]

The triumph of assumpsit over debt was thus assured, wager of law became a matter of legal history, and the legal status of the promise was elevated to an unprecedented level.

Baker makes the interesting observation that opposition of the Common Pleas to recognition of assumpsit at the expense of debt was based upon the inherent conservatism of its judges, proud of their paramount status in the courts of common law and conscious of the court's medieval origins, which were traceable to *Magna Carta*.[22] Coke described the court as

> the lock and the key of the common law in common pleas, for herein are reall actions, whereupon fines and recoveries (the common assurances of the realm) do passe . . .[23]

Pitted against the reactionary stance of Common Pleas was the progressive, modernising tendency of King's Bench, which Baker characterises as representing 'the

---

[19] Ibbetson, above n 17, at 297.
[20] *Slade's Case* (1602), Coke, 4 *Reports* (1604) 2: 93a.
[21] *Ibid*, 94a.
[22] On the founding of Common Pleas (*communia placita*) in *Magna Carta*, see Sir Edward Coke, *The Fourth Part of the Institutes of the Laws of England, Concerning the Jurisdiction of the Courts* (London, E and R Brooke, 1797) 98.
[23] *Ibid*.

legal renaissance of the sixteenth century',[24] anxious to extend its influence and business, and encroaching upon the traditional domain of Common Pleas.[25] The theme of unyielding ancient law colliding with a flexible modern alternative that was capable of responding to prevailing social and economic conditions, is addressed by Shakespeare in the first few lines of *The Comedy of Errors*. The merchant Egeon, condemned to death as an enemy alien in accordance with Ephesian statute, is informed by the Duke that, despite his apparent innocence of any crime other than being a Syracusian in Ephesus, 'I am not partial to infringe our laws' (1.1.4) and therefore Egeon must die.[26] The Duke's conscience dictates that 'were it not against our laws' (1.1.143),[27] he should 'favour thee in what I can' (1.1.150); but at the end of the play, persuaded by the mitigating circumstances of the particular case before him, the Duke overturns this inequitable law and frees Egeon without extracting the lawfully-sanctioned ransom of 1,000 marks (5.1.391).

Returning to the issue of debt and assumpsit, the problem of uncertainty for Elizabethan litigants was laid bare when cases were heard *nisi prius*,[28] on which occasion the particular decision invariably depended upon whether the assize judge was of Common Pleas or King's Bench. This unsatisfactory state of judicial affairs, in which the jurisdiction of one court overlapped and conflicted with that of another, was compounded by the peculiar process of surveillance, whereby King's Bench acted as a court of error for decisions made in Common Pleas. Coke records this role as

> regularly to examine and correct all and all manner of errors *in fait*, and in law, of all the judges and justices of the realm in their judgements, processe, and proceeding in courts of record . . .[29]

---

[24] Baker, 'New Light on Slade's Case', above n 14, at 412.

[25] The primary function of King's Bench was to hear 'all pleas of the crowne; as all manner of treasons, felonies, and other pleas of the crown which *ex congruo*, are aptly called *propriæ causæ regis*, because they are *placita coronæ regis*', Coke, above n 22, at 71. Quoting from Sir Matthew Hale CJ, Sacks notes that 'this "multiplication of Actions upon the Case, which were rare formerly," also accounts in large measure for the huge increases in business in the central courts' and that the promotion of assumpsit in King's Bench was 'part of this market-driven process', D H Sacks, 'The Promise and the Contract in Early Modern England: Slade's Case in Perspective', in V Kahn and L Hutson (eds), *Rhetoric and Law in Early Modern Europe* (New Haven, Conn, Yale University Press, 2001) 31, 37.

[26] All references to the text of the play are from *The Comedy of Errors*, (ed) S Wells (Harmondsworth, Penguin, 1972).

[27] Heinze argues that the play 'symbolises the commercial forces of early modernity unsettling a traditional feudal-aristocratic power structure', E Heinze, '"Were it not against our laws": Oppression and Resistance in Shakespeare's *Comedy of Errors*' (2009) 29 *Legal Studies* 230, 232. Drawing on the symbolism of the mythical ancient firebird, Heinze asserts that the home of Antipholus of Ephesus, the Phoenix, 'stands for the new man of the new law', *ibid* at 242. It is possible that Shakespeare chose the phoenix in veiled homage to Gray's Inn, whose emblem was the griffin. Like the phoenix, the griffin was used in the medieval church as a symbol of the Resurrection of Christ: the eagle's head representing his divinity, the lion's body his humanity.

[28] *Nisi prius* signified a trial by jury before a single judge at the assizes: sheriffs were required to bring jurors to the courts in Westminster on a specific day, 'unless before that day' (*nisi prius*) justices of assize came into the county.

[29] Coke, above n 22, at 71.

King's Bench routinely overturned the decisions of Common Pleas; but to add one further layer of judicial contrivance, error lay from King's Bench to the Exchequer Chamber (created by statute in 1585), in which Barons of the Court of Exchequer (who had been serjeants-at-law) sat in judgment alongside their brethren of the Common Pleas, who had no compunction in regularly overturning the decisions of King's Bench.[30]

As the above process demonstrates, error was writ large in the procedural apparatus of Elizabethan contract law. The mechanism of farce is driven by a series of mistaken assumptions and the frenetic pursuit of particular ends, motivated by an erroneously held belief. The complex institutional apparatus of Elizabethan private law and the conflicting stances of rival jurisdictions within the same legal system made it an obvious subject for farcical treatment by a skilful dramatist.[31] Farce is recognised in performance by the acceleration of an absurd plot, executed with mechanical precision, in which the artfully exploited situation takes precedence over the development of character. In terms of style, *The Comedy of Errors* contains more farcical elements than any of Shakespeare's plays, but it is not a farce—or rather it is more than a farce. Taking *Menaechmi* as his primary source,[32] Shakespeare humanises Plautus' efficiently comedic but cynical (and often cruel) work,[33] framing the action of the Roman play with the dramatic and potentially tragic tale of Egeon.

The themes of familial separation and reconciliation, the imminence of death, the search for identity and the discovery of happiness through individual immersion in and engagement with community are not conventional subjects for farce. In *The Comedy of Errors* these issues are fundamental to the play, and generally are

---

[30] On the various functions of Exchequer Chamber, see *ibid* at 117–19; Baker states that '[t]he Common Pleas judges sitting in the Exchequer Chamber treated their King's Bench brethren with open contempt, refusing even to allow argument in support of the King's Bench judgments', Baker, above n 13, at 344; see also, Ibbetson, above n 17, at 299.

[31] See, eg, plays by two of Shakespeare's contemporaries: John Marston, *Histrio-Mastix Or, The Player Whipt!* (London, T Thorp, 1610); and John Day, *Law-Trickes or, Who Would Have Thought It. As it hath bene divers times Acted by the Children of the Revels* (London, R More, 1608); see ch 5, nn 10, 19 and 20, below. For a discussion of *Slade's Case*, assumpsit and Ben Jonson's *Bartholomew Fair*, see L Wilson, 'Ben Jonson and the Law of Contract' (1993) 5 *Cardozo Studies in Law and Literature* 281.

[32] The identical *Menaechmi* twins, indistinguishable to all but each other, provided Shakespeare with the main farcical mechanism for *The Comedy of Errors*. *Menaechmi* was translated into English by the lawyer, William Warner, and was entered in the Stationers' Register on 10 June 1594. According to Whitworth, the date of entry lends credibility to the idea that Shakespeare referred to Warner's translation when writing *The Comedy of Errors* for performance during the Christmas season, 1594; see Whitworth (ed), above n 3, Introduction, 21–25. It is probable, though, that Shakespeare had read *Menaechmi* in Latin as part of his boyhood education at the King's New School in Stratford. The other important source is Plautus' *Amphitruo*, from which Shakespeare took the idea of identical and indistinguishable twin servants, thus multiplying the potential for confusion. *Amphitruo* was the inspiration also for Act 3, scene 1, in which Antipholus of Ephesus is locked out of his house by his wife, who is dining inside with his twin brother, whom she takes to be her husband. *Mother Bombie*, written by John Lyly and performed in the early 1590s, includes a servant called Dromio, although as Foakes notes, 'this name is a variant of *Dromo*, a type-name for a slave in several of Terence's comedies', Foakes (ed), above n 3, Introduction, xxxiii, n 4.

[33] Nuttall describes *Menaechmi* as 'a marvellous contraption', A D Nuttall, *Shakespeare The Thinker* (New Haven, Conn, Yale University Press, 2007) 57.

expressed throughout not in prose but in extended passages of lyrical poetry, allowing the characters to articulate their humanity in a manner alien to the plot-driven imperatives of traditional farce. Shakespeare takes the raw material of Plautus' stock characters—the unfaithful husband, the jealous wife, the long-suffering slave, the freeloading friend, the courtesan, the wife's father, the doctor—and not only transforms them into multidimensional human beings (discarding along the way the wife's father and the freeloading friend) but relocates them to a place which Nuttall describes as 'an ideological Illyria'.[34] The particular ideology to which the inhabitants of this Ephesian Illyria subscribe is that of *laissez-faire* market forces. It is a society in which the law intervenes only when the stability of the market is threatened by the failure of its members to conform with the law of contract. To illustrate this point Shakespeare introduces a long list of characters from the worlds of commerce and the law: Angelo, the goldsmith; Balthazar, the merchant; the First Merchant, who befriends Antipholus of Syracuse; the Second Merchant, Angelo's creditor; an Officer of the Law; a Jailer; and the supreme magistrate, Solinus, Duke of Ephesus.

III. The Chain: Symbol of Commerce, Love and Law

The subjects of legal dispute to which I refer above would have been of great interest to a contemporary dramatist intent on writing an urban comedy, whose plot hinged on a disputed debt and a contested promise to pay for the manufacture and delivery of a gold chain. The evidential status of the promise, described above, in which formal juridical criteria were applied to an act of moral, ethical and spiritual obligation, provides Shakespeare with a useful dramatic tool, as the 'promise' over the purchase of the chain propels the play's protagonists into the distorted realm of contractual dispute. As indicated above, the stance taken by King's Bench in the dispute over the status of the promise involved the recognition by law of an illusion: a non-existent promise was conjured by the judges from the factual evidence of the transaction.[35] It was the formal acknowledgment by King's Bench of an illusion to which Common Pleas objected. As early as 1567, Sir James Dyer, Chief Justice of the Common Pleas (1559–82), expressed unequivocal opposition to inclusion of an implied promise in the original transaction: '[W]ithout alleging a promise in fact, such as a subsequent promise to pay, no action lies in the case'.[36]

---

[34] *Ibid* at 59.
[35] Regarding *Slade's Case*, Zurcher refers to '[t]he 'imaginary' quality of the implied promise', Zurcher, above n 6, 36, n 27.
[36] *Lord Grey's Case* (1567), CUL MS li 5.15 fo 3.*v*; see also, *Michell v Dansden* (1595) CUL MS li 5.24 fo 50, in which it was noted that '[t]he opinion of Lord Dyer was that if the debtor made an actual promise to pay it, then an action on the case would lie against him, but not on the implied promise on the debt only'.

The Comedy of Errors *and the Meaning of Contract*

The choice of Ephesus as the location for *The Comedy of Errors* was not coincidental. Renowned not only as a commercial centre during the period of the Roman Empire, the city was famed also for the peculiar interest which its citizens took in conjuring, magicians and illusion. In *The Epistle of Paul to the Ephesians*, its author specifically warns his addressees 'to have no fellowship with the unfruitful works of darkness' and attempts to turn them 'against principalities, against powers, against the rulers of the darkness of this world, against spiritual wickedness in high places'.[37] Upon arrival in Ephesus, Antipholus of Syracuse immediately senses the forces of darkness to which St Paul refers:

> They say this town is full of cozenage,
> As nimble jugglers that deceive the eye,
> Dark-working sorcerers that change the mind ... (1.2.97–99)

Lorna Hutson has noted that recent literary criticism seeks to explain 'Shakespearean dramatic mimesis' by analogy with the dark arts of magic and illusion, suggesting that Shakespeare was a form of renaissance magus, summoning the presence of spirits through his use of language.[38] Hutson is alert to the peculiar language of sorcery in *The Comedy of Errors*, and of its noticeable similarity to the legal language of testament or proof, which is instanced throughout the last two acts of the play as claim and counter-claim are repeatedly made, concerning payment for the purchase of the gold chain.[39] The innocent Antipholus of Ephesus wages his law in defence of the honest claim that 'I never saw the chain, so help me heaven' (5.1.268). The various characters who have become involved in the contractual dispute act as compurgators or oath-takers, swearing as to the veracity of their testimony. 'And I am witness with her that she did' (4.4.87), swears Luciana in support of her sister's mistaken insistence that she gave a purse of ducats to Dromio of Ephesus, as bail for the arrest of her husband; to which the Ephesian Dromio honestly replies: 'God and the rope-maker bear me witness / That I was sent for nothing but a rope' (4.4.88–89); 'My lord, in truth, thus far I witness with him' (5.1.255), swears Angelo in rightful support of the defendant's claim to have been locked out of the Phoenix by his wife, but who wrongly believes Adriana to be a 'perjur'd woman' (5.1.212) for mistakenly swearing that she dined with her husband at home; 'I will be sworn these ears of mine / Heard you confess you had the chain of him' (5.1.260–61), avows the Second Merchant in the honest but mistaken belief that Antipholus of Ephesus had received the chain from Angelo.

The above oaths and testaments bear a strong if exaggerated resemblance to the juridical procedure of wager of law, which was available to the defendant in an action for debt but not in an action for assumpsit, the facts of which were tried by

---

[37] *The Epistle of Paul the Apostle to the Ephesians*, 5.11, 6.12; references to the text are from the Authorised King James Version of the Bible. On the influence of the *Epistle to the Ephesians* over the play, see Whitworth (ed), above n 3, Introduction, 39–41.

[38] L Hutson, *The Invention of Suspicion: Law and Mimesis in Shakespeare and Renaissance Drama* (Oxford, Oxford University Press, 2007) 148–49; Hutson cites an example of recent criticism in this vein: S Greenblatt, *Hamlet in Purgatory* (New Jersey, Princeton University Press, 2001).

[39] Hutson, above n 38, at 150.

The Chain: Symbol of Commerce, Love and Law

jury. This was another major source of contention in *Slade's Case*: was it fair and just to deprive the defendant of his right to wage law in an action for debt by forcing him into an action for assumpsit? In the early modern English legal system parties to an action were not permitted to give evidence on their own behalf, giving the plaintiff an unfair advantage. Even if the defendant had already paid money owed, or provided goods or services according to the terms of the original transaction, in a trial for assumpsit it was difficult if not impossible for him to counter the claims of an unscrupulous plaintiff that he had breached the terms of the contract.[40]

Moral as well as legal concerns of conscience, truth and honesty were central to the issue of wager of law; matters of obvious interest to jurist and dramatist alike. Under this system a defendant would present 11 oath-takers or compurgators, all of whom swore to the veracity of the defendant's claim. At a local level this system worked well, as friends, neighbours and business acquaintances of the defendant might testify on his behalf: a frenetic and distorted version of this practice is represented in Act 5 of *The Comedy of Errors*, as described above. David Harris Sacks argues that a tradesman would be unlikely to perjure himself in such circumstances, as a finding that he had sworn falsely under oath would instantaneously destroy his creditworthiness among lenders and fellow tradesmen[41]: an argument which is of particular relevance to the situation in which Antipholus of Ephesus finds himself, regarding the gold chain. The 'farce' of wager of law was exposed when such cases came to the courts of common law at Westminster. It was impractical for 11 compurgators, known to the defendant, to travel to London to swear on his behalf, as a consequence of which the defendant paid professional compurgators (who were completely unknown to him) to so testify.

Despite the obvious shortcomings of wager of law, trial by jury was by no means exemplary: apart from the fact that the parties were not permitted to give evidence, as David Ibbetson has noted, it was an easy task for an influential litigant to pack a jury with his supporters. The advantage of jury trial over wager of law was that it at least created the illusion of reason and probity.[42] The question of conscience and its intrinsic link with Judaeo-Christian theology was one which exercised Coke, both in his reporting of *Slade's Case* and in *The First Part of The Institutes*. In the latter he places great symbolic emphasis on the number 12, noting the link between:

---

[40] See, eg, *Turges v Becher* (1596) Yale MS GR 29.9 fo 197, in which it was reported that Owen J, in conversation with Wray CJ, posed the hypothetical instance: '[I]f one bought goods from a merchant and paid for them, and they continued to trade together for several years ... if afterwards the merchant bought assumpsit for all the contracts between them, now if the defendant was not admitted to wage his law he would not be able to prove that which had happened a long time before'. A party was allowed to give evidence on his own behalf only after the passing of the Evidence Act 1851. To prevent fraudulent claims by plaintiffs, the Shop Books Act 1610 made account books of merchants inadmissible as evidence, where the disputed contract was more than one year old; see Ibbetson, above n 17, at 314.

[41] Sacks, above n 25, at 35.

[42] Ibbetson, above n 17, at 312.

12. Jurors for the triall of matters of fact, but 12. Judges of ancient time for triall of matters in Law, in the Exchequer Chamber. Also for matters of State there were in ancient time twelve Counsellors of State. He that wageth his Law must have eleven others with him which thinke he says true. And that number of 12. is much respected in holy Writ, as 12. Apostles, 12. Stones, 12. Tribes, &c.[43]

In *Slade's Case*, Coke invokes the fear of eternal damnation as the inevitable consequence of perjury, a reason which he argues is sufficient to justify the non-appearance of a party in his own cause: 'for *Jurare in propria causa* (as one saith) *est saepenumero hoc seculo praecipitium diaboli ad detrudendas miserorum animas ad infernum*'.[44] Coke is referring to the criminal offence of perjury, the intentional giving of false evidence under oath. The equation of divine and municipal law (made here with Coke's characteristic recourse to Latin maxim) is by no means unusual in a legal system whose apologists depicted common law as the earthly manifestation of God's law. This rhetorical commonplace notwithstanding, the development of contract law in the 16th century was notable for a burgeoning emphasis on the individual conscience as a binding factor in commercial transactions.

In his description of the events preceding trial in *Slade's Case*, Coke's report conflates temporal and spiritual obligations: the plaintiff, John Slade, had sown wheat and rye on his land in Halberton, Devon, which the defendant, Humphry Morley,

> did assume, and then and there faithfully promised, that he the said Humph. 16l. of lawful money of Engl. to the afores. John in the feast of St. John the Baptist, then next following, would well and truly content and pay . . .

Not only, it was alleged by the plaintiff, was the defendant 'little regarding' of his assumption and promise, but also he intended 'subtilly and craftily to deceive and defraud, the said 16l. to the said John, according to his assuming and promise'.[45] The unconscious coupling of the plaintiff's Christian name, John, with St John the Baptist, of course contributes to the sense (as so often elsewhere in *The Reports*) that Coke is enacting a Biblical parable for the spiritual enlightenment of his readers.[46]

---

[43] Sir Edward Coke, *The first part of the institutes of the laws of England. Or, a commentary upon Littleton* (London, Societie of Stationers, 1628) 155, nn (b) and (c).

[44] Coke, *Slade's Case* (1602), 4 *Reports* (1604) 2: 95a.

[45] *Ibid* (1597) 91a–91b; the report makes evident why an action on the case for assumpsit was preferable to an action for debt: Slade claimed that, as a result of Morley's non-payment, he 'hath sustained damage to the value of 40l. and thereof he bringeth suit', *ibid*, 91b. Slade was eventually awarded compensation of £26: the original sum of £16, plus damages of £10, 'which damages in the whole do amount to 26l.', *ibid*, 92a; in an action for debt, he would have been awarded only the original £16.

[46] As, eg: 'For thy comfort and encouragement, cast thine eye upon the sages of the law, that have been before thee, and never shalt thou find any that hath excelled in the knowledge of these laws, but hath sucked from the breast of that divine knowledge, honesty, gravity, and integrity, and by the goodness of God hath obtained a greater blessing and ornament than any other profession to their family and posterity, as by the page following, taking some for many, you may perceive; for it is an undoubted truth, *that the just shall flourish like the palm-tree; and spread abroad as the cedars of* Libanus (Psalm 91.13)', Coke, 2 *Reports* (1602) 1: Preface, x–xi. Sir Francis Bacon criticised *The Reports* for their preponderance of opinion over fact: 'A Memorial Touching the Amendment of Laws' (*c* 1614), in J Spedding (ed), *The Letters and Life of Francis Bacon*, 7 vols (London, Longman, 1869) 5: 86. Baker

The Chain: Symbol of Commerce, Love and Law

But the coupling of 'assumption' and 'promise' is significant also in signalling the incorporation of Judaeo-Christian injunctions to love one another (and specifically in *The Epistle of Paul to the Ephesians*, the insistence upon mutual trust between 'fellow-citizens')[47] into common law doctrine, especially into those doctrines governing private relations between subjects of law. In symbolic terms, the judgment in *Slade's Case* represented the formal acknowledgment of civic responsibility, which hitherto had been unrecognised by the courts: the bonds of trust between citizens that are essential not only for the growth of a commercial society, but also for the development of *societas* and the cohesion of English society as a whole.[48]

Returning to *The Comedy of Errors*, some critics have argued that the chain represents the social harmony to which I refer above.[49] For others it is an 'associative object', signifying the various bonds in the play: between merchant and customer; husband and wife; servant and master; parent and child; and, of course, twin siblings.[50] But like the precious stones which decorate the 'carcanet' itself (3.1.4),[51] the symbolism of the chain is multifaceted, standing for many things. The diversity of critical elucidation, regarding the chain, testifies to the amorphous power of theatrical metaphor (be it in the form of text, actor, costume or prop) continually to change its meaning, depending on the imaginative skill of the dramatist and the interpretive will of the audience.[52] Theatre and law inhabit a shared rhetorical scheme, in which the persuasive power of the image is dominant and the physical object can be interpreted metonymically or more precisely as a visual form of synecdoche[53]: the part signifying the whole. Coke was especially alert to the

observes that although Coke's *Reports* do not usually differentiate between record and authorial comment, in *Slade's Case* the published report is identical to that which Coke wrote at the time of the trial, demonstrating that it was not subsequently amended by the author to reflect his opinion on the decision: BL MS.Harl 6686; Baker, 'New Light on Slade's Case', above n 14, at 394.

[47] *Ephesians*, 2.19.

[48] On the growth and effects of commercial society in early modern England, see C Muldrew, *The Economy of Obligation: the Culture of Credit and Social Relations in Early Modern England* (Basingstoke, Macmillan, 1998).

[49] For example, 'Shakespeare's chain ... symbolizes the cohesion of society', R Henze, '*The Comedy of Errors*: A Freely Binding Chain' (1971) 22 *Shakespeare Quarterly* 35.

[50] A B Dawson, 'Props, pleasure, and idolatry', in A B Dawson and P Yachnin, *The Culture of Playgoing in Shakespeare's England: A Collaborative Debate* (Cambridge, Cambridge University Press, 2001) 142.

[51] A carcanet is a necklace, decorated with precious stones: 'Nay Ile be matchless for a carckanet, / Whose Pearles and Diamonds plac'd with ruly rocks / Shall circle this faire necke to set it forth', Marston, above n 31, (3.1) D3.*v.*

[52] Commenting on Prospero's long exposition of plot to Miranda, laden with compressed images of keys, hearts, ivy and trees (*The Tempest*, 1.2.83–86), Kermode refers to 'flurries of metaphor', see F Kermode, *Shakespeare's Language* (London, Penguin, 2000) 288.

[53] For the iconoclastic reformers of the early modern period, the persuasive power of theatrical metaphor was associated with idolatry; eg, the 17th-century lawyer and polemicist, William Prynne, condemned plays as 'the common Idole, and prevailing evill of our dissolute, and degenerous Age ... That which had its birth, and primarie conception from the very Devill himselfe', W Prynne, *Histrio-Mastix: The Players Scourge, or, Actors Tragedie* (London, Michael Sparke, 1633) B.*v*, C.*r*; it is noteworthy that Prynne contrasted the idolatry of theatre with the iconic status of the Inns of Court, whose members were 'heires of heaven, coheires with Christ, yea, Kings and Priests unto God your Father', *ibid*, 'The Epistle Dedicatory' **4.*r.* On the law against images, see P Goodrich, *Oedipus Lex: Psychoanalysis, History, Law* (Los Angeles, University of California Press, 1995) 56–77; also, D Freedberg, *The Power of Images: Studies in the History and Theory of Response* (Chicago, Ill, University of Chicago Press, 1990).

representational power of the sign and its effect as metaphor, when he asserted in *Postnati. Calvin's Case* that 'a King's crown is an hieroglyphic of the laws, where justice, &c is administered'.[54] Similar rhetorical tropes work subliminally in the law reports of the period, especially in those cases relating to contract law, where objects and goods are items of dispute[55]; so, in *Slade's Case*, the plaintiff's eight acres' worth of wheat and rye act as a metonym: they are contiguous with the toil of English farmers, whose rightful reward is recompense for their honest labour and skilled husbandry of the land.

Shakespeare's choice of theatrical metaphor in *The Comedy of Errors* has strong historical connections with the representation of law in literature. The equivalent prop to the chain in Plautus' *Menaechmi* is a bracelet, which in the course of the play never takes on any metaphorical significance. It remains a physical object with no meaning beyond the superficial and the literal: an item of adornment for a prostitute. Shakespeare's gold chain, on the other hand, has a juristic link which is traceable at least to *The Laws* of Plato, in which the public law of the State is compared to a 'golden and holy' cord.[56] In his satire on the legal profession, *Law-Trickes*, Shakespeare's contemporary, John Day, derides common lawyers for their venality and trickery: 'Law-trickes, words of Art Demurs and quillets'.[57] Before debunking the myth of the lawyer as sacerdotal agent of divine law, he describes the law thus:

> . . . tis divine:
> And ile compare it to a golden chaine,
> That links the body of a common-wealth,
> Into a firme and formall Union.[58]

Day's simile of the golden chain passes in an instant, as soon as the line has been uttered, its poetic aspiration subsumed into the acerbic comedy of the principal narrative. In *The Comedy of Errors* the chain is not only a physical object of actual and metaphorical value; it is a central conceit of the play, driving the action, affecting relationships, passing among the characters and, in so doing, strengthening the bonds of a vibrant community.[59]

---

[54] Coke, *Postnati. Calvin's Case*, 7 *Reports* (1608) 4: 1a, at 11b. Watt notes that 'the crown as prop forms a well-trodden bridge between the worlds of stage and law in Shakespeare's plays', G Watt, 'The Law of Dramatic Properties in *The Merchant of Venice*', in Raffield and Watt (eds), above n 6, at 237.

[55] There was an actual legal dispute over a gold chain: at the hearing of *Slade's Case* in 1598 at Serjeants Inn, reference was made to *Lord Dudley v Lord Powles* (1489), in which 'a man, being indebted to another, licenses the debtee to take his gold chain and to retain it until he pays the money', translated and collated from BL MS.Add. 25203, ff 12.*r*–12.*v* and BL MS.Stowe 398, ff 10.*v*–11.*r* in Baker, 'New Light on Slade's Case', above n 14, at 397.

[56] Plato, *The Laws*, (tr) T J Saunders (London, Penguin, 2004) 31, Bk 1.II.645a. Note also St German on the derivation of the word 'law': 'For the law is derived of *ligare*, that is to say, to bind', C St German, *Dialogues Between a Doctor of Divinity and a Student in the Laws of England*, (ed) W Muchall (Cincinnati, Ohio, Robert Clarke, 1874) 10. I discuss the tropes of 'corda', from which the words for law derive, in ch 1, n 75, above.

[57] Day, above n 31, (Act 5) H4.*v*.

[58] *Ibid*, (Act 1) B.*v*.

[59] Henze notes that it is only his contact with the chain that draws Antipholus of Syracuse into Ephesian society, and out of his melancholic isolation: Henze, above n 49, at 38.

IV. Consideration, Conscience and the Gray's Inn Revels, 1594

Antipholus of Ephesus and Angelo the goldsmith had an agreement: Angelo would make a gold chain, or more precisely a carcanet, which Antipholus of Ephesus would buy from him, as a present for his wife, Adriana. The original transaction created obligations for both parties: Angelo to make and deliver the chain; Antipholus of Ephesus to pay Angelo the agreed sum upon delivery of the chain. If either breached the terms of the arrangement then an action of debt would lie. But Antipholus of Ephesus asked Angelo to bring the chain to the Porpentine, and Angelo promised to 'meet you at that place some hour hence'. (3.1.122) Angelo did not attend their agreed rendezvous, even though, as Antipholus of Ephesus later reminds him, 'I promised your presence and the chain' (4.1.23); indeed Angelo delivered the chain to the wrong person, Antipholus of Syracuse. The audience did not witness the original agreement between Antipholus of Ephesus and Angelo, whereby the former promised to pay the latter for manufacture and delivery of the chain, but we presume such a promise was enacted. What then is the value of these promises, and are they enforceable in law through assumpsit? Note the tenses used in the above narrative: Angelo and Antipholus of Ephesus *had* an agreement; Angelo *would make* a gold chain; Antipholus of Ephesus *asked* him to bring it to the Porpentine; Angelo *promised* to meet him there. Time is a central character in the play, and tense was a crucial factor in the juridical determination of contractual disputes.

Apart from *The Tempest*, *The Comedy of Errors* is the only play of Shakespeare which respects the classical unities of time, place and action: the single plot is enacted in one place (the Ephesian mart or street) in the course of a day. In the first scene of the play, Egeon is condemned to die, 'Unless a thousand marks be levied' (1.1.22) by the end of the day: time is elevated to the status of a major character. The audience is continually reminded of the passing of time: 'Within this hour it will be dinner-time' (1.2.11); 'soon at five o'clock, / Please you, I'll meet with you upon the mart' (1.2.26–27); 'The clock hath strucken twelve upon the bell' (1.2.45); 'Sure, Luciana, it is two o'clock' (2.1.3); 'At five o'clock / I shall receive the money for the same'. (4.1.10–11) The sense of urgency and the relevance of time to decisions and outcomes are compounded by precise references such as these. Indeed, in Act 2, scene 2, Antipholus of Syracuse and Dromio have a protracted discussion in which the word 'time' occurs 12 times in 60 lines; amongst other time-related themes, they discuss 'dinner-time' (2.2.56), 'Father Time' (2.2.75) and 'time for a man to recover his hair' (2.2.77–78). Of course, the repetition of the word 'time' is a dramatic device, which has the important effect of emphasising the fatal plight of Egeon; but Egeon appears only at the beginning and end of the play, framing the comedy of confused identity with a narrative of genuine pathos. Time is of equal importance to the commercial dealings which lie at the heart of Shakespeare's Ephesus.

The Comedy of Errors *and the Meaning of Contract*

For the lawyers in the audience at Gray's Inn, on 28 December 1594, the continual references to time, specifically in relation to the contract for the purchase by Antipholus of Ephesus of the gold chain, would have had especial resonance. In the formal framing of a contract there was indeed 'a time for all things'. (2.2.70) This applies not only to the original contract between the Ephesian Antipholus and Angelo, but also to the peripheral contracts which are affected by the dispute over the chain. The Second Merchant has lent money to Angelo, enabling the goldsmith to purchase the precious metal with which to make the chain. At the start of Act 4, scene 1, he informs Angelo (in front of the arresting officer) that

> You know since Pentecost the sum is due,
> And since I have not much importuned you;
> Nor now I had not, but that I am bound
> To Persia, and want guilders for my voyage. (4.1.1–4)

The Second Merchant would have an action for debt against Angelo for the amount he lent him, which was due to be repaid on the Feast of Pentecost.[60] Again, the question of assumpsit arises: what of the tortious loss suffered by the Second Merchant in association with his imminent and imperilled business trip to Persia? For the early modern lawyer (as for the dramatist), timing was crucial. The original contracts (between Antipholus of Ephesus and Angelo, and between Angelo and the Second Merchant) would usually have been described in the pluperfect tense, as, for example:

> Whereas Antipholus of Ephesus in consideration that the said Angelo at the special instance and request of the said Antipholus *had* bargained and sold to the defendant a gold chain at a price of . . .

The subsequent promise to pay would have been in the perfect tense:

> Antipholus of Ephesus then and there *assumed* and faithfully *promised*, that he the said Antipholus would well and truly pay the said Angelo the sum of . . .[61]

Thus it may be seen that the law distinguished between the original consideration and the subsequent promise to fulfil the terms of the contract. When did the promise occur? '*Adtunc et ibidem*' ('Then and there') was the formulaic phrase; but

---

[60] It is noteworthy that payment was invariably recorded as becoming due on a religious feast-day: as I have noted, in *Slade's Case*, the payment of £16 was meant to be paid on the feast of St John the Baptist (24 June), see text to n 45, above; Coke further notes that the case was to be tried by jury 'before the said lady the Q at Westm. on Thursday next after eight days of the Purification of the blessed Mary', Coke, *Slade's Case* (1597), 4 *Reports* (1604) 2: 91b. On the ecclesiastical origins of the law terms, see Sir Henry Spelman, 'The Original of the Four Terms of the Year' (1614) in *The English Works of Sir Henry Spelman, Kt. Published in his life-time; together with his posthumous works, Relating to the Laws and Antiquity of England*, 2 vols (London, D Browne, 1723) 2: 67; see also ch 4, text to nn 30–34, below.

[61] Emphasis added. Similar wording may be seen in *Slade's Case*: '[T]he said Humphrey . . . did assume, and then and there faithfully promised, that he the said Humph', etc, Coke, *Slade's Case* (1597), 4 *Reports* (1604) 2: 91a. The alternative to the above formula was the *indebitatus* clause: 'Whereas the said Angelo was indebted to the Second Merchant in the sum of 500 ducats, the same Angelo then and there assumed and faithfully promised that he the said Angelo would well and truly pay the said Second Merchant 500 ducats.'

was this after the consideration for the contract had been specified, or at the same time as it was made? During the 1590s, King's Bench decided that the promise was contemporaneous with the consideration (and, as I have noted above, that the promise may be implied rather than express); and so, something which was done in the present purported to govern the future.[62] The subject of law thus bound himself to the legal institution through the semantics of juridical discourse. As Shakespeare suggests in *The Comedy of Errors* (especially through his depiction of the troubled marriage between Antipholus of Ephesus and Adriana), the rapid elevation of contract to an unprecedented level of influence posed an immediate danger to the well-being of the household or *domus* (and, by extension, to the *polis* itself). In submitting himself to the formal bonds of contract law, the subject risked exclusion from the human bonds of love, friendship and community.[63]

And what of Angelo's response to the Second Merchant's demand for immediate payment of the debt?

> He [Antipholus of Ephesus] had of me a chain. At five o'clock
> I shall receive the money for the same.
> Pleaseth you walk with me down to his house,
> I will discharge my bond, and thank you, too. (4.1.10–13)

This returns us to the issue of mutual trust and the promise. A bare promise was worth nothing in contract law: *ex nudo pacto non oritur actio*. The promise was binding only if consideration was provided for it. The juridical scenarios which Shakespeare presents would have posed numerous questions of a doctrinal nature to the audience of lawyers at Gray's Inn. What did the Second Merchant give in return for Angelo's promise of deferred payment, to bind the parties into a formal and enforceable legal agreement? The lawyer's answer, which was acceptable to the Elizabethan King's Bench, would have been that the forbearance of the Second Merchant to sue Angelo until five o'clock that afternoon was sufficient consideration for the goldsmith's promise to pay him then.[64] Consideration is a symbol, a sign, evidence of a promise. Its increased relevance in Elizabethan contract law was at least partly to do with the expansion of informal commercial transactions, which were the subject of 'parol' (oral) agreements rather than being recorded in the form of a deed. In the 1598 hearing of *Slade's Case*, the juridical interpretation of consideration was included in the definition of a binding contract:

---

[62] See, eg, *Lyne v Neale* (1596) LI MS Mayn 55 fo 238a.v; '*adtunc et ibidem*' is discussed extensively in Ibbetson, above n 17, at 296–97; on the metaphysics of contract, see P Goodrich, *Languages of Law: From Logics of Memory to Nomadic Masks* (London, Weidenfeld & Nicolson, 1990) 170–75.

[63] I discuss Aristotle's thesis that the bonds of friendship form the basis of the ideal community in ch 5, text to nn 89–92, below; on the bonds of friendship which form the basis of the Aristotelian *polis*, see A Macintyre, *After Virtue: a Study in Moral Theory* (London, Duckworth, 1981) 146.

[64] On forbearance as consideration, see Baker, above n 13, at 343. Provided there was sufficient consideration, its adequacy was never considered by the courts; eg, in 1525, Rastell recorded that a penny was sufficient consideration for the conveyance of land: J Rastell, *Expositiones Terminorum* in Baker and Milsom, above n 16, at 483.

[A] mutual agreement between the parties for something to be performed by the defendant in consideration of some benefit which must depart from the plaintiff, or of some labour or prejudice which must be sustained by the plaintiff.[65]

The final judgment in *Slade's Case*, in 1602, appeared to conform to the principle that a counter-promise was sufficient consideration for the original promise. In Coke's opinion (expressed with his customary candour, at the end of the report of *Slade's Case*), there was no doubt as to the binding status of the promise: 'I am surprised that in these days so little consideration is made of an oath, as I daily observe'[66]; thus he neatly blurred the juridical and social meanings of consideration.

Shakespeare incorporates these twin meanings into his depiction of relationships in *The Comedy of Errors*. In the legalistic sense, consideration refers to the exchange of benefits and burdens, without which an agreement remains unenforceable; while in its social context consideration implies fraternity, respect, courtesy and kindness: a code of honour based upon mutual trust, without which *civitates* may not exist. In the play, only the former meaning of consideration is apparent in the relationship between Antipholus of Ephesus and the Courtesan: she gives him her diamond ring, 'worth forty ducats, / And for the same he promised me a chain'. (4.3.83–84)[67] Their relationship is defined by the law of contract. He dines regularly at the Porpentine and presumably pays for the pleasure of her company: '[A] wench of excellent discourse, / Pretty and witty' (3.1.109–10). Shakespeare contrasts this juridical form of consideration with its social counterpart, based upon less restrictive categories of benefit and burden: those which are engendered by community, love and friendship. Hence, Adriana seeks a more amenable *quid pro quo* with her husband, Antipholus of Ephesus; the melancholic merchant, Balthasar, tired (it seems) of the world of commerce, informs the Ephesian Antipholus that 'I hold your dainties cheap, sir, and your welcome dear' (3.1.21); while Antipholus of Syracuse (although given a gold chain by Angelo, tendered money by strangers, offered 'commodities to buy' (4.3.6) and presented with a bag of gold coins by his servant) is profoundly unhappy because he has spent seven years searching unsuccessfully for a binding relationship, based upon natural love and affection, with his lost twin brother.

The separate paths of juridical and social consideration, although appearing from the above description to be running parallel with each other, converged in a case of 1565, reported by Plowden. The treatment in *The Comedy of Errors* of the ambiguous nature of consideration suggests that Shakespeare may have read Plowden's report of *Sharington v Strotton*. The case concerned the validity of a use or trust, and the beneficiary's contested equitable right under it to profit from land which was the subject of the disputed use. The defendant claimed that consideration for the creation of the use was provided by the natural love and affection owed by one brother to another. Plowden argued that

---

[65] *Slade's Case* (1598), quoted in Baker and Milsom, above n 16, at 429.
[66] Coke, *Slade's Case* (1602), 4 *Reports* (1604) 2: 95b.
[67] Zurcher argues that private law of the Elizabethan period regulated commodities and possessions rather than people, A Zurcher, *Shakespeare and Law* (London, Arden Shakespeare, Forthcoming) ch 5.

[t]he third consideration here is, the brotherly love ... For those who descend from one same parentage, and are joined nearest in blood, are by nature joined in love.[68]

It is perhaps surprising that judgment in King's Bench was given against the plaintiff; Catlyn CJ declaring that 'the brotherly love which he bore to his brothers, are sufficient consideration to raise the uses in the land'.[69] Only two years after *Sharington v Strotton*, in Common Pleas, Dyer CJ is reported to have said in judgment that 'whatever goes in ease and benefit of my friend is my ease and benefit also'.[70]

The importance of natural love and affection to the question of sufficiency of consideration is linked to questions of conscience, and to the moral obligation of the autonomous subject of law to conduct his relations according to the Christian injunction to love thy neighbour. In general historical terms, this may be associated both with the influence of renaissance humanism and the ecclesiastical forebears of the common law judiciary. It is likely also that the collegiate environment of the Inns of Court, the constitutions of which resembled those of scholastic, Christian communities, acted as a subliminal directive to judicial decision-making.[71] Of profound importance to an understanding by lawyers of the perceived correlation between common law and conscience was the publication between 1528 and 1531 of Christopher St German's *Doctor and Student*, which remained a set text for students at the Inns of Court throughout the 16th century.[72] In Chapter XXIV, entitled 'What is a nude contract, or naked promise, after the laws of England, and whether any action may lie thereon', St German distinguishes clearly between 'a promise made to God', which binds the promisor 'in conscience to do it, though it be only made in the heart', and 'other promises made to a man upon a certain consideration'. While he is emphatic that a 'nude contract ... is void in the law and conscience', he repeatedly invokes the importance to social relations of 'the intent inward in the heart'.[73]

The dichotomy or tension between the external evidence of contract and the invisible presence of conscience lies at the heart of the Gray's Inn revels of 1594. The overriding theme of the revels is that of the brotherly love that exists between the host, Gray's Inn, and its illustrious guest, the Inner Temple. Reference is made variously to 'the Bond of our ancient Amity and League' and the 'tender Love and Good

---

[68] *Sharington v Strotton*, *The Commentaries or Reports of Edmund Plowden*, 2 vols (Dublin, H Watts, 1792) 1: 298, at 306; *Sharington v Strotton* is discussed in J H Baker, 'Origins of the "Doctrine" of Consideration, 1535–1585' in Baker, *The Legal Profession and the Common Law*, above n 14, at 376–77.

[69] Plowden, *Sharington v Strotton, Commentaries*, above n 68, 1: 309.

[70] *Lord Grey's Case* (1567), HLS MS 2071, fo 18.*v*; Baker notes that by 1588, 'love and affection' was ruled out as sufficient consideration in assumpsit actions, Baker, above n 68, at 377; see also, A W B Simpson, *A History of the Common Law of Contract: the Rise of the Action of Assumpsit* (Oxford, Clarendon, 1975) 434–37.

[71] On the ecclesiastical foundations of English law, see Dugdale, above n 4, at 10; F Pollock and F W Maitland, *The History of English Law*, 2 vols (Cambridge, Cambridge University Press, 1898) 1: 2, 4, 40; P Brand, *The Origins of the English Legal Profession* (Oxford, Oxford University Press, 1992).

[72] Part I of *Doctor and Student* was published in 1528, Part II in 1530; further additions were published in 1531. On the constitutional significance of St German's work, see ch 1, n 33, above.

[73] St German, above n 56, at 176, 175, 177.

Will' which characterise relations between the two Inns.[74] Initial examination of the fictional realm of Purpoole (whose supreme magistrate, the Prince, Arch-Duke of Stapulia and Bernadia, has been elected 'upon good Consideration')[75] suggests a highly-organised mercantile society, in which vast wealth is expended as consideration for the patronage of the Prince. Various 'dignitaries' contribute to the Prince's coffers, in return for the grant of certain privileges; for example, Alfonso de Stapulia and Davillo de Bernardia 'relieve all Wants and Wrongs of all Ladies, Matrons, and Maids within the said Arch-Dutchy', as consideration for which they render to the Prince 'a Coronet of Gold, and yearly five hundred Millions, *Sterling*'.[76] The theatrical representation of payment in return for patronage mirrors the grant of monopolies in late-Elizabethan England, a subject to which I shall return.

The mirror image is a central theatrical device in *The Comedy of Errors*.[77] It facilitates the plot of mistaken identity; but also, when the two sets of twins are reunited at the end of the play, it gives the characters pause for reflection on their relationships with fellow citizens. 'Methinks you are my glass and not my brother' (5.1.418), remarks Dromio of Ephesus to his twin. The Duke, gazing in disbelief at the Antipholi twins, comments that '[o]ne of these men is *genius* to the other' (5.1.333)—'genius' here meaning an attendant or a custodial spirit.[78] The revels play a similar attendant role on the law itself; sometimes distorting, but always reflecting the manner in which law engages with and affects its subjects. The device of the mirror image is further complicated by the fact that Shakespeare's play to a great extent illuminates specific aspects of the 1594 revels, as well as the quotidian life of the legal community at Gray's Inn. Thus the subject matter is refracted into several distinct though related images, enabling multiple but simultaneous perspectives on the form and content of law and the legal institution: the symbolic community of law in the Hall of Gray's Inn, the exaggerated representation of law in the fictional realm of Purpoole, and the hyper-fictional depiction of law in *The Comedy of Errors*.[79]

---

[74] Bland (ed), above n 2, at 10, 30.
[75] *Ibid* at 9.
[76] *Ibid* at 17.
[77] On the use of the mirror image throughout the works of Shakespeare, see Kermode, above n 52, at 70.
[78] Whitworth (ed), above n 3, 175, note to 5.1.333.
[79] For a theoretical basis to the manipulative power of the image and the poetics of law, see P Legendre, *Law and the Unconscious: a Legendre Reader*, (tr) P Goodrich, with A Pottage and A Schütz, (ed) P Goodrich (Basingstoke, Macmillan, 1997). Of relevance to the symbolic realm of the revels are the following words of Legendre: '. . . no society has yet been governed without song, without music, without the discourse of the celebrational', in P Goodrich and R Warrington, 'The Lost Temporality of Law: An Interview with Pierre Legendre', (tr) A Pottage (1990) 1 *Law and Critique* 3, 17. With particular reference to the image of law, as reflected in the mirror, see P Goodrich, 'Specula Laws: Image, Aesthetic and Common Law' (1991) 2 *Law and Critique* 233, 234: 'In its strongest definition, law itself proceeds through the representation of likeness or resemblance . . . in reflections or specula of the law, fixations of the image'. On the theory of the mirror and *imago*, see J Lacan, 'The Mirror Stage as Formative of the *I* Function as Revealed in Psychoanalytic Experience' in *Écrits*, (tr) B Fink (New York, W W Norton & Co, 2006) 75.

More than one week before 'The Night of Errors', *Gesta Grayorum* records that on the first grand night, 20 December, the revels were pre-empting many of the themes and characters of Shakespeare's play, which was performed in the Hall of Gray's Inn on 28 December. The Prince of Purpoole governs in accordance with the principle of limited monarchy: members of the judiciary, legislature and executive are included in the long list of 'Officers and Attendants at his honourable Inthronization'.[80] The constitution of Purpoole adheres to St German's theory of the King in Parliament, that the law may not be altered without the formal approval of the legislative assembly.[81] It is noteworthy in this respect that Shakespeare should allude, at the start of *The Comedy of Errors*, to a similar constitution, under which Ephesus is governed: 'It hath in solemn synods been decreed' (1.1.13), declares the Duke, with reference to the law which prohibits the admission of Syracusians to Ephesus. The treatment of foreign merchants is a subject that recurs throughout the revels: at the start of his reign the Prince of Purpoole issues a general pardon to all those who have transgressed his laws, with several exceptions, including

> [a]ll Merchant-Adventurers, that ship or lade any Wares or Merchandize, into any Port or Creek, in any *Flemish*, *French*, or *Dutch*, or other Outlandish Hoy, Ship, or Bottom.[82]

On 5 January a letter is sent 'from *Knights-bridge*, to the Honourable Council' of Purpoole, claiming

> that in His Excellency's Canton of Knights-bridge, there do haunt certain Foreigners, that sieze upon all Passengers, taking from them by force their Goods, under a pretence that being Merchant Strangers, and using Traffick into His Highness's Territories of Clerkenwell, Islington, and elsewhere, they have robbed of their Goods.

So it continues: on 10 January, three weeks after the revels have begun, a letter is sent 'from Sea, directed to the Lord Admiral', stating that

> [h]is Excellency's Merchants of *Purpoole* began to surcease their Traffick to *Clerkenwell*, *Newington*, and *Bank-side*... because they feared lest certain Rovers, which lay hovering about the Narrow Sea, should intercept them in their Voyages.[83]

The reception of foreign merchants by a host nation is recognisably an outstanding motif in the Gray's Inn revels of 1594, as it is in *The Comedy of Errors*, suggesting perhaps a degree of complicity between Shakespeare and the author(s) of the

---

[80] Bland (ed), above n 2, at 10.

[81] '... the said courts ne their authorities, may not be altered, ne their names changed, without parliament', St German, above n 56, at 19; on St German's interpretation of the King in Parliament, see M D Walters, 'St German on Reason and Parliamentary Sovereignty' (2003) 62 *Cambridge Law Journal* 335.

[82] Bland (ed), above n 2, at 26; a 'Hoy' was a freight barge or coastal trading vessel. 'Bottom' here alludes to the bottomry bond, whereby the owner of a ship obtained a loan by pledging the bottom of his ship, the keel, as security; see Watt, above n 54, at 247–49.

[83] Bland (ed), above n 2, at 64, 65.

revels, as to the substantive content of each text.[84] Although mercantilism and freedom of trade are notable thematic features of both works, the chief purpose of these conceits is to enable through metaphor the exploration of a more fundamental and profound aspect of society: the human bonds of association and friendship, whose links are forged not through external evidence of contractual obligation or juridical consideration, but through the exercise of conscience or social consideration; in the words of St German, 'the intent inward in the heart'.

Arguably, the most striking image of the 1594 revels is the extraordinary religious ceremony, enacted in the Hall of Gray's Inn on 3 January 1595, at which the fractured relations between Gray's Inn and the Inner Temple were formally healed. An altar to the Goddess of Amity was erected on one side of Hall. Attended by archetypal representations of male love and friendship drawn from the ancient world, *Grayus* and *Templarius* 'came lovingly, Arm in Arm, to the Altar, and offered their Incense as the rest'. After some nymphs had sung hymns to the Goddess of Amity, *Grayus* and *Templarius* were pronounced

> to be as true and perfect Friends, and so familiarly united and linked with the Bond and league of sincere Friendship and Amity, as ever were *Theseus* and *Perothous*, *Achilles* and *Patroclus*, *Pilades* and *Orestes*, or *Scipio* and *Lelius*; and therewithal did further divine, that this Love should be perpetual.[85]

At the end of the ceremony, in perhaps the most resonant echo of *The Comedy of Errors*, the Prince of Purpoole placed around the neck of the Inner Temple's ambassador a carcanet or bejewelled collar: the symbol of 'the Knighthood of the Helmet, an Order of his own Institution'.[86] Through an act of transubstantiation the secular community of lawyers becomes a sacred community, a sacerdotal citizenry, for whom amity is elevated to the level of the divine. The religious rite enacted by Gray's Inn and the Inner Temple represents the sacrifice of self for the sake of *societas*, association or fellowship.[87] The death of the ego enables the emergence of a social body. Infused with a spiritual presence, the community of lawyers

---

[84] For example, Shakespeare's Abbess finds a bawdy echo in '*Lucy Negro*, Abbess *de Clerkenwell*', ibid at 17; Cormack, above n 2, suggests that this character in the Gray's Inn revels alludes to a brothel-keeper in the neighbouring area of Clerkenwell; see also M Bly, 'Playing the Tourist in Early Modern London: Selling the Liberties Onstage' (2007) 122 *Publication of the Modern Language Association of America* 61, 63–65. The 'Sorcerer or Conjuror', who supposedly caused the confusion and errors of 28 December, finds his equivalent in the conjuror of *The Comedy of Errors*, Doctor Pinch; Bland (ed), above n 2, at 32. The mock trade mission from Moscow to Gray's Inn, on Twelfth Night 1595, in which the 'Ambassador from the mighty Emperor of *Russia* and *Moscovy*... came in Attire of *Russia*, accompanied with two of his own Country, in like Habit,' was possibly a source of inspiration for the scene in *Love's Labour's Lost*, in which the King of Navarre and his lords disguise themselves as Russians in order to woo the Princess and her ladies-in-waiting (Act 5, scene 2): Bland (ed), above n 2, at 59; see D W Palmer, *Writing Russia in the Age of Shakespeare* (Aldershot, Ashgate, 2004) 71–96.

[85] On the theory of homosociality, especially in relation to professional institutions, see M Borch-Jacobson, *The Freudian Subject*, (tr) C Porter (Stanford, Conn, Stanford University Press, 1988).

[86] Bland (ed), above n 2, 36–37.

[87] On the inauguration through sacrifice of a foundational space, from which law emerges, see G Bataille, *Theory of Religion*, (tr) R Hurley (New York, Zone, 1989) 45, 50; also, P Legendre, *L'Inestimable Objet de la Transmission: Etude sur le principe généalogique en Occident* (Paris, Fayard, 1985) 67.

is reborn as *corpus mysticum*, a microcosm of the ideal State. A promise of brotherly love forms the basis of their social contract, as consideration for which the other party counter-promises to act at all times in good conscience, and in the best interests of the common-weal.

V. Breaking the Bonds of Servitude: Trade, Markets and the Law

Change or rebirth is a central injunction of *The Epistle of Paul to the Ephesians*. If the people reject the bogus teaching of dupes and rogues, and accept in its place the Word of God, then the love of Christ will bring unity to a disjointed society, binding individuals into a single body, with Christ at its head.[88] It is noteworthy that Sir Edward Coke made a similar plea for unity, incorporating the Pauline metaphor of the body into a speech delivered to the Grand Jury of the Norwich assizes, after his appointment as Chief Justice of the Court of Common Pleas in 1606:

> [A]s wee are all of one Nation, so let us be all of one Church, and Christ beeing onely our head, let us all desire as in one sheepfolde, to be the sanctified members of his glorious bodie.[89]

In *The Comedy of Errors*, the unification of Ephesian society is partly facilitated by Solinus' decision to overrule the draconian statute under which Egeon was condemned to die (and which presumably would have consigned Antipholus of Syracuse to the same fate), signalling at least the beginning of the end to the trade war between Ephesus and Syracuse. The choice of name for the Duke may have been inspired by Shakespeare's reading of *The Excellent and Pleasant Works of Julius Solinus Polyhistor*, which was translated into English in 1587 by Arthur Golding, and which contains several references to the city of Ephesus.[90] Given the interest shown by Shakespeare's Solinus in mercantile relations with neighbouring States, and his reform of those domestic laws which restricted freedom of trade, it seems more likely that any historical resemblance was to the Athenian lawmaker and reformer, Solon. There are several indications that Plutarch's description of

---

[88] *Ephesians*, 4.14–17. St Paul uses the anatomical image elsewhere in *Ephesians*: 'And hath put all things under his feet, and gave him to be the head over all things to the church, Which is his body, the fulness of him that filleth all in all' (1.22–23); and again, in his *Epistle to the Romans*: 'For as we have many members in one body, and all members have not the same office: So we, being many, are one body in Christ, and every one members one of another' (12.4–5). See also 1 *Corinthians* 12–27, which I discuss in relation to the creation of a Christian commonwealth of interdependent citizens, in ch 4, text to nn 131–32, below.

[89] Sir Edward Coke, *The Lord Coke His Speech and Charge. With a Discoverie of the Abuses and Corruption of Officers* (London, Christopher Pursett, 1607) F3.*v*.

[90] Also, John Lyly's *Campaspe* (1584) includes a character named Solinus; see Foakes (ed), above n 3, Introduction, xxx.

Solon inspired Shakespeare's portrayal of Solinus, not the least of which was that Solon

> repealed the laws of Draco, all except those concerning homicide, because they were too severe and their penalties too heavy. For one penalty was assigned to almost all transgressions, namely death . . .[91]

As far as the regulation of commercial relationships was concerned, and with particular relevance to Shakespeare's play, Solon introduced legislative reforms which forbade a borrower's person being used as security for the loan of money.[92] The economic reforms of Solon were notable also for the encouragement they gave to foreign tradesmen to settle in Athens with their families, thereby gaining Athenian citizenship (represented in the play by the reunion and rehabilitation in Ephesus of the Syracusian Egeon, Emilia and their two sons).[93]

In constitutional and political terms, the reputation of Solon for extensive reform rests mainly on the actions which he took to democratise the Athenian State and abolish slavery.[94] The theatrical treatment of slavery might have been problematic for the Elizabethan adaptor of Roman domestic comedy, were it not for the fact that the farcical convention required a stereotypical and comedic dramatisation of the master and servant relationship. In particular, domestic farce demanded a stylised depiction of the physical violence which symbolised the oppressive dominion of one party over the other. Maurice Hunt has noted that Shakespeare's portrayal of the Dromios accurately reflects certain aspects of Elizabethan society, in relation variously to those employed in service, the institution of marriage and what he terms 'the individual's ordering of his or her inner faculties'.[95] The Dromios are referred to throughout as 'slave' (1.2.87), 'knave' (1.2.72) and 'villain' (1.2.19),[96] references to them as slaves far exceeding in number those to servants or attendants.[97] Their subservient status as slaves to the Antipholi twins is at odds with

---

[91] Plutarch, 'Solon' in *Lives I*, (tr) B Perrin (Cambridge, Mass, Harvard University Press, 1914) 449, XVII. Shakespeare mentions Solon in *Titus Andronicus*: 'But safer triumph is this funeral pomp / That hath aspired to Solon's happiness / And triumphs over chance in honour's bed' (1.1.179–81). These lines of Marcus Andronicus refer to Solon's fatalistic assertion that no man is happy until he is dead: 'For the future which is advancing upon every one is varied and uncertain, but when the Deity bestows prosperity on a man up to the end, that man we consider happy', Perrin (tr), 'Solon' 483, XXVII.

[92] Perrin (tr), above n 91, 443, XV.

[93] *Ibid*, 471, XXIV.

[94] Aristotle discusses the extent and success of these reforms in *The Politics*, Bk II.XII.1273b27–1274a22.

[95] M Hunt, 'Slavery, English Servitude, and *The Comedy of Errors*' (1997) 27 *English Literary Renaissance* 31; Hunt notes that in *Menaechmi*, the slave Messenio is never beaten, *ibid* at 35. Ward, above n 11, at 138, identifies the Dromios as a peculiarly English creation, 'determined by a residual semi-feudal sense of community and affiliation which is preserved despite their masters' obsession with the alienating regime of the markets'. On freedom and the mythical birthright of all Englishmen, see E P Thompson, 'The Free-Born Englishman' in *The Making of the English Working Class* (London, Victor Gollancz, 1980) ch 4.

[96] 'Villain' here in the medieval sense of 'villein': a peasant bound to his lord. For an Elizabethan account of bondmen, *servi* and 'villens', see Sir Thomas Smith, *De Republica Anglorum*, (ed) M Dewar (Cambridge, Cambridge University Press, 1982) 135–42.

[97] Egeon refers to Dromio of Syracuse as an 'attendant' to Antipholus of Syracuse (1.1.128).

the depiction of Ephesian society, which appears in all other respects to have abandoned adherence to feudal notions of governance, adopting instead as its governing principle the *laissez-faire* doctrines of the market.

Crucial though the decision in *Slade's Case* was in establishing the centrality of the mutual promise to modern contract law, this development would have had little practical effect if the necessary conditions for the enablement of free trade did not exist. It is important therefore to consider briefly the contribution made by the courts of common law to the expansion of commercial enterprise, and the enfranchisement thereby of a hitherto restricted class of skilled craftsmen, tradesmen and merchants. The sense of an economic and political practice being anachronistic and inflexible was reflected in the 1590s by the reaction of the courts to the prerogative grant of Crown monopolies. As Coke argued, the restrictive nature of monopolies posed an insuperable monetary obstacle to

> poor tradesmen, that many times are by ordinances made by incorporations (whereby the public good is pretended, and private respects intended) barred or hindered of the freedoms of their trade.[98]

The divisive social impact of monopolies manifested itself in the threat of civic rebellion. Hunt refers to the jest, made by Dromio of Ephesus, about whether he will repay the beatings he has received from his master, for whom he mistakes Antipholus of Syracuse: 'If I should pay your worship those again, / Perchance you will not bear them patiently'. (1.2.85–86) Hunt claims that an Elizabethan audience would have regarded these words, containing an oblique threat of rebellion, 'as ominously subversive'.[99] Such fears were well-founded during the 1590s, as prices rose and real wages fell sharply.[100] Popular protest was not uncommon in late-Elizabethan England: in London, apprentices rioted in 1590, and in 1595 there was a series of riots in protest at the high price of food. Certainly, the possibility of violent rebellion against proposed monopolies was not discounted by the City Fathers of London. In 1592, concerning one such proposal, the Privy Council was warned that 'popular multitudes being once incited and assembled together can hardly be suppressed and kept within obedience by any authority of magistrate whatsoever'[101]; while in a speech delivered in the House of Commons in 1601, Robert Cecil announced that

---

[98] Coke, 11 *Reports* (1615) 6: Preface, xii.

[99] Hunt, above n 95, at 32.

[100] On prices of food in Tudor London, see S Rappaport, *Worlds Within Worlds: Structures of Life in Sixteenth-Century London* (Cambridge, Cambridge University Press, 1989) ch 5.

[101] Quoted in I W Archer, *The Pursuit of Stability: Social Relations in Elizabethan London* (Cambridge, Cambridge University Press, 1991) 8; for a general perspective on the government of late-Tudor London, and rebellions therein, see P Williams, *The Later Tudors: England 1547–1603* (Oxford, Oxford University Press, 1998) 162–75; on the late-Elizabethan apprentices' riots in London and its suburbs, see R B Manning, *Village Revolts: Social Protest and Popular Disturbances in England, 1509–1640* (Oxford, Clarendon, 1988) 200–19.

The Comedy of Errors *and the Meaning of Contract*

I have hearde my selfe, beinge in my coache, these wordes spoaken alowde: 'God prosper those that further the overthrowe of these monopolies. God send the prerogative touche not our libertie'.[102]

The Case of the Taylors, &c of Ipswich and the more celebrated *The Case of Monopolies* (*Darcy v Allein*) are both concerned with the grant of monopolies by the Crown and the punitive effect of these on individual tradesmen. Although Coke's reports of these cases were not published until 1615, they both concern monopolies granted during or before the reign of Elizabeth and provide powerful illustrations of an archaic system of patronage, which ran counter to the commercial exigencies of late-Elizabethan society. The monarch was personally aware of public antipathy towards the grant of monopolies: in 1601, following a meeting to which he had been summoned by the Queen, the Speaker of the House of Commons informed MPs that

> [s]he saith that partlye by intimacion of her Counsell, and partlye by diverse peticions that have bene delivered unto her, both goeinge to the chapple and alsoe to walke abroad, she understood that dyvers pattentes which she had graunted were greivious to her subiectes.[103]

The Case of Monopolies and *The Case of the Taylors, &c of Ipswich* elicited from Coke explicit re-statements of classical, republican theory and insistence upon its application to English common law. It is significant that Coke should admit in the Preface that *The Case of Monopolies* was decided in 1602 (the same year as *Slade's Case*), some 13 years before the publication of Part XI of *The Reports*. Coke made no apology for the retrospective inclusion of a case that had been decided during the reign of Elizabeth I, arguing that

> though it cometh not in sequence of time, yet the case of Monopolies cannot come out of time, wherein divers things concerning monopolies, are clearly resolved . . .[104]

The report is unequivocal in its statement that all trades

> are profitable for the commonwealth, and therefore the grant to the plaintiff to have the sole making of them [playing cards] is against the common law . . .

The decision of the court was perhaps surprising, given that the case concerned the grant of a monopoly for the making, importation and sale of playing cards, which (according to the plaintiff) were 'things of vanity' and

> causes of want, which is the mother of woe and destruction, and therefore it belongs to the Queen (who is *parens patriae, & paterfamilias totius regni*, and as it is said in 20 H.7. fol. 4. *Capitalis Justiciarius Angliae*) . . .[105]

---

[102] T E Hartley (ed), *Proceedings in the Parliaments of Elizabeth 1*, 3 vols (Leicester, Leicester University Press, 1995) 3: 398. Thomas Dekker's *Westward Hoe*, written c 1604, includes a character named Monopoly; to his boast that 'I'll sticke wooll upon thy back', Mistress Birdlime replies, 'all the kinred of the *Monopolies* are held to be great Fleecers': R H Shepherd (ed), *The Dramatic Works of Thomas Dekker*, 4 vols (London, John Pearson, 1873) 2: 309.

[103] Hartley (ed), above n 102, 3: 394.

[104] Coke, 11 *Reports* (1615) 6: Preface, xiv.

[105] *Ibid, The Case of Monopolies*, 84b, at 86a, 85b.

Despite the idolatrous nature of the subject matter, the court found for the defendant, whose appeal to the custom of the ancient city of London, which recognised as right the freedom to sell all things, found favour with the judges. The antique, civic virtues of the commonwealth were accorded legal precedence over the Royal Prerogative on the pragmatic, republican grounds that all trades 'prevent idlenes the bane of the commonwealth'.[106]

The plaintiff in *The Case of Monopolies*, Edward Darcy, was a person of rank: 'an Esquire, and a groom of the Queen's Privy Chamber'.[107] The defendant was a skilled artisan and merchant who, in defiance of the Royal Charter, manufactured '80 grosses of playing cards, and as well those, as 100 other grosses of playing cards, none of which were made within the realm'.[108] The plaintiff conceded that he possessed no skills in the manufacture of playing cards. This disability notwithstanding, it was argued that

> [i]n matters of recreation and pleasure, the Queen has a prerogative given her by the law to take such order for such moderate use of them as seems good to her.[109]

The question of Darcy's rank is relevant to the thesis that this case was paradigmatic in establishing a contractual model of society in which the role of hierarchic status was permanently diminished. In 1586, John Ferne wrote *The Blazon of Gentrie*, in which he delineated the strict hierarchy of English society according to the patriarchal principles of ancient law. *The Blazon of Gentrie* emphasises the primacy of genealogy as a determinant of legitimacy in the individual and the State: 'Gentleman of bloud and coat-armor perfect, might only challeinge the benefit and priviledges of that law, called *Ius Gentilitatis*'.[110] The plaintiff in *The Case of Monopolies* was an 'esquire', which was an office in the gift of the monarch, by virtue of the Royal Prerogative. The inclusion of this rank in the 'dignities of regalitie'[111] entitled him to bear arms. But Ferne distinguished between the power of the king to bestow 'coat-armor' on a worthy subject and the superior authority of an unwritten law that bestowed the title of 'gentleman' on an individual by reference to flawless ancestry, which was traceable to no particular act of foundation. Ferne protested that

> I am not ignorant how some have labored to shew, that if the coat-armor be given him by the King, that in such a case three Discents (as aforesaid) shal make a Gentleman of bloud, whereunto I cannot subscribe.[112]

It was to ancient custom that Coke appealed in justification of the decision to declare unlawful the grant of a monopoly to Edward Darcy. Apart from the obvious

---

[106] *Ibid* at 86a.
[107] *Ibid* at 87a.
[108] *Ibid* at 85a.
[109] *Ibid* at 85b.
[110] J Ferne, *The Blazon of Gentrie* (London, Toby Cooke, 1586) 86.
[111] *Ibid* at 88.
[112] *Ibid* at 87; on the criteria for inclusion in the category of 'Gentilitie', see also Sir George Buc, 'The Third Universitie of England' (1612]) in J Stow, *The Annales or Generall Chronicle of England* (London, Thomas Adams, 1615) 968.

constitutional implication of *The Case of Monopolies* that the powers of the king were defined by the common law, the case was an important symbol of social and economic developments towards the end of Elizabeth's reign. Ferne had delineated four classes of person that were excluded from *nobilitas Polytica*, and which therefore exercised no influence over the polity of the State: these were '*Villani, Mercatores, Burgenses, Servi*'.[113] Allein, the skilled manufacturer and vendor of playing cards, belonged to two of these categories: *Mercatores* (merchants), 'the practise thereof consisteth of most ungentle parts, as doublenes of toong, violation of faith'; and *Burgenses*, 'comprehending all those which practise mechanicall and handycrafts'.[114] Sixteen years after the publication of *The Blazon of Gentrie*, *The Case of Monopolies* established the capacity of a disenfranchised tradesman to challenge the restrictive practices of a governing élite and thereby to engage in the direction of polity within the State. The judgment represented an unprecedented recognition of the right of subjects to engage freely, and without interference, in private contractual relations. Monopolies were adjudged prejudicial not only to others in the same trade, but to all subjects of law, 'for the end of all these monopolies is for the private gain of the patentees'.[115] Monopolies offended against the tenets of natural law, because they were inherently inequitable. But as Richard Baxter was later to observe, they were irreconcilable also with the equitable foundations of Christian theology. Baxter enjoined tradesmen to conduct their businesses in the spirit of a public service, 'for the advantage of his neighbour as much as, and, if his neighbour be poor, more than, for his own'.[116] Coke noted that not only was the granting of monopolies 'against the ancient and Fundamentall laws of this kingdome' but, because the law of England was grounded in the law of God, '[a]gainst these Inventers and Propounders of evil things, the holy ghost hath spoken, *Inventores malorum*, &c *digni sunt morte*'. Monopolists offended God because they destroyed a man's trade, which 'is accounted his life, because it maintaineth his life; and therefore the Monopolist that taketh away a mans trade, taketh away his life'.[117] It is apparent from the decision in *The Case of Monopolies* that within a Christian social framework, which recognised the moral rectitude of freedom of trade, the court was rejecting the narrow self-interest of the ruler in favour of the wider interests of the commonwealth and its citizens.

---

[113] The Dromio twins are described in *The Comedy of Errors* as both *Villani* and *Servi*; Angelo would be a member of *Burgenses*; Balthazar, First Merchant and Second Merchant are demonstrably *Mercatores*.

[114] Ferne, above n 110, at 7.

[115] Coke, *The Case of Monopolies*, 11 *Reports* (1615) 6: 86b.

[116] Quoted in R H Tawney, *Religion and the Rise of Capitalism* (Harmondsworth, Penguin, 1984) 221; on monopolies and natural law in medieval societies, see *ibid* at 50–52. On monopolies during the reigns of Elizabeth I and the early Stuart kings, see R Ashton, *Reformation and Revolution, 1558–1660* (London, Paladin, 1985) 182–84, 236–37, 248–49; also, M Weber, *The Protestant Ethic and the Spirit of Capitalism*, (tr) T Parsons (London, Routledge, 1992) 42, 122.

[117] Sir Edward Coke, *The Third Part of the Institutes of the Laws of England* (London, W Lee and D Pakeman, 1644) 181; on Coke and monopolies, see S D White, *Sir Edward Coke and the Grievances of the Commonwealth* (Manchester, Manchester University Press, 1979) 86–141.

Breaking the Bonds of Servitude: Trade, Markets and the Law

Novelty, particularly in the form of prerogative acts of the Crown, was abhorrent to Coke: it represented dissemblance or falsehood, and so was a perversion of law.[118] In *The Case of the Taylors, &c of Ipswich* (1614), as related by Coke, innovation is a metaphor for injustice, oppression and the subjugation of the commonweal to the private interest of the ruler. The case is symbolic also of the failure of sumptuary legislation to enforce (through the regulation of costume) a figurative scheme of social rank. Following the Act of Supremacy, 1534, an intended effect of sumptuary legislation was to project the *Imperium* of the monarch by restricting the use of particular kinds and colours of fabric to those of a specified status. For example, *24 H.8. cap. 13* declared that subjects were forbidden to wear

> any silke of the colour of purpure, ne any cloth of Gold of tissue, but only the King, the Queene, the kings mother, the kings children, the kings brethren and sisters, the kings uncles and aunts ...[119]

The control of tailors by a centralised authority (through the grant of Royal Charters) was an important means of ensuring conformity to imperial edict. 'The Taylors of Ipswich' were an incorporated body, with full power and authority (granted by the king) to make reasonable laws, ordinances and constitutions, and to impose fines in accordance with those rules. One such rule was that no tailor could practise his craft within the town of Ipswich until he had presented himself to the master and wardens of the Society of Taylors and proved that he had served seven years as an apprentice. Failure to comply with this regulation was punishable by a fine of five marks. The defendant in *The Taylors of Ipswich*, one William Sheninge, practised as a tailor in Ipswich for 20 days before presenting himself to the wardens. He was consequently fined, despite the fact that he did not have his own premises and was working in the household of one Anthony Penny, to whom he was contractually bound not only as a domestic servant, but also to make 'divers cloaths and garments for him, his wife and children'. Repeating the familiar adage that 'the common law abhors all monopolies', Coke reported that the case (decided in favour of the defendant) resolved the issue that

> at the common law, no man could be prohibited from working in any lawful trade, for the law abhors idleness, the mother of all evil ...[120]

In declaring the superior legal status of the 'common profit of the people' to 'any of the ordinances made by any corporation',[121] Coke implied the existence of an

---

[118] As, eg: 'I have ever holden all new or private interpretations, or opinions, which have no ground or warrant out of the reason or rule of our books, or former precedents, to be dangerous', Coke, 7 *Reports* (1608) 4: Preface, vib.

[119] W Rastall, *Collection in English of the Statutes now in force* (London, Deputies of C Barker, 1594) 105; on sumptuary legislation and the emergence of class as a pervasive form of social relations, see A Hunt, *Governance of the Consuming Passions: A History of Sumptuary Law* (Basingstoke, Macmillan, 1996) 9–11; P Goodrich, 'Signs Taken for Wonders: Community, Identity, and *A History of Sumptuary Law*' (1998) 23 *Law & Social Inquiry* 707; P Raffield, 'Reformation, Regulation and the Image: Sumptuary Legislation and the Subject of Law' (2002) 13 *Law & Critique* 127.

[120] Coke, *The Case of the Taylors, &c of Ipswich*, 11 *Reports* (1615) 6: 53a, at 53b.

[121] *Ibid* at 54b.

Aristotelian model of society, in which the exercise of the classical virtues enabled the individual achievement of *eudaimonia* or prosperity, and in which law and morality were coterminous.[122] It was to natural law that the defendant successfully appealed in *The Taylors of Ipswich*: the law abhorred idleness because it was synonymous with disorder. Reason was central to the equitable governance of the common-weal, and (according to common law orthodoxy) interference with existing laws or custom was irrational because such precipitate action would necessarily lead to uncertainty and chaos. It is paradoxical that Coke should have appealed to antiquity and ancient custom in order to empower and enfranchise an unprecedented, emergent class in English society. The public interest that Coke expressed with certitude, and which the common law facilitated, was the extension of wealth to a greater proportion of the population: the craftsmen, tradesmen and merchants who were the ultimate beneficiaries of the decisions in *The Case of Monopolies* and *The Taylors of Ipswich*.

Sir Francis Bacon complained to Coke that 'you make the Law to leane too much to yor opinion'.[123] In identifying the tendency of Coke to blur the distinction between opinion and law, Bacon unconsciously acknowledged the imaginary quality of law. Law is indeed bound up with opinion if, by opinion, we mean the inheritance of tradition or manners and the continuous adaptation of custom to the current circumstances of the institution.[124] In 1616, at the king's direction, Coke was subjected to an 'examination' by Lord Chancellor Ellesmere and 'other senior counsel', concerning the accuracy of his observations in *The Reports*. In particular, he was questioned about his assertion in *The Case of Monopolies*

> [t]hat the Dispensation or License of Q. Eliz. to Darcie to have the Sole Importation of Cards. Notwithstanding the Statute: 3. E. 4; is Agst. law.[125]

Coke's report of *The Case of Monopolies* challenged the insidious, oppressive means by which trade and the markets were controlled. Coke postulated an alternative constitution, in which the contractual form of association represented the perfect synthesis of human reason and divine will. The contract symbolised the

---

[122] On the relevance of *eudaimonia* to the *telos* of the Athenian city-State, see Macintyre, above n 63, at 139. On the influence of Aristotle and Cicero over Christian political theology, especially that of St Paul, see A J Carlyle, *The Influence of Christianity Upon Social and Political Ideas* (London, A R Mowbray, 1912) 76–77.

[123] *Letter to Coke from Sir Francis Bacon*, BL Sloane. 1775 ff 79.*v*–80.*r*; Bacon's letter is undated, but as he refers in it to the recent prosecution by Coke of the Gunpowder Plotters (the trial took place on 27 January 1606) it is probable that he wrote it in 1606, after Coke's appointment as Chief Justice of the Common Pleas (30 June 1606). Coke held part-time judicial office between 1585 and 1604, as Recorder of Coventry (1585); Recorder of Norwich (1586); Recorder of London (1591–92); Recorder of Orford (1593); Recorder of Harwich (1604). It is more likely though that Bacon was referring to Coke's recent appointment to the office of Chief Justice when he wrote in the same letter: 'in discourse you delight to speak too much, not to hear other men, this some say becomes a pleader not a judge', *ibid* at 79.*r*.

[124] On Coke's alleged failure to distinguish between law and opinion, see D Powell, 'Coke in Context: Early Modern Legal Observation and Sir Edward Coke's Reports' (2000) 21 *The Journal of Legal History* 33.

[125] *Exception to Coke's Reports, and examination of Coke by Ellesmere (Lord Chancellor)* (1616), BL Add MS 4107, fo 268.*r*.

classical bond of friendship or *amicitia*, which provided the moral foundation of the *polis*. Coke associated the social or supra-legal character of the contract with the supremacy of a higher, unwritten law; superior in constitutional status to the restrictive edicts of the monarch. The fusion in *The Reports* of law and opinion, which antagonised Bacon, testifies to Coke's belief that English law was inscribed upon the memory of man. As Foucault noted in connection with Nietzsche's theory of genealogy and the documentation of history, '[t]he body is the surface of the inscription of events'.[126] The jurisprudence enshrined within *The Reports* embodies the classical principle that law was not to be narrowly circumscribed in the interests only of the supreme magistrate: the strength, unity and consent of the common-weal were paramount,

> and this admirable unity and consent in such diversity of things, proceeds only from God the fountain and founder of all good laws and constitutions.[127]

---

[126] M Foucault, 'Nietzsche, Genealogy, History' in *Aesthetics, Method, and Epistemology*, (ed) J D Faubion, (tr) R Hurley (London, Penguin, 1998) 375; more generally, on genealogy and the inscription of events on the body, see *ibid* at 369–76; also, F Nietzsche, *The Genealogy of Morals*, (tr) H B Samuel (New York, Boni and Liveright, 1913).

[127] Coke, 3 *Reports* (1602) 2: Preface, iiia.

3

Reflections on the Art of Kingship: *Richard II* and the Subject of Law

I. 'Landlord of England' or 'deputy elected by the Lord'?

IN 1992, DURING restoration work on the Wilton Diptych, a discovery was made which goes some way towards enlarging and illuminating our understanding of the complicated metaphysical notion of divine kingship. The left interior panel of the Diptych depicts King Richard II, wearing cloth-of-gold and vermilion robes emblazoned with white harts and branches of rosemary, the emblems respectively of the King and his first wife, Anne of Bohemia, who died in 1394. Around his neck he wears a collar of broom cods,[1] the emblem of Charles VI of France, whose daughter, Isabella, Richard II married in 1396. On his breast he wears the badge of the white hart. He is kneeling in front of three saints, two of them English: St Edmund the Martyr (d 869), holding the arrow which killed him; and St Edward the Confessor (d 1066), holding the ring which according to legend he gave to the disguised St John the Evangelist.[2] Closest to Richard is his patron saint, St John the Baptist, holding the paschal lamb in his left hand and presenting the King to the Virgin and Child, who provide the central figures of the right interior panel.[3] Mary and the infant Christ are surrounded

---

[1] Broom cods are the seeds of the common broom, whose Latin title, *planta genista*, gave its name to the Plantagenet dynasty. Most scholars agree that the Diptych dates from around 1395. On the Wilton Diptych, see D Gordon, 'A New Discovery in the Wilton Diptych' (1992) 134 *The Burlington Magazine* 662; also, J H Harvey, 'The Wilton Diptych—A Re-examination' (1961) 98 *Archaeologia* 1; F Wormald, 'The Wilton Diptych' (1954) 17 *Journal of the Warburg and Courtauld Institutes* 191; more generally, see D Crouch, *The Image of Aristocracy in Britain, 1000–1300* (London, Routledge, 1992); J Alexander and P Binski (eds), *Age of Chivalry: Art in Plantagenet England, 1200–1400* (London, Royal Academy of Arts, in assoc with Weidenfeld & Nicolson, 1987).

[2] The composition of the painting may allude to the worship of Christ by the three wise men (Matthew, 2.11): Richard II was born on 6 January 1367. His baptism in Bordeaux was attended by three kings: Jaime IV of Majorca, Richard of Armenia, and Pedro of Castile; see N Saul, *Richard II* (New Haven, Conn, Yale University Press, 1999) 12; Saul notes that the names of the Biblical 'Three Kings' were engraved on a ewer belonging to Richard II: 'Jasper, Melcheser, Balteser', *ibid* at n 15.

[3] The exterior panels of the Diptych bear entirely secular heraldic emblems: the left panel bears the mythical arms of Edward the Confessor (martlets and cross fleurie), impaled with the arms of France and England (lilies and leopards), on which stands a helmet, surmounted by a cap of maintenance and a lion passant guardant; on the right panel the white hart, the emblem of Richard II, is couched among rosemary branches and other plants, a crown (with chain attached) around its neck. Each panel measures 47.5 × 29.2 cm.

'Landlord of England' or 'deputy elected by the Lord'?

by 11 angels (dressed, like the Virgin, in robes of lapis lazuli), all of whom wear Richard's emblem—the badge of the white hart—on their left breasts. They mirror the King by wearing broom-cod collars around their necks. Christ offers a blessing to Richard, who appears to extend his hands either in homage or prayer. Standing next to the Infant, an angel holds a flagstaff, which bears a banner with a red cross on a white background: the flag both of St George and the Resurrection.[4] The angel looks up at Christ and points a finger towards Richard (see **Figure 1**).

The discovery to which I refer above concerns a minute detail of the Diptych, namely the larger of the two orbs surmounting the banner, in the right interior panel. Prior to the restoration process, and upon investigation with infra-red photographic equipment, the tarnished orb (no more than one centimetre in diameter) revealed a landscape of a green island on which was painted a white, turreted castle with six black windows and, behind this, some trees with blue sky above; in the foreground a brown ship in full sail traverses a sea made of silver leaf (see **Figure 2**). In the context of Shakespeare's *The Tragedy of King Richard II* the miniature scene depicted in the orb recalls immediately the valedictory speech of John of Gaunt, and his lyrical description of England as 'this little world, / This precious stone set in the silver sea' (2.1.45–46).[5] The symbolism of the orb suggests that the banner may reasonably be interpreted as both the flag of England and the flag of the risen Christ, thereby conjoining the spiritual and temporal authority of the King. According to Dillian Gordon, the hands of the King are extended not in prayer but in anticipation of receiving back the banner from the angel, it having been given first by Richard to the infant Christ, who hands the flagstaff to the angel in order that He may bless the King.[6] The governance of an earthly realm by a devout civil magistrate and the patronage of an English king by the deity may therefore be seen as a central thematic feature of the Diptych.

The significance to the Diptych of the Virgin may be inferred from a lost altarpiece, pre-dating the Wilton Diptych and influencing its subject matter, which in the 17th century had been in the English College in Rome.[7] The altar-piece (which included depictions of St George, St John the Baptist and two other saints—probably St Edmund the Martyr and St Edward the Confessor) portrayed Richard II and his first wife, Anne of Bohemia, being presented by St John the Baptist to the Virgin, and offering her 'the globe or pattern of England'.[8] At the base of the panels was the inscription:

---

[4] See, eg, Piero della Francesca's *Resurrection* (1463) in the Museo Civico, Sansepolcro, in which the resurrected Christ emerges from a sarcophagus and plants the banner of the Resurrection in the ground outside the tomb, on which the Roman guards sleep. On the capacity of figurative art to represent the divinity of Christ, see A C Danto, *Embodied Meanings: Critical Essays and Aesthetic Meditations* (New York, Farrar, Straus and Giroux, 1995).

[5] All references to the text of the play are from *King Richard II*, (ed) C R Forker (London, Arden Shakespeare, 2002).

[6] '[T]he king waits to receive back the banner in order to rule Britain under the protection, and with the blessing, of the Virgin', Gordon, above n 1, at 667.

[7] Gordon argues that 'it is possible to argue that the Rome altar-piece was painted before 1394', *ibid* at 666.

[8] BL MS Harley 360, fo 98.v.

Reflections on the Art of Kingship: Richard II *and the Subject of Law*

> Dos tua, Virgo pia
> Haec est, quare rege, Maria.⁹

The spiritual devotion of Richard II to the Virgin is well documented. For example, in Book Two of *Chronicles,* in a chapter on the Peasants' Revolt, Jean Froissart records that the King prayed before the image of the Virgin in Westminster Abbey, 'dedicating himself to it' prior to his meeting with Wat Tyler, Jack Straw and John Ball at Smithfield in 1381.¹⁰ The explicit reference in the lost altar-piece to *dos* implies a symbolic marriage between Richard II and the Virgin, and the concomitant bestowal of a marriage gift. *Dos* referred in most legal systems to a dowry (a gift to the husband, or the husband and wife, usually from the bride's parents); but as Baker has observed, to English common lawyers *dos* translated as dower: a legal estate in the form of a tenancy for life in favour of the wife, following the husband's death. This was a gift from husband to wife, usually made at the church door on the day of their marriage.¹¹ Regarding the distinction between dowry and dower, the exact meaning of the inscription on the lost altar-piece is unclear, but in juridical terms it denotes intention to transfer an interest in property from donor to donee.

Ownership of title and possession of land are complex and contentious narrative themes both of Shakespeare's *Richard II* and the Elizabethan law relating to real property. The peaceful enjoyment of property and the occasional incursions by the Crown upon those traditional liberties associated with private dominion are notable themes in the history of English constitutional law. *The Commentaries or Reports* of Plowden record that during the reign of Elizabeth I enjoyment of property was adversely affected by the alienation of Crown lands and the effect of such action on feoffors, feoffees, tenants and beneficiaries of entailed estates, whose interests were often upset by the quasi-divine status which was claimed for the monarch. The subject matter of the Wilton Diptych depicts the synthesis of temporal and spiritual power in the person of the King. In his biography of Richard II, Nigel Saul argues that from the mid-1380s these two aspects of Richard's rule 'were fused in a single vision'.¹² A major task for any investigation into the impact on common law of the purported indivisibility of divine and municipal monarchic authority is to determine the legitimacy of each of these strands and the limits (if any) which the legal institution could impose upon the jurisdiction of the Crown. The leading cases concerning disputes arising over the ownership of interests in land, as reported by Plowden (and later by Coke), indicate that the judiciary devised its own ingenious formulae for conclusively resolving such disputes, based

---

[9] 'This is your dowry, O holy Virgin, wherefore O Mary, may you rule over it', Gordon, above n 1, at 665–66; see also Saul, above n 2, at 306. The description of the lost altar-piece was provided in C Coupe, 'An Old Picture' (1895) 84 *The Month* 229; Coupe translated two 17th-century accounts of the altar-piece, the latter of which (written by Silvestro Petrasancta in 1638) explicitly links it with Richard II, see S Petrasancta, *Tesserae Gentilitiae* (Rome, 1638) 677–78.

[10] J Froissart, *Chronicles*, (tr) and (ed) G Brereton (London, Penguin, 1978) 224.

[11] J H Baker, *An Introduction to English Legal History* (London, Butterworths, 2002) 269–71.

[12] Saul, above n 2, at 304.

upon the distinction between the body natural and the body politic of the king. The theory of supernatural kingship was expounded by Ernst H Kantorowicz in his study of medieval political theology, *The King's Two Bodies.* In section II. of this chapter I offer an alternative reading of the theory, based upon close analysis of Plowden's *Commentaries or Reports*.[13] The cases studied here provide irrefutable evidence of the pragmatism of the judiciary, and of the determination of its members to find an equitable and unequivocal solution to an indeterminable metaphysical issue: the eternal nature of kingship.

Returning to the symbolism of the Wilton Diptych, the right exterior panel reproduces the emblem of Richard II, the white hart. The devotion of Richard to his first wife, Anne of Bohemia, may be inferred from the fact that the white hart is lying on a bed of rosemary, which was Anne's emblem. But arguably the most notable feature of the painting is that the hart is tethered to the ground by a chain. The chain is connected to a crown, which is situated not on the head of the hart but around its neck, like a collar (see **Figure 3**). The imagery suggests that the Crown is restricted in its exercise of power, bound to the realm by its office. In the painting the chain is firmly embedded in the earth of England, rendering the white hart subject to *lex terrae*: the unwritten constraints of the ancient constitution, the immemorial *suprema lex* or common law, whose jurisdiction is unchallengeable and whose judges are the ultimate arbiters of juridical disputes. The question of subjection, of being a subject of, and being subjected to, the law in its several manifestations (the public trial, the Royal Prerogative, ownership of title in land) is a recurring motif in Shakespeare's *Richard II* and is one that I consider in this chapter. Following analysis of the juridical resolution of disputes over land, in section III. I examine the concept of betrayal in the context of the treason trial. Shakespeare's Richard likens his downfall to the betrayal of Christ. Characteristically, he self-dramatises his own plight:

> So Judas did to Christ, but He in twelve
> Found truth in all but one; I, in twelve thousand, none. (4.1.171–72)

The play asks pertinent questions about the legal status of a king, subjected to the law and accused in the High Court of Parliament by one of his subjects of

> ... grievous crimes
> Committed by your person and your followers
> Against the state and profit of this land ... (4.1.223–25)

---

[13] Lorna Hutson argues that Kantorowicz's interpretation of Plowden's *Commentaries* was unduly influenced by his reading of Maitland, who underestimated the influence of renaissance humanism over the development of English law. In particular, she suggests that Kantorowicz ignored the importance of Aristotelian equity (*epieikeia*) to the interpretation of statutes, see L Hutson, 'Not the King's Two Bodies: Reading the "Body Politic" in Shakespeare's *Henry IV, Parts 1 and 2*' in V Kahn and L Hutson (eds), *Rhetoric and Law in Early Modern Europe* (New Haven, Conn, Yale University Press, 2001) 170–71; F W Maitland, *English Law and the Renaissance* (Cambridge, Cambridge University Press, 1901). See also D Norbrook, 'The Emperor's New Body? *Richard II*, Ernst Kantorowicz, and the Politics of Shakespeare Criticism' (1996) 10 *Textual Practice* 329; J R Rust, 'Political Theology and Shakespeare Studies' (2009) 6 *Literature Compass* 175.

Reflections on the Art of Kingship: Richard II *and the Subject of Law*

In England, a king was not to be tried for treasonable offences such as these until the trial of Charles I in 1649, at which the indictment stated that he had been 'trusted with a limited power to govern by and according to the laws of the land'; a trust which he had betrayed in favour of

> a wicked design to erect and uphold in himself an unlimited and tyrannical power to rule according to his will, and to overthrow the rights and liberties of the people . . .

Charles I asked the court 'by what authority he was brought thither?',[14] raising questions about the status of the king as subject of law: could the king be tried in the king's court? Such a question returns us inevitably to the matter of the king's two bodies, the answer to the question posed by Charles I being that the king's body natural was tried in the name of the king's body politic.

Of equal interest to a critique of Kantorowicz's theory of the king's two bodies (especially when the discussion applies to fin-de-siècle Elizabethan England as opposed to fin-de-siècle Ricardian England) is not a discussion of the Bractonian principle of limited monarchy (with which in the last decade of Elizabethan rule Richard Hooker strongly aligned himself in *Of the Laws of Ecclesiastical Polity*) but an examination of the mask of kingship and the role of rhetoric in defining the authority of the monarch. This has particular relevance to the reign of Elizabeth I, the parallels of which to that of Richard II and the events portrayed in Shakespeare's play have been noted since its first performance in 1595.[15] The story of an heirless king towards the end of his reign, whose absolutist tendencies manifested themselves in excessive use of the Royal Prerogative, who depended for advice upon a court of self-interested sycophants, and who was eventually deposed in a popular coup d'état, was one of evident and obvious concern to Elizabeth I. Of course, the much-cited performance of *Richard II* on the afternoon of 7 February 1601, commissioned by the supporters of the Earl of Essex on the eve of the failed Essex Rebellion, instances the political significance of the play in late-Elizabethan England.[16] Its relevance to the events of 1601 is compounded by the conversation, which was supposed to have occurred on 4 August 1601, between Queen Elizabeth and the antiquary, William Lambarde. With reference to Essex, Elizabeth is reported to have said to Lambarde: 'He that will forget God will also

---

[14] *The Trial of Charles the First, King of England, before the High Court of Justice*, (ed) J Nalson (Oxford, R Walker and W Jackson, 1746) 24, 25, 28.

[15] On a private performance of *Richard II* in December 1595, to which Sir Robert Cecil was invited by Sir William Hoby, see *King Richard II*, (ed) A Gurr (Cambridge, Cambridge University Press, 2003) Introduction, 1–3.

[16] For interpretations of this performance, see P E J Hammer, 'Shakespeare's *Richard II*, the Play of 7 February 1601, and the Essex Rising' (2008) 59 *Shakespeare Quarterly* 1; J Bate, *Soul of the Age: the Life, Mind and World of William Shakespeare* (London, Penguin, 2008) 249–86. Worden argues that the play performed on 7 February was not Shakespeare's *Richard II* but a dramatised version of Sir John Hayward's *The First Part of the Life and Reign of King Henry IV*, see B Worden, 'Which Play Was Performed at the Globe Theatre on 7 February 1601?'(10 July 2003) 25 *London Review of Books* 22. Hayward's book was published in February 1599, and bore an ambiguous dedication to the Earl of Essex: '*futuri temporis expectatione*' ('and in expectation of future time'); see Forker (ed), above n 5, Introduction, 12–14.

forget his benefactors; this tragedy was played 40 times in open streets and houses'. More ominously she is supposed to have told Lambarde that 'I am Richard II, know ye not that?'[17] The presentation of a play the central scene of which depicted the deposition of a king was, to say the least, audacious. Mystery surrounds the omission from original published versions of *Richard II* of the deposition scene (Act 4, scene 1), which remained unseen until its publication in the Fourth Quarto of 1608, five years after the death of the Queen. Scholars are divided over whether this omission constituted an act of press censorship[18] although, as Jonathan Bate notes, there is no evidence that the play was censored, and it is at least possible that Shakespeare wrote the deposition scene either especially for the performance on 7 February, or after the Essex Rebellion as a scene of stately abdication, rather than as a subversive one of undignified deposition.[19]

Disquieting though the scenes of rebellion and usurpation must have been to Elizabeth and her Council, probably of greater concern was the evident capacity of political drama in general not merely to represent kingship as a form of theatre (Elizabeth had after all been doing this throughout her reign), but to expose the monarch as an actor playing a role: a subject, prone to the same frailties and faults as the rest of humankind. When Richard II publicly acknowledges his humanity, announcing to his followers that 'I live with bread like you, feel want, / Taste grief, need friends' (3.2.175–76), he invites the audience to question the authenticity of divinely ordained, hereditary kingship. More important to the Crown than whether the substantive content of *Richard II* was overtly subversive was the fact that in representing kingship at all, in presenting the institution of monarchy and the person of the king for scrutiny by a public audience, the theatre demonstrated

---

[17] Quoted in E K Chambers, *William Shakespeare: A Study of Facts and Problems*, 2 vols (Oxford, Oxford University Press, 1930) 2: 326–27; also, in F L, 'Queen Elizabeth and Richard II' (1913) 7 *Notes and Queries* 6. The reference to the play being performed 40 times in open streets and houses cannot refer to the performance of 7 February, as this took place at the Globe Theatre. According to the report of the conversation, although the Queen alludes to Essex, her acknowledgment of the analogy between herself and Richard II refers more specifically to a painting of the King, rather than to Shakespeare's *Richard II*; the Queen allegedly told Lambarde: 'The Lord Lumley, a lover of antiquities, discovered it fastened on the back-side of a door of a base room', *ibid*; the painting has never been found. The unidentified author of this article, 'F L', notes that the manuscript in which the conversation between Lambarde and the Queen is recorded was originally published in John Nichols' *Bibliotheca Topographica Brittanica*, no 42, in the 1780s. The location of the manuscript remains unknown; that it ever existed has not been proved.

[18] See,eg, C S Clegg, '"By the choise and Inuitation of al the realme"': *Richard II* and Elizabethan Press Censorship' (1997) 48 *Shakespeare Quarterly* 432; D M Bergeron, '*Richard II* and Carnival Politics' (1991) 42 *Shakespeare Quarterly* 33; J Clare, 'The Censorship of the Deposition Scene in *Richard II*' (1990) 41 *Review of English Studies* 89; L Barroll, 'A New History for Shakespeare and His Time' (1988) 39 *Shakespeare Quarterly* 441. More generally, see A Patterson, *Censorship and Interpretation: The Conditions of Writing and Reading in Early Modern England* (Madison, University of Wisconsin Press, 1984).

[19] Bate, above n 16, at 257. Gurr suggests that the deposition scene might always have been performed, but that it was cut by the publishers of the first three Quartos, only to be restored by the publisher of the 1608 Quarto (Mathew Law), Gurr (ed), above n 15, Introduction, 9; on events surrounding the deposition of Richard II, see M Bennett, *Richard II and the Revolution of 1399* (Stroud, Sutton, 1999); also, Saul, above n 2, at 405–34.

itself to be an inherently subversive medium.²⁰ As the Lord Mayor of London warned the Privy Council in July 1598,

> the said Staige playes were the very places of theire Randevous appoynted by them to meete with such otheir as wear to ioigne with them in theire designes & mutinus attemptes, beeinge allso the ordinarye places for maisterles men to come together.²¹

The liminal status of the playhouses, situated in London's Liberties, just beyond the boundaries of jurisdiction provided by the City of London and the Justices of Surrey and Middlesex, engendered suspicion and hostility in the organs of institutional authority. I discuss the theme of law, liberty and subversion in section IV. of this chapter. I consider in particular the depiction of kingship in the playhouses and the shared rhetoric of law and theatre, which drew attention both to the resilience and the fragility of the Crown.

II. *The Commentaries or Reports* of Plowden: Land and the Sacred Body of Law

The manuscript of the anonymous *Thomas of Woodstock, or King Richard the Second, Part One*, one of the sources of Shakespeare's *Richard II*, ends abruptly with a flurry of references to common law and the Elizabethan legal institution.²² Nimble, the treacherous servant to the corrupt Lord Chief Justice, Sir Robert Tresilian, claims that he 'was once a trampler in the law' (5.6.23), 'trampler' being one of many contemporary and derogatory slang words for an attorney.²³ In the following speech he refers to the writs of Habeas Corpus and Certiorari (or 'Habis Corpus' and 'Surssararis', as he terms them), and alludes to the law courts at Westminster Hall and the legal community in the Temple (5.6.26–31). The play ends precipitately, with Nimble informing the Earl of Arundel: '[F]or I have plodded in Plowden and can find no law...' (5.6.35–36) Whether Nimble would have

---

²⁰ David Scott Kastan argues that theatre created the cultural conditions which eventually allowed the people to put their king on trial for treason in 1649, 'not because the theatre approvingly represented subversive acts, but rather because representation became itself subversive', D S Kastan, 'Proud Majesty Made a Subject: Shakespeare and the Spectacle of Rule'(1986) 37 *Shakespeare Quarterly* 459, 461.

²¹ E K Chambers, *The Elizabethan Stage*, 4 vols (Oxford, Clarendon, 1923) 4: 321.

²² The manuscript is in a collection of 15 play-books: BL MS Egerton 1994. *Thomas of Woodstock* was written between 1591 and 1595; see P Corbin and D Sedge (eds), *Thomas of Woodstock, or King Richard the Second, Part One* (Manchester, Manchester University Press, 2002) Introduction, 4–8.

²³ Corbin and Sedge (eds), above, n 22, at 186, n 23. Abraham Fraunce refers to lawyers as 'so many upstart *Rabulae Forenses*': A Fraunce, *The Lawiers Logike, exemplifying the precepts of Logike by the practise of the common Lawe* (London, T Gubbin and T Newman, 1588) ¶.4.r; on Fraunce, see ch 5, text to nn 14 and 15, below. It is not clear whether Fulbecke was alluding to 'tramplers' and the unethical practices of some lawyers when he wrote that justice and law 'are together trodde under foote by such as neither care for God, nor goodness', W Fulbecke, *A Direction or Preparative to the study of the Lawe* (London, T Wight, 1600) B.v; see ch 1, text to nn 104 and 110, above.

The Commentaries or Reports *of Plowden: Land and the Sacred Body of Law*

gone on to explain that he arrested the fugitive Tresilian because he could find no statute or case to which Plowden refers that prevented him from lawfully so doing, we shall probably never know: the loss of the last sheet of the manuscript prevents our certain knowledge.

Frustrating though this loss is, the reference to Plowden in the unintended last lines of the play demonstrates to some extent the extraordinary importance of *The Commentaries or Reports* of Edmund Plowden to the Elizabethan writers of political drama. In chapter two I discuss Plowden in relation to the development of the doctrine of consideration in contract law, with particular reference to *Sharington v Strotton*.[24] In this chapter I concentrate on those cases reported by Plowden, concerning the inheritance and alienation of Crown lands and the effects of this upon interested parties. My purpose is to explain the pragmatic and equitable rationale, which underpinned the judicial construct of the king's two bodies. I argue that this particular interpretation of the theory of divine kingship demonstrated the intention of the judiciary to enforce compliance with the principle of limited monarchy, rather than to engage in metaphysical speculation for its own sake over the corporeal status of the king.

Near the start of *The King's Two Bodies*, Kantorowicz quotes from Fortescue's *Difference Between an Absolute and Limited Monarchy* in support of his thesis that the Lancastrian Chief Justice was proposing that the king shared with 'the holy sprites and angels' certain mystical powers. Kantorowicz claims that 'Elizabethan jurists "borrowed" from Fortescue', in elucidating the theory that the king was possessed of two bodies: the body natural and the body politic.[25] In particular he makes an explicit link between Fortescue's assertion in *Difference Between an Absolute and Limited Monarchy* that the angels do not 'grow old' and Plowden's report of the *Case of the Dutchy of Lancaster*, in which he wrote that the body politic of the king 'is utterly void of infancy, and old age'.[26] Arguably, it is conjectural in the extreme to correlate an Elizabethan law report with a work written approximately 90 years earlier, purely on the basis that both texts refer to the process of ageing. Insofar as the power of the king resembles *character angelicus*, the mystical quality of kingship is reflected in its suggestive capacity for good: the king acts at all times in the interests of *res publica*. This observation should be central to any discussion of Fortescue's delineation of positive powers and what he terms impotent 'non-powers'[27]: kings and angels exercised only the former.

---

[24] See ch 2, text to nn 68 and 69, above.

[25] E H Kantorowicz, *The King's Two Bodies: A Study in Medieval Political Theology* (New Jersey, Princeton University Press, 1957) 8.

[26] *Case of the Dutchy of Lancaster*, *The Commentaries or Reports of Edmund Plowden*, 2 vols (Dublin, H Watts, 1792) 1: 212, at 213.

[27] Sir John Fortescue, 'The Governance of England' in S Lockwood (ed), *On the Laws and Governance of England* (Cambridge, Cambridge University Press, 1997) 95; *Difference Between an Absolute and Limited Monarchy* was published in 1885 as *The Governance of England*; all references to *Difference Between an Absolute and Limited Monarchy* are from the 1997 edition of 'The Governance of England'. On Fortescue's constitutional model as 'a subtle blend of religious and secular ideas', see A Fox and J Guy, *Reassessing the Henrician Age: Humanism, Politics and Reform, 1500–1550* (Oxford, Blackwell, 1986) 119.

Nowhere in *Difference Between an Absolute and Limited Monarchy* does Fortescue claim for the king the metaphysical status of *character angelicus*. At most he asserts that, like the angelic choir, the institution of monarchy is a power for good; as such, it is incapable of sin, ageing or sickness. While it is undoubtedly true that Fortescue's political thought was informed by prevailing ideas in late medieval theology, Kantorowicz ignores completely the fundamental tenet of *Difference Between an Absolute and Limited Monarchy*, which is the secular observation that the ideal of kingship is predicated upon '*dominium politicum et regale*'.[28] In the context of Shakespeare's *Richard II* the word '*dominium*' has especial resonance, as it means not only 'lordship', but also 'ownership'.[29] The proprietary right to title is a central juridical theme of the play, whether in the context of Richard's illegal seizure of Bolingbroke's rightful inheritance or of Bolingbroke's usurpation of Richard's hereditary right to the Crown. In the deposition scene the line 'Here, cousin, seize the crown' (4.1.182), spoken by Richard to Bolingbroke, contains a pun on the word 'seize': 'seisin', denoting the legal possession of land, as in a freehold estate held in fee simple.[30] I quote the above invitation, extended by Richard to his cousin, to illustrate the significance of (and the distinction between) ownership and possession of land in Shakespeare's *Richard II*, but it is a crucial feature also of those cases reported by Plowden to which Kantorowicz refers. The selective use of quotations from Fortescue and (especially) Plowden serves well the argument of Kantorowicz that the mystical nature of the king's body politic came to dominate judicial thought in Elizabethan England, but this is not an accurate picture of the juridical landscape in relation to the resolution of disputes concerning real property.

The judiciary of the 16th century and early 17th century remained strongly influenced by the two major works of Fortescue: *De Laudibus Legum Angliae* and *Difference Between an Absolute and Limited Monarchy*. *De Laudibus*, an impassioned *apologia* for the English legal profession, ensured Fortescue's lasting talismanic status among common lawyers. But it was his elevation of the judiciary to something approaching supreme constitutional authority which probably endeared him most to lawyers and judges of the Elizabethan period. The resemblance between the respective powers of kings and angels is noted by Fortescue (and then, only incidentally) in chapter six of *Difference Between an Absolute and Limited Monarchy*, entitled 'Ordinances for the king's ordinary charges'.[31] In the interests of balance

---

[28] Fortescue, 'Governance of England', above n 27, at 83; see J H Burns, 'Fortescue and the Political Theory of *Dominium*' (1985) 28 *The Historical Journal* 777; also, N Doe, 'Fifteenth-Century Concepts of Law: Fortescue and Pecock' (1989) 10 *History of Political Thought* 257.

[29] Baker, above n 11, at 223.

[30] On the dual meaning of 'seize' and 'seisin' in *Richard II*, see W O Scott, '"Like to a Tenement": Landholding, Leasing, and Inheritance in *Richard II*' in C Jordan and K Cunningham (eds), *The Law in Shakespeare* (Basingstoke, Macmillan, 2007) 65.

[31] On expenditure and revenue-raising by the Crown during the 15th century, see K Mertes, *The English Noble Household, 1250–1600: Good Governance and Political Rule* (Oxford, Blackwell, 1988); also, A R Myers, *Crown, Household and Parliament in Fifteenth-Century England* (London, Hambledon, 1985). Kantorowicz cites only one Biblical source for the claim to monarchic *character angelicus*: the reference is less than authoritative, being the opinion expressed by the woman of Tekoah

The Commentaries or Reports *of Plowden: Land and the Sacred Body of Law*

and accuracy Kantorowicz should have quoted from chapter one, entitled 'The difference between "royal dominium" and "political and royal dominium"'. Using a Biblical analogy, with appropriate references both to Old Testament sources and St Thomas Aquinas's *On Princely Government*, Fortescue attributes to the judiciary a level of dominion within the constitution that was antithetical to the absolutist pretensions of Richard II and his Tudor (and early Stuart) successors:

> The children of Israel, as Saint Thomas says, after God had chosen them as 'his own people and holy realm', were ruled by Him under Judges 'royally and politically', until the time that they desired to have a king such as all the gentiles, which we call pagans, then had, but they had no king but rather a man who reigned upon them 'only royally'. With which desire God was greatly offended, as well for their folly, as for their unkindness since they had a king, which was God, who reigned upon them politically and royally.[32]

Fortescue concludes his republican meditation in chapter one of *Difference Between an Absolute and Limited Monarchy* with the thought (pertinent to the reigns both of Richard II and Elizabeth I) that, according to Aquinas, the prince who rules in accordance with political and royal dominium is less likely to 'fall into tyranny' than one who rules by royal dominium alone.[33] Shakespeare gives Richard numerous lines with which to make explicit the King's belief in the divinity of kingly office. It is Richard, rather than any of his subjects, who states that 'Not all the water in the rough rude sea / Can wash the balm off from an anointed king' (3.2.54–55), and who describes himself as 'The deputy elected by the Lord'. (3.2.57) It is certain that Richard II was particularly interested in the religious symbolism of anointing: he asked the Archbishop of Canterbury to anoint him with the holy oil of St Thomas of Canterbury, an ampoule of which Richard is supposed to have found in the Tower of London.[34] But the religious devotion of Richard and his emphasis on the divinity of kingship must be seen to a great extent as a response to the various rebellions and incursions upon the Royal Prerogative, which threatened his reign and eventually led to his deposition.[35] To assert that the distinction between the body natural of the king and his mystical body politic was central to the development of Elizabethan jurisprudence is to exaggerate the influence of medieval political theology over

---

to King David, ie 'for as an angel of God, so is my lord the king to discern good and bad' and 'my lord is wise, according to the wisdom of an angel of God', 2 *Samuel* 14.17, 20 (Authorised King James Version of The Bible).

[32] Fortescue, 'Governance of England', above n 27, at 84; Aquinas is thought to have written only the first book of *On Princely Government* and the first four chapters of the second book. Ptolemy of Lucca completed the work, and it is his contribution in Book II.VIII.IX to which Fortescue refers above; see Fortescue, *ibid* at 83, n 2 and at 84, n 5. The Biblical references in the passage quoted above are to: *Deuteronomy*, 14.2; *Exodus*, 19.6; 1 *Samuel* 8. On the interpretation of 1 *Samuel* 8 by Jean Bodin and James I, as justification for rule by divinely appointed princes, see ch 6, text to nn 53–59, below.

[33] Fortescue, 'Governance of England', above n 27, at 84.

[34] On the story of St Thomas's oil and Richard II, see N Saul, 'Richard II and the Vocabulary of Kingship' (1995) 110 *The English Historical Review* 854, 872.

[35] Saul argues that the problem of assertive and rebellious subjects during the 14th century was a pan-European phenomenon, and one to which monarchs responded by investing themselves with 'God-like attributes', *ibid* at 873.

the development of early modern common law.³⁶ As I discuss in chapter one, the judiciary sought increasingly to distance common law from the theological predications of canon and civil law; Coke in particular continually asserted the jurisdictional superiority of the 'temporal Judges' of the common law to their civilian counterparts.³⁷ This is not to deny the obvious parallel between the medieval principle of mystical kingship and the Elizabethan (and Jacobean) theory of the divine right of kings, both of which propositions served to justify absolute rule. But as the discussion of the king's two bodies in the cases reported by Plowden occurred in the early 1560s, and the theory of divine right was developed only from the late 1560s onwards, it is inconceivable that the judges intended such a parallel to be drawn.³⁸

Individual reports of cases in *The Commentaries or Reports* of Plowden are especially relevant to particular themes in the plays of Shakespeare. That Shakespeare was familiar with Plowden is evident from his informed allusion to *Hales v Petit* (1562) in the graveyard scene in *Hamlet* (Act 5, scene 1). The case of *Hales v Petit* concerned an action for trespass brought by Margaret Hales against Cyriack Petit, on the grounds that he, 'with force and arms' (*vi et armis*), caused damage to 'her grass to the value of 40l. there lately growing with certain cattle, eat up, trod down, and consumed, and other wrongs to her did, to the great damage of the said Margaret'.³⁹ In 1554, the plaintiff's husband, Sir James Hales, had committed suicide by drowning. According to the case report, he 'voluntarily entered into the said river and himself therein then feloniously and voluntarily drowned'. The issue at law was whether, suicide being a felony, his estate was forfeit to the Crown, thereby depriving his widow of any legal interest which she might have had in the land. The account in *Hales v Petit* of the death of Sir James Hales, 'not having God before his eyes, but seduced by the art of the Devil',⁴⁰ appears to have influenced Shakespeare's treatment of the burial of Ophelia.

Before turning to the line of cases that are relevant to the issue of property law in *Richard II*, it is instructive briefly to consider the extent to which Plowden's report of *Hales v Petit* influenced the depiction of certain themes in *Hamlet*. In the

---

³⁶ Saul suggests that Kantorowicz 'exaggerated the distinction between king and man', Saul, above n 2, at 446.

³⁷ *Nicholas Fuller's Case* in Part 12 (1655) of *The Reports of Sir Edward Coke, Knt. In English*, (ed) G Wilson, 7 vols (London, Rivington, 1777) 7: 42a; see ch 1, text to n 39, above.

³⁸ The theory of divine right was developed by John Whitgift, after his appointment in 1567 as Master of Trinity College, Cambridge; see J Whitgift, *The defense of the aunswere to the Admonition, against the replie of T C* (London, Henry Binneman, 1574). On the divine right of kings, the threat posed to the Crown by Presbyterianism, and specifically the claim of Thomas Cartwright that the governance of the Church and the State should be distinct, see J Guy (ed), 'The Elizabethan Establishment and the Ecclesiastical Polity' in J Guy (ed), *The Reign of Elizabeth I: Court and Culture in the Last Decade* (Cambridge, Cambridge University Press, 1995) 127; also, P Lake, *Anglicans and Puritans? Presbyterianism and English Conformist Thought from Whitgift to Hooker* (London, Unwin Hyman, 1988) 1–2; C Cross, *The Royal Supremacy in the Elizabethan Church* (London, Allen & Unwin, 1969).

³⁹ Plowden, *Hales v Petit, Commentaries*, 1: 253.

⁴⁰ *Ibid* at 255. Sir James Hales was appointed Justice of the Common Pleas in 1549: he was dismissed from office following the accession of Queen Mary in 1553; for an extensive discussion of *Hamlet* and *Hales v Petit*, see A Zurcher, *Shakespeare and Law* (London, Arden Shakespeare, Forthcoming) ch 7.

The Commentaries or Reports *of Plowden*: Land and the Sacred Body of Law

report of *Hales v Petit* it is not only the suicide by drowning of the plaintiff's husband, Sir James Hale, and the subsequent forensic analysis of the offence (known as *felo de se*) which have particular thematic resonance with the graveyard scene in *Hamlet*. The grave-digger demonstrates familiarity with the language and logic of the law when he explains to his assistant that 'if I drown myself wittingly, it argues an act, and an act hath three branches—it is to act, to do, to perform' (5.1.10–12).[41] There is a notable resemblance between the delineation by the grave-digger of 'an act' and the definition of suicide by drowning offered by counsel for the plaintiff in *Hales v Petit*:

> And the cause of the death is the act done in the party's lifetime, which makes the death to follow. And the act which brought on the death here was the throwing himself voluntarily into the water.[42]

The more general, philosophical theme of action and meditation in relation to the act of suicide is considered at some length in *Hales v Petit*. Indeed, the particular arguments of counsel, which dwell on the mental state of Sir James Hale and the possible link between his introspection and the fatal action which he took, have strong echoes of thoughts expressed by Hamlet. Serjeant Walsh, counsel for the defendant, argued that the act of suicide had three constituent parts:

> The first is the imagination, which is a reflection or meditation of the mind, whether or no it is convenient for him to destroy himself, and what way it can be done. The second is the resolution, which is a determination of the mind to destroy himself, and to do it in this or that particular way. The third is the perfection, which is the execution of what the mind has resolved to do. And this perfection consists of two parts, viz the beginning and the end. The beginning is the doing of the act which causes the death, and the end is the death, which is only a sequel to the act.[43]

The opening sentence of Serjeant Walsh's speech, above, bears an obvious thematic resemblance (and to a lesser extent a stylistic similarity) to Hamlet's most famous soliloquy:

> To be, or not to be, that is the question:
> Whether 'tis nobler in the mind to suffer
> The slings and arrows of outrageous fortune,
> Or to take arms against a sea of troubles
> And by opposing end them. (3.1.56–60)

It seems that the crucial influence of Plowden's *Commentaries* over the plays of Shakespeare lay in the juridical conflation of the metaphysical and the corporeal, of which the judicial construct of the king's two bodies is an obvious example. Sir James Dyer, Chief Justice of the Common Pleas, said in judgment that the act of suicide by Sir James Hale was an offence against nature, against God and

---

[41] References to the play are from *Hamlet*, (ed) H Jenkins (London, Arden Shakespeare, 1982).
[42] Plowden, *Hales v Petit*, *Commentaries*, 1: 258.
[43] *Ibid* at 259.

[a]gainst the king, in that hereby he has lost a subject, and . . . he being the head has lost one of his mystical members.[44]

Here, the biblical principle of the *corpus mysticum* of the Church, with Christ as its head, is adapted to the secular notion of the king as head of the *corpus mysticum* of the State, with his loyal subjects making up the rest of the body.[45]

The mysterious authority of an invisible power, vying for sovereignty with the tangible presence of a physical phenomenon, is the theme of the *Case of the Dutchy of Lancaster* (1561). Plowden's comment in his report of this case that 'the king has in him two bodies, *viz* a body natural and a body politic' provided the historical and intellectual foundation, as well as the title, for Kantorowicz's book.[46] Kantorowicz emphasises the relevance of Plowden's statement to Shakespeare's *Richard II*, which he describes as 'the tragedy of the King's Two Bodies'.[47] It is an irony, on which Kantorowicz does not remark, that the *Case of the Dutchy of Lancaster* involved a dispute over land which had devolved to the body politic of Henry IV after Henry Bolingbroke (heir to the dukedom of Lancaster) had deposed Richard II and replaced him as king. The case concerned a contested lease of land which originally belonged to the House of Lancaster:

> [T]he dutchy of Lancaster came to the said king Henry 4. by descent on the part of his mother, and in this case if he had not afterwards been king, his possessions should have passed by livery and seizin, and attornment, &c. in the same manner as the possessions of other subjects ought to pass. But after he had deposed king Richard 2. and had assumed upon him the royal estate, and so had conjoined to his natural body the body politic of this realm, and was become king, then the possessions of the dutchy of Lancaster were in him as king.[48]

The legitimacy of succession lies at the heart of the case. By virtue of the mysterious, binding power of the body politic, the land subsequently passed from the House of Lancaster to successive monarchs, until Edward VI made a lease of it during his minority. Plowden succinctly records the issue before the court:

---

[44] *Ibid* at 261; regarding Hale's suicide, Dyer stated (reflecting contemporary legal opinion) that 'the quality of the offence is murder', *ibid*; in his discourse to the court on the constituent parts of a felony, Serjeant Walsh argued that 'the doing of the act is the only point which the law regards; for until the act is done, it cannot be an offence to the world, and when the act is done it is punishable', *ibid* at 259. The allusion to murder and the repeated use of the word 'done' recall Macbeth's: 'If it were done when 'tis done, then 'twere well / It were done quickly'. (1.7.1–2) On St Augustine and Macbeth's 'need to do in order to possess what is by that act done', see F Kermode, *Shakespeare's Language* (London, Penguin, 2000) 208.

[45] Kantorowicz, above n 25, at 15, makes a similar observation about the *corpus mysticum*, quoting Coke's remark in *Postnati. Calvin's Case* that the body politic of the king is 'called a mystical body'; see also, *ibid*, ch 5, 'Polity-Centered Kingship: Corpus Mysticum', at 193.

[46] Plowden, *Case of the Dutchy of Lancaster, Commentaries*, 1: 213.

[47] Kantorowicz, above n 25, at 26. Coke refers to the *Case of the Dutchy of Lancaster* in *Postnati. Calvin's Case*, 7 Reports (1608) 4: 1a, at 10a.

[48] Plowden, *Case of the Dutchy of Lancaster, Commentaries*, 1: 214; on political language and literature of the early Lancastrian period, see J Nuttall, *The Creation of Lancastrian Kingship: Literature, Language and Politics in Late Medieval England* (Cambridge, Cambridge University Press, 2007).

The Commentaries or Reports *of Plowden: Land and the Sacred Body of Law*

[I]f the present queen shall be bound by this lease made by king Edward 6 or if she shall avoid it by reason of the nonage of the said king Edward 6.

The lease was binding, because of the supernatural authority of the body politic:

> [A]lthough he has or takes the land in his natural body, yet to this natural body is conjoined his body politic, which contains his royal estate and dignity, and the body politic includes the body natural, but the body natural is the lesser, and with this the body politic is consolidated.[49]

A vision of good governance, the body politic, is held to be of greater legitimacy than a corporeal entity, the body natural. Although it is at least arguable that the judgment was based upon an equitable interpretation of the law,[50] the decision in the *Case of the Dutchy of Lancaster* (in particular its reference to the subsumption by the body politic of the body natural) appears to mark the triumph of metaphysics over reason, and demonstrates also the importance of the anatomical image as a persuasive tool in early modern forensic rhetoric. But the significance of the judgment in constitutional terms (as well as in terms of substantive law) is that the judges unanimously agreed 'that the queen should not avoid the lease'.[51] Like the rest of her subjects, she was subject to the law, as interpreted by her judges. Regarding the law of real property, and in particular the law relating to inheritance and alienation of title, the Royal Prerogative did not endow the monarch with special, extra-legal powers.

In terms of the power to dispose of property, *Willion v Berkley* (a case which was decided only a few months before the *Case of the Dutchy of Lancaster*, in Trinity term, 1561) offers an explicit delineation of the limited powers of the king. In his discussion of *Willion v Berkley* in *The King's Two Bodies*, Kantorowicz is even more selective in the use of quotations from Plowden's report than he is in relation to the *Case of the Dutchy of Lancaster*. He attributes arguments to judges when they were actually made by counsel for the respective parties (thereby implying that such remarks were at least *obiter dicta*, if not part of the *ratio decidendi*). He fails even to mention the remarkable decision of a majority of judges, which was that in this particular instance, land inherited by the Crown was held by the body natural of the king and the heirs of his body. With reference to the claim of a subject for the repossession of land of which he had been unlawfully dispossessed, *Willion v Berkley* is arguably of greater relevance than the *Case of the Dutchy of Lancaster*. The former case has particular resonance with the plot of *Richard II* and the just claim of Bolingbroke to his inheritance, which was unlawfully seized by Richard II following the death of John of Gaunt. Of course, there is an obvious titular

---

[49] Plowden, *Case of the Dutchy of Lancaster, Commentaries*, 1: 212, 213.

[50] Kantorowicz fails to note that in the earlier case of *Hill v Grange* (1556), 'the argument of the king's eternity, which he chooses to cite as an impressive ending to his chapter on Plowden, was actually rejected by the lawyers', Hutson, above n 13, at 177; Plowden, *Hill v Grange, Commentaries*, 1: 164.

[51] Plowden, *Case of the Dutchy of Lancaster, Commentaries*, 1: 213; Plowden reports that the assembled judges 'unanimously agreed', with the exception of 'Ruswel (who had but little time to consider the matter)', *ibid*.

connection between Bolingbroke and the Duchy of Lancaster; despite this, Bolingbroke's forthright assertion that 'I am a subject, / And I challenge law' (2.3.133–34) finds especial consonance with *Willion v Berkley*, which refers explicitly to 'saving every subject their right'.[52]

The subject of dispute in *Willion v Berkley* was an entailed estate, the tenants in tail of which were King Henry VII and 'the heirs male of his body lawfully begotten'. If the King were to die without such heirs then the land 'should wholly remain to the right heirs' of the Marquis of Berkley, whose descendant (Henry, Lord Berkley) was the defendant in the present case.[53] After the death of Henry VII, the land passed to his son, Henry VIII; upon his death, it passed to his son, Edward VI. During the lifetime of Edward VI, the King granted the fee simple to the Earl of Pembroke, 'to have and to hold to the same earl and to his heirs for ever'. The Earl of Pembroke then granted the fee simple to one Henry Cock. After the death of Edward VI, Henry Cock leased the land to the plaintiff, Henry Willion, for a period of seven years. The day after the lease was granted, the defendant entered the land and 'with force and arms, viz swords, staves, and knives . . . the said Henry Willion from his farm aforesaid thereof ejected'.[54] Willion subsequently brought an action for trespass against Berkley.

The case raised two issues of constitutional importance, in the settlement of which the court severely curtailed the prerogative power of the Crown and restricted the application of the king's mystical body politic, where to do so would flout the established law of inheritance. The first issue concerned The Statute of Westminster the Second 1285 (*13 Ed. I. cap. 1*), *De donis conditionalibus* ('Of conditional gifts'), and whether the Royal Prerogative excluded the monarch from the binding authority of this statute, regarding the alienation of entailed interests; the second related to whether the entail was held by the body politic or the body natural of the king, this being of crucial importance to Edward VI, who died without an heir to his natural body. The intention of *De donis conditionalibus* was to prevent the alienation of land, where an interest had been left to the feoffee and the heirs of his body. Prior to the enactment of *De donis*, the only two legal estates recognised by common law were the fee simple absolute and the fee simple conditional. In the latter instance, if the donee had no heirs of his body then the estate reverted to the donor upon the death of the donee. In practice, once the donee had

---

[52] Plowden, *Willion v Berkley, Commentaries*, 1: 223, at 231. Bolingbroke's 'I challenge law' has the medieval sense of 'I claim my legal right': see Gurr (ed), above n 15, at 120, note to 2.3.133; in Daniel's *The First Foure Bookes of the Civil Warres* (1595), the banished Bolingbroke declares: 'Dear Countrey . . . I am thy Champion; and I seek my Right', S Daniel, *The History of the Civil War* (London, R Gosling, 1718) 33, Bk I.XC. Regarding the deposition of Richard II, it is noteworthy that in *Willion v Berkley*, counsel for the defendant (Serjeant Southcote), pursuant to his general argument that the disputed entailed land vested in the body natural of the king and his heirs, stated that 'if he had been deposed or removed from the office of king, yet he should have held this land as purchased by him in his body natural', Plowden, *Willion v Berkley, Commentaries*, 1: 234–35.

[53] *Ibid* at 224; on the history of inheritance, estates and entails, see Baker, above n 11, at 259–77; on the medieval origins of the fee tail, see J Biancalana, *The Fee Tail and the Common Recovery in Medieval England* (Cambridge, Cambridge University Press, 2001).

[54] Plowden, *Willion v Berkley, Commentaries*, 1: 226.

an heir, he was able to alienate the land, thereby disinheriting his heir and often defeating the intention of the donor:

> [T]hat the donee might alien after issue had, was contrary to the will of the donor, as the preamble of the statute *de donis* says.⁵⁵

De donis sought to honour the intention of the donor by creating an inalienable estate in fee tail. The significance of this statute—not only to the law of inheritance, but also to the management of land—may be gleaned from the fact that more than 300 years after its enactment, Coke continued to rail against its inequitable consequences:

> Infinite were the scruples, suits, and inconveniencies that the statute of 13 E. 1. *de donis conditionalibus* did introduce, which intended to give every man power to create a new found estate in tail, and to establish a perpetuity of his lands, so as the same should not be aliened nor letten, but only during the life of tenant in tail, against a fundamental rule of the common law, that all estates of inheritance were fee-simple; whereupon these inconveniencies ensued, purchasers defeated, leases evicted, other estates and grants made upon just and good consideration were avoided, creditors defrauded of their just and due debts, offenders imboldened to commit capital offences, and many other inconveniencies followed.⁵⁶

As with restrictions on freedom of trade, so with limitations on the capacity to alienate interests in land: Coke perceived any such action (whether by exercise of the Royal Prerogative or by parliamentary means) as an unwarrantable interference with the liberty of the subject and a divergence from the immutable custom of common law.⁵⁷

Returning to the immediate relevance of *De donis* to *Willion v Berkley*, the case was heard at last resort before three judges in the Court of Common Pleas: Weston J, Anthony Brown J and Dyer CJ. In his analysis of the decision of the court, Kantorowicz misleads the reader as to the identity of speakers and the outcome of the case. Quoting Plowden, he attributes arguments made by counsel for the plaintiff to 'the judges':

> [Y]et they [the judges] said that he [the King] is not void of Prerogative in regard to Things which he has in his Body natural.⁵⁸

'They' to whom Plowden refers here are not 'the judges', as Kantorowicz claims, but counsel for the plaintiff: Serjeants Puttrel, Bendloe and Carus.⁵⁹ It is important to

---

⁵⁵ *Ibid* at 235.
⁵⁶ Coke, 4 *Reports* (1604) 2: Preface, vi. Lord Ellesmere said of the same statute that it had been 'made but upon a singularity of conceit and that it had been well for the commonwealth if it had never been made', W H Bryson (ed), *Cases Concerning Equity and the Courts of Equity, 1550–1660*, 2 vols (London, Selden Society, 2001–02) 1: 306.
⁵⁷ Thompson provides a credible explanation for Coke's forthright opposition to *De donis*: 'What was happening from the time of Coke to that of Blackstone, was a hardening and concretion of the notion of property in land, and a re-ification of usages into properties which could be rented, sold or willed', EP Thompson, *Customs in Common* (London, Merlin, 1991) 135.
⁵⁸ Plowden, *Willion v Berkley, Commentaries*, 1: 238 in Kantorowicz, above n 25, at 11 (parentheses added by Kantorowicz).
⁵⁹ Plowden, *Willion v Berkley, Commentaries*, 1: 228.

correct this inaccuracy because, as Plowden notes, 'as to the plaintiff, the strength of his title depends upon the making of his lease good'.[60] The lease would be good only if it could be established both that (by virtue of the Royal Prerogative) Edward VI was not bound by *De donis*, and that it was possible for the body politic of the King to have heirs even though his body natural had produced no issue. In the absence of an heir to Edward VI, the title would automatically revert to the defendant, Lord Berkley. In a dissenting judgment, finding for the plaintiff, Weston J argued that by virtue of the Royal Prerogative the king was not bound by *De donis*: '. . . the law shews him special favour in all his business and things, as being the cause and origin thereof'. He made the alarming, anti-Bractonian assertion that the king

> is not so strictly bound by the law as others are. And as the common law cannot bind him, so cannot private customs.[61]

Regarding the issue of the king's two bodies, of the three judges, only Weston J argued that although the disputed entail was vested in the body natural of the king, it was 'annexed' to his body politic. Despite the absence of a natural heir to Edward VI, Weston J stated that the lease made to the plaintiff was valid because the king 'may have heirs in his body politic' and

> the land which he takes in the capacity of his body natural he has not meerly as a common person, but as a natural man and as a king also, and as to such land he shall have the prerogatives of king, because the royal estate is conjoined to the person who holds the same.[62]

In the majority judgments of Dyer CJ and Anthony Brown J (finding for the defendant), the Bractonian principle of a king subject to the law was firmly restated. While the theory of the king's two bodies was not rejected in either judgment, the limits to the binding authority of mystical kingship were defined in the greater interests of the subject of law. Plowden reports Dyer's reiteration of arguments made by counsel for the defendant: Serjeants Harper, Southcote, Walsh and Cholmley (not '*Justice* Southcote, seconded by *Justice* Harper', as stated by Kantorowicz).[63] Of considerable relevance to *Richard II* and its continual references to subjects and subjection was the emphasis placed by Dyer on the relationship between the king's subjects and the king's body politic. The definition of the body politic in the *Case of the Dutchy of Lancaster* made no reference to subjects: it is described in metaphysical terms only, as 'a body that cannot be seen or handled'.[64] In *Willion v Berkley*, by contrast, Dyer argued that the king's subjects were 'members' of the body politic. Although subject to government by their king, together with the king 'he and his subjects compose the corporation, as *Southcote* said, and he is incorporated with them, and

---

[60] *Ibid* at 229.
[61] *Ibid* at 242–43.
[62] *Ibid* at 242.
[63] Kantorowicz, above n 25, at 13 (emphasis added); Plowden, *Willion v Berkley*, *Commentaries*, 1: 228.
[64] Plowden, *Case of the Dutchy of Lancaster*, *Commentaries*, 1: 213.

they with him'.⁶⁵ Of course, Dyer's definition of the body politic can be read as a secular interpretation of the *corpus mysticum*, but it must be conceded that he placed great emphasis on the status afforded the subject in determining the form of the 'corporation' of the State. As Plowden reports unequivocally, 'the whole court was of opinion [that] every subject has an interest in the king'.⁶⁶ Dyer's definition of an inclusive body politic, above, implies a level of popular consent. In this respect, the body politic as defined in *Willion v Berkley* is more directly related to the consensual body politic described (more than 40 years later) by Coke in *Postnati. Calvin's Case* than to the more absolute model described by Plowden in the *Case of the Dutchy of Lancaster*. In the latter, the body politic is 'constituted *for* the direction of the people'; while in the former 'it is framed *by* the policy of man'.⁶⁷

Although Kantorowicz quotes extensively from Dyer's judgment in *Willion v Berkley*, he does not mention that Dyer agreed with the argument of the defendant that the original entail in favour of Henry VII was made to him in the capacity of his body natural, rather than *in jure coronae*. Consequently, it cannot accurately be averred (not anyway in relation to the legal status of the king's property transactions) that the body politic of the king 'does away with the human imperfections of the body natural'.⁶⁸ Dyer seriously undermined the sacred authority of the king's two bodies when he stated that

> the donor limited it [the entail] to *Henry 7*. and to the heirs males of his body, and if the heirs of the other body should inherit it, it would be contrary to the limitation and will of the donor . . .

Further to this, in affirming that *De donis* restored to the donor of an entailed interest the original terms of his gift, Dyer restricted the extent to which the Royal Prerogative may interfere with the customary rights of the subject:

> So that the design of the act is to give restitution, and in restitutions the king has no favour, nor has his prerogative any exemption, but the party restored is favoured.⁶⁹

Anthony Brown J was even more forthright in asserting the subjection of king to law. His judgment was antithetical to Weston's, which argued for the extra-legal force of the Royal Prerogative and the mystical power of the king's body politic. If evidence were needed of the practical application by the early modern judiciary of Bracton's dictum, *lex facit regem*, we need look no further than the following extract from Anthony Brown's judgment in *Willion v Berkley*:

> For the person of the king is not to be respected in gifts of land, but the quality of the estate is to be considered; and the person of the king shall not rule the estate in the land, but the estate in the land shall rule the person of the king.⁷⁰

---

⁶⁵ Plowden, *Willion v Berkley, Commentaries*, 1: 234.
⁶⁶ *Ibid* at 231.
⁶⁷ Plowden, *Case of the Dutchy of Lancaster, Commentaries*, 1: 213; Coke, *Postnati. Calvin's Case*, 7 *Reports* (1608) 4: 10a (emphasis added).
⁶⁸ Kantorowicz, above n 25, at 13.
⁶⁹ Plowden, *Willion v Berkley, Commentaries*, 1: 250, 252.
⁷⁰ *Ibid* at 245.

Reflections on the Art of Kingship: Richard II *and the Subject of Law*

The question of the king's conscience was raised throughout Anthony Brown's judgment, reminding the reader that the king is bound not only by his coronation oath but by the common law itself, to act in the best interests of his subjects. Rejecting Weston's insistence that the Royal Prerogative implicitly exempted the king from the provisions of *De donis conditionalibus,* Anthony Brown retorted:

> [H]e that will maintain that the king is in a degree to make such alienation, must at the same time maintain that the king may do wrong, and that the law suffers him to do wrong, which none can maintain; and it is a difficult argument to prove that a statute, which restrains men generally from doing wrong, leaves the king at liberty to do wrong.[71]

The emphasis placed by Anthony Brown J on 'wrong' is striking. At the heart of his and Dyer's judgments is the unspoken assumption that conscience is an integral facet in the philosophical ideology and practical application of the common law. Anthony Brown J refers to the intention of the donor in *Willion v Berkley,* stating that 'if it was contrary to the minds of the givers, then it was ill done'.[72] In other words, any attempt by the king to alienate title called into question the king's conscience. The influence of St German's *Doctor and Student* in particular, and the equitable tenets of renaissance humanism in general, are demonstrable features of Anthony Brown's judgment. He is describing an equitable system of justice, not necessarily in terms recognisable to the Court of Chancery (this was, after all, the Court of Common Pleas), but in the Aristotelian sense of judges as poets and sovereign artists,[73] applying the imaginary precepts of natural law to the tangible pragmatics of common law; the first of those precepts being to do good and avoid evil. It is axiomatic of English juridical procedure that the adversarial system contributes to polarised opinion within the courtroom, but *Willion v Berkley* is especially notable for the moral distinction, made by Anthony Brown J, between right and wrong: his judgment embodied Aquinas's first precept of law, outlined above, that 'good is to be done and pursued, and evil is to be avoided'.[74]

The theory of mystical kingship, of a monarch endowed with divine and irrefutable power, was one which Richard II expounded and exploited in order to justify the extension of prerogative powers at a time of civil unrest and, on occasion, open rebellion.[75] But to argue as Kantorowicz does that the Elizabethan judges of the common law were united in their professional commitment to the

---

[71] *Ibid* at 245, 248.
[72] *Ibid* at 247.
[73] Given the exaggerated juridical importance with which Kantorowicz invests the theory of the king's two bodies, it is noteworthy that in a later work he describes pre-modern judges in terms of their sovereignty and poetic judgments: see E H Kantorowicz, 'The Sovereignty of the Legal Artist: a Note on Legal Maxims and Renaissance Theories in Art' in E H Kantorowicz (ed), *Selected Studies* (New York, J J Augustin, 1965) 118.
[74] St Thomas Aquinas, *Summa Theologica (Pars Prima Secundae)* (Teddington, The Echo Library, 2007) 421, Q94, 'Of the Natural Law'.
[75] On the king's two bodies as 'sanction to the idea of the crown as inherited property', see Gurr (ed), above n 15, Introduction, at 19; see also, E Z Boris, *Shakespeare's English Kings, the People and the Law: A Study in the Relationship between the Tudor Constitution and the English History Plays* (New Jersey, Fairleigh Dickinson University Press, 1978).

theory of the king's two bodies, and that such unity was represented in their various judicial decisions, is inaccurate. Of course, certain judges (of whom Weston was one) stood in apparent awe of the king's divine majesty, according the monarch a level of extra-legal power which was antithetical to the limited powers invested in the king by Bracton and Fortescue. But in all of the cases in which the theory of the king's two bodies is discussed, a majority of judges demonstrate adherence to an equitable doctrine, predicated upon the classical principle of *epieikeia*.[76] Aristotle's idea of equity was not bound by formalism: *epieikeia*, with its implications of fairness and equability, envisages the ideal good of society, in much the same way as *gnomé* prefigures sympathy or consideration (as well as good judgment) and Platonic *dikaiosuné* envisages right relations between men.[77] Above all, most of the judges in the cases considered here demonstrated adherence to St German's injunction:

> [T]hat thou do justice to every man as much as in thee is: and also that in every general rule of the law thou do observe and keep equity. And if thou do thus, I trust the light of the lantern, that is, thy conscience, shall never be extinct.[78]

It is notable that St German refers to a 'general rule of the law' that equity should be observed: *epieikeia* was not the exclusive domain of a specialist jurisdiction but rather a quality of fairness, which the judges in all of the king's courts should seek to embody. The general principle of equability is evident in all of the cases discussed in this chapter. The judges were not displaying slavish devotion to a mystical interpretation of kingship; rather they were harnessing their poetic imaginations and their intellects to a metaphor—the king's two bodies—in order 'to relieve the people from trouble, and to take away mischief from them'.[79]

III. Through a Glass, Darkly: Treason, Law and the Discovery of Self

In chapter two I noted Shakespeare's interest in the mirror image as a theatrical device.[80] In *The Comedy of Errors* this was manifested in the two pairs of

---

[76] On *epieikeia* and English law, see G Watt, *Equity Stirring: the Story of Justice Beyond Law* (Oxford, Hart Publishing, 2009) 18–19.

[77] Aristotle, *The Nicomachean Ethics*, Bks V.X.1137a30–1138a3, VI.XI.1143a19–1143b17; on Plato and *dikaiosuné*, see ch 1, text to nn 62–65, above.

[78] C St German, *Dialogues Between a Doctor of Divinity and a Student in the Laws of England*, (ed) W Muchall (Cincinnati, Ohio, Robert Clarke, 1874) 44.

[79] Plowden, *Hill v Grange, Commentaries*, 1: 178; see G Behrens, 'Equity in the Commentaries of Edmund Plowden' (1999) 20 *The Journal of Legal History* 25.

[80] See ch 2, text to nn 77–79, above. The complete verse from the Authorised King James Version of The Bible reads: 'For now we see through a glass, darkly; but then face to face: now I know in part; but then shall I know even as also I am known', 1 *Corinthians* 13.12; more prosaic renderings include: 'Now we see only puzzling reflections in a mirror' (New English Bible); and 'For now we see in a mirror dimly' (Revised Standard Version).

indistinguishable identical twins. 'Methinks you are my glass, and not my brother' (5.1.418), remarks Dromio of Ephesus to his twin, recognising immediately the reflection of himself in his brother. In *Richard II*, written less than a year after the 1594 performance of *The Comedy of Errors* at Gray's Inn, the mirror image is a primary motif in the play. In the deposition scene Richard calls for a mirror, so that he may 'read' himself (4.1.276). *Richard II*, of course, contains no twins: the device of the mirror is utilised not for comic purposes, but rather for the introspective examination and analysis of self.[81] Richard sees in Bolingbroke an image of kingship, which during his own reign he was never able to represent. It is with uncomprehending admiration of Bolingbroke, as well as envy, that Richard

> Observed his courtship to the common people;
> How he did seem to dive into their hearts
> With humble and familiar courtesy ... (1.4.24–26)[82]

All this, while Bolingbroke was still a mere subject of Richard, but conducting himself '[a]s were our England in reversion his' (1.4.35). The technical language of real property—reversion—is used by Richard to comment on his relationship with his other self, Bolingbroke. The use of the word 'reversion' serves also to remind the audience that Richard has conducted his kingship like a tenant for life, one who has 'wasted' or injured the inheritance by despoiling the land.[83] The language of law recurs when the Queen likens her grief at being separated from Richard, upon his departure for Ireland, to a 'reversion that I do possess' (2.2.38). Later, when Bolingbroke orders his guards to convey Richard to the Tower, Richard replies: 'O, good – "Convey"! Conveyors are you all' (4.1.317), demonstrating his awareness that title to the Crown has been conveyed, or legally transferred, to his cousin.[84]

Seizure of property, despoliation of land and disputed claims to lawful title provide the narrative foundations of the plot in *Richard II*, but property serves also as

---

[81] Nuttall observes that while in *The Comedy of Errors* 'the doubled self is allowed to dance free from individual psychology into a fairyland of twins', in *Richard II* the dramatisation of the split identity is a device with which to analyse the self, A D Nuttall, *Shakespeare the Thinker* (New Haven, Conn, Yale University Press, 2007) 133; for an introduction to psychoanalytic theory of the self and the other, see J Lacan, 'Psychoanalysis and Its Teaching' in J Lacan, *Écrits*, (tr) B Fink (New York, W W Norton & Co, 2006) 364.

[82] Forker describes Richard's speech as 'carping', of betraying 'a new note of jealousy', but he notes also that it emphasises the play's theme of *Realpolitik*, Forker (ed), above n 5, 236, notes to 1.4.24–36. Harrison saw in Richard's description of Bolingbroke in Act 1, scene 4 a prophetic image of the Earl of Essex's ambition, G B Harrison, *Times Literary Supplement* (20 November 1930) 974; *ibid* (15 October 1931) 802.

[83] The most explicit reference to Richard as a tenant is made by John of Gaunt, who laments that England '[i]s now leased out—I die pronouncing it—/ Like to a tenement' (2.1.59–60); later in the same scene, he tells Richard: 'The waste is no whit lesser than thy land'. (2.1.103) Waste was the subject of much litigation in the Elizabethan period: in particular, in those cases involving disputes over alienation of title, as discussed above; eg, Plowden notes that 'the common law suffered tenant for years or for life to make wast and destruction of houses and woods, yet the doing thereof was discommendable and wrong', Plowden, *Willion v Berkley, Commentaries*, 1: 247.

[84] Gurr notes a third meaning of 'convey' as 'to steal', Gurr (ed), above n 15,159, note to 4.1.315–16.

a metaphor for the divided self, illuminating and lending form to the idea of the king's two bodies.[85] The Latin word '*proprium*' is the source not only of the word 'property', meaning one's own; it translates also as a characteristic quality (or property) which distinguishes a person. The theme of two becoming one, but remaining distinct (echoing the theological premise of the Trinity) was addressed by Shakespeare in his love poem, 'The Phoenix and the Turtle', in which the unification of two separate bodies is celebrated in the following stanza:

> Property was thus appalled
> That the self was not the same.
> Single nature's double name
> Neither two nor one was called.[86]

Richard discovers his true quality, his 'single nature', only when, stripped of his kingship and confined in a prison cell, he finds love in the simple acts of kindness of his fellow beings: in the playing of music—'a sign of love' (5.5.65)—and the visit of a faithful groom, whose only motive is to comfort his former master (5.5.67–97).

As far as the persona of the monarch is concerned, the image of the king which Richard reflects is distorted: in the first half of the play Richard's kingship is depicted by Shakespeare as idolatrous rather than iconic, the embodiment of falsehood, a lie.[87] In chapter two I noted Coke's observation, in *Postnati. Calvin's Case*, that 'a King's crown is an hieroglyphic of the laws',[88] but if the king is corrupt then the Crown is no longer a legitimate image of law. Insofar as common law is the perpetuation of custom or tradition,[89] it is reliant for its continuation on recollection and the truthful reflection of memory in its texts and iconography. The memory of law is reflected of course in the year books and law reports, but it is also made apparent through the institutional *arcana* of the legal community: costume,

---

[85] Klinck has commented on the 'preoccupation with property law in the play', noting especially the depiction of Richard as both profligate landlord and wasteful tenant, D R Klinck, 'Shakespeare's *Richard II* as Landlord and Wasting Tenant' (1998) 25 *College Literature* 21; Bradin Cormack argues that in the language of property law 'there was an operative metaphysics which Shakespeare looked to for its affective content', B Cormack, 'Shakespeare Possessed: Legal Affect and the Time of Holding' in P Raffield and G Watt (eds), *Shakespeare and the Law* (Oxford, Hart Publishing, 2008) 85.
[86] 'The Phoenix and the Turtle' in S Wells and G Taylor (eds), *William Shakespeare: The Complete Works* (Oxford, Clarendon, 2005) 810; 'The Phoenix and the Turtle' was published in 1601, in Robert Chester's *Love's Martyrs, or, Rosalin's Complaint*; on 'The Phoenix and the Turtle' and the theology of the Trinity, see Kermode, above n 44, at 70.
[87] On Shakespeare's Richard as 'an empty monarch, a king of nothing', and the depiction of history as 'an empty formalist gesture', see T Betteridge, *Shakespearean Fantasy and Politics* (Hatfield, University of Hertfordshire Press, 2005) 58.
[88] Coke, *Postnati. Calvin's Case*, 7 *Reports* (1608) 4: 11b. See ch 2, text to n 54, above.
[89] See, eg, Fortescue: 'Know then, that all Human Laws are either the Law of Nature, Customs, or Statute', Sir John Fortescue, *De Laudibus Legum Angliae*, (ed) J Selden (London, R Gosling, 1737) 28; also, St German, above n 78, at 18: 'And because the said customs be neither against the law of God, nor the law of reason, and have been alway taken to be good and necessary for the commonwealth of all the realm; therefore they have obtained the strength of a law, insomuch that he that doth against them, doth against justice: and these be the customs that properly be called the common law'.

architecture, heraldry, ritual.[90] The public monuments to its genealogy or history may be described as *specula* or mirrors of the law, reflecting the collective memory of the legal institution.[91] Given the concern of renaissance jurists, such as Coke, that memory should be accurately inscribed in the reflective texts of the law, it should not be surprising that the mirror figures so prominently in the bibliography of early modern jurisprudence. Hence, in the Preface to Part IX of *The Reports*, Coke refers to 'a very ancient and learned treatise of the laws and usages of this kingdom', entitled *The Mirror of Justices*.[92] The various books of heraldic emblems, published during the late renaissance period, provided graphic reflections of '*nobilitas polytica*' and '*ius gentilitatis*'[93]: these included *The Mirrour of Maiestie*, which depicted through pictorial allegory and accompanying poetic text the inherent rectitude and antiquity of the English nobility.[94] Shakespeare looked to *The Mirror for Magistrates* (first published in 1559) for its salutary portrayal of Richard II as the personification of corrupt kingship and 'evyll governaunce deposed from his seat, and miserably murdred in prison'.[95] *The Mirror for Magistrates* was distinctive amongst the texts which constituted a genre of reflective juristic literature, in that the specula which it provides—of kings and noblemen—illustrate not the virtues but rather the corruption, venality and self-

---

[90] Goodrich argues that such examples of 'legal art . . . provide popular consciousness with a Justice which can be seen and so remembered', P Goodrich, 'Specula Laws: Image, Aesthetic and Common Law' (1991) 2 *Law and Critique* 233, 234–35. Regarding the symbolism of costume, it is indicative of Richard's falsehood that he is influenced by 'Report of fashions in proud Italy, / Whose manners still our tardy-apish nation / Limps after in base imitation'. (2.1.21–23) The wearing of 'foreign' clothes was provided as evidence of treason at the trial in 1547 of Henry Howard, Earl of Surrey: see J Ashelford, *Visual History of Costume: Sixteenth Centry* (London, Batsford, 1983) 56–57. For a contemporary account of Italian fashions in clothes and late-Elizabethan costume, see R Greene, *A Quip for an Upstart Courtier: Or, A quaint dispute between Velvet breeches and Cloth-breeches* (London, Iohn Wolfe, 1592); on *A Quip for an Upstart Courtier*, see ch 4, text to nn 45–48, below.

[91] Foucault develops a textual analogy, arguing that genealogy 'operates on a field of entangled and confused parchments, on documents that have been scratched over and recopied many times', M Foucault, 'Nietzsche, Genealogy, History' in J D Faubion (ed), *Aesthetics, Method, and Epistemology* R Hurley (tr) (London, Penguin, 1998) 369.

[92] *The Mirror of Justices* was written by Andrew Horne (d 1328) in the 14th century, and remained a popular juristic text for the next three centuries.

[93] The Latin phrases above are used by John Ferne to describe respectively '[a] civill nobilitie: which onely appertaineth to mankind' and 'a law for the discents of Gentillity, that is, of the bloud of noble families', J Ferne, *The Blazon of Gentrie* (London, Toby Cooke, 1586) 6, 86; on *nobilitas polytica*, see ch 2, text to n 113, above.

[94] H G, *The Mirrour of Maiestie: or, the Badges of Honour Conceitedly Emblazoned: with Emblems Annexed, Poetically Unfolded* (London, W Jones, 1618); see also A Alciatus, *Emblemata* (Lugudini, M Bonhomme, 1550). For a discussion of *The Mirrour of Maiestie*, see P Raffield, *Images and Cultures of English Law in Early Modern England: Justice and Political Power, 1558–1660* (Cambridge, Cambridge University Press, 2004) 67–74.

[95] *The Mirror for Magistrates*, (ed) L B Campbell (Cambridge, Cambridge University Press, 1938) 111. The primary source for *Richard II* was Raphael Holinshed's *Chronicles of England, Scotland and Ireland* (1586–87), which paints a generally unsympathetic portrait of Richard. Shakespeare also drew on the following works: Samuel Daniel's *The First Foure Bookes of the Civil Warres* (1595); Edward Hall's *The Union of the Noble and Illustre Famelies of Lancaster and York*, popularly known as Hall's *Chronicle* (1548); the anonymous *Thomas of Woodstock, or King Richard the Second, Part One* (c 1591–95); and Jean Froissart's *Chronicles* (c 1369–1400). On the sources, see Gurr (ed), above n 15, Introduction, at 10–16; also, Saul, above n 2, at 1–5.

destructive ambition of its subjects: 'And tell them this from me that tryed it true. / Who reckless rules, right soone may hap to rue'.⁹⁶

Richard II is unusual in the plays of Shakespeare for the number and variety of formal trials and ad hoc tribunals which punctuate the action and drive the plot. The common feature of all these trials is the nature of the offence which has been alleged: each of them involves the charge of treason. The play presents several variations on the treason trial: the opening confrontation between Bolingbroke and Mowbray, 'to appeal each other of high treason' (1.1.27); the aborted trial by combat between Bolingbroke and Mowbray in the lists at Coventry (1.3); the summary trial by Bolingbroke of Bushy and Green for numerous offences committed against the Crown (3.1); the pre-trial accusations in the High Court of Parliament against Aumerle for his complicity in the murder of Gloucester (4.1.1–107); the quasi-trial of Richard in the same court for his 'weaved-up follies' (4.1.229) against the State; and the highly theatrical (and oddly comic) trial of Aumerle for his participation in the conspiracy to assassinate Henry IV at Oxford (5.3.23–145). The Statute of Treasons of 1352 (*25 Ed.3. cap. 2*) had specified that

> when anyone attempts to compass or imagine the death of our lord the king . . . what extends to our lord the king and to his royal majesty must be adjudged treason; and from such manner of treason the forfeiture of the escheats pertains to our lord the king . . .⁹⁷

The reference to escheat (from the old-French, *eschier*, meaning 'to fall') or forfeiture reminds us that the consequences to the convicted traitor were the same as those to the entailed tenant who died without an heir: his lands were forfeit to his lord. The repeated references to the treason trial in *Richard II*, with its implication of escheat, remind us of the centrality of land to the theme of the play: with each convicted traitor, the Crown stands to benefit from the forfeiture of the traitorous subject's estate.⁹⁸ References to 'England's ground' and its 'sweet soil' (1.3.306), to 'this dear dear land' (2.1.57), to '[t]his earth of majesty' and '[t]his other Eden' (2.1.41–42) illuminate the theme of patriotism.⁹⁹ Land here is a metonym, but its associations are more profound, more personal, than an expression merely of contiguity with patriotism. Shakespeare endows the earth with an anthropomorphic quality: a stylistic device which is never more apparent than when Richard is expressing his love of English earth, upon returning from the campaign in Ireland:

---

⁹⁶ *Mirror for Magistrates*, above n 95, 'The complaint of Henrye duke of Buckingham', at 345.

⁹⁷ On the Statute of Treasons of 1352, see J G Bellamy, *The Law of Treason in England in the Later Middle Ages* (Cambridge, Cambridge University Press, 1970) 59–101; regarding the various alterations and additions to the law of treason in the reign of Richard II, in particular the forfeiture of entailed interests as well as fees simple, see *ibid* at 114–15; see also, C D Ross, 'Forfeiture for Treason in the Reign of Richard II' (1956) 71 *The English Historical Review* 560.

⁹⁸ Holdsworth notes the material benefits that accrued to the Crown through forfeiture for treason, commenting also that convictions for treason were more easily obtained than those for 'more precisely defined felonies', W S Holdsworth, *A History of English Law*, 17 vols (London, Methuen, 1924) 3: 290.

⁹⁹ On the proliferation in *Richard II* of the words 'earth', 'land' and 'ground', see R D Altick, 'Symphonic Imagery in *Richard II*' (1947) 62 *Publication of the Modern Language Association of America* 341.

> Dear earth, I do salute thee with my hand,
> Though rebels wound thee with their horses' hoofs.
> As a long-parted mother with her child
> Plays fondly with her tears and smiles in meeting,
> So weeping, smiling, greet I thee, my earth,
> And do thee favours with my royal hands. (3.2.6–11)

The profession by Richard of love for his realm is antithetical to his ruthless exploitation of the land through the exercise of illegal or unconstitutional procedures. These include the seizure of Bolingbroke's estate, the enforcement of 'benevolences' (2.1.250) or forced loans and the issue of 'blank charters' (1.4.48). Richard's confiscation of Bolingbroke's 'plate, his goods, his money and his lands' (2.1.210) is patently unlawful: *28 Ed.3. cap. 3* (1354) states that

> no Man of what Estate or Condition that he be, shall be put out of Land or Tenement, nor taken, nor disinherited, nor put to Death, without being brought in Answer by due Process of the Law.[100]

As well as being in breach of the above statute, Richard has flouted the unwritten law of the land that he professes to love. It is Richard, rather than the rebels, who wounds the land by violating *lex terrae*—the ancient constitution of immemorial origin, which places peculiar emphasis on the right to private enjoyment of land by English subjects. In 1605, only 10 years after the first performance of *Richard II*, *Semayne's Case* averred as law

> [t]hat the house of every one is to him as his castle and fortress, as well for his defence against injury and violence, as for his repose.[101]

The same disregard for the liberty of the subject is displayed by Richard with regard to the imposition of blank charters.[102] The levying of this tax calls into

---

[100] Clause 52, *Magna Carta* of 1215, read as follows: 'If anyone has been disseised or deprived by us without lawful judgment of his peers of lands, castles, liberties or his rights we will restore them to him at once', in M Evans and R I Jack (eds), *Sources of English Legal and Constitutional History* (Sydney, Butterworths, 1984) 58; the clause was excised from the reissues of 1216, 1217 and from *Magna Carta* of 1297. St German, above n 78, at 30, states that 'there is a maxim in the law of England, that the king may disseise no man'.

[101] Coke, *Semayne's Case*, 5 *Reports* (1605) 3: 91a, at 91b.

[102] Holinshed records the unpopularity of this revenue-raising measure with the populace: 'manie blanke charters were devised, and brought into the citie, which manie of the substantiall and wealthie citizens were faine to seale, to their great charge, as in the end appeared. And the like charters were sent abroad into all the shires within the realme, whereby great grudge and murmuring arose among the people'; and later, 'Moreover, they were compelled to put their hands and seales to certeine blankes, wherof ye have heard before; in the which, when it pleased him, he might write what he thought good', R Holinshed, *Chronicles of England, Scotland and Ireland*, iii.496/1/11, iii.496/2/30 in W G Boswell-Stone, *Shakespeare's Holinshed: The Chronicle and the Historical Plays Compared* (London, Chatto and Windus, 1907) 90. In dramatic terms, the inequitable nature of 'blank charters' is dealt with more fully in *Thomas of Woodstock* than in *Richard II*. In the former play, Cowtail describes blank charters thus: 'I heard of them afore, and therefore I made such haste away. They're sent down to the high shrieve with special charge that every man that is of any credit or worship i'th'country must set their hands and seal to them, for what intent I know not'. (3.3.82–87)

question the constitutional validity of general or non-specific warrants, the illegality of which was established in the 18th century in the cases of *Wilkes v Wood* and *Entick v Carrington*.¹⁰³ In the former case, such warrants were declared 'an outrage to the constitution itself' and 'totally subversive of the liberty of the subject'; while in the latter case, the court—referring explicitly to the ancient constitution—declared that 'our law holds the property of every man so sacred, that no man can set his foot upon his neighbour's close without his leave'. Of course, it would be wrong to impute to Ricardian or Elizabethan jurisprudence the same regard for the sanctity of private property as demonstrated by the 18th-century courts, but the language of *Wilkes v Wood* and *Entick v Carrington* is the language of *Semayne's Case* and (as Coke would probably have stated) it is also the language of *Magna Carta*.¹⁰⁴ In the words of counsel for the plaintiff (Serjeant Glynn) in *Wilkes v Wood*, the courts (of whichever period in history) have 'ever been the protector of the liberty and property of the subject'.

The references to 'farming' of 'our royal realm' (1.4.45) to replenish the royal 'coffers', which 'with too great a court / And liberal largesse are grown somewhat light' (1.4.43–44), have clear parallels with the sale of Crown lands during the 1590s. These echoes are reinforced in Gaunt's lament for a lost England, when he declares that Richard has 'leased out' the country, '[l]ike to a tenement or pelting farm' (2.1.59–60)¹⁰⁵; and, later in the same scene, when he confronts Richard with the accusation: 'Landlord of England art thou now, not king. / Thy state of law is bondslave to the law' (2.1.113–14). In the early 1590s, in order to finance war against Spain, the Crown sold lands worth a total of £15,593.¹⁰⁶ Most of these transactions involved the sales of land in fee simple, but in the 1590s a market grew for sales of land in fee farm (whereby a perpetual rent, payable by the freeholder, issued out of lands held in fee simple). As Richard Hoyle has noted, the holder of an interest in fee farm owed no obligation to the Crown other than to pay the agreed rent: in such instances, the Crown was literally 'Landlord of England'.¹⁰⁷

---

¹⁰³ *Wilkes v Wood* (1763) 19 St Tr 1153; *Entick v Carrington* (1765) 19 St Tr 1029. In discussing these two cases, Goodrich refers to 'the inviolability of soil' and the immemorial law of unwritten tradition that guarantees protection of proprietary interests by the courts, P Goodrich, *Languages of Law: From Logics of Memory to Nomadic Masks* (London, Weidenfeld & Nicolson, 1990) 215.

¹⁰⁴ Both *Wilkes v Wood* and *Entick v Carrington* confirm the principle, stated by Coke (reiterating Bracton and Hooker), that 'the law makes the King: therefore let the King attribute that to the law, which from the law he hath received, to wit, power and dominion: for where will, and not law doth sway, there is no King', Coke, 4 *Reports* (1604) 2: Preface, xixa. In the 1628 Parliamentary debates over the Petition of Right, the MP Henry Sherfield said that '[o]thers object it is not the language of parliaments to bind kings and the Council by express words. Answer: it is the language of Magna Carta', R C Johnson, M F Keeler, M Jansson Cole and W B Bidwell (eds), *Proceedings in Parliament 1628*, 6 vols (New Haven, Conn, Yale University Press, 1977) 3: 187.

¹⁰⁵ In *Thomas of Woodstock*, Richard boasts that 'to ease our wanton youth', he will '[b]ecome a landlord to this warlike realm, / Rent out our kingdom like a pelting farm' (4.1.146–48).

¹⁰⁶ This compares to sales of land worth £11,711 between 1559 and 1565; sales ceased during the middle period of Elizabeth's reign. Figures are from R Hoyle, 'Introduction: aspects of the Crown's Estate, c. 1558–1640' in R W Hoyle (ed), *The Estates of the English Crown, 1558–1640* (Cambridge, Cambridge University Press, 1992) 29.

¹⁰⁷ *Ibid* at 30–31.

Gaunt's use of the word 'bondslave' is also significant: for the Elizabethan jurist it implied the distinction between a commonwealth 'united by common accord' and a disparate 'host of men', made by Sir Thomas Smith in De Republica Anglorum (first published in 1583).[108] In chapter X of De Republica, entitled 'What is a Common Wealth, and the Partes Thereof', Smith argued that in ancient Rome 'the bondman hath no communion with his master'; crucially, 'there is no mutuall societie' because 'the bondman or slave which is bought for monie is so'.[109] Shakespeare's Richard recognises no such mutual society, no communion with his subjects and no common accord. He is the master; his subjects the bondslaves. He has betrayed the principle of amity upon which the Aristotelian, communitarian polis is founded.[110] In his prison cell he claims with some justification that 'love to Richard / Is a strange brooch in this all-hating world' (5.5.65–66)[111]; but before his deposition he spurned the true bonds of love or friendship upon which the foundations of the commonwealth are based, his narcissism blinding him to the needs of his country and its people. He listened only to the 'flatt'ring sounds' (2.1.17) and '[l]ascivious metres' (2.1.19) of his sycophantic courtiers and 'all too late comes Counsel to be heard' (2.1.27).

As king, Richard acted in his own interests, rather than in the best interests of the commonwealth. The comparisons made by Richard to the betrayal of Christ by Judas (3.2.132, 4.1.171) call for the audience's sympathy, but they call also for an examination of the meaning of treason. In The Third Part of the Institutes, Coke wrote that 'Treason is derived from trahir which is treacherously to betray. Trahue, Betrayed, and Trahison, per contractionen, Treason, is the betraying it selfe'.[112] Could a king betray his country, and be tried for treason as a consequence? At the time that Richard II was written, no English king had stood trial for treason. In 1327, proceedings in Parliament had been instigated against Edward II, charging him with High Treason against his subjects on several counts, including:

> That he regarded nothing but his own Profit, and enriching his evil Ministers: And lastly, that he had abandoned (or abdicated) the Kingdom, and was become incorrigible; for which Reasons they declared he had forfeited his Crown.[113]

---

[108] Sir Thomas Smith, De Republica Anglorum (1583), (ed) M Dewar (Cambridge, Cambridge University Press, 1982) 57; see ch 1, text to n 82, above.

[109] Smith, above n 108, De Republica, at 57; Hamilton argues that '[f]or Smith, the keystone of a commonwealth is not the king's royal prerogative, his power, or his supremacy, but the well-being of those he rules', D B Hamilton, 'The State of Law in Richard II' (1983) 34 Shakespeare Quarterly 5, 7.

[110] 'Friendship also seems to be the bond that holds communities together', Aristotle, The Nicomachean Ethics, (tr) J A K Thomson (London, Penguin, 2004) 201, Bk VIII.I.1155a20–25.

[111] There are echoes of Richard's contemplative lines on love and friendship, expressed in the prison cell, in Bk VIII of The Nicomachean Ethics, entitled 'The Kinds of Friendship': 'Indeed those who hold wealth and office and power are thought to stand in special need of friends; for what is the use of such prosperity to them if they are denied the opportunity for beneficence, which is most commonly and most commendably directed towards friends?' Aristotle, above n 110, 200, Bk VIII.I.1155a5–10.

[112] Sir Edward Coke, The Third Part of the Institutes of the Laws of England (London, W Lee & D Pakeman, 1644) 4.

[113] 'Proceedings in Parliament against King Edward II, for High Treason against his Subjects' in T Salmon (ed), A Collection of Proceedings and Trials against State Prisoners (London, J Wilcox, 1741) 44.

But Edward II did not stand trial: he formally resigned the crown at Kenilworth Castle in January 1327 and was murdered at Berkeley Castle in October 1327.[114] In *Richard II*, the deposition scene is a fictionalised version of Richard's abdication. King Richard II abdicated on 29 September 1399 in the Tower of London; it was reported to Parliament at Westminster the following day.[115] After his abdication Richard did not appear before Parliament: from the Tower he was dispatched to Leeds Castle in Kent, before being sent to his final place of imprisonment (and to his death) at Pontefract Castle in Yorkshire.[116] His appearance in Shakespeare's play at Westminster Hall is entirely imaginary and suggestive of a trial for treason in the 16th century. It was in this great theatre of law (which Richard II had had extensively rebuilt only two years before his deposition) that trials for the offence of High Treason were usually staged during the Tudor era.

The treason trial of this period provided a spectacular dramatisation of the act of betrayal. A striking feature of the numerous trials for High Treason during the reign of Elizabeth I is the personalisation of the relationship between Queen and subject; of the depicted love, demonstrated by the monarch for the defendant through the various acts of patronage; and of the inexplicable betrayal of that love by the defendant. The issue for the court was not primarily one of establishing the guilt or innocence of the defendant,[117] but rather of providing a stage upon which the narrative of betrayal might be enacted. The defendant on a charge of High Treason had no legal advisers in court; the constitutional principle of *audi alteram partem* ('hear the other side') was considered irrelevant and inappropriate, as Coke explains:

> And after the plea of not guilty, the prisoner can have no Councell learned assigned to him to answer the king's Councell learned, nor to defend him. And the reason thereof is, not because it concerneth matter of fact, for *Ex facto jus oritur*: but the true reasons of the law in this case are: First, that the testimonies and the proofs of the offence ought to be so clear and manifest, as there can be no defence of it.[118]

Coke was writing with the hindsight of having served as Attorney-General between 1594 and 1606, and of acting as leading counsel for the Crown in many of the trials for High Treason during this period, notably that of the Earl of Essex in February

---

[114] See I Mortimer, 'The Death of Edward II in Berkeley Castle' (2005) 120 *The English Historical Review* 1175; also, R M Haines, *King Edward II: Edward of Caernarfon, His Life, His Reign, and its Aftermath, 1284–1330* (Montreal, McGill-Queen's University Press, 2003).

[115] Saul, above n 2, at 420–22.

[116] *Ibid* at 424.

[117] A guilty verdict was not necessarily predetermined; Coke is at pains to point out that the trial procedure was fair, and that no argument might be offered by counsel for the Crown unless the defendant was present: '[A]s it was resolved by all the Justices of England in the reign of king H. 8. in the case of the Lord Dacres of the North . . . and upon so just a resolution the case succeeded well, for the Peers found the Lord Dacres not guilty', Coke, above n 112, at 30.

[118] *Ibid* at 29; regarding the rule against counsel, Baker argues that Coke 'confused the forensic presentation of the case with what we would regard as evidence', J H Baker, 'Criminal Courts and Procedure, 1550–1800' in J H Baker, *The Legal Profession and the Common Law: Historical Essays* (London, Hambledon, 1986) 287; on the law of treason in the 16th century, see J Bellamy, *The Tudor Law of Treason: An Introduction* (London, Routledge & Kegan Paul, 1979).

1600. The trial of Essex is memorable for the emotive rhetoric employed by the actors—counsel, witnesses and defendant—and for the conspicuous emphasis placed upon love and loyalty. Coke argued that Essex and his conspirators

> not only carried [High Treason] in their Hearts, but, for a continual Remembrance, kept in a black Purse, which my Lord of Essex wore on his Breast next to his Skin.[119]

The image of a memory being inscribed on the surface of the body is familiar,[120] but here it is inverted—the memory is false, disloyal: the image is that of a lie. In his address to the court, Serjeant Yelverton alluded to the love of the Queen for her subjects, emphasising the personal betrayal by Essex:

> I much wonder that his Heart could forget all the Princely Advancements given him by her Majesty, and be so suddenly beflinted . . .[121]

The emotive language of betrayal was most apparent in the evidence of Sir Robert Cecil, the Secretary of State, who declared to Essex that

> I have loved your Person . . . but you have a Sheep's Garment in show . . . I stand for Loyalty, which I never lost; you stand for Treachery, wherewith your Heart is possess'd . . .[122]

It is perhaps not surprising, given the personalisation in the Elizabethan treason trial of relations between the Queen and her subjects, that in 1597 the Middle Temple should have presented a masque entitled *Le Prince d'Amour or The Prince of Love* as part of its Christmas revels, in which a trial for High Treason is the dramatic climax. As with the Gray's Inn revels of 1594, a Prince was elected to govern the Inn for the duration of the revels: at the Middle Temple he was described as 'this one most worthy Title of all, The Prince *d'Amours*'.[123] The 1597 revels bear a stylistic resemblance to Shakespeare's *Richard II*; most obviously they share the chivalric rhetoric of medieval law. The action of both starts with a challenge to trial by battle, in which the themes of love and treason are immediately emphasised.[124] In *The Prince of Love*, one of the Prince's champions throws down a gauntlet and invites challengers to the lawful authority of the Prince to engage in trial by combat. A 'strange Knight' takes up the challenge, identifying the Prince as a usurper to the throne of Elizabeth I. While his description of England as '[h]er Kingdom seated in the midst of the Waters'[125] lacks the alliterative splendour of '[t]his

---

[119] 'The Trial of Robert Earl of Essex, and Henry Earl of Southampton, before the Lords, at Westminster, for High-Treason, the 19th of February 1600. 43 Eliz.', *A Complete Collection of State-Trials, and Proceedings for High Treason*, 11 vols (London, C Bathurst, J & F Rivington, 1776–81) 1: 199; after listening to Coke's opening address, Essex asked the court: 'Will your Lordships give us our turns to speak, for he playeth the Orator', *ibid*. His request was refused.

[120] See ch 2, text to n 126, above.

[121] 'The Trial of Robert Earl of Essex', above n 119, at 198.

[122] *Ibid* at 205.

[123] All references to *The Prince of Love* are from the 1660 edition (published by William Leake of Fleet Street), reproduced in A Arlidge, *Shakespeare and the Prince of Love: The Feast of Misrule in the Middle Temple* (London, Giles de la Mere, 2000) Appendix II, 129.

[124] On the procedure of trial by combat in medieval England, see M J Russell, 'Trial by Battle in the Court of Chivalry' (2008) 29 *The Journal of Legal History* 335.

[125] *Prince of Love*, above n 123, at 131.

Figure 1 Richard II presented to the Virgin and Child by his Patron Saint John the Baptist and Saints Edward and Edmund. 'The Wilton Diptych' (c 1395–99). Unknown artist. © The National Gallery, London.

Figure 2 Infra-red detail of orb (right interior panel). 'The Wilton Diptych' (*c* 1395–99). Unknown artist. © The National Gallery, London.

Figure 3 Royal arms of England and France Ancient, impaled with the arms of Edward the Confessor, surmounted by helmet with cap of maintenance and lion passant guardant (left exterior panel); white hart lying among branches of rosemary (right exterior panel). 'The Wilton Diptych' (*c* 1395–99). Unknown artist. © The National Gallery, London.

Figure 4 'The Coronation portrait' of Elizabeth I (*c* 1600, copy of lost original, *c* 1559). Unknown artist. © National Portrait Gallery, London.

Figure 5 Portrait of Richard II, wood panel painting (*c* 1395). Unknown artist. © Dean and Chapter of Westminster.

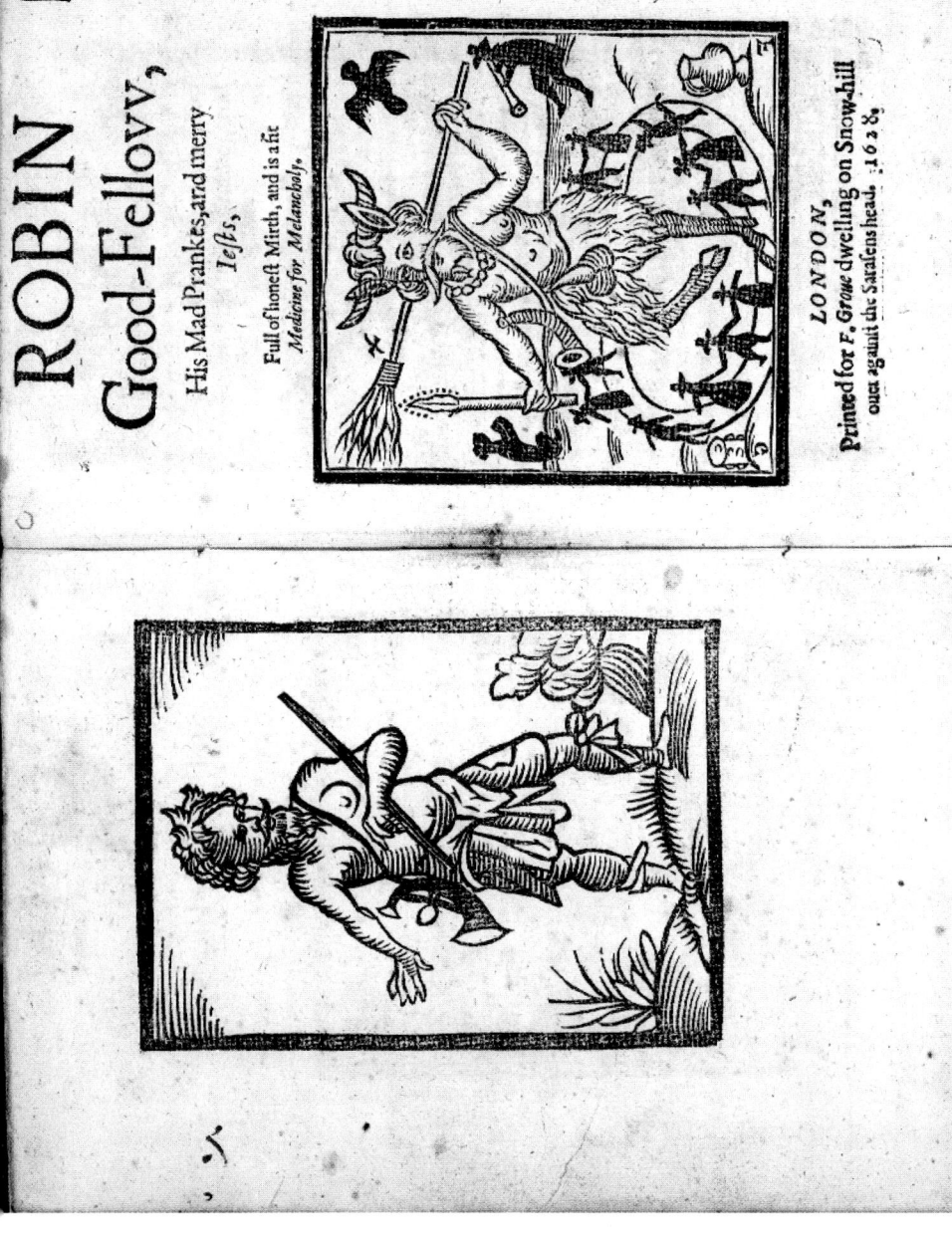

Figure 6 Anonymous, *Robin Good-Fellow, His Mad Prankes, and merry Iests, Full of honest Mirth, and is a fit Medicine for Melancholy* (London, F Grove, 1628) Title-page. This item is reproduced by permission of the Huntington Library, San Marino, California.

Figure 7 Monument to Sir John Fortescue (c 1397–1479), the parish church of St Eadburgha, Ebrington, Gloucestershire.

precious stone set in the silver sea' (2.1.46), there is no mistaking the debt owed by the author(s) to *Richard II*. *The Prince of Love* imitates Shakespeare's play to the extent even of replicating Richard's dramatic intervention immediately prior to the trial by combat (1.3.119–22):

> The Prince seeing both the Champions resolute, and ready to encounter each other, gave order to stay them . . . And in the mean space advised with his counsel . . .[126]

The masque concludes with a trial for 'most heinous Treasons against our Prince, and the mighty name and Power of Love', while loyal subjects of the Prince are described as '[s]oldiers under the sweet Banner of Love'.[127]

The cult of Elizabeth was driven by the persona of kingship as reflected in the female mask: Astraea, Venus, Gloriana and Diana figure largely in the literary and pictorial iconography of the Queen.[128] The subject of law was drawn into an imaginary relationship with the monarch: his loyalty, devotion and emotional attachment were captured by the image of the Virgin Goddess and his imagined love for her.[129] But the cult of Elizabeth depended for its efficacy on something more than belief in the transformative power of her iconic signs. It depended on the profession of love, and the willing subjugation of the individual to his divine (and therefore unattainable) inamorata. In chapter one, I noted the historical characterisation of law as a feminine body: 'the queen of all things divine and human' and 'the Lady Common Law'.[130] The iconography that was created around Elizabeth I depicts her not only as *Imago Dei* but also as the Goddess of Justice, tempering the rigour of law with the virtue of natural equity, which (according to Selden) may be 'adapted, applied, and fitted' as appropriate to particular circumstances. See, for example, the depiction of youthful femininity and beauty in 'The Coronation portrait' of Elizabeth I[131] (see **Figures 4 and 5**). Selden refers to the Ovidian Golden Age, when subjects were governed not by positive law but 'by the guidance of vertue, and of those Laws which the Platonicks call the

---

[126] *Ibid* at 134.

[127] *Ibid* at 163, 152.

[128] See S Doran, 'Virginity, Divinity and Power: The Portraits of Elizabeth I' in T F Freeman and S Doran (eds), *The Myth of Elizabeth* (London, Palgrave Macmillan, 2003) 171; also, R Strong, *Gloriana: The Portraits of Queen Elizabeth I* (London, Pimlico, 2003). Christopher Haigh argues that 'the public Elizabeth was not a real person, but a cluster of images', C Haigh (ed), *The Reign of Elizabeth I* (Basingstoke, Macmillan, 1984) Introduction, 5. Haigh quotes from Thomas Dekker's play *Old Fortunatus* (1599), in which an old man is travelling to the temple of Eliza: 'Even to her temple are my feeble limbs travelling. Some call her Pandora, some Gloriana, some Cynthia, some Belphoebe, some Astraea, all by several names to express several loves', in Haigh (ed), above, Introduction, 5–6.

[129] On 'the manipulation of subjective attachment through the play of images' and 'the capture of the subject by the institution', see P Legendre, *Law and the Unconscious: a Legendre Reader*, (tr) P Goodrich, with A Pottage and A Schütz, (ed) P Goodrich (Basingstoke, Macmillan, 1997) 258.

[130] Justinian, *The Digest*, 1.3.2; J Selden, *Titles of Honor* (London, Iohn Helme, 1614) a3v; see ch 1, nn 59 and 60, above.

[131] The portrait, by an unknown artist, was painted *c* 1600 and is probably a copy of the lost original, painted *c* 1559. 'The Coronation portrait' of the Queen is notably similar to the painting of Richard II in Westminster Abbey, the earliest known portrait of an English monarch (*c* 1395).

Laws of Second Venus'.[132] The law of love refers us back to the Aristotelian principle that amity or friendship is the basis of the *polis*, more important even than justice itself.[133] To commit treason, then, is to reject the law of love: the ultimate betrayal not only of the Queen, but of the community or *corpus mysticum* of which she is the head and her subjects the members.

In the complex metaphysical language of the king's two bodies (as expounded by Coke in *Postnati. Calvin's Case*), '[i]n all indictments of treason, when any do intend or compass *mortem & destructionem domini Regis* (which must needs be understood of his natural body, for his politic body is immortal, and not subject to death) . . . the ligeance is due to the natural body'.[134] Coke's definition of treason is logical but, if applied to the alleged betrayal of England by Shakespeare's Richard II and later to the actual trial of Charles I, inadequate: the charge against Charles I was predicated upon allegiance owed by the body natural of the king to the body politic. More comprehensible is Yelverton's appeal to the court in the trial of Essex:

> That if any Man do but intend the Death of the King, it is Death by the Law: for he is the Head of the Commonwealth, and all his Subjects as Members ought to obey and stand by him.[135]

Yelverton alludes to the body politic as a *corpus mysticum* in which (as Foucault noted of all post-medieval western legal systems) 'the representation of power has remained under the spell of monarchy'.[136] In the case of Elizabeth I, the representation of power was predicated also upon a complex image of female divinity, whose emotional appeal to the subject of law was more personal, more human and more profound than intellectual adherence to the theory of the king's two bodies.

IV. Theatre, Mimesis and the Counterfeiting of Monarchy

The social range of the audiences at the Elizabethan playhouses was extensive. As the playwright Thomas Dekker observed, the theatres were

> so free in entertainment, allowing a stoole as well to the Farmers sonne as to your Templer: that your Stinkard has the selfe same libertie to be there in his Tobacco-Fumes, which your sweet Courtier hath: and that your Car-man and Tinker claime as strong a

---

[132] J Selden, *The Reverse or Back-Face of the English Janus*, (tr) R Westcot (London, Thomas Basset & Richard Chiswell, 1682) 11; on Selden and the 'laws of Venus', see P Goodrich, *The Laws of Love: a Brief Historical and Practical Manual* (Basingstoke, Palgrave Macmillan, 2006) 6–12.
[133] Aristotle, above nn 110 and 111, Bk VIII.
[134] Coke, *Postnati. Calvin's Case*, 7 Reports 4: 10b.
[135] 'Trial of Robert Earl of Essex', above n 119, at 198.
[136] 'In political thought and analysis we still have not cut off the head of the king', M Foucault, *The History of Sexuality: An Introduction*, (tr) R Hurley, 3 vols (New York, Random House, 1978) 1: 88–89.

voice in their suffrage, and sit to give iudgement on the plaies life and death, as well as the prowdest Momus among the tribe of Critick.[137]

Of greater concern to the monarchy than the dramatisation in *Richard II* of the king's deposition would have been the threat to hierarchic order posed by the imitation of kingship and its presentation to an audience as socially diverse as the one described by Dekker. The authority of the king is threatened by the unrestricted scrutiny of him by the audience, especially where the king in question describes himself as '[b]eing now a subject' (4.1.307). In May 1559, Elizabeth I issued a Proclamation, ordering the mayors of all cities and towns and the Lieutenants of the shires to prohibit the performance of plays in which

> either matters of religion or of the governaunce of the estate of the common weale shalbe handled or treated, beyng no meete matters to be wrytten or treated upon, but by menne of auchoritie . . .[138]

In London, the City Fathers were assiduous in their organised opposition to the performance of plays, in particular to those of an irreligious or seditious nature. For example, in December 1574 an Act of Common Council decreed that

> no playe, Commodye, Tragidye, enterlude, nor publycke shewe shalbe openlye played or shewed within the liberties of the Cittie, whearin shalbe uttered anie wourdes, examples, or doynges of anie unchastitie, sedicion, nor such lyke unfytt and uncomelye matter, upon paine of Imprisonment . . .[139]

The municipal authorities were successful in driving the companies of players from the City of London, barring them access to the improvised stages which the yards of city hostelries had hitherto provided. In 1567, a purpose-built (albeit primitive) amphitheatre was built at the Red Lion in Stepney, and the era of the playhouse was born.[140]

Of great importance to the survival of the playhouses and the subject matter of the plays which were performed there was the fact that they were built in areas outside the jurisdictions of the City of London, Middlesex and Surrey. The Theatre and The Curtain were north of the Thames in the suburb of Shoreditch; The Rose, The Swan and The Globe were south of the Thames on Bank-side (situated in the Liberty of the Clink). In juridical terms, the geographical situation of the playhouses in the Liberties—outside the City's boundaries—meant that they inhabited

---

[137] T Dekker, *The Guls Horne-booke* (London, RS, 1609) 28; on the social range of audiences for Shakespeare's plays during this period, see A Gurr, *The Shakespearean Stage, 1574–1642* (Cambridge, Cambridge University Press, 1992) 212–22; also, A Gurr, *Playgoing in Shakespeare's London* (Cambridge, Cambridge University Press, 1987).

[138] Chambers, above n 21, 4: 263.

[139] *Ibid* at 274.

[140] On the early history of the London playhouses, see Gurr, *The Shakespearean Stage*, above n 137, at 115–36; more specifically, see J S Loengard, 'An Elizabethan Lawsuit: John Brayne, his Carpenter, and the Building of the Red Lion Theatre' (1983) 34 *Shakespeare Quarterly* 298; also, H Berry, 'The First Public Playhouses, Especially the Red Lion' (1989) 40 *Shakespeare Quarterly* 133.

a liminal space, on the threshold of established civic jurisdictions.[141] While not exempted from the law, they were not subjected either to the full force of municipal jurisprudence.

With the establishment of the permanent playhouses, a more complicated relationship was established between the royal court and the playing companies, which were patronised by the nobility (for example, Essex's Men, Leicester's Men, Pembroke's Men and Sussex's Men). Government regulation of the plays and playhouses was the responsibility of the Lord Chamberlain, but the quotidian managerial role was enacted by the Master of the Revels, to whom was entrusted not only the censorship and licensing of plays and playhouses, but also the selection of dramatic entertainments which were deemed suitable for performance at the royal court during the long Christmas season. To this extent, the relationship between the playing companies and government was one of mutual self-interest, which may account partly for the absence of prosecutions merely on the basis of submitting a manuscript to the Master of the Revels.[142] In February 1598 the Privy Council informed the Master of the Revels and the Justices of Middlesex and Surrey that licences to perform in public had been granted to the Lord Chamberlain's Men and the Admiral's Men (creating a duopoly of playing companies in the playhouses),

> to use and practise stage playes, whereby they might be better enhabled and prepared to shew such plaies before her Majestie as they shalbe required at tymes meete and accustomed, to which ende they have bin cheefelie licensed and tolerated as aforesaid . . .[143]

Despite the Queen giving plays her official patronage in 1583 with the establishment of the Queen's Men, the City authorities remained vocal in their opposition to all dramatic entertainments. The following extract from a letter written in September 1595 by the Lord Mayor to the Privy Council exemplifies the institutional hostility which was directed towards the performance of plays:

> [N]either in policye nor in religion they [stage plays] ar to be permitted in a Christian Common wealthe, specially being of that frame & making as usually they are, & conteyning nothing but profane fables, Lascivious matters, cozonning devizes, & other unseemly & scurrilous behaviours, which ar so sett forthe, as that they move wholy to imitacion & not to the avoyding of those vyces which they represent, which wee verely think to bee the cheef cause, aswell of many other disorders & lewd demeanors which appeer of late in young people of all degrees, as of the late stirr & mutinous attempt of those fiew apprentices and other servantes, who wee doubt not drew their infection from these & like places.[144]

---

[141] Mullaney refers to the playhouses' 'marginal yet commanding situation on the threshold of early modern London', S Mullaney, 'Civic Rites, City Sites: The Place of the Stage' in D S Kastan and P Stallybrass (eds), *Staging the Renaissance: Reinterpretations of Elizabethan and Jacobean Drama* (London, Routledge, 1991) 18.

[142] R Dutton, *Mastering the Revels: The Regulation and Censorship of English Renaissance Drama* (Iowa, University of Iowa Press, 1991) 25.

[143] Chambers, above n 21, 4: 325.

[144] *Ibid* at 318; on the apprentices' riots in London during the 1590s, see ch 2, text to nn 100–102, above.

Theatre, Mimesis and the Counterfeiting of Monarchy

The references in the above passage to imitation and representation are significant, as they suggest that mimesis was perceived by the Lord Mayor as both a direct threat to the maintenance of civil order and the obvious cause of insurrection and social unrest. If imitation *per se* was a subversive act, the imitation of a king might be interpreted as an incitement to rebellion. Indeed the representation of the death of a king might even be described as an imaginative act of treason, as 'when anyone attempts to compass or imagine the death of our lord the king'.[145]

It has long been noted that rulers in the early modern period expressed their power by theatrical means.[146] The remark of Elizabeth I that '[w]e princes are set as it were upon stages in the sight and view of all the world'[147] (made in 1586 to a deputation of the Lords and Commons) might have served as a maxim for the mimetic quality of the Shakespearean history play. As Stephen Greenblatt observed, Elizabethan royal power was 'manifested to its subjects as in a theatre'; but he included the important proviso that although the monarchy was dependent for its successful reception on its 'privileged visibility', it was crucial also that the Queen's subjects be kept 'at a certain respectful distance from it'.[148] The problem with *Richard II*, as far as the image of the Elizabethan monarchy was concerned, is that this most theatrically self-conscious of all Shakespeare's history plays presents the king as an actor, playing a role. Richard is the actor-king, manipulating the emotions of his subjects, both within the artificial framework of the play and beyond, in the audience. Even when imprisoned in Pomfret Castle, deprived of the public forum to which as king he was accustomed, he remains acutely aware of his dramatic role: 'Thus play I in one person many people, / And none contented'. (5.5.31–32) Far from being kept at a respectful distance, the audience is invited to watch in close-up the humiliating disintegration of monarchic power and to hear the public confession of Richard that he shares their lowly status: 'Subjected thus, / How can you say to me I am a king?' (3.2.176–77)

Richard self-dramatises his predicament, deliberately submitting himself to the scrutiny and criticism of his subjects. During the deposition scene he calls for a mirror, to 'see the very book indeed / Where all my sins are writ' (4.1.274–75). The continual recurrence in *Richard II* of the word 'subject' reminds us that in the history play the king is the principal focus not only of the author's imagination, but of the audience's judgement as well. Theatre demystifies power by the very act of exposing the means through which power is manifested, and inviting the audience to comment on the process. The king who proclaims himself '[t]he deputy elected by the Lord' (3.2.57) admits only three scenes later that he is 'no man's lord! I have no name, no title' (4.1.255). *Richard II* raises the subversive possibility that the

---

[145] The Statute of Treasons of 1352 (*25 Ed.3. cap. 2*).
[146] See R Strong, *Art and Power: Renaissance Festivals 1450–1650* (Berkeley, University of California Press, 1984); also, S Orgel, *The Illusion of Power* (Berkeley, University of California Press, 1975).
[147] Quoted in J E Neale, *Elizabeth I and her Parliaments, 1584–1601*, 2 vols (London, Cape, 1965) 2: 119.
[148] S Greenblatt, 'Invisible bullets: Renaissance authority and its subversion, *Henry IV* and *Henry V*' in J Dollimore and A Sinfield (eds), *Political Shakespeare: Essays in Cultural Materialism* (Manchester, Manchester University Press, 1994) 44.

Reflections on the Art of Kingship: Richard II and the Subject of Law

king is merely an actor and that kingship is a fragile persona, concealing a vacuous self. It is a small step from there to the anti-monarchic sentiment that the Crown is the embodiment of falsehood: a counterfeit, idol, or lie.[149] Writing in 1579, Stephen Gosson employed the reformist invective of the period to rail against the inherent falsehood of theatre:

> [P]ul off the visard that poets maske in, you shall disclose their reproch, bewray their vanitie, loth their wantonnesse, lament their follie, and perceive their sharpe sayings to be placed as Pearles in Dunghils, fresh pictures on rotten walles, chaste Matrons apparel on common Curtesans.[150]

Representation of the monarchy involved a risk to the Crown of damnation by association; anti-theatrical iconoclasts such as Gosson might accuse the Crown of dissimulation, much as they levelled the charge at the theatre itself. The representation of monarchy in the theatre was an effective means of projecting an image of spiritual unity and nationhood, of the king as *parens patriae*. An audience is always a necessary condition of monarchic authority,[151] but if the subject of the audience's attention is scrutinised too closely there is a risk of over-exposure: that the 'fresh pictures' will be seen to cover 'rotten walles'. The danger posed to the stability of the Crown by the staging of *Richard II* was not that the play depicted the deposition of a king but that it depicted a king at all, and an actor-king at that. The greatest danger of all was that *Richard II* portrayed the vulnerable and flawed human body beneath the tarnished raiment of kingship.

---

[149] In *1 Henry IV*, counterfeit King Henrys appear on the battlefield at Shrewsbury; upon eventually encountering the real King Henry, the rebel Douglas exclaims 'Another king! They grow like Hydra's heads' (5.4.24), and confides to the King that 'I fear thou art another counterfeit' (5.4.34). Kastan argues in connection with Shakespeare's history plays that theatre's 'counterfeit of royalty raises the possibility that royalty is a counterfeit', Kastan, above n 20, at 464; see also, M Breitenberg, ' ". . . the hole matter opened": Iconic Representation and Interpretation in "The Quenes Majesties Passage" ' (1986) 28 *Criticism* 1.

[150] S Gosson, *The Schoole of Abuse Conteining A Pleasaunt Invective Against Poets, Pipers, Plaiers, Iesters, and Such Like Caterpillers of a Comonwealth* (London, Thomas Woodcocke, 1579) A2.v; in a similar diatribe against theatre, published in 1583, Philip Stubbes argued that 'if you will learne to murther, slaie, kill, picke, steale, robbe and roue: If you will learn to rebel against Princes, to comit treasons . . . you need to go to no other schoole, for all these good Examples, may you see painted before your eyes in enterludes & playes', P Stubbes, 'Of Stage-playes and Enterluds, with their wickednes' in *The Anatomie of Abuses* (London, Richard Iones, 1583) L.9.v. On Gosson and Stubbes, see L Levine, 'Men in Women's Clothing: Anti-theatricality and Effeminization from 1579 to 1642' (1986) 28 *Criticism* 121.

[151] With reference to *Richard II*, Ward notes that 'the strength of a constitution, ultimately, rests with the political authority granted by its audience', I Ward, *Shakespeare and the Legal Imagination* (London, Butterworths, 1999) 39.

4

The Poetic Imagination, Antique Fables and the Dream of Law

I. Festival, Subversion and Misrule

AT THE INNER TEMPLE in 1561 a 'magnificent Christmas' was celebrated, at which Lord Robert Dudley was honoured for his 'earnest intercession to the Queen'[1] concerning a dispute between the Inner Temple and the Middle Temple over the ownership of Lyon's Inn, one of the Inns of Chancery. Dudley's intervention was successful in ensuring that Lyon's Inn maintained its institutional links with the Inner Temple.[2] Dudley played an active part in the Christmas revels that year, enacting the role of Palaphilos (High-Constable of Pallas Athene and defender of her temple) and presiding over the period of feasting and entertainment.[3] That the Inner Temple revels of 1561 were exceptional can be inferred from Sir William Dugdale's record of the events. The presence of so eminent a guest as Dudley was enough in itself to ensure that the organisers created an extraordinary event, spectacular even by the extravagant standards of Christmas revels at the Inns of Court. In other respects the 1561 revels conformed to the style and content which had prevailed since these annual seasonal rites were first established in the calendar of the Inn. Most notable in this respect is the peculiar interest shown in the theatrical manifestation of order, the inversion of hierarchy and the temporary subversion of rules. At the start of the feasting, on Christmas Eve, Lord Robert Dudley (as Palaphilos) was attended by the following 'officers', played by members of the Inn: Lord Chancellor, Lord Treasurer, Lord Privy Seal, Chief Justice of the King's Bench, Chief Justice of the

---

[1] Sir William Dugdale, *Origines Juridiciales or Historical Memorials of the English Laws* (London, F & T Warren, 1666) 150.
[2] On the Elizabethan Inns of Chancery, see ch 5, n 62, below.
[3] For a personal account of a visit to the Inner Temple revels of 1561, see G Legh, *The Accedens of Armory* (London, Richard Tottill, 1562) 202.*v*–32.*v*; Dugdale includes extracts from *The Accedens* in his description of the 1561 revels, above n 1, at 151. On Legh and the symbolic iconography of the Inns of Court, see P Goodrich, 'Eating Law: Commons, Common Land, Common Law' (1991) 12 *The Journal of Legal History* 246; also, P Raffield, *Images and Cultures of Law in Early Modern England: Justice and Political Power, 1558–1660* (Cambridge, Cambridge University Press, 2004) 99–106; P Raffield, 'The Inner Temple Revels and the Elizabethan Rhetoric of Signs: Legal Iconography at the Early Modern Inns of Court' in J Archer, E Goldring and S Knight (eds), *The Cultural and Intellectual World of the Early Modern Inns of Court* (Manchester, Manchester University Press, Forthcoming).

The Poetic Imagination, Antique Fables and the Dream of Law

Common Pleas, Chief Baron of the Exchequer, Steward of the Household, Marshall of the Household, Chief Butler, Master of the Game (played by the future Lord Chancellor, Christopher Hatton), Lieutenant of the Tower, Carver, Ranger of the Forests, Sewer, '[a]nd there were fourscore of the Guard; besides divers others not here named'.[4] The pageantry, processions, music, dancing and dramatic entertainments were choreographed by four Masters of the Revels. Gerard Legh recorded the feasting and spectacle thus:

> [T]ender meates, sweet frutes and deinte delicates, confeccioned with curious Cookerie: as it semed wonder, a world to serve the provision. And at every course, The Trompetts blew the coragious blast of deadly warre with noise of drome and fyffe, with ye swete Armony of violetts [violins], shakbutts, recorders, & cornetts, with other instruments of musicke, as it semed Apollos harpe had tewned ther strock [stroke].[5]

The ordered dreamland of Apollo was soon to be threatened (albeit temporarily) by the chaotic excess of Dionysus.[6] I shall return to the Inner Temple revels of 1561 later in this chapter, when I consider the Arcadian representation of the English landscape and its people, which itself constitutes a literary sub-genre of utopian fantasy. For now, I wish only to note the late appearance in the revels' *dramatis personae* of a mysterious, nocturnal character: the Lord of Misrule. Dugdale is punctilious in recording the names of all those members of the Inns who participated in the revels, and the roles which they acted: Mr Onslow played the Lord Chancellor; Christopher Hatton (as noted above), the Master of the Game; and Messrs Blaston, Yorke, Penston and Jervise, the four Masters of the Revels.[7] The Lord of Misrule is not mentioned in the cast list, neither is the actor who played him. After pages of narrative in which Dugdale records every item of food, every piece of music, and every elaborate procession and theatrical device, he reports that, following supper on St Stephen's Day, 'the Lord of Misrule addresseth himself to the Banquet', after which the night ended in 'Minstralsye, mirth, and dancing'. His appearance only during the hours of darkness is noteworthy. The following day, 27 December, was the feast of St John the Evangelist:

> About seaven of the Clock in the Morning, the Lord of Misrule is abroad . . . After Breakfast ended, his Lordships power is in suspence, until his personal presence at night, and then his power is most potent.[8]

---

[4] Dugdale, above n 1, at 150–51.
[5] Legh, above n 3, at 213.*r*–213.*v*.
[6] On Nietzsche's distinction in *The Birth of Tragedy* between the 'Apollonian world of pictures' and 'the mystical cheer of Dionysus', see ch 2, text to n 6, above; also, P Raffield, 'The Separate Art Worlds of Dreamland and Drunkenness: Elizabethan Revels at the Inns of Court' (1997) 8 *Law and Critique* 163.
[7] Dugdale, above n 1, at 150.
[8] *Ibid* at 156. Hutton discusses the Inner Temple revels of 1561 with reference to the Tudor tradition of Christmas Lords of Misrule in R Hutton, *The Rise and Fall of Merry England: the Ritual Year, 1400–1700* (Oxford, Oxford University Press, 1994) 114–15.

Festival, Subversion and Misrule

He resembles a spirit rather than a person: in the parlance of medieval and early modern England, he is a Hobgoblin, a Robin Goodfellow, a Puck.[9] Dugdale (consciously or otherwise) incorporates a technique which is itself a major theme of Shakespeare's *A Midsummer Night's Dream*: the blurred distinction between reality and illusion. Is the Lord of Misrule a character in the revels, played by a student member of the Inn, or is he a restless spirit of the night, intent upon subversion of the strict rules governing the conduct of honourable members of the Inner Temple? This is not to embark on a prolonged journey of metaphysical conjecture, still less on a Lacanian discourse about the improbability of existence.[10] Rather, it is to emphasise the shared imaginary sources of law and theatre, and to acknowledge the centrality of the poetic imagination to the successful reception by its audience of either artistic enterprise.

In earlier chapters I have concentrated on discrete, substantive areas of law that developed partly as a response to social, political and economic conditions in the second half of the 16th century. The emergence in embryonic form of a body of constitutional law, which attempted to protect the rights of the citizen from the tyranny of imperial rule, was examined by reference to Shakespeare's first Roman tragedy (and his first revenge tragedy), *Titus Andronicus*. The tightly plotted and classically constructed urban comedy of *The Comedy of Errors*, whose characters are impelled by the commercial society that they inhabit, and whose action is driven by the threat of juridical proceedings for unpaid debt, provided the framework for an exploration of contract law and its unprecedented significance in the governance of societal relations in late-Elizabethan England. The image of the king's two bodies in *Richard II* enabled analysis of the lawful limits to 16th-century monarchic governance, refracted through the lens of late-medieval kingship. The play's peculiar emphasis on ownership, inheritance and unlawful dispossession of land also facilitated discussion of English property law and its imaginative application by the Elizabethan judiciary in order to establish the boundaries of the Royal Prerogative. In this chapter I explore something altogether less formal, more amorphous, but no less recognisable for its distinct lack either of shape or

---

[9] The terms were generic, referring to a class of terrestrial spirits. Robert Burton categorised them thus: 'Terrestrial devils, are those *Lares, Genii, Faunes, Satyrs*, Wood-nymphs, Foliots, Fairies, *Robin Goodfellows, Trulli*, &c which as they are most conversant with men, so they do them most harme . . . A bigger kinde there is of them, called with us *Hobgoblins,* & *Robin Goodfellows*, that would in those superstitious times, grinde corn for mess of milk, cut wood, or do any maner of drudgery work', R Burton, *The anatomy of melancholy what it is*, 6th edn (Oxford, Henry Cripps, 1651) 47, 48. On spirits and fairies, see K M Briggs, *A Dictionary of Fairies: Hobgoblins, Brownies, Bogies, and Other Supernatural Creatures* (London, Lane, 1976); K M Briggs, *The Fairies in English Tradition and Literature* (Chicago, University of Chicago Press, 1967). The English 'Puck' derives from several sources, including old Norse 'puki'; Frisian 'puk'; Welsh 'pwca'; and Irish 'púca'. See K M Briggs, *The Anatomy of Puck: An Examination of Fairy Beliefs Among Shakespeare's Contemporaries* (New York, Arno, 1977); also, W Schleiner, 'Imaginative Sources for Shakespeare's Puck' (1985) 36 *Shakespeare Quarterly* 65.

[10] 'By definition, there is something so improbable about all existence that one is in effect perpetually questioning oneself about its reality': J Lacan, 'Ego in Freud's Theory and in the Technique of Psychoanalysis' in *The Seminar of Jacques Lacan. Book 2*, (tr) S Tomaselli, (ed) J-A Miller (Cambridge, Cambridge University Press, 1988) 226.

The Poetic Imagination, Antique Fables and the Dream of Law

juridical features: the unwritten law of England, *lex terrae* or *leges non scriptae*. In short, I am talking of custom, by reference to which English jurists of the early modern period defined and distinguished the common law.[11]

It is perhaps more accurate in this context to talk of plural 'customs' rather than singular 'custom', as the purpose of the chapter is to investigate, with specific reference to *A Midsummer Night's Dream*, the antique practices and rituals of English folklore, and the role of these customs in articulating an aspiration to spiritual unity and political community. At a political level the seasonal mimetic rites of ancient folklore or carnival may be interpreted as an expression of discontent, a staged (and therefore artificial) rebellion against prevailing models of governance.[12] As with Dugdale's description of the Lord of Misrule at the Inner Temple, so the distinction in carnival between reality and illusion is blurred, the participants inhabiting a liminal zone between life and art. Mikhail Bakhtin notes the lack of differentiation between actor and audience; unlike the theatre,

> carnival does not know footlights ... [c]arnival is not a spectacle seen by the people; they live in it, and everyone participates because its very idea embraces all the people.[13]

There is disagreement among scholars regarding the level of subversive intent in these seasonal festivities. Theories of festival or carnival tend to be characterised by their diametric opposition to each other; accordingly, festive rites either 'affirm' or 'subvert' the extant hierarchical order. On the one side is the conciliatory theory of C L Barber, who interprets festive rites as 'a temporary license, a "misrule" that implied rule'.[14] On the other side is Bakhtin, for whom the laughter provoked and engendered by these rites is darker and more ambivalent; in intent, it is destructive of authority and assertive of popular renewal. This laughter is 'gay, triumphant, and at the same time mocking, deriding. It asserts and denies, it buries and revives'.[15]

---

[11] For example, 'England has nevertheless been constantly governed by the same Customs, as it is at present', Sir John Fortescue, *De Laudibus Legum Angliae*, (ed) J Selden (London, R Gosling, 1737) 30; '[t]he third ground of the law of England standeth upon divers general *customs* of old time used through all the realm', C St German, *Dialogues Between a Doctor of Divinity and a Student in the Laws of England*, (ed) W Muchall (Cincinnati, Ohio, Robert Clarke, 1874) 21; '... many Grounds and Rules of the Lawes of this Realme are derived from Common use, Custome, and Conversation amonge men, Collected out of the general Disposition, nature and condition of human kinde', Sir John Doddridge, *The Lawyers Light: or, A due direction for the study of the law* (London, Benjamin Fisher, 1629) 13. On the selective interpretation by Sir Edward Coke of custom, and judicial reason as 'the distilled knowledge of many generations of men', see J G A Pocock, *The Ancient Constitution and the Feudal Law: A Study of English Historical Thought in the Seventeenth Century* (Cambridge, Cambridge University Press, 1987) 35.

[12] See T Pettitt, ''Here comes I, Jack Straw': English Folk Drama and Social Revolt' (1984) 95 *Folklore* 3; also, M D Bristol, *Carnival and Theater: Plebeian Culture and the Structure of Authority in Renaissance England* (New York, Methuen, 1985).

[13] M Bakhtin, *Rabelais and His World*, (tr) H Iswolsky, (Bloomington, Indiana University Press, 1984) 7.

[14] C L Barber, *Shakespeare's Festive Comedy* (Cleveland, Ohio, World Publishing, 1968) 10.

[15] Bakhtin, above n 13, at 11–12. Patterson contrasts Barber's message 'that both the archaic festivals and their Elizabethan echoes functioned to reaffirm, through reconciliatory symbolic action, the hierarchical structure of society' with Bakhtin's thesis 'that popular festival forms and inversion rituals were actually subversive in intent and function all along', A Patterson, *Shakespeare and the Popular*

Festival, Subversion and Misrule

For most citizens, resort to the institutional formality of juridical procedure for the resolution of disputes and complaints was not an option. It is from this huge class of subjects that the actors in the seasonal festive rites were mainly drawn.[16] As E P Thompson noted in *Customs in Common*, the law reports

> are not packed with cases in which poor commoners challenged their lords or great landowners in the highest courts of the land.

Thompson includes the addendum that recourse to the Courts of King's Bench and Common Pleas 'was not the cottagers' nor the labourers' thing'.[17] For citizens such as these, justice was a local affair; and justice included not only the settlement of private altercations and the punishment of wrongdoing, but also (in the communitarian, Aristotelian sense of justice) the festive performance of communal rites in which grievances were aired through the medium of subversive comic drama. The Lord of Misrule played as prominent a role in the summer rites of rural England as he did in the exclusive Christmas revels of the Inns of Court. Writing in 1583, Philip Stubbes records that the Lord of Misrule was chosen by 'all the wilde-heds of the Parish', who crowned him their king. The newly ennobled Lord then appointed up to a hundred parishioners 'to guarde his noble person':

> [T]hen marche this heathen company towards the Church and Church-yard, their pipers pipeing, their drummers thundring, their stumps dauncing, their bels iyngling, their handkerchefs swinging about their heds like madmen, their hobbie horses and other monsters skirmishing amongst the route: & in this sorte they go to the Church (I say) & into the Church (though the Minister be at praier or preaching) dancing & swinging their handkercheifs over their heds, in the Church, like devils incarnate with such a confuse noise, yt no man can hear his own voice.[18]

Voice (Cambridge, Basil Blackwell, 1989) 60, 61. On the application of 'subversive' theory to the study of Shakespeare, see R Weimann, *Shakespeare and the Popular Tradition in the Theater: Studies in the Social Dimension of Dramatic Form and Function*, (tr) & (ed) R Schwartz, (Baltimore, Md, Johns Hopkins University Press, 1978).

[16] On parallels between the participants in English holiday rituals and the characters in Shakespeare's comedies, see Barber, above n 14, at 11–13.

[17] E P Thompson, *Customs in Common* (London, Merlin, 1991) 141.

[18] P Stubbes, 'Lords of Mis-rule in Ailgna' in *The Anatomie of Abuses* (London, Richard Iones, 1583) M2.r–M2.v. For a discussion of Stubbes and the summer Lords of Misrule, see Hutton, above n 8, at 115–18; as Hutton notes, the 'satanic' dance to which Stubbes refers was the morris, *ibid* at 117; on the morris dance in Tudor England, see *ibid* at 33–34. Dance is a major stylistic feature of *A Midsummer Night's Dream*: eg, Oberon and Titania 'rock the ground' to celebrate their reconciliation (4.1.83); while towards the end of the play, the dance by the fairies acts as an apotrope, warding off evil spirits (5.1.378). Following the performance of 'Pyramus and Thisbe' in *A Midsummer Night's Dream*, Bottom offers to dance a 'Bergomask' for Theseus and his guests (5.1.334); this would more accurately have been described as a morris than the rustic dance of Bergamo in northern Italy that is suggested. 'The nine-men's-morris' (2.1.98) to which Titania refers was, as Stanley Wells notes, 'a sort of open-air draughts, in which each player has nine pieces', *A Midsummer Night's Dream*, (ed) S Wells (Harmondsworth, Penguin, 1967) 135. Enid Welsford describes the entire structure of *A Midsummer Night's Dream* as 'dance-like', E Welsford, *The Court Masque: a Study in the Relationship between Poetry and the Revels* (Cambridge, Cambridge University Press, 1927) 331–32; Peter Holland argues that 'the whole action of the play can be viewed as dance', *A Midsummer Night's Dream* (ed) P Holland (Oxford, Oxford University Press, 2008) Introduction, 65.

Parodic festive rites of the winter season derived mainly from medieval, Continental Europe and were ecclesiastical in origin; in one way or another they mocked the authority of the Roman Catholic Church. 'The Feast of the Ass', 'The Feast of Fools' and 'The Feast of the Boy Bishop' are obvious examples. *Festum Asinorum* was celebrated on 14 January and was originally intended to commemorate the Flight of the Holy Family to Egypt.[19] At some stage in its development it became an occasion for mockery of the Liturgy: 'asinine masses' were offered, at which the congregation brayed their responses to the priest and the celebrant would 'hee-haw' the final blessing and 'Amen'. *Festum Stultorum* or the Feast of Fools took place on or around the Feast of the Circumcision (1 January) and was celebrated in cathedrals by inferior members of the clergy: hence its alternative title of 'Feast of the Subdeacons'. The licensed foolery of the junior clerics was presided over by a Lord of Misrule, *Precentor Stultorum*, who wielded the Precentor's staff of office and was permitted by the church authorities to exclaim '*Laetemur gaudiis*' within the cathedral. The Feast of Fools was eventually abolished by the Council of Basle in 1435. During the Feast of the Boy Bishop, a chorister from the cathedral was elected on the feast of St Nicholas (6 December), at which the real bishop ceded his authority to the boy until the Feast of the Innocents (28 December). The Feast of the Boy Bishop was abolished in England by Henry VIII, revived by Mary I and finally abolished by Elizabeth I.[20]

The imagery of the Feast of the Ass has much in common with that of the Christmas festivities at the Inns of Court. The ass's head is of course the most memorable visual image in *A Midsummer Night's Dream*, but the ass is also a recurring motif of the Inns' of Court revels. The entrance on an ass of the old satyr Silenus (because he was too drunk to stand) was a notable feature of *The Maske of Flowers*. This entertainment was performed before James I at the Palace of Whitehall by members of Gray's Inn, in celebration of the marriage in 1613 between the Earl of Somerset and Lady Frances Howard Carr, daughter of the Earl of Suffolk, the Lord Chamberlain.[21] More than 50 years earlier, at the Inner Temple revels of 1561, following the New Year's Day banquet, 'cometh into the Hall the Constable-Marshall, fairly mounted on his Mule'.[22] The old wood-demon—humane (but not human) and fatalistic—is one of the subjects that I

---

[19] *Matthew* 2.13–15. In figurative art of the renaissance period, the Flight is usually depicted with the Virgin and Child riding an ass, led by Joseph; see, eg, 'The Flight Into Egypt' (*c* 1304–06), by Giotto di Bondone, Scrovegni Chapel, Padua; 'The Flight Into Egypt' (*c* 1515), Workshop of the Master of 1518, National Gallery, London.

[20] For an example of 'sermons', preached by Boy Bishops in 16th-century England, see J Gough Nichols (ed), 'Two Sermons Preached by the Boy-Bishop, One at at St Paul's, Temp. Henry VIII., the Other at Gloucester, Temp. Mary', 7 [New Series XIV] *The Camden Miscellany* (London, The Camden Society, 1875) 1–29. On the Feast of the Ass, see Bakhtin, above n 13, at 78; on the Feast of Fools (including the election of 'the all-clowns' pope'), see *ibid* at 218–19. See also 'The Feast of Beans', celebrated on Twelfth Night, *ibid* at 219; Barber, above n 14, at 25.

[21] J Coperario, *The Maske of Flowers. Presented by the Gentlemen of Graies-Inne, at the Court of White-hall, in the Banquetting House, upon Twelfe night, 1613* (London, Robert Wilson, 1614); for an extended discussion of this masque, see P Raffield, '"Lex facit regem" v "Quod principi placuit": Dramatic Symbols of Crown and Common Law' (1999) 20 *The Journal of Legal History* 45.

[22] Dugdale, above n 1, at 157.

Festival, Subversion and Misrule

consider later in this chapter when I examine the mythography surrounding Shakespeare's Puck and the shared imaginative power of theatre and law.

The association of the above bestial imagery with Biblical narrative is obvious, but as striking (if not more so) is the association with classical mythology and the identification of the ancient deities with natural law. Although the presiding figure of the Lord of Misrule is shared by the summer and winter celebrations of medieval England, his origins are traceable to the Roman festival of Saturnalia: the winter feasts in honour of Saturn. During this period of licensed social inversion, feasting and revelry, the participants commemorated a utopian golden age when slavery was unknown, men had all things in common and the land poured forth its fruit.[23] The rejection of societal hierarchy implied the existence of a higher order than the institutions of earthly governance to which citizens traditionally owe allegiance. Although ownership of property was the domain of human laws, it was believed that regulation of the earth itself belonged to God. In the words of the early modern judge and antiquary, Sir Henry Spelman: 'The Possession of Lands is *ex jure homino*, but the Earth is the Lord's *ex jure divino*'.[24] It is not divine law itself so much as the earthly interpretation of divine law that is the subject of mockery in the parodic rites of *ecclesia* described above; the institutional authority of the Church therefore becomes a target of satire. Similarly, at the Inner Temple revels the Lord of Misrule holds up the institutional authority of law (represented by the Benchers, the governing body of the Inn), rather than the law itself, to the satirical gaze of its critics.[25]

In the sense that the Saturnalian rites of winter are related to the governance and husbandry of the earth,[26] there is a strong thematic link between the festive rites of winter and those of summer. A general but important distinction to be made between the two seasonal festivities is that the Christmas Saturnalia which I have considered here were exclusive, to the extent that the principal instigators and

---

[23] See C A Miles, *Christmas in Ritual and Tradition, Christian and Pagan* (London, T F Unwin, 1912); also, Sir James Frazer, *The Golden Bough: a Study in Magic and Religion* (Ware, Wordsworth, 1993).

[24] Sir Henry Spelman, '*De non Temerandis Ecclesiis*: Of the Rights and Respects Due unto the Church' (1613) in *The English Works of Sir Henry Spelman, Kt. Published in his life-time; together with his posthumous works, Relating to the Laws and Antiquity of England*, 2 vols (London, D Browne, 1723) 1: 71.

[25] For an analysis of the legal profession as the subject of early modern satirical drama, see P Raffield, 'A Discredited Priesthood: The Failings of Common Lawyers and Their Representation in Seventeenth Century Satirical Drama' (2005) 17 *Law & Literature* 365. Concerning the satirical idiom, Goodrich has noted that '[t]he dramatic form of the satire, a genre that combines vehemence, conceit, and polemic is entirely appropriate and historically exemplary of the critique of law', P Goodrich, 'Translating Legendre, or the Poetical Sermon' in P Goodrich and D G Carlson (eds), *Law and the Postmodern Mind: Essays on Psychoanalysis and Jurisprudence* (Ann Arbor, University of Michigan Press, 1998) 232.

[26] In the Golden Age over which Saturn presided, he is supposed to have taught the people to cultivate the land; as well as giving the people their laws, Saturn is traditionally associated with the invention of viticulture. Ovid describes the earth in the Golden Age as an Edenic place of natural bounty: 'Flowers which had never been planted were kissed into life by the warming breath of the gentle zephyrs; and soon the earth, untilled by the plough, was yielding her fruits, and without renewal the fields grew white with the swelling corn blades', Ovid, *Metamorphoses*, (tr) D Raeburn (London, Penguin, 2004) 10, Bk I.106–10.

actors were members of institutional communities, those of the Church and the Law.[27] The summer rites were inclusive in that they were accessible to all; being held largely outdoors, they were more difficult to control than their winter counterparts. Incipient rebellion and the threat to traditional models of authority were inherent characteristics of these annual events. The fear of an uncontrollable mob, of descent into ungodly chaos, was expressed by Philip Stubbes:

> Against May, Whitsonday or other time, all the yung men and maides, olde men and wives run gadding over night to the woods, groves, hils & mountains, where they spend all the night in pleasant pastimes, & in the morning they return bringing with them birch & branches of trees, to deck their assemblies withal, and no mervaile, for there is a great Lord present amongst them, as Superintendent and Lord over their pastimes and sportes, namely, Sathan prince of hel: But the chiefest iewel they bring from thence is their May-pole, which they bring home with great veneration.

The may-pole—'this stinking Idol rather'—is drawn into position by between 20 and 40 oxen, their horns decorated with nosegays. Once the may-pole is erected the celebrants 'daunce about it like as the heathen people did at the dedication of the Idols'. Stubbes explicitly complained of the abandoned, irreligious sexual conduct that was the inevitable consequence of the summer rites:

> I have heard it credibly reported (and that, *viva voce*) by men of great gravitie and reputation, that of fortie, threescore, or a hundred maides going to the wood over night, there have scarcely the third part of them returned home againe undefiled.[28]

These are the revels with which Shakespeare is concerned in *A Midsummer Night's Dream*: the Mayday festivities of rural England. The entire emphasis of the summer rituals is on the liberation of subjects from the constraints of a hierarchic society and the rediscovery of their natural rights; the social contract is breached and a natural *pactum* is renewed through enjoyment of 'pleasant pastimes' in the wood. They differ in this respect from the civic Saturnalia of the Inns of Court, which lack the pagan dimension of idolatrous worship in the form of fertility rites. Suffused with symbols of rebellion, renewal, procreation and fecundity, the mystical customs of rural England provide the narrative background of the play: 'No doubt they rose up early to observe / The rite of May' (4.1.129–30),[29] observes Theseus on discovering the sleeping lovers in the wood.

Municipal law was laid aside on these days, which were dedicated to the law of nature. As Spelman admits in his discourse on the origins of the four law terms:

---

[27] Hutton notes that the Christmas Lords of Misrule appeared in 'some wealthy households, and in colleges, urban corporations, and Inns of Court', Hutton, above n 8, at 114.

[28] Stubbes, above n 18, at M3.*v*–M4.*r*.

[29] All references to the text of the play are from *A Midsummer Night's Dream*, (ed) R A Foakes (Cambridge, Cambridge University Press, 2003). Barber notes that there is no discrepancy between the title of Shakespeare's play and the reference by Theseus to the rites of May: 'people went Maying at various times . . . even on Midsummer Eve itself', Barber, above n 14, at 120. The principal festival days of late spring and summer were: Hocktide (second Tuesday after Easter), May Day, Whitsuntide, Midsummer Eve and Harvest-home. On the ritual year in Tudor England, see Hutton, above n 8, at 5–48; also, C Davidson, *Festivals and Plays in Late Medieval Britain* (Aldershot, Ashgate, 2007).

Festival, Subversion and Misrule

> The *Latian* Laws do no man now molest,
> But grant this weary season Peace and Rest;
> The Courts are stopt when Harvest comes about,
> The Plaintiff or Defendant stirs not out.[30]

It is noteworthy that Spelman should quote these lines from Book IV of Statius' pastoral poems, *Silvae*, and suggest that they represented the law of peoples or nations, *Ius Gentium*.[31] Spelman's 'The Original of the Four Terms of the Year' is an important work, not least because it acknowledges the influence of the earth and the seasons over the institutional structures of English law. The summer months and the impending harvest were of particular importance: Spelman notes that when, during the reign of Henry III, the date for the end of Trinity term was fixed on or around 12 July (two or three days after the Quindene of St John the Baptist), the effect was to

> so hinder Hay-seed and Harvest following, that either the course of it must be shortned, or it must still usurp upon the time allotted by Nature to collect the fruits of the Earth. [Consequently] *Trinity-Term* is alter'd and shortned by the Statute of 32. *Hen*.VIII.*cap*.21 . . .[32]

Spelman is forthright in his assertion that the summer is a season of 'Feasting and Merriment, for receiving the Fruits of the Earth' and attending to 'the Store-house of the Common-wealth', rather than pleading suits in the courts of law.[33] Dispensation for a prescribed period from the rigours of lawsuits and farm-labour was approved by Cicero in *De Legibus*:

> Next, our provision for *holidays* and festivals ordains *rest from lawsuits and controversies for free men, and from labour and toil for slaves*. Whoever plans the official year ought to arrange that these festivals shall come at the completion of the various labours of the farm.[34]

---

[30] Sir Henry Spelman, 'The Original of the Four Terms of the Year' (1614) in *English Works*, above n 24, 2: 84. The origins of the four law terms are traceable to the Church calendar: Hilary ('the Term was begun at *Octabis Epiphaniae* . . . we begin it not till the 23d of January', *ibid* at 83); Easter ('which now beginneth two Days after *Quindena Paschae*' and ended 'before the Vigil of Ascension', *ibid*); Trinity (starting 'the Friday after *Corpus Christi* Day, and to continue nineteen Days', *ibid* at 87); and Michaelmas (starting 'the third day after the *Octaves* [of St Michael]' and ending 28 November: 'it may not extend into Advent', *ibid* at 86).

[31] Spelman does not attribute a translator; presumably he translated it himself. Statius' *Silvae* were written in the reign of Domitian (AD 81–96); on Statius and the Flavian poets, in particular the challenge posed by *Silvae* to imperial majesty and private wealth, see C E Newlands, *Statius' Silvae and the Poetics of Empire* (Cambridge, Cambridge University Press, 2010).

[32] Spelman, above n 30, at 84, 87.

[33] *Ibid* at 85. Plague also played its part in foreshortening Trinity term: 'The Altering and Abbreviation of this Term is declared by the Preamble of the Statute to have risen out of two Causes; one for Health, in dismissing the Concourse of People in that contagious time of the Year: the other for Wealth, that the Subject might attend his harvest, and gathering in the Fruits of the Earth', *ibid* at 87.

[34] 'Tum *feriarum* festorumque dierum ratio in liberis *requietem litium habet et iurgiorum, in servis operum et laborum*; quas compositor anni conferre debet ad perfectionem operum rusticorum', Marcus Tullius Cicero, *De Legibus* in *De Re Publica, De Legibus*, (tr) C Walker Keyes (Cambridge, Mass, Harvard University Press, 2006) 407, Bk II.XII.29.

The Poetic Imagination, Antique Fables and the Dream of Law

That the law of nature should take precedence over the law of man is a prominent theme in *A Midsummer Night's Dream*. The 'sharp Athenian law' (1.1.162) that would have condemned Hermia to death (or else '[t]o live a barren sister all your life' (1.1.72)) for her steadfast love of Lysander is eventually supplanted by a more flexible model. Later in this chapter I consider the societal impact of an irrational law that compels obedience to the Father, in the context of a *polis* lacking an equitable legal system, whose citizens exist in a perpetual state of incipient rebellion. It should be remembered that the comedic confusions of *A Midsummer Night's Dream* are precipitated by one such rebellious act: the decision of Lysander and Hermia to reject their civil obligations and fly to a *locus amoenus*, a rural location of comfort and safety beyond the reach of municipal Athenian law. The faith that the two young lovers place in the Arcadian idyll is misplaced, as Shakespeare confounds their expectations by inverting the pastoral convention. The labyrinthine wood near Athens is a dark place, in which the subject's imagination conjures monstrosity and horror. That it is not ultimately the scene of violence and violation that we associate, for example, with *Titus Andronicus* is due to the apotropaic effect not only of the magic exerted by the fairies, but also of the laughter engendered in the audience.[35] Actor and audience collaborate in a creative rite of benediction and exorcism. The last lines, spoken by Puck, are a celebration both of the play's artistry and the unifying power of theatre: 'Give me your hands, if we be friends, / And Robin shall restore amends'. (5.1.415–16) The metadrama of *A Midsummer Night's Dream* is concerned with lending dramatic shape to ideas about the family, the State and the theatre.[36] It is concerned also with the role of law in nature and society, and the transformative power of the legal imagination to generate and reinforce 'gentle concord in the world' (4.1.140): the bond of community upon which the ideal *polis* is founded.

II. Satyrs, Fairies and the Oneiric Imagination

Three months after the death of Elizabeth I, the queen consort of the new king visited a country estate in Northamptonshire, accompanied by her eldest son, Henry, Prince of Wales. We learn from E K Chambers that

> [t]he host, Sir Robert Spencer of Althorp, Northants, was created Lord Spencer of Wormleighton on 21 July 1603. On arrival (25 June) the Queen and Prince were met in the park by a Satyr, Queen Mab, and a bevy of Fairies.[37]

---

[35] See A D Nuttall, '*A Midsummer Night's Dream*: Comedy as *Apotrope* of Myth' (2000) 53 *Shakespeare Survey* 49.
[36] See L A Montrose, '"Shaping Fantasies": Figurations of Gender and Power in Elizabethan Culture' (1983) 2 *Representations* 61, 86.
[37] E K Chambers, *The Elizabethan Stage*, 4 vols (Oxford, Oxford University Press, 1923) 3: 391.

Satyrs, Fairies and the Oneiric Imagination

There was more to it than that: a sylvan masque written by Ben Jonson, entitled *A Particular Entertainment of the Queen and Prince at Althorpe* and subtitled *A Satyr*, was performed in honour of the visit by Queen Anne of Denmark and Prince Henry, during their triumphal journey from Edinburgh to London following the accession of James I. The script of *A Satyr* was altered to accommodate the fact that the royal visit 'was expected there on *Midsummer* day at night, but came not till the day following'.[38] The stage direction on the title page of the masque demonstrates the blurred distinction between reality and illusion that characterises much of the action in *A Midsummer Night's Dream* and on which I comment above regarding the Inner Temple revels of 1561.[39] A satyr was to greet Queen Anne and Prince Henry, as they walked through the wood:

> The Invention was, to have a Satyr lodged in a little Spinet, by which Her Majesty and the Prince were to come who (at the report of certain Cornets that were divided in several places of the Park, to signify her Approach) advanced his head above the top of the wood, wondering, and (with his Pipe in his hand) began as followeth.[40]

The inclusion in the cast of Queen Mab and 'a Bevy of fairies' evidences Jonson's homage to Shakespeare.[41] According to Mercutio in *Romeo and Juliet*, Queen Mab is the enabler of dreams: 'In shape no bigger than an agate-stone' (1.4.55), she 'gallops night by night' (1.4.70), facilitating the ambitions of those who sleep (including lawyers, 'who straight dream on fees' (1.4.73)). The late-Elizabethan period produced numerous books and treatises on the interpretation of dreams, many of them drawing on *Oneirocritica*, written in the 2nd century by Artemidorus of Daldis. Artemidorus provided a rational framework for the classification of dreams. To Elizabethan writers, well-versed in the literary tropes of classical rhetoric, the emphasis placed by Artemidorus on the significance of allegorical dreams (a sub-category of *oneiroi*, or predictive dreams) would have been immediately credible. Artemidorus described such dreams as

---

[38] 'A Particular Entertainment of the Queen and Prince at Althorpe' in *The Works of Ben Jonson. In six volumes. Adorn'd with cuts*, 6 vols (London, J Walthoe, M Wotton, 1716–17) 3: 245.

[39] Holland notes 'the disjunction of actor and role' following a Sunday performance in 1631 of *A Midsummer Night's Dream*, when the actor playing Bottom was put into the stocks with a sign around his neck, which read: 'Good people I have played the beast / And brought ill things to pass: / I was a man, but thus have made / Myself a silly Ass', E K Chambers, *William Shakespeare: a Study of Facts and Problems*, 2 vols (Oxford, Oxford University Press, 1930) 2: 348–50, in Holland (ed), above n 18, Introduction, 79–80.

[40] Jonson, above n 38, at 242.

[41] The mischief-making of Jonson's Queen Mab has more in common with the Puck of *A Midsummer Night's Dream* than the Queen Mab of *Romeo and Juliet*: 'This is she that empties Cradles, / Takes out Children, puts in Ladles: / Trains forth Midwives in their slumber, / With a Sieve the holes to number', Jonson, above n 38, at 245. Jonson's satyr offers Lord Spencer's eldest son a 'Dog of Sparta Breed' (*ibid* at 249) with which to hunt. The similarity to Theseus's hunting dogs in *A Midsummer Night's Dream* is striking: 'My hounds are bred out of the Spartan kind' (4.1.116). Also, Jonson's masque contains an allusion to the amateur theatricals of Shakespeare's mechanicals: the stage directions describe 'a Morris of Clowns thereabout, who most officiously presented themselves'. Their spokesman delivers a rhyming prologue to the royal party, similar to the doggerel addressed by Quince to Theseus and the other newlyweds prior to the performance of 'Pyramus and Thisbe' in Act 5, scene 1 of *A Midsummer Night's Dream*: 'If my outside move your Laughter, / Pray Jove, my inside be thereafter. / Queen, Prince, Duke, Earls, / Countesses, you Courtly Pearls!', Jonson, above n 38, at 250.

allegorical, and by one thing signifie another. Whereupon our soule doth naturally advise us, that under them their is somewhat abstruse, secret, hidden.[42]

Writing in 1594, two years before the first performance of *A Midsummer Night's Dream*,[43] Thomas Nashe distinguished (as Artemidorus had done) between those dreams which are 'nothing els but a bubling feum or froath of the fancie, which the day hath left undigested' and those which are recognisable not only by their allegorical content, but also (and especially) by their capacity to foreshadow political events:

> Some will obiect unto mee for the certainety of Dreames, the Dreames of *Cyrus*, *Cambyses*, *Pompey*, *Cesar*, *Darius*, & *Alexander*. For those I answer, that they were rather visions than Dreames, extraordinarily sent from heaven to foreshow the translation of Monarchies.[44]

Discernible from Nashe's analysis of the allegorical vision is the idea that the dream is as much a rhetorical device as the allegory that it contains. The form of dream described above by Nashe is a metaphor for the political imagination, a device used also by Robert Greene in *A Quip for an Upstart Courtier*, written in 1592. Here, Greene employs the dream as a means of facilitating discourse on the threat posed to societal hierarchy by deregulation of the sartorial image, which had been controlled throughout the 16th century by the enforcement of sumptuary legislation.[45] Through exploitation of this narrow conceit, Greene's political imagination explores a range of contemporary issues, from the emergence of a power-

---

[42] D Artemidorus, *The iudgement, or exposition of dreames, written by Artimodorus, an auncient and famous author, first in Greek, then translated into Latin, after into French, and now into English*, (tr) R W (London, William Iones, 1606) 1. On the distinction made by Artemidorus between *enhypnion* ('anxiety dreams and petitionary dreams') and *oneiroi*, see Holland (ed), above n 18, Introduction, 5–7. For recent editions of Freud and Jung on dreams, see S Freud, *The Interpretation of Dreams*, (tr) J Crick (Oxford, Oxford University Press, 1999); C G Jung, *Memories, Dreams, Reflections*, (tr) R Winston and C Winston, (ed) A Jaffé (London, Fontana, 1983).

[43] The exact date of composition of *A Midsummer Night's Dream* is unknown. Its style and subject-matter (in particular the parodic treatment of tragic love in 'Pyramus and Thisbe') suggest that it came after *Romeo and Juliet* (1595–96) and before *The Merchant of Venice* (1596–97). The nuptial theme of the play possibly indicates that it was written in celebration of an actual marriage; either between Elizabeth Vere and the Earl of Derby in January 1595, or between Elizabeth Carey and Thomas Berkeley in February 1596. It is possible also that Titania's lines regarding recent meteorological and climatic confusion (2.1.88–117) refer to the bad summer of 1594, although as Wells observes in this respect, 'bad summers were, we may suppose, no less common than now', Wells (ed), above n 18, Introduction, 12. On the date and occasion of its first performance, see Foakes (ed), above n 29, Introduction, 1–4; Holland (ed), above n 18, Introduction, 110–12; see also, A J Riess and G Walton Williams, '"Tragical Mirth": From *Romeo* to *Dream*' (1992) 43 *Shakespeare Quarterly* 214; W B Hunter, 'The First Performance of *A Midsummer Night's Dream*' (1985) 32 *Notes and Queries* 45; Barber, above n 14, at 152.

[44] T Nashe, *The Terrors of the night Or, A Discourse of Apparitions* (London, William Iones, 1594) C3.v, D4.r. Shakespeare employs the dramatic device of the prophetic vision to great effect in *Julius Caesar*, in which Calpurnia's dream foretells the assassination of Caesar: 'She dreamt tonight she saw my statue, / Which, like a fountain with an hundred spouts, / Did run pure blood' (2.2.76–78). It is noteworthy that the character who unsuccessfully attempts to warn Caesar of the assassination plot against him should be a teacher of rhetoric, aptly named Artemidorus (2.3, 3.1.1–10).

[45] On sumptuary legislation in the 16th century, see ch 2, text to n 119, above.

ful class of artisans to the threat posed to the English economy by the import of foreign goods. As in *A Midsummer Night's Dream*, the *mise-en-scène* is an Arcadian idyll in which the imagination distorts the conventions of that genre:

> It was iust at that time when the Cuckoulds quirrister began to bewray Aprill Gentlemen with his never chaunged notes, that I damped with a melancholy humor, went into the fields to cheere up my wits with the fresh aire: where solitarye seeking to solace myself I fell in a dreame, and in that drowsie slumber, I wandered into a vale al tapistred with sweete and choice flowers.

The dream soon turns from images of flower-clad vales to more disturbing visions of social inversion and rebellion. The author sees 'certain clownes in clowted shoone' picking and devouring a herb (which he describes as thyme), and

> no sooner was sunke into their mawes, but they were metamorphosed, and lookt as proudlye though pesants, as if they had beene borne to be princes companions.[46]

Greene is drawing here on fictional sources other than his own political imagination. The reference to 'clowted shoone' echoes another deluded rebel, Shakespeare's Jack Cade, who (once he has killed all the lawyers) will '[s]pare none but such as go in clouted shoon' (*2 Henry VI*, 4.2.174).[47] Greene's dreamer (the author narrates in the first person) continues to conjure images of the most extraordinary hallucinatory intensity, culminating in an encounter with 'Velvet-breeches' and 'Cloth-breeches'. The former is 'an uncouth headless thinge . . . it wanted a body, yet seeing legges and hose, I supposed it to bee some monster'. Cloth-breeches is also an anthropomorphic manifestation of outsize Elizabethan hose, the only difference between the two being that, as Cloth-breeches explains to Velvet-breeches:

---

[46] Robert Greene, *A Quip for an Upstart Courtier: Or, A quaint dispute between Velvet breeches and Cloth-breeches* (London, Iohn Wolfe, 1592) A3.r. Herbs have a similar transformative effect in *A Midsummer Night's Dream*: Oberon orders Puck to bring him 'love-in-idleness': 'The juice of it on sleeping eyelids laid / Will make or man or woman madly dote / Upon the next live creature that it sees' (2.1.170–72); the juice of another herb, squeezed into the eyes of Lysander (3.2.453–63) and Titania (4.1.68–72) while they sleep, is an antidote to the charmed effect of love-in-idleness.

[47] On Jack Cade's rebellion and Shakespeare's possible ambivalence towards lawyers, see ch 5, text to nn 1–4, below; also, C Hobday, 'Clouted Shoon and Leather Aprons: Shakespeare and the Egalitarian Tradition' (1979) 23 *Renaissance and Modern Studies* 63. *Henry VI, Part 2* was the first play in the *Henry VI* trilogy to be written and performed (1590–91), under the title of *The First Part of the Contention*. Philip Henslowe recorded receipts of £3 16s 8d for a performance by Lord Strange's Men of a 'new' play at the Rose Playhouse in March 1592, which Henslowe entitles 'harey the vj', R A Foakes (ed), *Henslowe's Diary* (Cambridge, Cambridge University Press, 2002) 16; Wells argues that the play to which Henslowe refers was probably *The First Part of Henry VI*, the last in the trilogy to be written and performed: S Wells and G Taylor (eds), *William Shakespeare: The Complete Works* (Oxford, Clarendon, 2005) 125. Greene disparaged Shakespeare in *Greene's Groatsworth of Wit*, written shortly before he died in September 1592 (the title page of the first edition, published in the year of Greene's death by William Wright, includes the line, 'Written before his death and published at his dyeing request'): '[T]here is an upstart Crow beautified with our Feathers, that with his Tygers heart, wrapt in a Players hyde, supposes he is as well able to bombast out a blank verse, as the best of you', R Greene, *Greenes Groatsworth of Wit, Bought with A Million of Repentance* (London, Henry and Moses Bell, 1637) C3.v. The reference by Greene to the tiger's heart is a parody of a line spoken by the Duke of York to Queen Margaret in *3 Henry VI*: 'O tiger's heart wrapped in a woman's hide!' (1.4.138)

The Poetic Imagination, Antique Fables and the Dream of Law

> I belong to the old aunciant yeomanry, yea and Gentility, the fathers, and thou to a company of proud and unmannerly upstarts the sonnes.

The greatest fault of Velvet-breeches is to be foreign; specifically, to be Italian. On that basis alone, Cloth-breeches accuses Velvet-breeches of importing 'nothing but infectious abuses, and vaine glory, selfelove, sodomie, and strange poisonings, wherewith thou hast infected this glorious Iland'.[48]

The transformative power of the dream was of evident fascination to Greene, as it was to Shakespeare. The storyteller of Greene's *A Quip for an Upstart Courtier* observes, records and comments upon the fantastical events that befall him. He is a critic, analysing the behaviour of all those he encounters, howsoever unworldly and irrational their behaviour may be. In many respects he fulfils the role of the licensed fool, commenting from an objectified distance on the folly of those around him. Such is the role played by the eponymous satyr in Jonson's Althorp masque, and such is the role played by Shakespeare's Puck in *A Midsummer Night's Dream*. 'Lord, what fools these mortals be' (3.2.115), Puck remarks, not only of the young lovers in the wood but of the human condition in general. The resemblance of Puck or Robin Goodfellow to the satyr is demonstrated by his pictorial depiction on the title page of *Robin Good-Fellow, His Mad Prankes, and merry Iests*, published in 1628 (see **Figure 6**). The illustration portrays a summer rite, in which the male and female celebrants dance in a circle (in the manner to which Philip Stubbes vehemently objected in *The Anatomie of Abuses*). Here, Robin Goodfellow is presented unequivocally as a satyr, with horns, cloven hooves and erect penis.

As we saw in *Titus Andronicus*, the depiction of an antique foreign world, far removed from late-Elizabethan England, enabled an implied critique of prevailing modes of governance. The same observation applies to the depiction in the theatre (and in the texts of imaginative works such as Greene's *A Quip for an Upstart Courtier*) of dreams.[49] Returning briefly to Thomas Nashe's description of allegorical dreams, did Jonson intend to effect a 'translation of Monarchies' when his masque was presented at Althorp to Queen Anne and Prince Henry? He almost certainly did not (if by 'translation' Nashe was referring to a transformation),[50] but he was clearly aware of the capacity of theatre to reflect an image of governance (however benign and fanciful) and to have an affective influence over the imagination of its audience, which in this instance included the Queen. It is Queen Anne whom Jonson addresses in the epilogue to his masque as 'Mirror of

---

[48] Greene, above n 46, at A4.*v*–B2.*r*.

[49] In a chapter entitled 'The Art of Government', Ward notes of *A Midsummer Night's Dream* that '[t]he entire play is a testimony to this appreciation of imagination as a political force', I Ward, *Shakespeare and the Legal Imagination* (London, Butterworths, 1999) 209.

[50] This sense of the word is intended by Shakespeare in the line addressed by Quince to Bottom, following the latter's entrance with the ass's head: 'Bless thee, Bottom, bless thee! Thou art translated!' (3.1.98)

Satyrs, Fairies and the Oneiric Imagination

Queens'[51]: an actual queen, but the reflected image also of the fictional Queen Mab—facilitator of dreams—whom Queen Anne has encountered in the actual surroundings of the Althorp estate.[52]

The subject-matter of *A Satyr*, its setting, and the presence in the audience of Queen Anne and Prince Henry demonstrate the relevance of the 'Apollonian dreamland' to the representation of power in early modern England. As Nietzsche observed, it was in dreams that 'the glorious divine figures first appeared to the souls of men'.[53] The fantastical figures of the satyr, Queen Mab and the fairies offer a stylised mirror-image of the royal party, in whose divine presence they have materialised.[54] Of particular interest here is the representation of a satyr: simultaneously the archetype of man and a 'sublime and godlike' being.[55] The satyr was a familiar character in the masques presented to the royal court during the reigns of Elizabeth I and James I. I refer in the previous section to the performance by members of Gray's Inn of *The Maske of Flowers*, in which the character of Silenus sat astride 'an artificiall Asse . . . attended by a Satyre'.[56] Despite his drunkenness and obesity, Silenus is wise, equable and humane: qualities which Sir John Fortescue and his judicial descendants attributed to the common law and its practitioners. A benevolent and sagacious presence, Silenus is both omniscient observer of the pitiful human condition and embodiment of powerful atavistic emotions. When asked what was best for all men, Silenus replied: '. . . not to be born, not to be, to be nothing. The second best for you, however, is soon to die'.[57] The identical sentiment is expressed by the Chorus in Sophocles' *Oedipus at Colonus*, watching the horrific scene unfold in Athens:

> Say what you will, the greatest boon is not to be;
> But, life begun, soonest to end is best,
> And to that bourne from which our way began
> Swiftly return.[58]

Awareness of the desperation of the human condition is demonstrated by Puck in *A Midsummer Night's Dream*, the main difference from Sophocles' Chorus being

---

[51] The epilogue was not performed on this occasion: the stage directions inform us that it 'was to have been presented in the person of a Youth, and accompanied with divers Gentlemens younger Sons of the Country: But by reason of the multitudinous press, was also hindered', Jonson, above n 38, at 252.

[52] On '[t]he mystical presence of the Crown' in early modern England, see Goodrich, above n 25, at 237: 'The image, symbol, or rite represents the stake of law and enacts, again in a parable, in allegory or image, the institution of legal writing as the lawful institution of life.'

[53] F Nietzsche, *The Birth of Tragedy*, (tr) WA Haussmann (Edinburgh, Foulis, 1909) 22.

[54] On Narcissus gazing at his reflection and the 'bond between body and image', see P Legendre, *Law and the Unconscious: a Legendre Reader*, (tr) P Goodrich, with A Pottage and A Schütz, (ed) P Goodrich (Basingstoke, Macmillan, 1997) 211.

[55] Nietzsche, above n 53, at 63.

[56] *Maske of Flowers*, B3.r; see text to n 21, above.

[57] Nietzsche, above n 53, at 34.

[58] Sophocles, 'Oedipus at Colonus' in E F Watling (tr), *The Theban Plays* (Harmondsworth, Penguin, 1947) 109, lines 1225–27.

the style in which Shakespeare communicates this sensibility.[59] Puck's is an almost entirely comic mode of expression, but his critical observations are profound as well as serious, challenging the audience to confront their preconceptions about reality and illusion:

> If we shadows have offended,
> Think but this, and all is mended:
> That you have but slumbered here
> While these visions did appear . . . (5.1.401–04)

As A D Nuttall has noted of the final speech in the play, when Puck deliberately fractures the theatrical illusion of reality by talking to the audience, his words of reassurance are not as comforting as they initially appear.[60] The audience may 'think' that they have witnessed an illusion, but is their rational belief obscuring a more profound reality than their reason permits them to entertain?

In 1596, when *A Midsummer Night's Dream* was first performed, imagination had distinct pejorative connotations to do with falsehood, lies and (especially in a reformist context) idolatry.[61] In chapter two, I note the antagonism expressed by Sir Francis Bacon towards the imaginative approach to legal judgment and law-reporting demonstrated by Sir Edward Coke.[62] In a private letter written to Coke in 1606, Bacon castigated Coke for his imaginative interpretation of law, which Bacon perceived as a threat to certainty and legitimacy:

> While you speake in yor own Element, the Law, no man ordinarily equals you, but when you wander (as you often delight to doe) you then wander indeed, and give never such satisfaction as the Curious time requires . . . you having a living fruitfull mind should not soe much labour what to speak, as to find what to leave unspoken, rich soyles are often to be weeded . . . you converse with books not man, and books especially humane.[63]

The reference by Bacon to 'books especially humane'—the literature of the classical world and of renaissance humanism—is illuminating. Throughout *The Reports*, Coke refers to the ancient Greeks as sources of authority for English law, as for example:

---

[59] Puck demonstrates particular affinity with the restless spirits of the damned: 'Damnèd spirits all, / That in crossways and floods have burial, / Already to their wormy beds are gone'. (3.2.382–84) Foakes notes that '[s]uicides were buried at cross-roads, or carried away by water if they drowned themselves', Foakes (ed), above n 29, at 108. On Plowden's report of *Hales v Petit*, concerning the suicide by drowning of Sir James Hales and the influence of this case over the treatment of Ophelia's suicide in *Hamlet*, see ch 3, text to nn 39–44, above.

[60] Regarding these lines, Nuttall makes an analogy with the language of law: 'The use of "think" here is a little like the use of "deem" in law, to cover a threatened chasm in due sequence: "If we deem that the payment was made before 1 July, none of the above applies"', A D Nuttall, *Shakespeare the Thinker* (New Haven, Conn, Yale University Press, 2007) 131.

[61] Nuttall notes a chapter entitled 'The Dangerous Prevalence of Imagination' in Samuel Johnson's *Rasselas* (1759), *ibid* at 124.

[62] See ch 2, nn 46 and 123, above.

[63] *Letter to Coke from Sir Francis Bacon*, BL Sloane. 1775, ff 79.r–79.v.

> There are (saith Euripides) three virtues worthy our meditation: to honour God, our parents who begat us, and the common laws of Greece; the like do I say to thee ... yield due reverence and obedience to the common laws of England: for of all laws (I speak of human) these are most equal and most certain, of greatest antiquity, and least delay, and most beneficial and easy to be observed.[64]

The above passage is ambiguous: does Coke intend the reader to understand that the laws of Greece or those of England are 'of greatest antiquity', and in political terms what does the pointed reference to equality imply? It is ambiguity such as this that infuriated Bacon: the imagery employed by Coke in *The Reports* was invariably drawn from the philosophical and political texts of the ancient world. Coke incorporated Aristotle's principles of justice and natural equity (*epieikeia*), discussed in Book V of *The Nicomachean Ethics*, not only into the prefaces to *The Reports*, but into reports of the cases themselves. It is therefore inevitable that Coke's *Reports* imply a level of empathy between the reality of English law and the illusion of the ideal State, in which the best interests of the common-weal was the ultimate aim of law. Hence, in his report of *Postnati. Calvin's Case*, during discussion of the political sovereignty of James I and the primacy of natural law, Coke refers approvingly to Aristotle as 'nature's secretary'. He further notes that the seminal jurists of late medieval and early modern England—Bracton, Fortescue and St German (all of whose theories emphasised the republican notion of limited monarchy)—thoroughly approved Aristotle's equitable ideology.[65] Given that *Postnati. Calvin's Case* was ostensibly concerned with the disputed ownership of a freehold interest in a property in Shoreditch, Bacon might be excused a level of annoyance at the extent to which Coke's political imagination dominated his report of that and numerous other cases. Like Shakespeare's Puck or Greene's anonymous dreamer in *A Quip for An Upstart Courtier*, like the satyr in Jonson's Althorp masque or the Chorus in Sophocles' *Oedipus at Colonus*, Coke the law-reporter was commenting on the human condition. He was no less imaginative a critic for the fact that the vision of humanity which he recorded was manifested in the artificial environment of the courtroom and interpreted in the language of English law. In *The Reports* he stands at a distance from human activity, noting its foibles and idiosyncrasies, incrementally shaping the development of English law through the application of political imagination to the exercise of artificial reason.

III. Violence on the Edge

Like Romulus, his Roman counterpart, Theseus is an archetype of nationhood. According to classical legend, Romulus founded Rome and Theseus united the

---

[64] Part 2 (1602) of *The Reports of Sir Edward Coke, Knt. In English*, G Wilson (ed), 7 vols (London, Rivington, 1777) 1: Preface, vii–viii.
[65] Coke, *Postnati. Calvin's Case*, 7 *Reports* (1608) 4: 1a, at 12b.

scattered residents of Attica in the metropolitan commonwealth of Athens. Each shared with the other a notorious distinction, as Plutarch relates: '[E]ach resorted to the rape of women'.[66] Plutarch records that the banishment and eventual death of Theseus were caused by his rape of Helen, 'who was not of marriageable age'.[67] Insofar as rape serves as a metaphor for the violation and conquest of nations, the violence perpetrated by Theseus balances the depiction of him as the beneficent founder of Athenian democracy, acting 'for the common interests of all'.[68] Sir Thomas North's translation of Plutarch's *Lives* (published in 1579), which probably influenced Shakespeare's depiction of the Duke in *A Midsummer Night's Dream*, provided an ambivalent portrait of Theseus. It is noteworthy in the context of a discussion of ideal governance that the violence associated with the sexual conduct of Theseus is explicitly linked by North to the degeneration into tyranny of Theseus's rule:

> [H]e that is more severe or remisse then he should be, remaineth now no more a King or a prince, but becommeth a people pleaser, or a cruel tyrant: and so causeth his subiects to despise or hate him.[69]

In the first scene of the play, Theseus refers to the violent means by which he 'conquered' Hippolyta: he boasts that 'I wooed thee with my sword, / And won thy love doing thee injuries' (1.1.16–17). As well as the obvious connotations of military conquest by Theseus, the above lines recall the violent sexual conduct related by Plutarch. Further reference is made to Plutarch when Oberon rebukes Titania for her 'love to Theseus' (2.1.76). The King of the Fairies asks her:

> Didst thou not lead him through the glimmering night
> From Perigenia, whom he ravishèd,
> And make him with fair Aegles break his faith,
> With Ariadne, and Antiopa? (2.1.77–80)

---

[66] Plutarch, 'Theseus' in *Lives 1* (tr) B Perrin (Cambridge, Mass, Harvard University Press, 2005) 5, II; I refer below to Sir Thomas North's translation of Plutarch's *Lives*, which Shakespeare read, but Perrin's translation is both more accurate and comprehensive. North's English translation was based on a translation from Greek into French: *The Lives of the Noble Grecians and Romanes, Compared together by that grave learned Philosopher and Historiographer, Plutarke*, (tr) T North (London, Thomas Vautroullier, 1579).

[67] Perrin (tr), above n 66, at 71, XXXI; according to Homer's *Iliad*, Helen of Troy was the daughter of Zeus and Leda.

[68] Perrin (tr), above n 66, at 51, XXIV. In the words of Thompson, 'freedom was the coinage of patrician, demagogue and radical alike', E P Thompson, *The Making of the English Working Class* (London, Victor Gollancz, 1980) 85; relevant to a discussion of Theseus's 'conquests' is the remark of Tom Paine's, quoted in *The Making of the English Working Class*, that all governments (with the exception in his opinion of revolutionary France and America) 'derived their authority from conquest and superstition: their foundations lay upon "arbitrary power"', Tom Paine, *Rights of Man* in Thompson, *Making of the English Working Class*, at 99.

[69] North (tr), above n 66, at 42; on North's depiction of Theseus, see Holland (ed), above n 18, Introduction, 53–54. A source for Theseus's wedding celebrations in Shakespeare's play is Chaucer's *The Knight's Tale*, which also refers to the conquest of Hippolyta by Theseus (lines 866–83); on Shakespeare's sources, see Holland (ed), above n 18, at 49–59.

Violence on the Edge

Perigenia (Perigune), Aegles, Ariadne and Antiopa were abandoned lovers of Plutarch's Theseus.[70]

I emphasise the importance of Plutarch's depiction of violence because Theseus is the ultimate source of lawful authority in Shakespeare's play; he is literally the body of law upon whom Athenian citizens depend for the impartial administration of the legal system.[71] Apart from the above indirect references to the pathological violence of Theseus as described in the *Lives*,[72] the 'historical' background ascribed him by Plutarch is not developed by Shakespeare. This omission notwithstanding, the implication of serious violence remains in the background of *A Midsummer Night's Dream*; its proximity is always sensed by the astute reader and audience. Hermia faces sentence of death for her refusal to marry Demetrius in accordance both with her father's will and Athenian law; but there are numerous other, more indirect means by which Shakespeare communicates the imminence of physical danger and oppression.

In *Titus Andronicus*, Shakespeare had shown that a forest just beyond the city walls was a dark place fraught with danger of the most savage kind. In *Titus*, Demetrius (and his brother Chiron) raped and mutilated Lavinia in the forest; in the wood of *A Midsummer Night's Dream* another Demetrius raises the possibility of rape and murder when he says to Helena (whose name is obviously associated with Helen of Troy, the victim of a rape committed by Theseus):

> You do impeach your modesty too much,
> To leave the city and commit yourself
> Into the hands of one that loves you not . . . (2.1.214–16)

The associative links between Hippolyta and violence extend beyond her 'conquest' by Theseus. In Greek legend (dramatised by Euripides and later by Seneca), Hippolytus is the son of Theseus. Having rejected the sexual advances of his stepmother (Theseus's wife), Phaedra, Hippolytus is unjustly accused by Phaedra of raping her. Believing Hippolytus to be guilty, Theseus curses his son,

---

[70] '*Theseus* faults touching women and ravishements, of the twaine, had the lesse shadowe and culler of honestie. Bicause *Theseus* dyd attempt it very often: for he stale awaye *Ariadne, Antiope,* and *Anaxo*', North (tr), above n 66, at 43. Perigune, 'after consorting with Theseus, bore him Melanippus, and afterwards lived with Deïoneus, son of Eurytus the Oechalian, to whom Theseus gave her', Perrin (tr), above n 66, at 19, VIII; Plutarch records of the war between Athens and the Amazons that Theseus 'made a voyage into the Euxine Sea, as Philochorus and sundry others say, on a campaign with Heracles against the Amazons, and received Antiope as a reward of his valour', *ibid* at 59, XXVI; after three months, 'a treaty of peace was made through the agency of Hippolyta; for Hippolyta is the name which Cleidemus gives to the Amazon whom Theseus married, not Antiope', *ibid* at 63, XXVII.

[71] I use the word 'citizen' here in its republican sense: Theseus promised the people 'government without a king and a democracy, in which he should only be commander in war and guardian of the laws, while in all else everyone should be on an equal footing', Perrin (tr), above n 66, at 53, XXIV.

[72] As, eg: '[H]e is said to have carried off Anaxo, a maiden of Troezen, and after slaying Sinis and Cercyon to have ravished their daughters; also to have married Periboea, the mother of Aias, and Phereboea afterwards, and Iope, the daughter of Iphicles; and because of his passion for Aegle, the daughter of Panopeus, as I have already said, he is accused of the desertion of Ariadne, which was not honourable nor even decent; and finally, his rape of Helen is said to have filled Attica with war, and to have brought about at last his banishment and death', *ibid* at 67, XXIX.

who dies a violent death, torn to pieces by his horses.[73] Throughout *A Midsummer Night's Dream*, the shade of Theseus lurks in the subconscious, the unspoken hinterland of terror that provides the imaginary counterpoint to the comic ecstasy of the play. Even in what Peter Holland describes as 'the play's structural centre'—the transformation of Bottom—the mythography of Theseus looms large.[74] The stage directions tell us that the bewitched Bottom enters 'with the ass head' (3.1.84): the remainder of his body is not 'translated'. Direct comparison with the myth of the Minotaur—half-man and half-beast, the product of sexual union between Pasiphae and the bull sent to Minos by Poseidon—was made in Book X of Apuleius' *The Golden Ass*, translated into English in 1566 by William Adlington, and an obvious literary source for Bottom's transformation. In Apuleius' work Lucius is transformed completely into an ass, and has sexual intercourse with a 'delicate Matron':

> But nothing greved me so much, as to think how I should with my huge and great legges embrace so faire a matron, or how I should touche her fine, deintie, and silken skinne, with my hard hoofes, or how it was possible to kisse her soft, her prettie and ruddie lippes, with my monstrous mouthe and stony teeth, or how she, who was so yonge and tender, could be able to receive me . . . and therewithal she eftsones embrased my bodie round about, and had her pleasure with me, whereby I thought the mother of Minotaurus, did not causeless quenche her inordinat desire with a Bull.[75]

Unlike the encounter between Lucius and the delicate matron, the relationship between Bottom and Titania is not consummated. Throughout this interlude Bottom is entirely concerned with sensual activities of a non-sexual nature, such as shaving (because he is 'marvellous hairy about the face' (4.1.23)), eating ('I could munch your good dry oats' (4.1.29)) and drinking ('Methinks I have a great desire to a bottle of hay' (4.1.30)).

Bottom's childlike naivety notwithstanding, the mental image of the Minotaur's conception—of violent bestial coupling—is ineradicable. Puck reports to Oberon that '[m]y mistress with a monster is in love' (3.2.6),[76] although the monstrosity that we witness is fantastical rather than abominable. The above line of Puck serves to conjure in the imagination a Bottom whom we never actually see onstage: the beast that impregnated Pasiphae or the ass copulating with his 'delicate matron' in *The Golden Ass*. In this imaginative sense, Jan Kott's description of the transformed Bottom as a 'monster' is not inaccurate; although his claim that the picture of

---

[73] Holland draws attention to the possibility that Shakespeare's Helena and Demetrius are versions of Phaedra and Hippolytus, transformed from the tragedy of Seneca's *Hippolytus* to the comedy of *A Midsummer Night's Dream*: P Holland, 'Theseus' Shadows in *A Midsummer Night's Dream*' (1994) 47 *Shakespeare Survey* 139, 142. Holland finds the above lines of Demetrius (2.1.214–16) unthreatening, arguing that 'we do not really imagine for a moment that he is likely to rape her', *ibid* at 148; this is probably true, but the possibility of rape is registered notwithstanding.

[74] *Ibid* at 150.

[75] Apuleius, *The xi. Books of the Golden Asse conteininge the Metamorphosie of Lucius Apuleius*, (tr) W Adlington (London, Henry Wykes, 1566) 109.*v*–110.*r*; on the influence of *The Golden Asse* over the transformation of Bottom, see Holland (ed), above n 18, Introduction, 69–71.

[76] Later in the same scene Oberon also refers to Bottom as a monster: 'And then I will her charmèd eye release / From monster's view' (3.2.376–77).

Titania caressing the head of an ass was 'closer to the fearful visions of Bosch' is excessive.[77] Kott incorrectly elevates the status of sex in the play to the level of the graphically violent, but he is right to emphasise its phantasmal presence, albeit that we glimpse it only through the mythographical imagination. Onstage, in keeping with the theme of Ovidian metamorphosis that governs the play, the sex between a woman and a beast that Apuleius explicitly describes in *The Golden Ass* is transformed into fantastical comedy.[78] As with Helena and Demetrius, so too with Bottom and Titania: the mythography of Theseus is an absent presence, in a transformed setting. To borrow Holland's evocative phrase (which he applies to the eponymous hero of Seneca's *Hippolytus* and the Cretan Minotaur), Theseus is the man on the stair from Hugh Mearns' 'The Psychoed'.[79] Theseus slew the Minotaur, but as important an aspect of the story is that (with the help of the thread provided by Ariadne) he escaped from the labyrinth.[80] For Shakespeare's Theseus, the labyrinth from which he eventually escapes is that of unquestioning and perpetual conformity to immutable law. Until the moment when he pardons Hermia and condones her marriage to Lysander, the archetypal lawgiver has refused to apply imagination to the resolution of juridical and moral conundrums such as that posed by Hermia's refusal to marry Demetrius.[81] Prior to that instant of imaginative liberation, supplicants such as Hermia would have been sacrificed to the violent imperatives of Athenian law, just as in legend young Cretan men and women were sacrificed each year as tribute to the Minotaur.[82]

---

[77] J Kott, *Shakespeare Our Contemporary* (New York, W W Norton & Co, 1974) 229; Kott associates Titania with Pasiphae, claiming that '[t]he slender, tender, and lyrical Titania longs for animal love', *ibid* at 228; Nuttall rejects the sexual explicitness of Kott's claim as 'simply ludicrous', noting that '[t]he twentieth century is marked by a prejudice in favour of the discordant', Nuttall, above n 35, at 51.

[78] On Ovidian metamorphosis and the transformation of Bottom as 'the play's most remarkable "higher imitation" of Ovid', see J Bate, *Shakespeare and Ovid* (Oxford, Clarendon, 1993) 142; Bate argues that the inversion of traditional gender roles, in which 'the rapacious divinity is female' and the male is 'a wise fool', ensures that the intimacy between Titania and Bottom is defused into comedy, *ibid* at 143. In 'Pyramus and Thisbe', *Shakespeare* parodies the style of Arthur Golding, whose translation into English of Ovid's *Metamorphoses* was published in 1567; see A B Taylor, 'Golding's Ovid, Shakespeare's "Small Latin", and the Real Object of Mockery in "Pyramus and Thisbe"' (1990) 42 *Shakespeare Survey* 53.

[79] Holland, above n 73, at 144: 'As I was going up the stair / I met a man who wasn't there. / He wasn't there again today. / I wish, I wish he'd stay away', H Mearns, 'The Psychoed' in *The Oxford Dictionary of Quotations* (Oxford, Oxford University Press, 1979) 336.

[80] The only explicit reference to mazes in the play is Titania's: 'And the quaint mazes in the wanton green / For lack of tread are undistinguishable' (2.1.99–100); these are the benign turf mazes of rural England. On the origins of mazes and the rites associated with them, see W H Matthews, *Mazes and Labyrinths: their History and Development* (New York, Dover Publications, 1970).

[81] A similar, literal interpretation of the text bedevils the attempts of the mechanicals to stage 'Pyramus and Thisbe'. They doubt they can perform the play without a real wall and real moonshine, and that the illusion of death and the presence onstage of an artificial lion will be unacceptable to 'the ladies' in the audience (3.1.8–55). As Bate notes, Peter Quince 'is bounded by the letter and accordingly fails to perceive the spirit', Bate, above n 78, at 132: until his decision to overturn the 'sharp Athenian law', the same may be said of Theseus.

[82] Relevant to a discussion of sacrificial rites and primitive law is the comment of Girard that '[t]he king's sovereignty—real or imagined, permanent or temporary—seems to derive from an original, generative act of violence inflicted on a surrogate victim', R Girard, *Violence and the Sacred*, (tr) P Gregory (Baltimore, Md, Johns Hopkins University Press, 1977) 120.

The Poetic Imagination, Antique Fables and the Dream of Law

Discussion of the imaginative application of law in *A Midsummer Night's Dream* inevitably brings us to the last character over whom the mythographical shadow of Theseus is cast: Egeus, the father of Hermia. According to legend, Theseus was the son of Aegeus and Aethra (the daughter of Pittheus, who founded the city of Troezen).[83] The symbolism of the Father is a crucial factor in understanding the legal significance of Egeus' insistence that his daughter be put to death for refusing to marry the husband of his choice. There is no reason given by Shakespeare why Egeus should want his daughter to marry Demetrius instead of Lysander. As Lysander informs the Duke:

> I am, my lord, as well-derived as he,
> As well-possessed: my love is more than his,
> My fortunes every way as fairly ranked . . . (1.1.99–101)

There is little, if anything, of material worth to distinguish the two young men. Indeed, if past experience is relevant, Lysander is likely to prove the more faithful of Hermia's two suitors. In a further echo of Plutarch's Theseus, Demetrius has a record of abandoning his lovers, as Lysander avers: 'Demetrius, I'll avouch it to his head, / Made love to Nedar's daughter, Helena' (1.1.106–07). The only explicable reason for Egeus' intransigence is to do with the exercise of paternal power. For Egeus, Hermia is his property, to bestow as he wishes, in accordance with the patriarchal law of Athens: 'I beg the ancient privilege of Athens; / As she is mine, I may dispose of her' (1.1.41–42). Upon discovery of the sleeping lovers in the wood, Egeus demands vengeance: 'I beg the law, the law upon his head!' (4.1.152) His resort to the awful retributive power of positive law recalls the demand of another vengeful patriarch, Shylock.[84] The unexpected decision of Theseus to 'overbear' (4.1.176) the will of Egeus (and also incidentally the law of Athens) and to approve the marriage of Hermia and Lysander represents the triumph of the legal imagination over an oppressive and irrational law.

Since the 12th century, children could be 'espoused' by their parents, by means of an engagement process known as *sponsalia per verba de futuro*: a verbal promise to marry at a future date. Parents were entitled to espouse their children when they reached the age of 7 years, until infancy officially ended at the age of 14 for a boy and 12 for a girl. A subsequent marriage would be valid only if both parties to it

---

[83] On the genealogy, birth and upbringing of Theseus and his eventful journey to Athens, see Perrin (tr), above n 66, at 7–25, III–XII. Plutarch's Theseus inadvertently brought about the death of Aegeus. He informed his father that, if he slew the Minotaur, then upon his safe return to Attica the ship which carried him would bear a white sail rather than a black one. On its return from Crete, as the ship drew near the coast of Attica, Theseus forgot to hoist the white sail. Seeing in the distance the black sail, Aegeus took it as a sign of his son's death and in despair jumped from a cliff to his death, *ibid* at 45, XXII.

[84] Shakespeare expands the theme of positive law and its inherent potential for injustice in *The Merchant of Venice*, which he wrote soon after *A Midsummer Night's Dream*. *The Merchant of Venice* was entered in the Stationers' Register on 22 July 1598, but was probably written in 1596–97; *The Merchant of Venice*, (ed) J Russell Brown (London, Arden Shakespeare, 2006) Introduction, xxi–xxvii. In demanding enforcement of the penalty clause attached to his bond with Antonio, Shylock echoes the above line of Egeus: 'My deeds upon my head! I crave the law' (4.1.202). Like Egeus, Shylock wishes the death of his daughter when she elopes with her lover: 'I would my daughter were dead at my foot' (3.1.80–81).

consented.⁸⁵ Despite the invalidity at English law of a 'forced' marriage, early modern juristic opinion would probably have divided over the idea that Hermia was morally bound to obey her father. The first line of Dugdale's *Origines Juridiciales* emphasises the symbolic importance of the father to governance of the State: the original of all government 'was in the Father of the Household' and obedience was 'the fruit of natural reverence'.⁸⁶ Opposition to uncritical acceptance of irrational laws was expressed unequivocally by Richard Hooker in *A Learned Sermon of the Nature of Pride*. Demonstrating adherence to the Ciceronian principle that '[t]rue law is right reason in agreement with nature' ('*Est quidem vera lex recta ratio naturae congruens*'),⁸⁷ Hooker states that

> [a] law simply commaunding or forbidding is but dead in comparison of that which expresseth the reason wherefore it doth the one or the other.⁸⁸

Although Hooker's ostensible theme in this work is the law of God and specifically the divine injunction against the sin of pride, as in *Of the Laws of Ecclesiastical Polity*, the particular theology expressed here is 'politic' and 'public' in the sense that the spiritual and the temporal are conflated.⁸⁹ Pride was the cause of civil unrest, as well as ecclesiastical rift:

> [B]y tyrannie of potentates, ambition of nobles, rebellion of subiects in civill states; by heresies, schismes, divisions in the Church; naming pride wee name the mother which brought them forth, and the only nurse that feedeth them.⁹⁰

Adherence to divine law (and its expression through public worship) effected continual personal transformation, shaping the political and social, as well as the

---

⁸⁵ One such example of a daughter refusing to marry in accordance with the espousal arranged by her parents was recorded in 1598 at Lichfield, concerning *sponsalia per verba de futuro* between Thomas Waterhous and Sibille Bancrofte: 'the sayd Sibill and this Respondent being marryed together when they were but x years of age by the procurement and entysement of their parents and friends the sayd Sibell after she came to better discretion would never Lyke of this respondent nor take him for her husband but by all meanes she could devyse did denye and forsake him and soe still doeth and sayeth that neither by any means this Respondent could ever worke nor by any persuasion of other frend whatsoever the sayd Sibell would not nor as yet can be brought to lyve with him', LJRO B/C/5/1598/Matrimonial: *Bancrofte v Waterhous* in A Tarver, *Church Court Records: An Introduction for Family and Local Historians* (Chichester, Phillimore, 1995) 84. Pope Alexander III (1159–1181) decreed that marriage could be contracted by consent alone, without church ceremony, so long as consent was notified in the present tense: *sponsalia per verba de praesenti*. For an introduction to the law of marriage in the 16th century, see L Stone, *Road to Divorce, 1530–1987* (Oxford, Oxford University Press, 1990) 51–71; also, M Ingram, *Church Courts, Sex and Marriage in England, 1570–1640* (Cambridge, Cambridge University Press, 1987); F G Emmison, *Elizabethan Life*, 5 vols (Chelmsford, Essex Records Office, 1973) vol 2: 'Morals and the Church Courts'.

⁸⁶ Dugdale, above n 1, at 1. On *paterfamilias* in ancient Rome and the power of the father as a reflection of imperial authority, see ch 5, text to n 124, below.

⁸⁷ Cicero, *De Re Publica*, Bk III.XXII.33

⁸⁸ R Hooker, *A Learned Sermon of the Nature of Pride* (London, John Barnes, 1612) A2.r.

⁸⁹ McGrade suggests that where Aristotle acknowledged the place of religion in the *polis*, Hooker regarded religion as 'the *chief* good of the soul for which a body politic will naturally "care"', A S McGrade (ed), *Of the Laws of Ecclesiastical Polity* (Cambridge, Cambridge University Press, 1989) Introduction, xxv. In Book VIII of *Of the Laws*, Hooker distinguished between 'secular and Ecclesiastical affairs' while commenting on their indivisibility: 'The *Church* and the *Commonwealth* therefore are in this case personally one society', *ibid* at 132, 133, Bk VIII.I.IV.

⁹⁰ Hooker, above n 88, B4.*v*.

religious. Hooker's insistence that the will of man—'will in all things'—should be 'framed by reason; reason directed by the law of God and nature'[91] finds a close correlative in the quasi-divine argument of Coke that common law was 'the absolute perfection of reason'.[92]

For Hooker, reason must be receptive to imagination in order that the will of God might be manifested on earth. I refer in chapter one to the belief of Hooker that the written word, the statute or *leges scriptae*, was not the exclusive repository of truth.[93] The 'spiritual influence'[94] over Man's exercise of reason legitimated the use of religious ritual; only through the licit use of symbols could the invisible and intangible be represented and comprehended. Hence the sacraments of the Anglican church 'are resemblances framed according to things spiritually understood, whereunto they serve as a hand to leade, and a way to direct'.[95] The role that Hooker attributes to the choir of angels, acting as benevolent intermediaries between God and mankind, mirrors the role played by the fairies in *A Midsummer Night's Dream*. Invisible ministers of divine will, they intervene in the mortal world, guiding the actions of human souls and liberating their imaginations from the deadening constraints of literal exactitude. The only difference noted by Hooker between humans and angels is the omniscience of the latter: 'Angels already have full and complete knowledge in the highest degree that can bee imparted unto them'.[96]

---

[91] Ibid, B1.v.

[92] Sir Edward Coke, *The Second Part of the Institutes Of the Lawes of England* (London, E Dawson, R Meighen, W Lee & D Pakeham, 1642) 179. Schoeck argues that Hooker's writing fuses 'Erasmian humanism and Christian theology', R J Schoeck, 'From Erasmus to Hooker: An Overview' in A S McGrade (ed), *Richard Hooker and the Construction of Christian Community* (Binghampton, Medieval & Renaissance Texts & Studies, 1997) 61. Hooker's affinity with renaissance humanism is traceable to his education at Corpus Christi College, Oxford, founded in 1517 by Richard Fox (Bishop of Winchester and a political adviser to Henry VIII); as Schoeck notes, Fox offered 'a humanistic curriculum, in which enterprise much was owing to the ideas of Erasmus', *ibid*.

[93] See ch 1, text to n 117, above.

[94] R Hooker, *Of the Lawes of Ecclesiastical Politie* (London, William Stansbye, 1622) 56, Bk II.I.

[95] *Ibid* at 130, Bk IV.I. The Preface to a 1705 edition of Hooker's works contains the following *apologia* for his devotion to the rites of the Anglican church: 'As St. Paul fought with a Beast at Ephesus, so he [Hooker] encountered a certain Number of Men called Puritans, Righteous in Shew, Positive in Opinion, who were endued with a certain Squamishness of Conscience, suck'd in from the Dregs of Geneva, that any Ceremonies decent in themselves, and allowable by the Church, were peuk'd at, and would not go down with them: A Set of Men who were always more dash'd with Prejudice and Opposition, than fortified with Argument: A Set of Men who stopt at nothing to carry on their Cause, and to gratify their peevish Conceits, would not have cared if Church and State had but been one Pile of Ruin, could but John Calvin's Form of Worship and Principles been established. These Books of the Ingenious Mr Hooker are levelled against these Enemies of Ecclesiastical Power', *A Faithful Abridgment of the Works of that Learned and Judicious Divine, Mr. Richard Hooker* (London, Benjamin Bragg, 1705) Preface.

[96] Hooker, above n 94, at 12, Bk I.VI. According to Isaak Walton, as Hooker lay on his deathbed he confided to his confessor, Dr Saravia, '[t]hat he was meditating the number and nature of Angels, and their blessed Obedience and Order, without which, Peace could not be in Heaven; and oh that it might be so on Earth', I Walton, 'The Life of Mr Richard Hooker' in *The Works of that Learned and Judicious Divine, Mr Richard Hooker* (London, R Scot, 1670) 23. McGrade notes of Book I of *Of the Laws* that it 'is thus an especially promising text for reading Hooker as an Anglican angelic doctor, serenely above the controversies of his day', McGrade (ed), above n 89, Introduction, xx.

For Gerard Legh, the distinction between members of the Inner Temple and the Heavenly Choir was less obvious. Legh describes the transformation of lawyers into angels at the formal ceremony that ended the Inner Temple revels of 1561. In chapter two, I noted the ritual at the Gray's Inn revels of 1594, during which members of the Inn were dubbed Knights of the Helmet, thereby creating a sacred community dedicated to the classical principles of *societas*.[97] At the Inner Temple in 1561, Palaphilos presided over a ceremony in which members were initiated into the Knighthood of Pallas:

> Advaunce your honours by your dedes,
> to lyve for evermore,
> As Pallas knightes, by Pallas helpe,
> Pallas serve ye therefore.[98]

The rites of initiation precede and enable metamorphosis or transubstantiation, from corporeal beings to celestial hierarchs. Legh concludes his eulogy to 'these houses of honour'—the Inns of Court—with the following assertion of their members' seraphic qualities:

> Herein I might compare your state (but yt you are men) unto the heavenly Ierarches, for that you have all the three things that Ierarches have, that is, Order, cunnyng, and woorking. In your order, is office, in your cunning, readiness, and in your woorkyng, is service.[99]

The benevolent intervention of spirits in the earthly affairs of mortals was, as I have outlined above, a theme explored by Hooker in *Of the Laws of Ecclesiastical Polity* and by Shakespeare in *A Midsummer Night's Dream*, angels and fairies both acting as agents or messengers of the supreme deity. Legh's *The Accedens of Armory* works on two distinct levels. One is that of the heraldic manual, delineating and explaining the significance of armorial devices. The other is related entirely to the fantastical description of the author's visit to the Inner Temple (which is at the end of the book and runs to only 30 of the 232 folio sheets in the first edition of 1562). Here the style of the heraldic manual is replaced by an imaginative (at times almost hallucinatory) exploration of the origins of law in classical mythography and Judaeo-Christian theology. In Legh's account, the angels of the Judaeo-Christian God co-exist with Pallas Athene and Palaphilos, 'high constable of the Goddesse her selfe, marshall of thinner Temple'.[100] His inventive and illusory account of the English legal institution is peculiar for its recognition of the foundations of English law in the antique fables of ancient worlds, both classical and Judaeo-Christian. Elucidation of the angelic theme may be found in another Elizabethan manual of heraldic devices, *Workes of Armorie*, by John Bossewell. Although Bossewell does not make the direct correlation between angels and lawyers, he includes familiar

---

[97] See ch 2, text to nn 85–87, above.
[98] Legh, above n 3, at 224.*v.*
[99] *Ibid* at 232.*r.*
[100] *Ibid* at 203.*v.*

allusions to the unwritten traditions of honour, nobility and virtue that Legh identified with the Inns of Court and their members:

> [A]lmightie God is the originall author of honouring Nobilitie, who, even in the heavens hathe made a discrepance of his heavenly Spirites, giving them severall names, as Ensigns of honour. And these heavenly Spirites, when they are sent of God, are called, *Angeli*, Angels: which in the Greeke tongue signifieth, sent . . . in the Latine tongue, they be interpreted, *Nuntù*, Messengers.[101]

In the pragmatic and institutional forum of the courtroom, the invocation of the supernatural invariably had real (as opposed to imaginary) and violent consequences. I refer in chapter one to the trials for High Treason of suspected papists and the gruesome public executions that inevitably followed their convictions.[102] In the reports of the Elizabethan witchcraft trials, we witness a ghastly theatrical parody of the forensic process, in which the supernatural is associated not with the Heavenly Choir but with the destructive power of Satan. In the words of Thomas Nashe, 'the divell can transform himself into an angell of light, appeare in the day aswell as in the night'.[103] At the trials for witchcraft, imagination was equated unequivocally with idolatry, falsehood and rebellion.[104] Indeed, Nashe links the mythical spirits of rural England, the 'Robbin-good-fellowes, Elfes, Fairies, Hobgoblins of our latter age,' to 'idolatrous former daies'.[105]

It seems likely that Shakespeare's depiction of Puck was as much influenced by the lurid details of contemporary witchcraft trials as it was by English folk-tales. As Reginald Scot noted, writing in 1584:

> Robin goodfellowe ceaseth now to be much feared, and poperie is sufficientlie discovered. Neuertheles, witches charms, and coniurors cousenages are yet thought effectuall.[106]

One such trial was that of 'the three Witches of Warboys', held at Huntingdon Assizes in 1593. A man, his wife and their daughter (John, Alice and Agnes Samuell) were convicted of bewitching 'the five daughters of Robert Throckmorton Esquier', 12 of his maidservants, '[a]nd also for the bewitching to death of the Lady

---

[101] J Bossewell, *Workes of Armorie* (London, Richardi Totelli, 1572) 10.*r*.

[102] See ch 1, text to n 120, above.

[103] Nashe, above n 44, B2.*v*. While Legh compares members of the Inns of Court to 'the heavenly Ierarches', Nashe links with the devil those lawyers who make their living in the courts at Westminster: 'If in one man a whole legion of divells have bin billetted? how manie hundred thousand legions retaine to a Tearme at *London*. If I said but to a Taverne, it were an infinite thing. In *Westminster Hall* a man can scarce breath for them: for in every corner they hover as thick as moates in the sunne', *ibid* B4.*r*.

[104] See B P Levack, *The Witch-Hunt in Early Modern Europe* (Harlow, Pearson Longman, 2006); C Larner, *Witchcraft and Religion: the Politics of Popular Belief*, (ed) A Macfarlane (Oxford, Blackwell, 1984); A Macfarlane, *Witchcraft in Tudor and Stuart England: a Regional and Comparative Study* (London, Routledge & Kegan Paul, 1970); K M Briggs, *Pale Hecate's Team: an Examination of the Beliefs on Witchcraft and Magic among Shakespeare's Contemporaries and his Immediate Successors* (London, Routledge & Kegan Paul, 1962).

[105] Nashe, above n 44, B2.*v*.

[106] R Scot, *The discoverie of witchcraft wherein the lewd dealing of witches and witchmongers is notablie detected* (London, William Brome, 1584) 'The Epistle', Bii.*v*.

Crumwell'.[107] Evidence of their supernatural powers was the effect the alleged witches had on the bodily functions of their victims. The Samuells were next-door neighbours of the Throckmortons in the village of Warboys, near Huntingdon. In November 1589, 10-year-old Jane Throckmorton 'fell upon the sodaine into a straunge kinde of sickenes and distemperature of body'. The sickness was characterised by prolonged bouts of sneezing, followed by 'a great trance', during which she 'lay quietly' for half an hour:

> Soone after she woulde begin to swell and heave up her bellie so as none was able to bende her, or keepe hir downe, sometime shee would shake one legge and no other part of her, as if the paulsie had bin in it, sometimes the other, presently she would shake one of hir armes and then the other and soone after hir head, as if shee had binne infected with the running paulsie: continuing in this case two or three days.[108]

Alice Samuells visited the sick child, whereupon her condition worsened. The child exclaimed to her grandmother:

> [L]ooke where the old witch sitteth (pointing to the said mother Samuell) did you ever see (said the Child) one more like a witch than she is: Take off her black-thrumbed cappe, for I cannot abide to looke on her.[109]

Jane's elder sister, Joan, was even more grievously tormented:

> [I]t forced her to neese, screetch & grone verie fearefullie . . . & many times sitting in a chaier having her fit, shee would with her often starting, and heaving, almost breake the chaier shee sate in.[110]

There is a notable resemblance here to the mischievous conduct of Shakespeare's Puck, who 'frights the maidens of the villag'ry' (2.1.35), changes his shape to resemble a 'three-foot stool' on which women sit (2.1.52) and causes the assembled company to 'neeze' (2.1.56).

Of interest to a discussion of the possible influence of *the Three Witches of Warboys* over the depiction of Puck is the 'confession' of Alice Samuell, made to the presiding minister, 'master Doctor *Chamberlin*, at the time and place of her execution being upon the ladder'.[111] She claimed to have summoned three spirits, who assisted her in bewitching the Throckmorton children. One of these familiars was called Pluck:

> Being demaunded, whether shee had bewitched Master Throckmortons children: Shee confessed, that shee had done it. Being asked, with which of her Spirites: Shee said, that it was Pluck. Being asked, what shee said to him, when shee sent him about that matter: Shee confessed, that shee willed him: go torment them, but not hurt them.[112]

---

[107] Anon, *The most strange and admirable discoverie of the three Witches of Warboys arraigned, convicted and executed at the last Assises at Huntington* (London, Thomas Man and Iohn Winnington, 1593) title page.
[108] *Ibid*, B.r.
[109] *Ibid*, B.v.
[110] *Ibid*, B2.v.
[111] *Ibid*, P3.v.
[112] *Ibid*, P4.r.

None of the above is to suggest that Shakespeare necessarily based the darker aspects of Puck's character on any of the events and characters described in the anonymous *Three Witches of Warboys* (it was published in 1593, a couple of years before *A Midsummer Night's Dream* was written). Puck belongs to the folkloric genre of poukes, puckles and púcas that Robert Burton described as terrestrial devils of '[a] bigger kinde'.[113] But the report of the trial is significant in demonstrating both the suggestive power of supernatural belief and the assimilation of English folklore into juridical procedure.

The trial of the 'Witches of Warboys' represented the administration of criminal justice at a regional level: clearly the court was sympathetic to the beliefs of customary folklore. It should be emphasised that the published report of the trial and events preceding the indictment of the Samuell family is not a law report in the institutional sense of Coke's or Plowden's *Reports*. The story of the 'witches' covers a four-year period, and the record of supernatural occurrences leading up to the trial was presumably compiled mainly from anecdotal reportage and the reminiscences of witnesses. At issue here is not the establishment of legal principle, but rather the recording in chronological fashion of the purported facts that led to the executions of the accused. Typical for a criminal trial of this period is the absence both of defence counsel and any rules or protocol governing the admissibility of evidence. The judge at the trial performed an inquisitorial role as well as a judicial one. Hence in April 1593 the judge at the assizes, Fenner J, was lodging at Huntingdon in the Crown Inn; so too was one of the witnesses, Joan Throckmorton. It was not considered a matter of procedural irregularity that Fenner J went to meet Joan in the garden of the inn, where she was 'then being in the company with other women'. The judge was accompanied by 'a great assembly of Justices & gentlemen'. When they met, 'Joan fel into one of her ordinarie fits',[114] whereupon 'many good prayers were made both by the Judge & all the company'. One of the accused, Agnes Samuell, happened also to be in the garden. Joan's father pointed her out to the judge and told him that 'if she would say certain words in the maner of a charge, y then the said mistr. Joan shalbe presently well'. The words of the 'charge' were as follows:

> [A]s I am a witch, & a worse witch then my mother, and did consent to the death of the La. Crumwell, so I charge the divel to let Mistres Ioan Throckmorton come out of her fit at this present.

The judge read the charge aloud, with no apparent effect on Joan. Again, he 'made many good prayers & petitions to God',[115] to no avail. Subsequently, Agnes Samuell was made to say aloud the formulaic charge, after which

---

[113] Burton, above n 9, at 48; Schleiner concludes that 'whether Pluck is an additional source or only an analogue, it seems to me that Shakespeare's Puck is deeply imbued with dark conceptions of devilish spirits', Schleiner, above n 9, at 68; see also, D P Walker, *Unclean Spirits: Possession and Exorcism in the Late Sixteenth and Early Seventeenth Centuries* (London, Scolar Press, 1981).
[114] Anon, above n 107, O4.r.
[115] *Ibid*, O4.v.

the said Mistres Ioan was well as ever shee was in her life, & so hath continued without any grife or fittes till this day.[116]

The accused were indicted before the jury on the following morning. Evidence was heard for five hours,

> until both the Judge, Justices, and Jury saide openly that the cause was most apparant: their consciences were wel satisfied, that the saide Witches were guilty, & had deserved death: and therewithal the gent. ceased to give any further evidence.[117]

They were executed the next day.

IV. A Most Rare Vision

The witches of Warboys were an enigma, a riddle. Unintelligible to the reason of the law, they were deemed obscene idolaters who merited their fate on the gallows. *Aenigma* was acceptable as a poetic device, but in a legal context it represented dissimulation or falsehood.[118] In 1589, George Puttenham made exactly this claim when he wrote that

> [w]e dissemble againe under covert and darke speaches, when we speake by way of riddle (*Enigma*) of which the sence can hardly be picked out, but by the parties owne assoile ...[119]

Writing in 1600, William Fulbecke stated that

> true is that saying of Cicero, *Omnia incerta sunt cum a iure discessum est*. If you depart from Law there is no certain state of any thing.[120]

Departure from immutable custom represented a threat to societal order. Hence, Fulbecke repeats his advice 'that there should be laws written, & that such laws should not be altered without urgent occasion'[121]; and again,

> [t]he writing or the engraving of lawes in Tables is a principall cause of ye certainty of the same, & without certainty, it should be of smal credit: for what authority or force should it have, if it did alwaies change like the Moone ...[122]

---

[116] *Ibid*, P.r.
[117] *Ibid*, P.v. On English criminal law in the early modern period, see J G Bellamy, *Criminal Law and Society in Late Medieval and Tudor England* (Gloucester, Alan Sutton, 1984); also, J A Sharpe, *Crime in Early Modern England, 1550–1750* (London, Longman, 1999).
[118] On the classical origin of the legal enigma and its discussion in renaissance rhetoric manuals, see P Goodrich, 'Legal Enigmas—Antonio de Nebrija, *The Da Vinci Code* and the Emendation of Law' (2010) 30 *Oxford Journal of Legal Studies* 71, 74–87.
[119] G Puttenham, *The Arte of English Poesie* (London, Richard Field, 1589) 156–57.
[120] W Fulbecke, *A Direction or Preparative to the Study of the Lawe Wherein is showed, what things ought to be observed and used of them that are addicted to the study of the Law* (London, T Wight, 1600) B4.v.
[121] *Ibid*, B5.v.
[122] *Ibid*, B6.r.

The Poetic Imagination, Antique Fables and the Dream of Law

The poetic imagination was a threat to the perfect reason of law: sufficient cause in itself for Plato to exclude poets from his ideal state.[123] Puttenham tells us that the *Areopagites*, the judges in the Athenian court of Areopagus, were expressly forbidden from exercising their imaginations when giving judgment: poetical devices such as allegory were harbingers of uncertainty, embodying as they did 'duplicitie of meaning or dissimulation under covert and darke intendments'. The figurative speeches of poets were 'meere illusions to the minde, and wresters of upright iudgement'.[124] Shakespeare allows his lawgiver, Theseus, to express similar doubts about the value and integrity of the imagination. He is mistrustful of 'antique fables' (5.1.3) even though, as we have seen, patently he belongs to them. The idea of dramatising the conflict between reason and imagination may well have come to Shakespeare from North's translation of Plutarch's *Lives*, at the start of which the author expounds his intention of dispelling the poetic mythology surrounding the life of Theseus (and the parallel life of Romulus) and divulging only the historical truth:

> Wherein I would wishe that the inventions of Poets, and the traditions of fabulous antiquitie, would suffer themselves to be purged and reduced to the forme of a true and historicall reporte...[125]

The notion that history is objective and definitive was a belief shared by early modern English jurists, as they sought to justify the claim that the common law had existed as a recognisable body of jurisprudence since time immemorial.[126]

Theseus's speech about '[t]he lunatic, the lover and the poet' (5.1.2–22) is not a paean by the Duke to the creative power of the imagination.[127] His homily is ambiguous in intent, suggesting at one point that the imagination employs 'tricks' (5.1.18) to attain the ends of its author. But within the space of 200 lines a transformation has been effected on Theseus, echoing his earlier metamorphosis where he 'overbears' both the will of Egeus and the law of Athens (4.1.176). When Hippolyta comments on the inadequacies of the mechanicals' performance of 'Pyramus and Thisbe', calling it 'the silliest stuff that ever I heard' (5.1.204), Theseus replies: 'The best in this kind are but shadows; and the worst are no worse,

---

[123] '...the only poetry that should be allowed in a state is hymns to the gods and paeans in praise of good men', Plato, *The Republic*, (tr) D Lee (London, Penguin, 1987) 375, Bk X.III.607a.

[124] Puttenham, above n 119, at 128.

[125] North (tr), above n 66, at 2. Perrin translates the same passage as: 'May I therefore succeed in purifying Fable, making her submit to reason and take on the semblance of History', Perrin (tr), above n 66, at 5, I. Holland observes that 'the world of "antique fables"' is one to which Theseus 'indissolubly belongs', Holland, above n 73, at 143.

[126] For example, Sir Thomas Wilson claimed with absolute certainty that 'this Kingdome is an absolute Imperiall Monarchy held nether of Pope, Emperor, nor any but of God alone, and so hath bene ever since the year of the World 2855, which was 1108 yeares before Christ', Sir Thomas Wilson, 'The State of England, Anno Dom. 1600' in F J Fisher (ed), 16 *The Camden Miscellany* (London, Offices of the Society, 1936) 1. Coke makes a similar claim, stating that Brutus, the mythical founder of English law, 'died after the Creation of the World 2860 years, and before the Incarnation of Christ 1103 years, Samuel then being Judge of Israel', Coke, 3 *Reports* (1602) 2: Preface, viiia.

[127] The speech of 21 lines incorporates the word 'imagination' three times and the word 'imagining' once.

146

if imagination amend them'. (5.1.205–206) The transformation from monolithic lawgiver and patriarch to flexible legislator and judge is complete: imagination has been formally admitted to the lexicon of the supreme magistrate. Although Puttenham argued that imagination facilitated dissimulation—acceptable in the poet but not in the judge—he acknowledged that even 'the great Emperour' appreciated the importance of imaginative skills: '*Qui nescit dissimulare nescit regnare*' ('he who is unable to dissemble is unable to rule').[128] Puttenham had in mind the governance of the ideal State and the imaginative treatment of that theme in the commonwealths of Plato's *Republic* and Thomas More's *Utopia*. As Puttenham concisely remarked of the utopian literary genre, with reference to both *The Republic* and *Utopia*, the exemplary constitution was 'easier to be wished then to be performed',[129] but in *A Midsummer Night's Dream* Shakespeare manages to convey both the wish and the performance of the exemplary. There is a sense at the end of the play that Theseus has become a 'philosopher king', thus enabling the realisation of the imaginary State, in accordance with Plato's exhortation that:

> The society we have described can never grow into a reality or see the light of day, and there will be no end to the troubles of states, or indeed, my dear Glaucon, of humanity itself, till philosophers become kings in this world, or till those we now call kings and rulers really and truly become philosophers.[130]

Discussion of Plato's *Republic* returns us to the idea that the development of the philosophical imagination is a *sine qua non* in the creation of spiritual unity and political community, prerequisites for the foundation of the *polis*. When Bottom awakes from his dream, the transformation that he has undergone is not confined merely to the removal of the ass's head. His political imagination has been aroused, signalled by his confused rendering of 1 *Corinthians* 2.9:

> The eye of man hath not heard, the ear of man hath not seen, man's hand is not able to taste, his tongue to conceive, nor his heart to report what my dream was! (4.1.205–7)[131]

St Paul elaborates the anatomical metaphor later in 1 *Corinthians* to describe an interdependent Christian community in which the active contribution of each

---

[128] Puttenham, above n 119, at 155; Puttenham is referring here to Louis XI of France, who devised the above maxim.

[129] *Ibid* at 32. More's *Utopia* was published in Latin in 1516; in 1551 it was translated into English by Ralph Robinson. On literary utopias, see F E Manuel and F P Manuel, *Utopian Thought in the Western World* (Oxford, Blackwell, 1979); R C Elliott, *The Shape of Utopia: Studies in a Literary Genre* (Chicago, Ill, University of Chicago Press, 1970).

[130] Plato, *Republic*, 202–3, Bk V.473d.

[131] 'Eye hath not seen, nor ear heard, neither have entered into the heart of man, the things which God hath prepared for them that love him', *The First Epistle of Paul the Apostle to the Corinthians* 2.9; all references to the text are from the Authorised King James Version of the Bible. Nuttall suggests that Bottom's confused rendering of the passage deepens St Paul's message, taking us beyond earthly values to 'a reality beyond categories', Nuttall, above n 60, at 127. Coke adapted the above passage from 1 *Corinthians* to describe *Postnati*. *Calvin's Case*: '. . . such a one as the eye of the law (our books and book-cases) never saw, as the ears of the law (our reporters) never heard of, nor the mouth of the law (for *judex est lex loquens*) the Judges our forefathers of the law never tasted', Coke, *Postnati. Calvin's Case*, 7 Reports (1608) 4: 4a.

member is valued as an integral part of the whole, regardless of the function each individual actually performs. The Pauline message is directed at the Christian commonwealth on earth, that good might be done for the benefit of all its citizens, irrespective of their rank, status or occupation:

> For the body is not one member, but many. If the foot shall say, Because I am not the hand, I am not of the body: is it therefore not of the body? And if the ear shall say, Because I am not the eye, I am not of the body: is it therefore not of the body? If the whole body were an eye, where were the hearing? If the whole were hearing, where were the smelling? But now hath God set the members every one of them in the body, as it hath pleased him. And if they were all one member, where were the body? But now are they many members, yet but one body.[132]

In 1608, some 12 years after *A Midsummer Night's Dream*, Shakespeare was to explore more fully, and in an overt political context, the Pauline metaphor of the body and its secular application: at the start of *Coriolanus*, the patrician Menenius addresses the mutinous citizens on the role assigned to each member of the body politic.[133] The interpretation given the anatomical metaphor by Menenius is hierarchic rather than communitarian, emphasising the Platonic principle of the correct ordering of parts and the performance by each part of its allotted function.[134] The particular exegesis offered by Menenius is antithetical to St Paul's explanation that 'those members of the body which we think to be less honourable, upon these we bestow more abundant honour'.[135]

Bottom's awakening instances a mimetic representation, rather than a comparative critique or an ideological perspective, of the Pauline communitarian thesis. Like St Paul, Bottom speaks in riddles or *aenigma* and, like the mechanicals, the audience is left in ignorance as to the exact nature of his vision. But it is reasonable to infer from Bottom's reference to 1 *Corinthians* that for a moment in his dream

---

[132] 1 *Corinthians* 12.14–20.
[133] *Coriolanus* 1.1.94–161; see also, ch 1, text to nn 51–52, above. The speech of Menenius to the citizens is derived directly from the defence of papal supremacy provided by Pope Adrian IV (1154–1159), as related by William Camden in *Remaines*: 'All the members of the body conspired against the stomacke, as against the swallowing gulfe of all their labors; for whereas the eies beheld, the eares heard, the hands labored, the feete traveled, the tongue spake, and all partes performed their functions, onely the stomacke lay ydle and consumed all. Hereuppon they ioyntly agreed al to forbeare their labors, and to pine away their lasie and publike enemy ... albeit the Princes gather much, yet not so much for themselves, as for others: So that if they want, they cannot supply the want of others; therefore do not repine at Princes heerein, but respect the common good of the whole publike estate', W Camden, *Remaines of a Greater Worke, Concerning Britaine, the inhabitants thereof* (London, Simon Waterson, 1605) 199.
[134] Plato, *Republic*, Bk IV.427d–434d; see also, Plato, 'Gorgias' in *Gorgias, Menexenus, Protagoras*, (tr) T Griffith, (ed) M Schofield (Cambridge, Cambridge University Press, 2010) 507e–508a. Patterson discusses the anatomical metaphor in 1 *Corinthians* with reference to Bottom's 'utopian vision'; she argues that after the Midland Rising of 1607, Shakespeare was disinclined to use again a comedic medium through which to express popular social and political grievances, Patterson, above n 15, at 68–69. On the Midland Rising and its influence over *Coriolanus*, see E C Pettet, '*Coriolanus* and the Midlands Insurrection of 1607' (1950) 3 *Shakespeare Survey* 34; A Gurr, '"Coriolanus" and the Body Politic' (1975) 28 *Shakespeare Survey* 63; D George, 'Plutarch, Insurrection, and Dearth in *Coriolanus*' (2000) 53 *Shakespeare Survey* 60.
[135] 1 *Corinthians* 12.23.

A Most Rare Vision

he saw face to face that which he had only ever seen through a glass, darkly: a Christian commonwealth of Aristotelian friends, of which the mechanicals are the microcosm and template.[136] Shakespeare was not the first writer to place St Paul's words in the mouth of a wise fool. Towards the end of *The Praise of Folly*, Erasmus quotes the lines (spoken by the character of Folly) from 1 *Corinthians* 2.9:

> was never mans eie sawe, nor eare heard, nor thought of hert yet compassèd, what, and how great felicitee god hath prepared unto such as dooe love him.[137]

It might have been the above translation by Sir Thomas Chaloner, with its reference to a thinking heart, that inspired Shakespeare's treatment of Bottom's synaesthesia on waking from his dream. Erasmus is influenced throughout *The Praise of Folly* by the meditation in 1 *Corinthians*, on 'the wisdom of the wise' and in particular the assertion of St Paul that 'God hath chosen the foolish things of the world to confound the wise'.[138] According to Erasmus, such people are blessed and, of particular relevance to Bottom in *A Midsummer Night's Dream*, 'those holy men shalbe altogether transformed and alterated'.[139] In the same passage, Erasmus conflates the life of the 'good Christian' with that of the wise fool, identifying along the way many of the traits that characterise Bottom's confused state when he awakes:

> [T]hey are subiecte to a certaine passion muche lyke unto madnesse or witrayving, whan ravished so in the sprite, or beyng in a traunce, thei dooe speake certaine thyngs not hangyng one with an other . . .[140]

Good Christians have glimpsed the incomprehensible wonders to which St Paul refers, but they will disclose the details of their vision to nobody:

> [T]hei denie plainly thei wote where thei became, or whether thei were than in theyr bodies, or out of their bodies . . . savyng as it were through a cloude, or by a dreame . . .[141]

In similar fashion, Bottom refuses to disclose the details of his dream to the other mechanicals, 'for if I tell you, I am not true Athenian'. (4.2.23) Of great importance to appreciating, if not fully understanding, the inexplicable ecstasy of Bottom's dream is the prophetic line of Folly's, spoken at the end of *The Praise of Folly*: 'remember the Greeke proverbe, that *oftentimes a foole maie speake to purpose*'.[142] Slavoj Žižek associates the fool and the knave respectively with 'left-wing'

---

[136] On Aristotelian friendship and community as the basis of the *polis*, see ch 5, text to nn 89–92, below. Patterson refers to the 'profound spiritual levelling' of Bottom's speech: Patterson, above n 15, at 68. Ward describes the mechanicals in *A Midsummer Night's Dream* as 'a mini-commonwealth of friends', representing a new social order in Tudor England: 'the emerging "middling" sort': Ward, above n 49, at 208.
[137] Desiderius Erasmus, *The Praise of Folie*, (tr) Sir Thomas Chaloner (London, Thomas Berthelet, 1549) T.iii.r.
[138] 1 *Corinthians* 1.19, 1.27.
[139] Erasmus, above n 137, T.ii.v.
[140] *Ibid*, T.iii.r.
[141] *Ibid*, T.iii.r–v.
[142] *Ibid*, T.iii.v.

and 'right-wing' political ideologies. He characterises the fool as the licensed court jester who casts a satirical light on the existing political structure, while the knave is a conformist figure whose argument in favour of the extant order is based on nothing more than the fact of its existence. Žižek makes the familiar observation that although the fool acts as a cultural critic, his comic mode of expression—or 'ludic procedures'—dissipates his satirical intent, thereby supplementing rather than subverting the status quo.[143] The nearest we have to a satirical fool in *A Midsummer Night's Dream* is Puck, whose objectified relationship both with the mortal *personae* of the play and the audience casts him as much in the role of critic as it does realistic character within the narrative frame of the drama.[144] Puck's critical propensity notwithstanding, it is Bottom who comes closest to expressing the vision of an alternative society—a world in which 'truth, reason and love' (3.1.120) are reunited and directed by the political imagination towards the realisation of his dream.[145]

Civil rebellion by a disaffected under-class is not an explicit theme of *A Midsummer Night's Dream*. Shakespeare had already directly addressed the subject in *Henry VI, Part 2*, but in *A Midsummer Night's Dream* the proximity of the rebel is sensed, even if he is never seen: he is on the edge, in the shadows, another man on the stair.[146] In the mid-1590s, when the play was written, organised rebellion had become a commonplace. The midsummer riots of Elizabethan apprentices in London are well documented.[147] Unemployment, high food prices, grain shortages, the perceived impact of monopolies on tradesmen and xenophobic anti-alien sentiments were all causes of unrest in late-Elizabethan London. As Roger

---

[143] Slavoj Žižek, *The Plague of Fantasies* (London, Verso, 1997) 45–46. Žižek bases his argument on Lacan's thesis that the left-wing intellectual is tolerated and his views adopted because, like the fool, he is 'clothed in the insignia of the jester'. The right-wing intellectual on the other hand is a knave: '[H]e doesn't retreat from the consequences of what is called realism; that is, when required, he admits he's a crook', J Lacan, *The Ethics of Psychoanalysis 1959–1960: the Seminar of Jacques Lacan. Book 7*, (tr) D Porter, (ed) J-A Miller (London, Routledge, 1992) 182–83. For a mid 20th-century, socialist interpretation of the utopian literary genre, one that 'take[s] its rise from the desires and hopes of the people', see A L Morton, *The English Utopia* (London, Lawrence & Wishart, 1952) 33.

[144] Betteridge describes Puck as the 'internal author of the play's narrative . . . embodying the dangerous possibility that the created artificial nature of the play will be exposed', T Betteridge, *Shakespearean Fantasy and Politics* (Hatfield, University of Hertfordshire Press, 2005) 74.

[145] G K Chesterton described *A Midsummer Night's Dream* as 'a psychological study . . . of a spirit that unites mankind'. For Chesterton, Bottom was saintly and heroic: '[H]e only differs from humanity in being as it were more human than humanity', G K Chesterton, *Chesterton on Shakespeare*, (ed) D Collins (Henley-on-Thames, Darwen Finlayson, 1971) 102, 108.

[146] Patterson mentions 'the repeated fears expressed by the artisans that violence is feared from them', Patterson, above n 15, at 57. She is referring to the rehearsal of 'Pyramus and Thisbe', in which the mechanicals express their concerns that the representation of violence in the play will be mistaken by its courtly audience for actual violence. Hence, Starveling warns the other mechanicals: 'I believe we must leave the killing out, when all is done'. (3.1.12)

[147] See, eg, R B Manning, *Village Revolts: Social Protest and Popular Disturbances in England, 1509–1640* (Oxford, Clarendon, 1988) 187–219; Manning records 35 instances of serious disorder in London between 1581 and 1602: *ibid* at 187. The London riots of 1595 'constituted the most dangerous and prolonged urban uprising in England': *ibid* at 208. See P Slack (ed), *Rebellion, Popular Protest and the Social Order in Early Modern England* (Cambridge, Cambridge University Press, 1984); also ch 2, texts to nn 100–102, above.

A Most Rare Vision

Manning has noted, these conditions were exacerbated by the presence there in large numbers of discharged and discontented soldiers and sailors.[148] In rural England too, mainly in protest at the enclosure of common land and the shortage of affordable corn, organised rebellion was not uncommon.[149] Notable in the individual reports of these outbreaks of disorder is the preponderance amongst the rioters of artisan tradesmen such as tailors, carpenters and weavers: '[a] crew of patches, rude mechanicals' (3.2.9).[150] John Marston deals directly with the topical issue of the London rebellions in *Histrio-Mastix*, in which 'a sort of Russetings and Mechanichalls' enters, demanding 'Liberty, liberty, liberty'. The mob engages in violent rebellion on the streets of London, threatening to 'pluck downe the Church, and set up an Ale-house' and to 'take what we will of the Marchants'.[151] There are allusions throughout the play to Shakespeare's mechanicals, not least in the inept troupe of players (known as Sir Oliver Owlet's Men): Belch the beard maker, Gutt the fiddle-string maker, Incle the Pedlar, Posthast the Poet, Gulch and Clowt.[152] Like Shakespeare's mechanicals, Marston's actors are concerned about their reception by the audience:

---

[148] Manning, above n 147, at 193–94; also, C G Cruickshank, *Elizabeth's Army* (Oxford, Oxford University Press, 1968); A L Beier, *Masterless Men: The Vagrancy Problem in England, 1560–1640* (London, Methuen, 1985) 93–95.

[149] On the Enslow Hill Rebellion of 1596, see Manning, above n 147, at 221–29; also, J Walter, 'A "Rising of the People"? The Oxfordshire Rising of 1596' (1985) 107 *Past & Present* 90. The organisers of the Enslow Hill Rebellion were charged with High Treason under the Treason Act 1571 (*13 Eliz. cap. 1*); they were tried (the prosecution was conducted by Sir Edward Coke) and convicted in June 1597.

[150] In 1594, a fight between a tailor and a clerk to the Court of Common Pleas led to an attack on Lyon's Inn, one of the Inns of Chancery: Manning, above n 147, at 203. The London riots in the summer of 1595 started when a silk-weaver insulted the Lord Mayor and was saved from commitment to Bedlam by the intervention of a crowd of 200–300: *ibid* at 209. The Enslow Hill Rebellion was instigated by a carpenter, Bartholomew Steere, and his brother John, a weaver: *ibid* at 221.

[151] J Marston, *Histrio-Mastix Or, The Player Whipt!* (London, T Thorp, 1610) (Act 5) F3.*v*.

[152] *Ibid* (1.1) B.*r*. On a possible date for the composition of *Histrio-Mastix*, see ch 5, n 19, below; the several allusions to *A Midsummer Night's Dream* suggest that it was written in or around 1596, although Chambers places it a few years earlier, without specifying an exact date, E K Chambers, *The Elizabethan Stage*, 4 vols (Oxford, Clarendon, 1923) 4: 18. In *Histrio-Mastix* specific words and actions of the troupe of players recall those of Shakespeare's mechanicals. For example, a prologue to their play, written in doggerel, is read out: 'When Authours quill, in quivering hand, / His tyred arme did take: / His wearied Muse, bad him devise, / Some fine play for to make', Marston, above n 151, (2.1) B5.*r*. One of the actors offers to perform the prologue 'extempore' (*ibid*, B5.*v*), recalling the advice to Snug that he should perform the part of the lion 'extempore' (1.2.56). A choice of performable plays is offered: '*Mother Gurtons neadle*; (a Tragedy.) / *The Divell and Dives*; (a Comedie) / *A russet coate, and a Knaves cap*; (an Infernall) / *A prowd heart and a beggars purse*, (a pastorall.) / *The Widdowes apron-strings*; (a nocturnall.)', Marston, above n 151, (2.1) C3.*r*, echoing the choice of plays at Theseus's wedding feast (5.1.44–60). A verse play on the subject of tragic adolescent love is performed: 'Troylus and Cressida' (Marston, above n 151, (2.1) C4.*r*), mirroring the performance of 'Pyramus and Thisbe'; on a possible reference by Marston to Shakespeare's *Troilus and Cressida*, see ch 5, n 19, below. The declamatory acting style of Gutt the fiddle-string maker is identical to Bottom's: 'Ile teare their turret toppes, / Ile beat their Bulwarks downe, / Ile rend such Raskalls form their ragges, / And whippe them out of towne', Marston, above n 151, (4.1) E4.*v*. Bottom's boast that he can play 'a part to tear a cat in' (1.2.22) is repeated almost verbatim by a soldier, who asks the players: 'Sirha is this you would rend and teare the Cat / Upon a Stage, and now march like a drown'd rat?' Marston, above n 151, (Act 5) G.*r*.

The Poetic Imagination, Antique Fables and the Dream of Law

> *Gulsh.* I but how if they doe not clap their hands.
> *Post.* No matter so they thump us not.[153]

It is as though Shakespeare's mechanicals have been caught up in a nightmarish parody of *A Midsummer Night's Dream*, in which the rule of law has been supplanted by the law of the mob. Marston's is a realistic portrayal of rioting apprentices; he appears even to borrow the most famous line in *Henry VI, Part 2*—Dick the Butcher's 'The first thing we do, let's kill all the lawyers' (4.2.71)—and to translate it less memorably into the following lines of dialogue between three of the rioters:

> 2. Nay, weele have a fling at the Lawyers too.
> 3. O, I, first of all at the Lawyers.
> 4. True, that we may have the law in our owne hands.[154]

It is noteworthy that Marston's 'Russetings and Mechanicalls' are not the troupe of players, Sir Oliver Owlet's Men, but rather the vengeful mob, intent on the destruction of extant societal order: their levelling battle-cry is '[a]ll shall be common'.[155] Meanwhile the players are pressed into military service and caught up in violent civil unrest, during which 'all the factions of Noblemen, Peasants, and Cittizens' fight on the streets, lawyers' books are burned and shops looted.[156] The last we see of them they are destitute, attempting to pawn their costumes to pay sixpence for a meal of one egg.[157] The play ends abruptly with the entrance of Astraea (described in the stage directions as Queen Elizabeth)—'Iustice perfection, / Whose traine is unpolute Virginity'[158]—and the allegorical figures of Plenty, Pride, Envy, War and Poverty surrendering their sceptres to Peace, 'sitting in Maiestie'.[159] The violence of *Histrio-Mastix* is far removed from the comedy of *A Midsummer Night's Dream*. In Shakespeare's play violence is held at bay. It prowls the shadows of the imagination. It is the discordant antithesis of Bottom's dream: the man on the stair, 'the dust behind the door'. (5.1.368)

---

[153] Marston, above n 151, (2.1) B5.*v.*
[154] *Ibid* (Act 5) F3.*v*–F4.*r.*
[155] *Ibid*, F4.*r.*
[156] *Ibid*, G.*r.* Concerning the impressment of players, Chambers quotes from an undated letter (*c* 1602) of Philip Gawdy: 'All the playe howses wer besett in one daye and very many pressed from thence, so that in all ther ar pressed ffowre thousand besydes five hundred voluntaryes, and all for flaunders', Chambers, *Elizabethan Stage* 4: 18.
[157] Marston, above n 151, (Act 6) H.*r*; there is an echo in Posthast's line, 'What sixepence an Egg', of Flute's 'Thus hath he lost sixepence a day during his life' (4.2.15–16).
[158] Marston, above n 151, (Act 6) H2.*v.*
[159] *Ibid*, I.*r.*

5

The Ancient Constitution, Common Law and the Idyll of Albion: Law and Lawyers in *Henry IV, Parts 1 and 2*

I. Kill *All* The Lawyers?

THERE IS ONE line in the Shakespearean canon that has been adduced, probably more than any other, as evidence of its author's personal ambivalence towards common lawyers in particular and the English legal system in general. The line is from *Henry VI, Part 2*, and is spoken by Dick the Butcher to his fellow rebel, Jack Cade: 'The first thing we do, let's kill all the lawyers'. (4.2.71)[1] It is unlikely that Shakespeare personally approved the political manifesto of a revolutionary mob, whose leader, immediately after Dick the Butcher has spoken, sentences to death the Clerk of Chatham on the singular grounds that 'he can write and read' (4.2.78).[2] This proviso notwithstanding, and despite the comic self-delusion of the rebels' leader, Jack Cade, the line undoubtedly raises numerous issues of legitimate concern regarding Shakespeare's relationship with the English legal institution. Although a fruitful source of conjecture, the full extent of Shakespeare's technical knowledge of common law and legal procedure is not known. We may never learn whether he spent the 'missing years' of the 1580s as a noverint—an attorney's clerk[3]—or whether his near

---

[1] For a discussion of Shakespeare's attitude towards lawyers, see D J Kornstein, *Kill All The Lawyers? Shakespeare's Legal Appeal* (Lincoln, Neb, University of Nebraska Press, 2005) 22–34. Holinshed records the demand made of Richard II by Wat Tyler, for 'a commission to put to death all lawyers, escheaters, and other which by any office had any thing to doo with the law', R Holinshed, *Chronicles of England, Scotland and Ireland*, iii.432/1/56 in W G Boswell-Stone, *Shakespeare's Holinshed: The Chronicle and the Historical Plays Compared* (London, Chatto & Windus, 1907) 271.

[2] Again referring to the Peasants' Revolt of 1381, Holinshed noted that 'it was dangerous among them to be known for one that was lerned, and more dangerous, if any men were found with a penner and inkhorne at his side: for such seldome or never escaped from them with life' (*Chronicles* iii.436/1/9), Boswell-Stone (ed), above n 1, at 272. On writing, violence and 'the politics of literacy' in *Henry VI, Part 2*, see O Arnold, *The Third Citizen: Shakespeare's Theater and the Early Modern House of Commons* (Baltimore, Md, Johns Hopkins University Press, 2007) 136.

[3] Given that he was writing in 1589, it is unlikely that Thomas Nashe was referring to Shakespeare (still less to Shakespeare's *Hamlet*, which was not recorded in the Stationers' Register until 26 July 1602) when he complained that '[i]t is a cōmon practise now a daies amongst a sort of shifting companions, that runne through every arte and thrive by none, to leave the trade of *Noverint* whereto they were borne, and busie themselves with the indevors of Art . . . and if you inteate him faire in a frostie

lifelong involvement in protracted lawsuits prejudiced him against the legal profession (it was enough certainly to give him a detailed understanding of lawyers and their practices).[4] That the legal profession of the late 16th century had expanded greatly and many of its practitioners become wealthy on the proceeds of their skills is indisputable.[5] As Sir Thomas Wilson noted,

> the Lawyer can never want living till the earth want men and all be voyde ... There is not a word in the Law, but it is a grote in the Lawiers purse.[6]

Shakespeare's Pompey makes a similar observation in *Measure for Measure*, assuring Mistress Overdone that 'good counsellors lack no clients' (1.2.89): the fact that the comment is made by a pimp to a brothel-keeper may be indicative of its author's ambivalence concerning the probity of common lawyers, or counsellors. The emergence in the 16th century of a standardised, self-regulating legal profession was instrumental in diminishing the relevance of its sacerdotal role, as propounded by Sir John Fortescue in *De Laudibus Legum Angliae*. Fortescue's characterisation of the judiciary as '*sacerdotes*' or priests, whose primary role was to teach 'Holy Things',[7] implies a jurisprudence that is coexistent with and indivisible from the Word of God. But as forensic rhetoric attained unprecedented levels of emphasis in the education of common lawyers throughout the 16th century, the practice of law and the practices of lawyers became associated in the public imagination more with trickery than divinity. Still less did the spiritual correlation between lawyers and priests, made in the previous century by Fortescue, appear to have any basis in reality. Late-Elizabethan jurists such as William Fulbecke conflated the temporal and spiritual aspects of common law, arguing that

morning, he will affoord you whole *Hamlets*, I should say handfulls of tragical speeches': T Nashe, 'An Epistle to the Gentlemen Students of the Two Universities' in R Greene, *Menaphon Camillas alarum to slumbering Euphues, in his melancholie Cell at Silexedra* (London, Sampson Clarke, 1589) **3.r. Given the Elizabethan predilection for puns, the reference in the same passage to 'the Kidde in *Æsop*' suggests that Thomas Kyd (the son of a scrivener) is probably the subject of Nashe's attack; see *Hamlet*, (ed) H Jenkins (London, Arden Shakespeare, 1982) Introduction, 83–84. Philip Henslowe records the performance at Newington Butts in 1594 of a play entitled *Hamlet*: '9 of June 1594, Rd at hamlet ... viijs', R A Foakes (ed), *Henslowe's Diary* (Cambridge, Cambridge University Press, 2002) 21; on the performances at Newington Butts until mid-June 1594 of the Chamberlain's Men and the Admiral's Men, see ibid, App I, 283–84; on the pre-Shakespearean '*Ur-Hamlet*', see Jenkins (ed), *Hamlet*, Introduction, 82–83.

[4] On the legal dispute that lasted for 20 years, concerning the contract for a loan of £40, made by Edmund Lambert (Mary Arden's brother-in-law) with William's father, John Shakespeare, see G Restivo, 'Inheritance in the Legal and Ideological Debate of Shakespeare's *King Lear*' in P Raffield and G Watt (eds), *Shakespeare and the Law* (Oxford, Hart Publishing, 2008) 170–71. On Shakespeare's involvement in the case of *Bellott v Mountjoy*, see C Nicholl, *The Lodger: Shakespeare on Silver Street* (London, Allen Lane, 2007).

[5] On the expansion of the Bar during this period, see W R Prest, *The Inns of Court Under Elizabeth I and the Early Stuarts, 1590–1640* (London, Longman, 1972); W R Prest, *The Rise of the Barristers: A Social History of the English Bar, 1590–1640* (Oxford, Clarendon, 1986).

[6] Sir Thomas Wilson, *The Arte of Rhetorique* (London, George Robinson, 1585) D.iii.*v*, D.iiii.*r*.

[7] Sir John Fortescue, *De Laudibus Legum Angliae*, (ed) J Selden (London, R Gosling, 1737) 4–5; see ch 1, text to n 127, above. In his Preface to *De Laudibus*, John Selden notes that 'The Reigns of Hen. VI. and Edw. abounded with Learned Men in the Law ... The Knowledge and Practice of the Law were then in high Credit ... at a Time when the Law was not so lucrative, as it became afterwards', Fortescue, *De Laudibus*, Preface, vi.

though the charge and calling be seculer, yet it must be religiously handled. For God is the author of the Law, and the revenger of the abuse thereof. . .[8]

Despite the biblical tone of Fulbecke's injunction against irreligious conduct, it seems that Sir John Doddridge more accurately reflected the popular perception of lawyers at the end of the 16th century, when he argued that '[t]he first and chiefest Natural gift [of the common lawyer] is sharpenesse, and dexterity of wit'.[9] Indeed, in his popular satirical comedy, *Law-Trickes or, Who Would Have Thought It*, John Day implies that the pre-eminent skills of the barrister are those of dissimulation. The character of Polymetes is described as:

> A parlous youth, sharpe and satyricall,
> Would a but spend some study in the law,
> A would prove a passing subtle Barrister.[10]

It was the acquisition merely of 'sharp' and 'subtle' skills at the Inns of Court to which the scholar, poet and lawyer, Abraham Fraunce objected most strongly in *The Lawiers Logike*, published in 1588. Fraunce was not opposed to the learning of rhetorical skills *per se*; rather, it was the absence of any logical, structural or ethical basis to legal education that he found most offensive and least conducive to the creation of a distinguished legal profession. Legal education of this period was predicated upon the rehearsal of disputatious skills. In *Origines Juridiciales*, Sir William Dugdale provides an account of educational exercises undertaken by law students during this period, all of which took place in the halls and libraries of their respective Inns. The most striking aspect of his description is the primacy accorded by the curriculum to performance and debating skills. Hence, at the Grand Vacation moots, cases were 'pleadyd and declared in homely Law-french' by inner-barristers (law students); after which, an utter-barrister (qualified advocate) 'doth reherse, and doth argue and reason to it in the Law-frenche'.[11] Similarly at 'readings', after the Reader had given a lecture on a particular legal issue he would offer up cases, which would be disputed by utter-barristers and

---

[8] W Fulbecke, *A Direction or Preparative to the study of the Lawe* (London, T Wight, 1600) B2.*v*.

[9] Sir John Doddridge, *Describing a Method for the managing of the Lawes of this Land* (London, I More, 1631) 4.

[10] J Day, *Law-Trickes or, Who Would Have Thought It. As it hath bene divers times Acted by the Children of the Revels* (London, R More, 1608) (Act 1) A4.*v*; see also ch 2, text to nn 57 and 58, above. Comic dramas of the period, notable for the satirical treatment of lawyers, include *Epicœne, or the Silent Woman* and *Volpone*, by Ben Jonson. On depictions of common lawyers in early modern drama, see E F J Tucker, *Intruder into Eden: Representations of the Common Lawyer in English Literature 1350–1750* (Columbia, SC, Camden House, 1984). Lawyers continued to provide subject-matter for popular comedies throughout the 17th century; see R Brathwaite, *Mercurius Britannicus, or the English Intelligencer: A Tragic-Comedy, at Paris* (London, Felix Kingston, 1641); E Ravenscroft, *The English Lawyer; a Comedy* (London, James Vade, 1678). On the satirical dramatic genre and the law, see ch 4, n 25, above.

[11] Sir William Dugdale, *Origines Juridiciales, or Historical Memorials of the English Laws* (London, F & T Warren, 1666) 193. On law-French, see Prest, *The Rise of the Barristers*, above n 5, at 108–09; also, J H Baker, *Manual of law-French* (Amersham, Avebury, 1979).

Benchers: 'The Judges and Benchers argue according to their antiquity, the puisne Bencher beginning first; and so everyone after another'.[12]

For many students, the rhetorical and procedural skills that they acquired at the Inns were applied to the administration of large country estates when they returned to their familial homes after several years of study in London. As Fortescue accurately noted, sons of the gentry were sent to the Inns of Court, 'not so much to make the Laws their Study, much less to live by the Profession (having large Patrimonies of their own)'[13]; but the acquisition of some basic tenets of property law would serve them well in the subsequent management of their land. Fraunce was highly critical of this practice, citing it as an example of the failings of an education that produced legal technocrats rather than juristic scholars:

> [H]aving in seaven years space met with six French words, home they ryde lyke brave Magnificoes, and dashe their poore neighboures children quyte out of countenance, with Villen in gros, Villen regardant, and Tenant per le curtesie . . .[14]

The absence of any philosophical, critical or ethical context to legal education prompted Fraunce to claim that the study of common law was 'hard, harsh, unpleasant, unsavory, rude and barbarous', as a consequence of which the lawyers produced were

> so many upstart *Rabulæ Forenses*, which under a prætence of Lawe, become altogeather lawlesse, to the continuall molestation of ignorant men, and generall overcharging of the country . . .[15]

While avarice and dissimulation were popularly considered to be institutional features of the legal profession, there were those who sought to defend lawyers from charges of impropriety and to restore the image of integrity, tradition and honour that Fortescue had ascribed to them in *De Laudibus Legum Angliae*. In *The Third Universitie*, George Buc argues that the wealth of lawyers is God's reward for 'their long continual, painfull and diligent Studies' and their 'vertue and honest industry'.[16] For John Ferne, author of *The Blazon of Gentrie*, the Inns of Court

---

[12] Dugdale, *Origines Juridiciales*, above n 11, at 160; on educational exercises at the early modern Inns of Court, see P Raffield, *Images and Cultures of Law in Early Modern England: Justice and Political Power, 1558–1660* (Cambridge, Cambridge University Press, 2004) 20–22.

[13] Fortescue, above n 7, at 112. Baker notes that the most intellectually accomplished law students might either practise at the Bar, or join the senior ranks of the civil service; others found work as attorneys, court advisers and in local government. Most graduates of the Inns of Court 'returned to the country to follow their fathers as country gentlemen, making use of their brief acquaintance with legal scholarship when acting as justices of the peace', J H Baker, 'Learning Exercises in the Medieval Inns of Court and Chancery' in J H Baker, *The Legal Profession and the Common Law: Historical Essays* (London, Hambledon, 1986) 8.

[14] A Fraunce, *The Lawiers Logike, exemplifying the præcepts of Logike by the practise of the common Lawe* (London, T Gubbin and T Newman, 1588) ¶.4.r–v.

[15] Ibid, ¶.2.v, ¶.4.r. For a discussion of Fraunce and the 'failure' of common law, see P Goodrich, *Languages of Law: From Logics of Memory to Nomadic Masks* (London, Weidenfeld & Nicolson, 1990) 15–52.

[16] Sir George Buc, 'The Third Universitie of England' (1612) in J Stow, *The Annales or Generall Chronicle of England* (London, Thomas Adams, 1615) 975.

contained 'many gentlemen of bloud and coate-armour, so perfect and auncient, that their number exceedeth, anye assembly of men, which I can remember'.[17] Given that Ferne and Buc were both educated at the Inns of Court and maintained links with them throughout their lives, the eulogistic tone of *The Third Universitie* and *The Blazon of Gentrie* is perhaps unsurprising.[18] Those who profited from professional and social advancement through membership of the Inns tended to depict lawyers as the embodiment of the immemorial custom of common law; but for popular dramatists such as John Day and John Marston, the avarice, pride and dissemblance of lawyers made them obvious targets for derision in their satirical plays. Hence, in Marston's *Histrio-Mastix Or, The Player Whipt!*, performed for an audience of lawyers at the Middle Temple in 1599, the two protagonists, lawyers called Furcher and Vourcher, describe 'sweet contention' as 'Lawyers best content'. Marston introduces into his farce the allegorical character of Pride; upon seeing Furcher and Vourcher (who were presumably attired in legal costume), Pride exclaims:

> O these be Lawyers! Concords enemies,
> *Prydes* fuell shall their fire of strife increase . . .
> . . . Then use your wisdom to enrich your selves,
> Make deepe successe high Steward of your store.[19]

In the self-referential environment of Middle Temple Hall, before an audience comprised exclusively of lawyers, lines such as these were guaranteed to provoke

---

[17] Sir John Ferne, *The Blazon of Gentrie* (London, Toby Cooke, 1586) 92. The grounds for Ferne's encomium to the gentility of members of the Inns should be regarded with a degree of scepticism; as Baker notes: 'Although the title of gentleman was bestowed on all entrants to the inns, and therefore confuses social origins for the historian, it is known that yeomen could gain admission', J H Baker, 'The English Legal Profession, 1450–1550' in Baker, *The Legal Profession and the Common Law*, above n 13, at 97.

[18] Ferne was an eminent genealogist and common lawyer; from 1595 to 1609 he served as Secretary in the Council of the North. Buc was appointed Gentleman of the King's Privy Chamber by James I; in 1603, he was appointed Deputy Master of His Majesty's Office of the Revels, assuming the office of Master of the Revels in 1610.

[19] J Marston, *Histrio-Mastix Or, The Player Whipt!* (London, T Thorp, 1610) (3.1) D1.*v*. Hotson argues that *Histrio-Mastix* was written and performed in 1599 in response to Shakespeare's *Troilus and Cressida*, which (he claims) was performed at the Middle Temple in 1598, J L Hotson, 'Love's Labours Won' in *Shakespeare's Sonnets Dated* (London, Rupert Hart-Davis, 1949) 37. Hotson bases his claim largely on the following lines: 'Come *Cressida* my Cresset light, / Thy face doth shine both day and night, / Behold, behold, thy garter blue, / Thy knight his valiant elboe weares, / That when he shakes his furious Speare, / The foe in shivering fearfull sort, / May lay him downe in death to snort', Marston, *Histrio-Mastix* (2.1) C4.*r*; but Chambers notes of *Histrio-Mastix* that 'the hit at Shakespeare, if there really is one, remains unexplained. There is nothing else which points to so early a date as 1599 for his *Troilus and Cressida*', E K Chambers, *The Elizabethan Stage*, 4 vols (Oxford, Clarendon, 1923) 4: 19. Chambers argues that the 1599 performance of *Histrio-Mastix* was a revival (with additional material), performed by the Children of Paul's: Chambers, *The Elizabethan Stage*, 4: 17–19. Given the extraordinarily large cast of *Histrio-Mastix* it is possible that parts were played by student members of the Middle Temple; see G L Geckle, *John Marston's Drama: Themes, Images, Sources* (New Jersey, Fairleigh Dickinson University Press, 1980) 34; T F Wharton (ed), *The Drama of John Marston: Critical Re-Visions* (Cambridge, Cambridge University Press, 2000) 30–31; Raffield, above n 12, at 26–37; also, text to ch 4, nn 151–59, above.

laughter. Marston knew his audience well: like his father, he was a member of the Middle Temple and lived in chambers there during the 1590s.[20] But while *Histrio-Mastix* and *Law-Trickes* were to a great extent written with an audience of lawyers in mind, Shakespeare never intended his references to law and lawyers to be appreciated exclusively by the legal profession.

Where Marston and Day directed their satire at the perceived venality of lawyers, Shakespeare's authorial interest in the law lies in exploring models of governance and their twofold effect: on the development of the State and on individual subjects of law. Of course, Shakespeare was not above making quips at the expense of lawyers; his personal experience of prolonged litigation probably engendered thoughts similar to those expressed by Jack the Butcher in *Henry VI, Part 2*. One of the many facets of Shakespeare's great diptych of the English State, *The History of Henry the Fourth* and *The Second Part of Henry the Fourth*,[21] is a mimetic reflection on both the role of law in English society and the immemorial custom of England's legal institution. In Tillyard's critical opinion, the two parts of the diptych should, for reasons of thematic continuity, be addressed as a single play. Tillyard argues that the action at the end of *1 Henry IV* is incomplete; that Shakespeare required the audience subsequently to watch *2 Henry IV* in order fully to share the vision of England that he imagines.[22] This is not to say that the tone of each play is not distinctive. Stephen Greenblatt compares the spaciousness of *1 Henry IV* and its emphasis on heroes and 'glittering' enemies with the claustrophobia of *2 Henry IV*, where betrayal is the motivating factor.[23] In terms of character, Tillyard's decision to regard the two parts as a consolidated whole is of particular importance with respect to the treatment of Prince Hal and Falstaff. Hal only emerges at the end of *2 Henry IV* from 'the foul and ugly mists / Of vapours that did seem to strangle him' (*1 Henry IV*, 1.2.200–201), to banish Falstaff in fulfilment of his prophecy in *1 Henry IV*. Of course, the plays represent much more than a dramatic representation of the education of a prince, but it is a theme that pervades the two parts of the diptych, especially when they are read as a single entity, and it is one to which I return throughout the chapter. In particular, in section II. I analyse the important role played by common lawyers in shaping

---

[20] See P J Finkelpearl, *John Marston of the Middle Temple: An Elizabethan Dramatist in his Social Setting* (Cambridge, Mass, Harvard University Press, 1969); at a Parliament of the Middle Temple, held on 8 February 1600, it was recorded that 'Mr John Marston was readmitted to the chamber to which his father was lately admitted with Mr Haule', C H Hopwood (ed), *Calendar of the Middle Temple Records*, 4 vols (London, Butterworths, 1903) 1: 401.

[21] Hereinafter *1 Henry IV* and *2 Henry IV*; the 1623 Folio describes *1 Henry IV* as *The First Part of Henry Fourth*, but it was entered in the Stationers' Register on 25 February 1598 as *The History of Henry the Fourth*. *The Second Part of Henry IV* was printed in 1600, but Ben Jonson alluded to the play in *Every Man Out Of His Humour* (5.2.20–22), written in 1599. For the argument that *2 Henry IV* was completed before the end of 1598, see *King Henry IV, Part 2*, (ed) A R Humphreys (London, Arden Shakespeare, 1981) Introduction, xiv–xvii. All references to the text of the play are from this edition.

[22] E M W Tillyard, *Shakespeare's History Plays* (London, Chatto & Windus, 1944) 264.

[23] S Greenblatt, 'Invisible bullets: Renaissance authority and its subversion, *Henry IV* and *Henry V*' in J Dollimore and A Sinfield (eds), *Political Shakespeare: Essays in Cultural Materialism* (Manchester, Manchester University Press, 1994) 34–35.

the development of the unwritten constitution with reference to two characters in *2 Henry IV*: the Lord Chief Justice and Justice Shallow. For this reason, while agreeing with Tillyard that for purposes of extrapolating a unified theme the two parts are better addressed as a single play, I place greater emphasis on *2 Henry IV*, and in particular on those scenes in which Shallow and the Lord Chief Justice appear. I consider the influence of several judges of the early modern period (the most significant of whom in this context is the Lancastrian Chief Justice, Sir John Fortescue) over the depiction of these two characters, both of whom constitute multifaceted representations of common lawyers.

Fatherhood is a ubiquitous theme in *1 Henry IV* and *2 Henry IV*, and in psychoanalytical terms is relevant to an understanding of the emotional power of law to control the imagination of its subjects, binding them into a state of allegiance to a symbolic father or original.[24] In section III. of the chapter I examine the various models of fatherhood offered in the plays, predicated upon Prince Hal's relationship with his actual father, King Henry IV; his surrogate and antithetical father, Falstaff; and the symbolic father of the law, the Lord Chief Justice. Lastly, in section IV., I consider the correlation between paternity, filial relations and the mystical nature of kingship, with particular reference to the classical and emblematic persona of *paterfamilias*, an archetypal figure to whom all subjects owe ultimate allegiance and obedience.

II. Common Lawyers and the Pastoral Idyll

Less than 10 miles to the south of Stratford-upon-Avon is the village of Ebrington. Along a narrow winding road, a couple of miles to the west of the main thoroughfare from Stratford to Cirencester (the ancient Fosse Way), Ebrington sits on top of a hill, just inside the Gloucestershire border with Warwickshire. The road, which leads to Chipping Campden, is lined intermittently with pretty sand-coloured cottages built from the local Cotswold stone. It winds upwards past the village inn, reaching its highest point at the parish church of St Eadburgha, from whose ancient churchyard the view extends over a landscape of meadows, orchards, copses and farm buildings to the Vale of Evesham in the west, Cirencester and the lower dip-slopes of the Cotswold Hills in the south, and the market town of Stratford-upon-Avon in the north. The surrounding countryside of Gloucestershire and Warwickshire presents a vision of rural England that Lord Denning regularly invoked in his more idiosyncratic judgments in the Court of Appeal; for example, in *New Windsor Corporation v Mellor*:

---

[24] For a psychoanalytical interpretation of law, see P Goodrich and D Carlson (eds), *Psychoanalysis and Jurisprudence: Essays in Law and the Postmodern Mind* (Ann Arbor, Michigan University Press, 1997).

The Ancient Constitution, Common Law and the Idyll of Albion

Today we look back far in time. To a town or village green. The turf is old. Animals have grazed there for hundreds of years. Nowadays there are pleasant stretches of grass where people sit and talk. Sometimes they play cricket or kick a ball about. But in medieval times it was the place where the young men mustered with their bows and arrows. There might be stocks there where offenders were put for their petty misdemeanours. In the month of May they set up a maypole and danced around it. We have no record of when it all began, but the poet tells us:

> On the green they watched their sons
> Playing till too dark to see,
> As their fathers watched them once,
> As my father once watched me.[25]

Lord Denning evokes a sense of timelessness, suggesting (as jurists of the early modern period commented of the common law itself) that the customs of rural England have existed since time immemorial.[26] It is axiomatic of Denning's judgment in *New Windsor Corporation v Mellor* and in other of his judgments that the England for which he yearns is a pastoral vision of nationhood rather than a statement of historical fact.[27] The study of common law is as much to do with the perusal of tradition as it is with the acquisition of technical knowledge; in which case, myth, memory and the image are as relevant to the accretion of a body of law as the law reports, statutes and the texts of jurists.[28]

In terms of historical accuracy, Lord Denning is referring in the above extract to an idealised past: a quasi-fictional merry England of maypoles, village cricket, grazing cattle and eternal summers. Had he visited the Gloucestershire village of Ebrington, Denning would have lauded the physical manifestation of the unwritten ancient constitution, which his judgments invariably evoke and that Ebrington appears to embody. A constitution, particularly when it is unwritten, represents an

---

[25] *New Windsor Corporation v Mellor* [1975] 1 Ch 380, at 386. The verse extract quoted by Lord Denning is from *Forefathers*, by Edmund Blunden. In this context, it is appropriate to quote from Coke on the etymology of Albion: 'I omit the name Albion, at the first Olbion, or the happy island in Greek', in Part 3 (1602) of *The Reports of Sir Edward Coke, Knt In English*, (ed) G Wilson, 7 vols (London, Rivington, 1777) 2: Preface, xb.

[26] As, eg, 'that which we call the Common Law is, out of question, no less antient than the beginning of differences betwixt man and man, after the first peopling of this land', Dugdale, above n 11, at 3. Noting Lord Denning's 'attraction to the pastoral', Klinck remarks of his judgment in *New Windsor Corporation v Mellor* that 'the nostalgia is almost palpable', D R Klinck, '"This Other Eden": Lord Denning's Pastoral Vision' (1994) 14 *Oxford Journal of Legal Studies* 25, 29, 30. Sales describes pastoralism as 'nostalgia for the good old days', implying that such days exist only in the imagination, R Sales, *English Literature in History 1780–1830: Pastoral and Politics* (New York, St Martin's Press, 1983) 15; 'nostalgia' derives from two Greek words: *nostos* (the yearning for a lost home) and *algos* (suffering).

[27] See, eg, *Corpus Christi College v Gloucester County Council* [1983] 1 QB 360, at 363: 'In the lovely Cotswold country there is the old parish of Little Rissington not far from Bourton-on-the-Water. It is a small place with only a few houses and the church. In the parish there is a meadow called Temple Ham Meadow of nearly 26 acres. It has been grazed by the residents of the parish for centuries'.

[28] In relation to early modern accounts of the origins of common law, Goodrich argues that '[t]he indefinite time of the originary refers to a past which was never present', P Goodrich, 'Poor Illiterate Reason: History, Nationalism, Common Law' (1992) 1 *Social & Legal Studies* 7, 11.

Common Lawyers and the Pastoral Idyll

aspiration rather than a set of rules. The aspiration takes the form of diverse images, drawn from the memory of an idealised past and the projection of an optimal future.[29] Lord Denning is not alone among the judiciary in appealing to an idealised past as a paradigm for the present and the future. Sir Edward Coke frequently adopted a similar rhetorical style, as, for example, in *Postnati. Calvin's Case*:

> [W]e are but of yesterday, (and therefore had need of the wisdom of those that were before us) and had been ignorant (if we had not received light and knowledge from our forefathers) and our days upon the earth but as a shadow, in respect of the old ancient days and times past, wherein the laws have been by the wisdom of the most excellent men, in many successions of ages, by long and continual experience.[30]

The judicial careers of Sir Edward Coke and Lord Denning, although separated by nearly 400 years, were identical in their dedication to preserving the unbroken chain of English law, by which the juridical past may be linked to the present.[31] The venerable sages of the English legal profession, the appellate judges, profess to protect and propound the timeless reason of common law for the benefit of its subjects.

The themes of time and timelessness, and the sense of past deeds acting upon the present, pervade the autumnal tone of *2 Henry IV*. Not only is the English countryside the nostalgic idyll of Lord Denning's poetic imagination; it is also the seat of Shakespeare's Justice Shallow, whose Gloucestershire house and surrounding orchard provide the location for much wistful reverie. In Justice Shallow, Shakespeare gives the legal profession its nostalgic counterpoint to the unsentimental pragmatism of his Lord Chief Justice, whose 'bold, just, and impartial spirit' (5.2.116) is in sharp contrast to the discursive meanderings of Shallow, the 'poor esquire of this county, and one of the King's justices of the peace'. (3.2.56–57) These two facets of the English legal tradition, the pragmatic and the nostalgic, were united in the person of Sir John Fortescue, Chief Justice of the King's Bench (1442–1461) and Lord Chancellor in the reign of King Henry VI.[32] The Preface to John Selden's edition of Fortescue's *De Laudibus Legum Angliae* informs the reader that

> He lies buried in the Parish Church belonging to *Ebburton,* (now written more frequently *Ebrington,*) where in the Chancel there is a Monument erected for him (see **Figure 7**).

---

[29] Ward defines a constitution as 'a mentality; a collective impression, of past, present and future', I Ward, *A State of Mind? The English Constitution and the Popular Imagination* (Stroud, Sutton, 2000) 6; see also Coleridge, who defined a constitution as 'an idea arising out of the idea of a state', S T Coleridge, *On the Constitution of the Church and State* (London, J M Dent, 1972) 9.

[30] Coke, *Postnati. Calvin's Case*, 7 *Reports* (1608) 4: 1a, at 3b.

[31] On the flawless and unbroken ancestry of the common law and its practitioners, see Ferne, *Blazon of Gentrie*, text to n 17, above.

[32] Fortescue described himself in *De Laudibus* as '*Cancellarius Angliae*', although Selden states that '[i]t seems, being with Henry VI driven into Scotland, he was made his Chancellor, the Memory whereof (as it could hardly be otherwise) wants in the Patent Rolls', Fortescue, above n 7, Preface, i.

Ebrington was Fortescue's home, 'where he was settled: Which Manor and Lands he had by Sale from Sir *Robert Corbett*, as by Deed declared 35 *Hen.* VI'.[33] The monument to a descendant of Sir John Fortescue, Denzil George (6th Earl Fortescue, 1893–1977), stands in the grounds of the same church as that of his illustrious predecessor, a testament to the immutable continuity of English law.

Ebrington Manor and its orchards may or may not have been the inspiration for the Gloucestershire scenes in *2 Henry IV*, but it is likely that *De Laudibus Legum Angliae* influenced the depiction of the English legal institution in *Parts 1 and 2*. In particular, Fortescue's portrayal of the relationship between the young Edward, Prince of Wales, and 'a certain grave old Knight, his Father's Chancellor'[34] finds echoes in the three models of fatherhood presented in the two plays: between Hal and his actual father, King Henry IV, and between Hal and his two surrogate fathers, the Lord Chief Justice and Falstaff. *De Laudibus* was written in or around 1470 and published in Latin in 1545.[35] In the Preface to the 1616 edition, Selden stated that '[t]his book was first translated and published, together with its *English* Version, by Robert Mulcaster, 8°. Lond. 1599'.[36] If Selden's claim was correct then Shakespeare would not have had access to a published English translation of *De Laudibus* prior to writing *2 Henry IV*. But Selden was wrong: the first edition of Mulcaster's translation was published in 1567 under the title, *A Learned Commendation of the Politique Lawes of England*.[37] So it is possible that Shakespeare's depiction of the Prince's relationship with his various 'fathers' was influenced by the paternalistic relationship between the Prince and the Chancellor, described by Fortescue in *De Laudibus*. I shall return to the paternal theme and its reflection of belief in an ultimate source of legitimate, patriarchal authority. For now, I remain in the orchards of Gloucestershire to analyse the central importance of rural England to Shakespeare's (and Fortescue's) interpretation of the English State and its governance. In his discussion of the Gloucestershire scenes in *2 Henry IV*, Tillyard refers to them as 'the symbol of the undefeated operating of the country life'.[38] Tillyard does not elaborate, but it is reasonable to infer from his comment the belief that in the midst of upheaval and rebellion the timeless values of rural existence, based on respect for custom and man's congruency with nature, will prevail and flourish.

The role of Justice of the Peace was crucial in establishing the authority of the monarch *in absentia*: he was the legitimate image in the shires of the King's law.

---

[33] *Ibid*, Preface, xlviii. Fortescue's origins were in south Devon; according to Selden, 'he came out of the House of *Wimondesham*, or *Wimston*, in the Parish of *Modberry* [Modbury], *Devon*; the most ancient Seat of this Name and Family in the Kingdom', *ibid*, Preface, xlv.

[34] *Ibid*, Introduction, lxiv.

[35] 'Ex Impress. *Ed. Whitchurch*, temp. *Hen.* VIII (*Mr Waterhouse*, Pref., Marg.)', *ibid*, Preface, liv.

[36] *Ibid*.

[37] The 1567 edition was published in London by Richard Tottell; a second edition was published in 1573. It is possible that Elizabeth I made her own translation of Fortescue's work, as her language tutor was another Sir John Fortescue—'being a great Master of the Greek and Latin Tongues'—a descendant of the author of *De Laudibus*. The Queen 'made him Chancellor of the Exchequer, and of her Privy Council. Her Saying was, "Two Men out-did her Expectation, Fortescue for Integrity, and Walsingham for Subtilty and officious Services"', *ibid*, Preface, lii.

[38] Tillyard, above n 22, at 303.

Common Lawyers and the Pastoral Idyll

The office of Justice of the Peace was established by statute in the reign of Edward III (*1 Ed.3. cap. 15*), although William Lambarde (writing in 1579) noted that 'before the tyme of K. Edward the third, there were sundry persons, that hadde interest in the keeping of the Peace'.[39] As prescribed by *34 Ed.3. cap. 1*, 'in everie Shire, one Lorde, and with him three (or foure) of the Best in the Countie, and some learned in the Lawes' were appointed by the King's Commission to keep the peace and restrain offenders.[40] In the reign of Richard II, two statutes were passed to restrict the number of justices in any county to five (*12 R.2. cap. 10* and *14 R.2. cap. 11*): the post brought with it power and payment, and 'ambition so multiplied the number of those Iustices, that it was afterward high time to make a contrarie law to diminish them'.[41] Centralisation of government and expansion of administration under successive Tudor monarchs necessitated large increases in the numbers of Justices of the Peace; as Lambarde notes,

> the growing number of the Statute lawes committed from time to time to the charge of the Iustices of ye Peace, hath bene the cause that they also are nowe againe increased to the overflowing of each Shire at this day.[42]

Lambarde interprets the primary role of the Justice of the Peace, from its earliest statutory inception in the reign of Edward III, as that of conducting vigilant surveillance of the king's subjects:

> [I]n every Shire, the king himselfe should place speciall eyes and watches over the common people, that shoulde be both willing & wise to foresee, and bee also enabled with meete auctoritie to repress al intention of uproare and force . . .[43]

This stark and oppressive analysis of justice in the shires calls into question the efficacy of the ancient constitution, which was claimed (by Fortescue and other early modern jurists) to protect the liberty of subjects and their inalienable rights, irrespective of social status. It is instructive briefly to consider the depiction of 'the common people' of the shires in *De Laudibus Legum Angliae*. In chapter XXXV, entitled 'The Inconveniencies in France by Means of the Absolute Regal Government', Fortescue is forthright in his condemnation of an unjust political system in which 'the Peasants live in great Hardship and Misery'.[44] The Chancellor leaves the Prince in no doubt that a major cause of 'this cruel oppressive

---

[39] W Lambard, *Eirenarcha: or of The office of the Iustices of Peace* (London, Assigns of Richard Tottell and Chr Barker, 1582) 11. In *De Republica Anglorum*, first published in 1583, Smith dedicates a discrete chapter to the office of Justice of the Peace, in which he emphasises that 'for the good government of the shire, the Prince putteth his confidence in them', Sir Thomas Smith, *De Republica Anglorum*, (ed) M Dewar (Cambridge, Cambridge University Press, 1982) 106.

[40] Lambard, *Eirenarcha*, above n 39, at 36.

[41] *Ibid* at 37; during the reign of Elizabeth I, 'every Justice of Peace, sitting in execution of the Statute of Laborers and Servauntes, shall have five shillings the day' (*5 Eliz. cap. 4*), *ibid* at 277.

[42] *Ibid* at 37–38; Gleason estimates that between the years 1588 and 1642 there were approximately 15,000 JPs in England: J H Gleason, *The Justices of the Peace in England, 1558–1640: A Later Eirenarcha* (Oxford, Clarendon, 1969) 4; see also T Skyrme, *A History of the Justices of the Peace* (Chichester, Barry Rose, 1991).

[43] Lambard, *Eirenarcha*, above n 39, at 21–22.

[44] Fortescue, above n 7, at 80.

Treatment'[45] is an inequitable system of taxation under which the French peasantry bear a disproportionate fiscal burden, while '[t]he Nobility and Gentry are not so much burthened with Taxes'.[46] At no point in *De Laudibus* does Fortescue refer specifically to the English peasantry. Rather, he describes in general terms, 'the Advantages consequent from that Political Mixt Government which obtains in England'. He alludes to a hierarchic social structure in which '[e]very one, according to his Rank, hath all Things which conduce to make Life Easy and Happy'.[47] Above all else, the England of *De Laudibus* is an agrarian society, 'constantly governed by the same Customs',[48] and the social rank of any English subject was the immutable product of those customs.

It is over the issue of customary law that Pocock has identified a central flaw in the deductive argument employed by Fortescue in *De Laudibus*. If laws are to be accounted rational and therefore just, they should be deduced from principles of natural justice, rather than being predicated upon national or local customs.[49] But Fortescue is adamant that the laws of England are better than those of any other nation-State or of any empire (notably those of the Venetians and the Romans), on grounds of their antiquity alone; on which basis 'the Laws and Customs of England are not only Good, but the very Best'.[50] As Pocock observes, logic such as this can hardly be described as rational, based as it is on a 'technical and traditional' interpretation of customary law[51]; but the justification that is offered by Fortescue for the superiority of English law over all rival legal systems is perhaps closest to the distinction, later to be made by Sir Edward Coke, that

> causes which concern the life . . . of [the King's] subjects, are not to be decided by natural reason, but by the artificial reason and judgment of law . . .[52]

What is the essence of this artificial reason, which makes the common law unique among western legal systems and renders it better than any of its rivals? Fortescue's Chancellor informs the Prince that the laws of England are 'excellent in their Nature and Reason', and describes a process of metamorphosis in which the love and knowledge of law changes the subject into the embodiment of law itself: 'For what is once loved do's by use transform the Person into its very Nature'.[53] Fortescue is developing a conceit whereby a person becomes the incarnation of an intangible ideal: perfect justice. Especially notable is Fortescue's insistence that this transformative process can occur only through 'use' or adher-

---

[45] *Ibid* at 79.
[46] *Ibid* at 81. Regarding this claim, Selden notes that '[t]he [French] Crown receives no other Advantage from the Barons, than in the Revenue for *Salt*; and never Taxes them but upon Extraordinary Occasions', *ibid*, n l.
[47] *Ibid* at 83.
[48] *Ibid* at 30.
[49] J G A Pocock, *The Machiavellian Moment: Florentine Political Thought and the Atlantic Republican Tradition* (New Jersey, Princeton University Press, 2003) 13.
[50] Fortescue, above n 7, at 34.
[51] Pocock, above n 49, at 16.
[52] Coke, *Prohibitions del Roy*, 12 Reports (1655) 7: 64a, at 65a.
[53] Fortescue, above n 7, at 10.

ence to custom. Only when the Chancellor's young charge has 'transcribed the Law' into his 'very Habit and Disposition' will he 'deservedly obtain the Character of a Just Prince'.⁵⁴ In his definition of nature, Fortescue implies the indivisibility of custom and the Law of God; furthering his thesis that the laws of England are primarily *leges non scriptae*, he argues that statutes represent nothing more than the reduction 'into Writing' of the laws of nature and custom.⁵⁵ Selden notes of Fortescue's assertion that human laws are derived from nature, customs or statutes that the law of nature is 'the Law of all Places, Persons and Times, without Alteration, One and the same Inscription of GOD's Power, and Goodness'.⁵⁶ Fortescue uses a metaphor that is drawn from his knowledge of the orchards of Gloucestershire, with which to illustrate how privileged access to artificial reason transforms the recipient of such knowledge from being a 'Stranger' to the common law into a personification of 'the Rule of Justice'.⁵⁷ The Chancellor likens the young Prince to 'an Apple-Stock', onto which a scion from a pear tree is grafted, with the felicitous result 'that both become a Pear-Tree, and are called so from the Fruit which they produce'.⁵⁸ The Ovidian imagery employed by Fortescue is intended to suggest that the fusion of 'nature' (the apple tree) with the artificial reason of law (the grafted pear tree) will transform the host body into a manifestation of law itself. The image of the ancient constitution that is evoked throughout *De Laudibus* is predominantly rural. For Fortescue, the customs of the shires represent the unity of human reason and natural law. This much is apparent from the metaphor of the grafted pear tree, above, and in the more general (but no less symbolic) and idealised description of the English subject of law:

> Every Inhabitant is at his Liberty fully to use and enjoy whatever his Farm produceth, the Fruits of the Earth, the Increase of his Flock, and the like . . .⁵⁹

In *2 Henry IV*, Justice Shallow's Gloucestershire orchard is a theatrical representation of Fortescue's bucolic imagery. Fortescue's vision of England is prevented from subsiding into pastoral sentimentality by the violent historical context in which *De Laudibus* is set: the dynastic war between the Houses of Lancaster and York. It is the same in Shakespeare's Gloucestershire: populated though it is by 'good varlet[s]' (5.3.12) and 'lusty lads' (5.3.20), the violent civil unrest beyond its borders reminds the audience of the fragility of ancient and immutable custom, and of the need to be vigilant in defence of the ancient constitution. Like

---

⁵⁴ *Ibid* at 11.
⁵⁵ *Ibid* at 28.
⁵⁶ *Ibid*, n (a).
⁵⁷ *Ibid* at 10, 11.
⁵⁸ *Ibid* at 10. The Shakespearean equivalent of the grafting metaphor employed by Fortescue can be found in *The Winter's Tale*, where Polixenes argues that the art which human reason applies to nature is a product of nature itself: 'Yet nature is made better by no mean / But nature makes that mean: so, over that art, / Which you say adds to nature, is an art / That nature makes. You see, sweet maid, we marry / A gentler scion to the wildest stock, / And make conceive a bark of baser kind / By bud of nobler race. This is an art / Which does mend nature—change it rather—but / The art itself is nature'. (4.4.89–97) See *The Winter's Tale*, (ed) J H P Pafford (London, Arden, 1963).
⁵⁹ Fortescue, above n 7, at 83.

The Ancient Constitution, Common Law and the Idyll of Albion

Fortescue's Chancellor, Justice Shallow is a true countryman, skilled in the horticultural technique of grafting described above: he invites Falstaff to 'see my orchard, where, in an arbour, we will eat a last year's pippin of mine own graffing' (5.3.1–2).

In *The Justices of the Peace in England, 1558–1640*, subtitled *A Later Eirenarcha*, in homage to William Lambarde, J H Gleason provides a valuable analytical insight into the local administration of justice in early modern England. Gleason's expansive claim, in the first sentence of the book, that '[t]he justices of the peace symbolize the polity of England',[60] finds dramatic resonance in the three Gloucestershire scenes of *2 Henry IV*. Justice Shallow is neither jurist nor judge. Indeed, from a strict reading of Shakespeare's play, it seems unlikely that he was a member of one of the Inns of Court. 'I was once of Clement's Inn, where I think they will talk of mad Shallow yet' (3.2.12–13), he boasts to his fellow justice, Silence. Clement's Inn was one of the Inns of Chancery in London, at which attorneys-at-law were trained.[61] Fortescue's Chancellor informs the Prince that in each of these (there were 10 Inns of Chancery when *De Laudibus* was written):

> [T]here are an Hundred Students at the least; and, in some of them, a far greater Number, tho' not constantly residing. The Students are, for the most part, young Men; here they Study the Nature of Original and Judicial Writs, which are the very first Principles of the Law: After they have made some Progress here, and are more advanced in Years, they are admitted into the Inns of Court.[62]

If Shallow had not progressed from Clement's Inn to one of the four Inns of Court, his knowledge of English law would have been rudimentary. He misses no opportunity to remind Falstaff and Justice Silence of his youthful experiences in London; therefore it seems unlikely that he would have failed to mention any adventures that befell him while a student at one of the Inns of Court. Characteristically, Shallow boasts to Silence of his acquaintance with young men from the 'superior' Inns of Court:

> . . . There was I, and little John Doit of Staffordshire, and black George Barnes, and Francis Pickbone, and Will Squele, a Cotsole man—you had not four such swingebucklers in all the Inns o'Court again . . . (3.2.18–21)

---

[60] Gleason, above n 42, at 1.

[61] On the junior branch of the legal profession in Elizabethan England, see C W Brooks, *Pettyfoggers and Vipers of the Commonwealth: the 'Lower Branch' of the Legal Profession in Early Modern England* (Cambridge, Cambridge University Press, 1986).

[62] Fortescue, above n 7, at 109–10; during Elizabeth's reign there were only eight Inns of Chancery. Each of these was affiliated to one of the Inns of Court. If Shallow had subsequently been admitted to an Inn of Court, it would most likely have been the Inner Temple, whose affiliated Inns of Chancery were Clement's Inn, Clifford's Inn and Lyon's Inn. Of the remaining five Inns of Chancery, Barnard's Inn and Staple's Inn were affiliated to Gray's Inn; Furnival's Inn and Thavie's Inn to Lincoln's Inn; and New Inn to the Middle Temple. By the time Coke was writing the Preface to Part 3 of *The Reports*, the numbers of Inns of Court men far exceeded those at the Inns of Chancery. Coke states that 'each of the Houses of Court consists of Readers above twenty; of Utterbarristers above thrice so many; of young Gentlemen about the number of eight or nine score, who there spend their time in study of law,' while each of the Inns of Chancery 'consist of forty or thereabouts': Coke, 3 *Reports* (1602) 2: Preface, xviiib.

While a student at Clement's Inn, Shallow almost certainly would have had friends and drinking companions at one of the nearby Inns of Court, but he never goes so far as to claim that he was a member himself. The four 'swinge-bucklers' of the Inns of Court were John Doit, George Barnes, Francis Pickbone and Will Squele: the fifth member of the gang (if his reminiscence is accurate)[63] was Robert Shallow, of Clement's Inn.

The traditional educational route for an aspiring common lawyer was to study for a degree at Oxford or Cambridge prior to a prolonged period as a student at one of the Inns of Court. After eight years as an inner barrister, during which time he would participate in 12 'grand moots' at his Inn and 24 'petty moots' at an Inn of Chancery, the student was called to the Bar and elevated to the status of utter barrister. Utter barristers from the Inns of Court gave readings on particular statutes or cases at the Inns of Chancery, and students there participated in moots, similar to those at the Inns of Court.[64] But as I have already noted, for many young men attendance at the Inns of Court was never intended as an introduction to a career in the legal profession. By the end of the 16th century the Inns of Court were, as J A Sharpe has observed, still functioning to a great extent as finishing schools for the English landowning classes, much as they had when Fortescue wrote *De Laudibus*.[65] Unlike Oxford and Cambridge, the 'Third University' offered no scholarships, so all but the wealthiest were precluded from admission. It is worth quoting at length from *De Laudibus* to gain an accurate impression of the social background from which students at the Inns of Court were drawn:

> [A] Student cannot well be maintained under Eight and twenty Pounds a Year: And, if He have a Servant to wait on him (as for the most part they have) the Expense is proportionably more: For this Reason, the Students are Sons to Persons of Quality; those of an Inferior Rank not being able to bear the Expences of maintaining and educating their Children in this Way. As to the Merchants, they seldom care to lessen their Stock in Trade by being at such large yearly Expenses. So there is scarce to be found, throughout the Kingdom, an eminent Lawyer, who is not a Gentleman by Birth and Fortune; consequently they have a greater Regard for their Character and Honour than those who are bred in another Way.[66]

For most students from the social background to which Fortescue refers, legal education provided them with an elementary knowledge of law, sufficient to manage their country estates when they returned permanently to the shires.[67] This point is

---

[63] As Falstaff observes of Shallow, '[t]his same starved justice hath done nothing but prate to me of the wildness of his youth, and the feats he hath done about Turnbull Street, and every third word a lie' (3.2.298–301).
[64] See Dugdale, above n 11, at 144, 158–60, 193–95; also Coke, 3 *Reports* (1602) 2: Preface, xviiia.
[65] J A Sharpe, *Early Modern England: A Social History 1550–1760* (London, Arnold, 1987) 270.
[66] Fortescue, above n 7, at 110–11.
[67] Sir Andrew Aguecheek is another of Shakespeare's characters, drawn from the shires, who appears to have 'benefited' from an education at one of the Inns but has never practised law. He shows an acquaintance with the customs of the Inns when he claims that 'I delight in masques and revels sometimes altogether', *Twelfth Night* (1.3.107–108); he demonstrates limited knowledge of law, though, when he threatens Sebastian with 'an action of battery' (4.1.33).

reinforced by W S Holdsworth, who comments on the necessity, in a litigious age, of landowners acquiring some technical knowledge of common law.[68] I refer above to Shallow's description of himself as 'a poor esquire of this county'; but while not a member of the nobility, nor even the son of a knight, his background was of a sufficiency to send him to London, where he spent many 'mad days' (3.2.32). If as a young man Robert Shallow had attended only Clement's Inn then (according to Dugdale) his education would have been sporadic and less than satisfactory. There was no tutorial system and, aside from the provision of readings and moots, students were left to their own devices. Dugdale contrasts the cloistered calm of the Inns of Court with the noisy commerce of the Inns of Chancery:

> [I]n the Terme time they are so unquieted by Clyents and servants of Clyents, that resort to such as are Attorneys and practysers, that the Students may as quietly study in the open streets, as in their Studies. Item, they have no place to walk in, and talk and confer their learnings, but in the Church.[69]

Among Justices of the Peace, the paucity of Shallow's formal education would have been by no means unusual. Gleason records that in Worcestershire, of the 52 justices extant in the year 1584, only 13 had attended Oxford or Cambridge as undergraduates and only 16 had been called to the Bar. Twenty of the 52 Worcestershire justices had attended neither Oxford nor Cambridge, nor one of the Inns of Court.[70] Shallow refers in passing to Oxford, when he says to Silence: 'I dare say my cousin William is become a good scholar; he is at Oxford still, is he not?' (3.2.8–10) But there is no textual evidence that Shallow himself was a student there. The only statutory qualification for appointment to the post of Justice of the Peace (beyond the vague requirement, expressed in *34 Ed.3. cap. 1*, that they should be 'learned in the Lawes') was that 'None shall bee assigned Iustice of the Peace, if he have not landes or tenements to the value of twentie pounds by the yeare'.[71] Of far greater importance than formal education or social status (beyond the requirement that a justice must be a landowner) was the more nebulous requirement that he should be 'of the Best in the Countie'.[72] As Tillyard observes of Shallow, it matters not that at times (particularly when recalling his rumbustious youth as a student at Clement's Inn) he appears ridiculous; the crucial point about his embodiment of unwritten law is that he 'is a good countryman'.[73] Although as a Justice of the Peace, Shallow is an important functionary in the administration of justice, his knowledge of statutes and case law is less relevant to the execution of his duties as one of the King's Justices than his affinity with the unchanging customs of the English countryside.

---

[68] W S Holdsworth, *A History of English Law*, 17 vols (London, Methuen, 1924) 2: 506–10; see also, B J Sokol and M Sokol, *Shakespeare's Legal Language: A Dictionary* (London, Athlone, 2000) 1–3.
[69] Dugdale, above n 11, at 195.
[70] Gleason, above n 42, at 86.
[71] Lambard, above n 39, at 34.
[72] *Ibid* at 36.
[73] Tillyard, above n 22, at 302.

Common Lawyers and the Pastoral Idyll

Colin Burrow makes a similar observation in connection with the Gloucestershire scenes in *2 Henry IV*, referring to the interconnections between the juridical process in the shires and the associated 'networks and affinities'[74] as an example of the manner in which early modern England was governed. As we see in the scene between Shallow and his servant Davy, Shallow's network encompasses his shared knowledge of the Gloucestershire countryside and its customs; his social affinity with the inhabitants; and his association with the local community, forged by his judicial office. Beyond that, Shallow's network is evidenced by his contribution towards the security of the realm (in his role as Justice of the Peace, and in particular by his mustering of 'half a dozen sufficient men' to fight for the King), ineffectual though his actions undoubtedly are, and (through his acquaintance with Falstaff) by his indirect relationship with the royal court itself. The powers attached to the role of Justice of the Peace were not inconsiderable; as Lambarde states, justices had powers of jurisdiction and '[c]oertion', including the lawful authority to pass capital sentences, 'as by hanging, burning, boyling, or pressing'.[75] But it is in the informal enforcement of unwritten law, as reflected in the dialogue between Shallow and his servant Davy, that the role of Justice of the Peace as guardian of the ancient constitution is more accurately represented. Tillyard describes Davy as 'both administrator and politician',[76] and his questioning of Shallow, concerning the sowing of wheat, the shoeing of horses and the payment 'of William's wages' (5.1.21–22), suggests that his role is more akin to that of estate manager than that of a mere servant.[77]

The professional relationship between Shallow and Davy appears to be similar to that of an attorney (which Shallow would have been, had he completed his education at Clement's Inn) and his clerk or noverint. Davy's first lines to Shallow, after greeting him, are: 'Marry, sir, thus: those precepts cannot be served; and again, sir—shall we sow the hade land with wheat?' (5.1.11–13) In his law dictionary entitled *The Interpreter*, John Cowell notes that a '[p]ræcept (*præceptum*) is diversly taken in the common law: sometime for a commaundement in writing sent out by a Iustice of peace'.[78] Humphreys makes the plausible suggestion that 'precepts' here refers to one of the *praecipe* writs[79]: a form of action in which a right to enjoyment of property by a plaintiff was asserted over a defendant. In *The Interpreter*, Cowell notes that '*Præcipe quod reddat*, is a writ of great diversitie touching both the forme and use'.[80] Such a writ 'properly signifieth in our common lawe, the taking possession of lands or tenements'; for example, 'where a man demandeth lands or tenements of his owne seisin, after the terme is expired'. The

---

[74] C Burrow, 'Reading Tudor Writing Politically: The Case of *2 Henry IV*', (2008) 38 *The Yearbook of English Studies* 234, 235.
[75] Lambard, above n 39, at 66, 68.
[76] Tillyard, above n 22, at 303; Tillyard makes the further claim that in respect of his political and administrative skills, Davy is 'perhaps in his little way the double of Henry IV', *ibid*.
[77] Falstaff refers to Davy as Shallow's 'husband' (5.3.11), ie a husbandman or steward.
[78] J Cowell, *The Interpreter: or Booke containing the signification of words wherein is set foorth the true meaning of all, or the most part of such words and termes, as are mentioned in the law writers* (Cambridge, Iohn Legate, 1607) Ddd1.*v*.
[79] Humphreys (ed), above n 21, at 157, note to 5.1.11.
[80] Cowell, above n 78, at Ddd1.*v*.

relevance of *praecipe* to the continuation of antique custom in the shires of England and therefore, in more general terms, to the perpetuation of the ancient constitution is that (as Cowell elaborates):

> The writs of entrie savour much of the right of propertie. As for example: some be to recover customes and services: in the which are contained these twoe words (*solet & debet*)...[81]

The symbolic importance of *solet* and *debet* to the claim of a higher, moral law and supreme constitutional status could not be more apparent, suggestive as they are of that which is customary and that which ought to be. Baker compounds the idea that Shakespeare was referring in this scene to the rectitude of ancient and immutable custom, by describing the writs of *praecepe* as 'the oldest and most solemn of actions'.[82] The action was concerned with exercising the right of the plaintiff over property currently in use by the defendant, rather than with compensation for a wrong committed by the defendant. Therefore, it is possible that Davy's question concerning the sowing of wheat on the 'hade land' refers to his preceding statement that the 'precepts' could not be served. In other words, the defendant was denying the plaintiff access to the 'hade land', thereby preventing the sowing of wheat. Davy had consequently attempted to serve a writ of *praecipe* on the defendant, demanding that the plaintiff be allowed to sow wheat, but had failed. As Baker remarks, defendants often ignored the initial serving of the writ, requiring several stages in the process before the plaintiff successfully claimed his right over the land.[83]

In response to Davy's inquiry about whether they should sow wheat, Shallow replies: 'With red wheat, Davy' (5.1.14), referring to the 'red Lammas' variety, grown locally in Gloucestershire since time immemorial.[84] For all his boastful and possibly fictitious reminiscences about his lusty youth, Shallow is at one with nature and the customs of rural life. Whether choosing the best variety of wheat or grafting 'pippins' onto rootstocks, he fulfils Tillyard's definition of a good countryman. Of course, Shallow has many obvious human flaws. He is vain, mendacious and venal; apart from boasting and lying about his past, he bribes Falstaff on the death of Henry IV in order to court favour with the new king (upon the death of the regnant monarch, the commissions of sitting justices were automatically terminated).[85] The last we see of him, he is committed by the Lord Chief Justice (albeit temporarily) to The Fleet prison, with Falstaff and 'all his company along

---

[81] *Ibid* at Bb4.r.

[82] J H Baker, *An Introduction to English Legal History* (London, Butterworths, 2002) 58.

[83] The particular writ would have been one of the following: *praecipe quod reddat* (concerning the performance of a covenant); *praecipe quod permittat* (ordering the defendant to allow the plaintiff to do something); or *praecipe quod permittat habere* (enforcing an easement or profit): *ibid*.

[84] Humphreys (ed), above n 21, at 158, note to 5.1.14; see also D H Madden, *The Diary of Master William Silence, a Study of Shakespeare and of Elizabethan Sport* (New York, Longmans, Green & Co, 1907) 381.

[85] 'By the death or demise of the Prince, also dieth the power of al the Commissioners of the Peace made by him . . . and the Justices of the next Prince they shall not be, unless he wil to make them, 4.E.4.44: &. 1.E.5.1.', Lambard, above n 39, at 78.

with him'. (5.5.92) Venality of the kind evinced by Shallow did not prevent two pre-eminent common lawyers of the Elizabethan and Jacobean era, Sir Edward Coke and Sir Francis Bacon, from attaining high judicial office.[86] Neither did dismissal from their posts (Coke as Chief Justice of the King's Bench in 1616, Bacon as Lord Chancellor in 1621) and imprisonment in the Tower diminish their status as archetypes of an equitable legal tradition. Shallow is digressive and prone to sentimental, unreliable reminiscence; so too, as I have indicated above, was Lord Denning. Like Denning, Shallow's interpretation of law is predicated upon his respect for the customs of rural life.[87] In Shallow's case, such respect extends to empathising with individual members of the rural community. Hence, Davy asks Shallow to 'countenance' or support his friend, 'William Visor of Woncot against Clement Perkes a'th'Hill'. (5.1.34–35)[88] Shallow knows Visor to be an 'arrant knave' (5.1.37), but Davy pleads for him on the grounds of amity, 'at his friend's request' (5.1.41) and because '[t]he knave is mine honest friend' (5.1.46). Swayed perhaps by Davy's loyalty towards his friend, Shallow declares that 'I say he shall have no wrong'. (5.1.49)

The system of justice described here by Shakespeare is Aristotelian, in the sense that it is dependent on the recognition of community, association or friendship to the creation and maintenance of the *polis*. In Book I of *The Politics*, Aristotle uses the microcosm of the village community with which to demonstrate the interdependency of the various constituent members of the State. They are 'homogalactic': literally, they suckle from the same source of milk.[89] Of even greater relevance to the scene between Davy and Shallow (and to the sense that this scene alludes to the fractious state of England in the reign of Henry IV) is the political importance that Aristotle attaches to friendship in Books VIII and IX of *The Nicomachean Ethics*. For Aristotle, friendship is the bond of communities and is, he claims, more important to lawgivers even than justice; the primary objective of lawgivers is the attainment of concord and the elimination of faction, and concord is synonymous with friendship.[90] In *The Book Named the Governor*, Sir Thomas Elyot's seminal work on governance, the commonweal and the education of a

---

[86] On the lives of Coke and Bacon, see respectively C D Bowen, *The Lion and the Throne: The Life and Times of Sir Edward Coke (1552–1634)* (London, Hamilton, 1957); L Jardine and A Stewart, *Hostage to Fortune: The Troubled Life of Francis Bacon* (London, Gollancz, 1998).

[87] On the description of his upbringing and family background in rural Hampshire, and its influence over his life and work, see the various volumes of autobiography by Lord Denning: *The Due Process of Law* (London, Butterworths, 1980); *The Family Story* (London, Butterworths, 1981); *Leaves from My Library* (London, Butterworths, 1986).

[88] Woncot is the Gloucestershire village of Woodmancote; see Humphreys (ed), above n 21, 159, note to 5.1.34–35; also, Madden, above n 84, at 84–85; J Bate, *Soul of the Age: the Life, Mind and World of William Shakespeare* (London, Penguin, 2008) 39; Burrow further suggests that 'th'Hill' to which Davy refers is the Gloucestershire location of Stinchcombe Hill: Burrow, above n 74, at 243.

[89] Aristotle, *The Politics*, (tr) T A Sinclair (London, Penguin, 1992) 58–59, 61, Bk I.II.1252b15–27, 1253a29–b1; Burrow observes of *De Republica Anglorum* that its author (despite his claims to the contrary) presents 'a single, Aristotelian model of what a commonwealth suited to the English temperament should be': Burrow, above n 74, at 240.

[90] Aristotle, *The Nicomachean Ethics*, (tr) J A K Thomson (London, Penguin, 2004) 200–201, Bk VIII.I.1155a1–32.

prince, the Aristotelian notion of friends is interpreted in the context of advisers or counsellors to the prince: *amici principis*. According to Elyot, those rulers who refuse the counsel of advisers are subject to 'most pernicious danger'. Discussing the best form of governance, Elyot quotes from Plutarch of Theopompus, King of Lacedaemonia:

> 'If' (said he) 'the prince give to his friends liberty to speak to him things that be just, and neglecteth not the wrongs that his subject sustaineth'.[91]

I shall return to Elyot, with particular reference to the exchange between Hal and the Lord Chief Justice in *2 Henry IV*, concerning Hal's committal to prison for publicly striking him (5.2.70–83). For now, I conclude my discussion of Shallow's Gloucestershire idyll with the observation that the Aristotelian notion of friendship was an essential component of common law principles of fairness, equability and social cohesion, forming the basis of community at a local and national level.[92]

Left alone, when Shallow and Davy retire to prepare for dinner, Falstaff reflects on 'the semblable coherence of his [Shallow's] men's spirits and his.' He misinterprets the exchange between Shallow and Davy, making the mistaken observation that Shallow's servants, 'by observing of him, do bear themselves like foolish justices; he, by conversing with them, is turned into a justice-like servingman'. (5.1.62–65) Far from acting foolishly, as Falstaff surmises, what has occurred between them is akin to the grafting process described by Shallow in Act 5, scene 3, and by Fortescue in *De Laudibus*. Whether by serving the writ of *praecipe* on their intransigent neighbour or by Shallow's 'countenancing' of Davy's friend, William Visor, the artificial reason of the law has been grafted onto ancient custom: the writ will enable the 'hade land' to be sown with 'red wheat', as it has been since time immemorial[93]; the countenancing of William Visor against Clement Perkes will allow Davy's honest friend to carry on his agrarian business (whatever it may be) as he always has. In their unity of purpose, which Falstaff mistakes for foolishness, Shallow and Davy display fidelity to the land and to ancient custom.[94] In their brief, pre-prandial dialogue, the two countrymen, Shallow and Davy, have amply demonstrated that the common or customary laws of England are, as Fortescue stated, 'deduced from the Law of Nature'.[95] Citing Aristotle as author-

---

[91] Sir Thomas Elyot, *The Book Named the Governor* (London, J M Dent, 1962) 111.

[92] Discussing Richard Hooker's Aristotelian political theory, instanced especially in Book VIII of *Of the Laws of Ecclesiastical Polity*, Carlyle states that '[t]he authority of the laws is derived not from the king, but from the whole community, as indeed is the authority of the king himself', A J Carlyle, 'Political Theory from 1300 to 1600' in A J Carlyle and R W Carlyle, *A History of Medieval Political Theory in the West*, 6 vols (Blackwood, Edinburgh, 1903–36) 6: 498.

[93] On the legal significance of the plough to the jurisdiction of early modern rural communities, and for the argument that '[t]he measurement of Law is the measurement of the productivity of arable land', see P Goodrich, 'Eating Law: Commons, Common Land, Common Law' (1991) 12 *The Journal of Legal History* 246, 260.

[94] Hachamovitch notes that all medieval land was 'held in fee, (*fide*) that is to say, faithfully', Y Hachamovitch, 'The Ideal Object of Transmission: An essay on the faith which attaches to instruments (*de fide instrumentorum*)' (1991) 2 *Law and Critique* 85, 99.

[95] Fortescue, above n 7, at 29.

ity for his claim that the law of nature is the ultimate source of English law, Fortescue quotes approvingly from Book V of *The Nicomachean Ethics*: ' "The Law of Nature is the same, and has the same Force all the World over" '[96] The quotation from Aristotle is an appropriate subtitle for the three Gloucestershire scenes in *2 Henry IV*. In his delineation of the various functions of Justices of the Peace, Lambarde ascribes to them a spiritual role, not dissimilar to the description by Fortescue of the judiciary as '*sacerdotes*'. Defining the word 'Peace', Lambarde argues that the word

> hath sundry significations in the holy Scripture: For there is an inwarde, and an outward Peace ... Out of this proceedeth an other inwarde Peace, named ye Peace of Conscience, for that our conscience is (by faith in Christ) at Peace, both with God and itself.[97]

For Lambarde, Elizabethan justices played a central role in the maintenance of the customary laws of England and the protection of the ancient constitution. They were the provincial guardians of the nation's conscience, considered by Gleason to be leaders of English society and, more portentously by Trevelyan, 'of the utmost significance for the future of our constitution and our law'.[98]

III. The Education of a Prince and 'the rusty curb of old Father Antic the law'

Critics of *2 Henry IV* have consistently noted the play's themes of time and timelessness. Humphreys goes so far as to argue that in the course of the play, time becomes a 'picture of the nation'.[99] There is a sense in much if not all of the play (not least in the Gloucestershire scenes discussed above) that the action may be set in the early 15th century, the late 16th century, or somewhere in between (or after). In the context of precedent in common law—of past decisions acting upon and directly affecting the present case—the observation of Lord Hastings that '[w]e are time's subjects' (1.3.110) is an accurate and concise description of every litigant who ever appeared before an English court. Each plaintiff and defendant is subject to time, in the sense that the present decision of the court is contingent upon past judgments.

The issue of the succession to Elizabeth provided an underlying and general theme for *1 Henry IV* and *2 Henry IV*; of particular relevance is that the Tudor rebellions of 1536, 1547 and 1569 (especially given the involvement of the Percys in the 1569 Northern Rebellion) provided Shakespeare with recent and resonant

---

[96] *Ibid*; Aristotle, *Nicomachean Ethics*, Bk V.VII.1134b18–20.
[97] Lambard, above n 39, at 4–5.
[98] Gleason, above n 42, at 119; G M Trevelyan, *English Social History: A Survey of Six Centuries from Chaucer to Queen Victoria* (London, Longman's, Green & Co, 1942) 171.
[99] Humphreys (ed), above n 21, Introduction, liii.

simulacra of the rebellions against the rule of Henry IV.[100] Indeed, the lawyer who, in 1570, was employed at the assizes in York, Carlisle and Durham to receive the submissions of the Northern rebels was to become known to Shakespeare's family for presiding over the trial in 1583 of two of their relatives, John Somerville and Edward Arden, charged with plotting to kill the Queen.[101] By then, Sir Christopher Wray had been appointed Lord Chief Justice, a post that he held from 1574 until his death in 1592.[102] The phantasms of leading members of the judiciary inhabit the two parts of *Henry IV*, casting long shadows over Shakespeare's portrayal of the English legal institution. I have commented on the powerful influence of Sir John Fortescue and *De Laudibus* over the depiction of the English countryside and its symbolic status as the embodiment of the ancient constitution. The guidance offered by *De Laudibus* is palpable also in the variations on the paternal relationship that exist respectively between Hal and Henry IV, the Lord Chief Justice, and Falstaff. Fortescue (like Bracton before him) was insistent that the model prince should be as familiar with the laws of England as he should with martial skills. Fortescue's Chancellor is pleased to see his young charge 'employ your self in such Manly and Martial Exercises', but he does not shirk from reminding the Prince, in chapter I, entitled 'An Exhortation to the Study of the Laws', that:

> [I]t is the Duty of a King to Fight the Battles of his People, and to Judge them in Righteousness. (1 *Kings* VIII.20) Wherefore, as You divert and employ your self so much in Feats of Arms, so I could wish to see You Zealously affected towards the Study of the Laws: because, as Wars are decided by the Sword, so the Determination of Justice is effected by the Laws.[103]

If Shakespeare reached back to the late 15th century and *De Laudibus* for the model of a paternal relationship between 'old Father Antic the law' (*1 Henry IV* 1.2.60) and the heir to the throne, he had recourse also to the early life of Sir John Popham, Lord Chief Justice from 1592 until his death in 1607. In *1 Henry IV*, the robbery scene at Gadshill, Kent, derives from anecdotal reportage of Popham's alleged criminal past. John Aubrey writes that Popham

> for several [years] addicted himself but little to the study of the laws, but [to] profligate company, and was wont to take a purse with them.[104]

---

[100] See T McAlindon, *Shakespeare's Tudor History: A Study of Henry IV, Parts 1 and 2* (Aldershot, Ashgate, 2001); for an earlier reflection on the same subject, see B T Spencer, '2 *Henry IV* and the Theme of Time' (1944) 13 *University of Toronto Quarterly* 397; on the development of the history play and its unique capacity to reflect continuity of existence, see B Griffin, *Playing the Past: Approaches to English Historical Drama, 1385–1600* (Woodbridge, D S Brewer, 2001).

[101] Somerville was son-in-law to Arden, the head of Shakespeare's mother's family. For an account of the trial and deaths of Somerville and Arden, see M Wood, *In Search of Shakespeare* (London, BBC Worldwide, 2003) 88–96.

[102] As Lord Chief Justice, Wray presided over the trial in 1581 of Edmund Campion. Prosecuting Counsel in the trial was Wray's successor as Lord Chief Justice, Sir John Popham, then Attorney-General. In 1585, Wray presided over the Star Chamber inquest at which the treason and suicide of the Earl of Northumberland were confirmed. Of possible relevance to Shakespeare's portrayal of country justices in *2 Henry IV*, in 1590 Wray initiated the revision of Commissions of the Peace, the processes of which had become notorious for their corruption.

[103] Fortescue, above n 7, at 1.

[104] J Aubrey, *Brief Lives* (London, The Folio Society, 1975) 255.

The Education of a Prince and 'the rusty curb of old Father Antic the law'

In his biography of Popham, Douglas Rice argues that, as a young man, Popham and his criminal associates gathered at a hostelry in Southwark, whence they set out to ambush travellers on the coach road to Kent, at Shooter's Hill, a notorious haunt for highwaymen.[105] Prevailed upon by his wife 'to lead another life, and to stick to the study of the law', Popham transformed himself from criminal to lawyer, becoming 'eminent in his calling',[106] to the extent that George Keeton asserted that '[t]he rugged personality and upright character of Popham must have been in Shakespeare's mind during the composition of the plays'.[107]

Another narrative, culled by Shakespeare from the repository of legal anecdotage, concerns the exchange between the uncrowned Henry V and the Lord Chief Justice in *2 Henry IV*. The new King asks his Chief Justice:

> How might a prince of my great hopes forget
> So great indignities you laid upon me?
> What! rate, rebuke, and roughly send to prison
> Th'immediate heir of England? Was this easy? (5.2.68–71)

The Lord Chief Justice reminds the King that he was imprisoned justifiably, for the offence of contempt of court:

> Your Highness pleased to forget my place,
> The majesty and power of law and justice,
> The image of the King whom I presented,
> And struck me in my very seat of judgment. (5.2.77–80)

Holinshed records as fact an incident in which Prince Henry 'had with his fist striken the cheefe iustice for sending one of his minions (upon desert) to prison'.[108] The earliest account of this story is in Elyot's *The Book Named the Governor*, published in 1531. Elyot does not record the Prince striking the Lord Chief Justice, merely that he 'all in a fury, all chafed, and in a terrible manner, came up to the place of judgment'. Elyot quotes the Lord Chief Justice's public rebuke of the Prince, in the Court of King's Bench, as follows:

> Sir, remember yourself; I keep here the place of the King, your sovereign lord and father. To whom ye owe double obedience, wherefore eftsoons in his name I charge you to desist of your wilfulness and unlawful enterprise, and from henceforth give good example to those hereafter shall be your proper subjects. And now for your contempt and disobedience, go you to the prison of the King's Bench, whereunto I commit you.[109]

---

[105] D W Rice, *The Life and Achievements of Sir John Popham, 1531–1607* (New Jersey, Fairleigh Dickinson University Press, 2005) 22–24.
[106] Aubrey, above n 104, at 255, 256.
[107] G Keeton, *Shakespeare's Legal and Political Background* (London, Sir Isaac Pitman & Sons, 1917) 7.
[108] Holinshed, above n 1, *Chronicles* iii.543/2/10.
[109] Elyot, above n 91, at 114–15; subsequent versions of the supposed altercation between Prince Henry and the Lord Chief Justice are reported in Robert Redman's *Vita Henrici V*, written between 1536 and 1544, and in Edward Hall's *The Union of the Noble and Illustre Famelies of Lancaster and York* (Hall's *Chronicle*), published in 1548.

The Ancient Constitution, Common Law and the Idyll of Albion

In an essay entitled 'The Story of Prince Henry of Monmouth and Chief-Justice Gascoign', Sir Frederick Solly-Flood argues that the 'quotation' by Elyot is fictitious. He states that spoken English 'was not used on the Bench' during the reign of Henry IV, implying that judges would have addressed the court in law-French or Latin.[110] Solly-Flood provides no authority for his claim, and as early as 1363 a statute had been enacted (*36 Ed.3. cap. 15*), decreeing that henceforth court proceedings should be conducted in English rather than law-French. Baker has indicated that the proceedings of the court were formally recorded in Latin text,[111] but *ex tempore* oral interventions from the Bench, such as that claimed by Elyot, might have been in English. It is likely, though, that Elyot was transposing events and locations from the reign of Henry VIII to that of Henry IV. In the reign of Henry VIII, when *The Book Named the Governor* was written, the King's Bench Prison (to which Elyot's Chief Justice commits the Prince) was extensively rebuilt, near Borough High Street, in Southwark. Froissart records that during the Peasants' Revolt of 1381 the rebels 'levelled several fine buildings and, in particular, the King's prisons, which are called Marshalseas'.[112] Solly-Flood argues that, during Sir William Gascoigne's tenure of the office of Lord Chief Justice (1400–1413), there was no 'prison of the King's Bench': convicted prisoners were committed to the custody of a marshal of the court ('*Committitur marescallo*'), who was responsible for their safekeeping. The prisoner was thus '*in custodia marescalli*' rather than '*in prisona Domini*'.[113] Solly-Flood plausibly suggests that Elyot derived the story from a report in the Court of King's Bench, in 1305, more than 80 years before Prince Henry of Monmouth was born. The relevant paragraph records that the then Prince of Wales, in contempt of the Court of King's Bench, had used gross and bitter language ('*verba grossa et acerba*') against the Chief Justice, for which offence the King (rather than, in Elyot's account, the Chief Justice) banished his son from his presence for six months ('*et hospicio suo fere per dimidium annum amovit*').[114] There is no record in the above account of the Prince of Wales striking the Chief Justice. Apart from Shakespeare's acquaintance with the story from

---

[110] Sir Frederick Solly-Flood, 'The Story of Prince Henry of Monmouth and Chief-Justice Gascoign' (1886) 3 *Transactions of the Royal Historical Society* 47, 57.

[111] J H Baker, 'The Three Languages of the Common Law' (1998) 43 *McGill Law Journal* 5, 10; Coke records that 'all judicial records are entered and enrolled in the Latin tongue: as it appeareth by an act of parliament in anno 36 Ed.3.c.15', 3 *Reports* (1602) 2: Preface, xixb. Despite the abolition of law-French from the courts, educational exercises in law-French continued at the Inns of Court throughout the 15th and 16th centuries, Dugdale, above n 11, at 194.

[112] J Froissart, *Chronicles*, (tr) and (ed) G Brereton (London, Penguin, 1978) 217. The rebels burned down the house of Richard Imworth, Keeper of the Marshalsea; see N Saul, *Richard II* (New Haven, Conn, Yale University Press, 1999) 64.

[113] Solly-Flood, above n 110, at 57; on the origins of the common law courts, see Baker, above n 82, at 37–52. In 1598, Stow records that there were five prisons in Southwark: 'The Clink on the Banke. The Compter, in the late parish church of St Margaret. The Marshalsey. The King's Bench. And the White Lion, all in Long Southwark', J Stow, *A Survey of London, Written in the Year 1598* (Stroud, Sutton, 2005) 340. On the King's Bench of the late medieval and early modern periods, see M Blatcher, *The Court of King's Bench, 1450–1550: A Study in Self-Help* (London, Athlone, 1978); also, J G Bellamy, *Criminal Law and Society in Late Medieval and Tudor England* (Gloucester, Alan Sutton, 1984).

[114] Quoted in Solly-Flood, above n 110, at 150–51.

The Education of a Prince and 'the rusty curb of old Father Antic the law'

Elyot's *The Book Named the Governor*, he would have seen a dramatised version of the altercation in the anonymous *The Famous Victories of Henry the Fifth*, entered in the Stationers' Register in May 1594, but performed in the mid-1580s by The Queen's Men.[115] In that play, the Prince 'giveth him [the Lord Chief Justice] a boxe on the eare' for passing sentence on one of his thieving companions, Cutbert Cutter. The Lord Chief Justice commits the Prince to Fleet Prison and Cutter to Newgate Prison, 'until the next Sises'[116]; there is no reference to Elyot's 'prison of the King's Bench'.

I have dwelt on the origins of the story in order to emphasise the importance of its derivation to Shakespeare. Holinshed's *Chronicles of England, Scotland and Ireland* and Hall's *The Union of the Noble and Illustre Fameliy of Lancaster and York* were both sources of the historical content in *Henry IV, Parts 1 and 2* (Hall's work begins with the accession of Henry IV in 1399 and includes a chapter entitled 'The unquiet time of King Henry the Fourth'). But with reference to the education of a prince and the impact of this upon his capacity to govern in the best interests of the common-weal, Elyot's *The Book Named the Governor* was obviously the greater influence. While Solly-Flood is almost certainly correct in doubting the veracity of Elyot's 'quotation' from Sir William Gascoigne, CJ, his statement that *The Book Named the Governor* 'has no claim whatever to be considered anything but a story book' is a major interpretive error.[117] As John Guy has suggested, the humanist literature of the Tudor era, heavily influenced as it was by the writings of Plato, Aristotle and Cicero, was republican in theme, to the extent that it displayed a preference for limited monarchy. Guy notes that *The Book Named the Governor* was interpreted by many commentators of the early modern period as a critique of the Henrician *Imperium*.[118] In view of its republican tone, it is unsurprising that *The Book Named the Governor* gained considerable critical attention after the abolition of the monarchy in 1649; indeed, in *Leviathan*, Thomas Hobbes explicitly criticised the type of humanist education advocated by Elyot. Hobbes was forthright in his condemnation of the classical texts to which Elyot refers, claiming that they instilled in those who read them a range of subversive and violent, republican sentiments.[119] His contemporary (and apologist for the theory of the divine right of kings), Robert Filmer, disagreed fundamentally

---

[115] Anon, *The Famous Victories of Henry the Fifth*, (ed) Chiaki Hanabusa (Manchester, Manchester University Press, 2007) Introduction, v, xxi; this edition is a reprint of the 1598 First Quarto, printed by Thomas Creede. For an argument that the play was performed by mid-1587, see S McMillan and S-B MacLean, *The Queen's Men and their Plays* (Cambridge, Cambridge University Press, 1998) 89, 196; also, G M Pinciss, 'The Queen's Men, 1583–1592' (1970) 11 *Theatre Survey* 50, 54.

[116] *Famous Victories*, above n 115, at 14–15. In *2 Henry IV*, Falstaff's Page announces that the Lord Chief Justice 'committed the Prince for striking him about Bardolph'. (1.2.55–56)

[117] Solly-Flood, above n 110, at 55.

[118] J Guy, 'Tudor Monarchy and its Critiques' in J Guy (ed), *The Tudor Monarchy* (London, Arnold, 1997) 81, 85; see also ch 1, text to nn 81–82, above. On *The Book Named the Governor* as an amalgam of various literary genres, including that of political tract, see C Carroll, 'Humanism and English literature in the fifteenth and sixteenth centuries' in J Kraye (ed), *The Cambridge Companion to Renaissance Humanism* (Cambridge, Cambridge University Press, 1996) 261–63.

[119] T Hobbes, *Leviathan*, (ed) J C A Gaskin (Oxford, Oxford University Press, 1996) 143.

with Hobbes's theory of the social contract but was similarly dismissive of the classical sources of *The Book Named the Governor*, describing Plato, Aristotle, Cicero and Polybius as 'heathen authors, who were ignorant of the manner of the creation of the world'.[120] At the core of Hobbes's opposition to humanist literature and its origins in the classical world was the distinction he made between *lex* and *ius*. For Hobbes, liberty of the citizen had been mistakenly elevated by the Athenians and the Romans to the harmful status of a positive right, thus threatening the sovereign power of the supreme magistrate. Hobbes made the identical observation of Sir Edward Coke, in *A Dialogue Between a Philosopher and a Student of the Common Laws of England*, accusing him of failing to recognise that a 'right' is a liberty only to do that which the law does not forbid.[121]

IV. Patriarchal Symbolism and the Common Law

The historical inaccuracy of the reported altercation between Prince Henry and Sir William Gascoigne, CJ is less important than its allegorical status as an illustration of the constitutional sovereignty of common law. Shakespeare's Lord Chief Justice informs Hal that he was imprisoned not for the assault upon his person, but for his assault upon the sacred institution that the office of Lord Chief Justice represents: the law itself. The Lord Chief Justice is conscious of the persuasive power of legal iconography, reminding Hal that the office he holds is '[t]he image of his [the King's] power' (5.2.74) and that it is '[t]he image of the King' (5.2.79) that he embodies when he sits in judgment. He poses Hal the hypothetical question whether, if he had a son, he would allow him to 'spurn at your most royal image' (5.2.89). He is mindful too of the symbolism inherent in the role of the Father, using the words 'father' and 'son' three and four times respectively in the same speech. His relationship with Hal is one of several variants on the paternal relationship that Shakespeare incorporates into the two plays. The symbol of fatherhood, of an imaginary father to whom all true subjects of law owe allegiance and from whom all law emanates,[122] is a metaphysical conceit to which judges and jurists of the early modern period made frequent allusion. Hence Coke refers variously to Moses, Brutus, the Druids and King Arthur as definitive founders and authors of English law.[123]

---

[120] R Filmer, 'Observations upon Aristotle's Politiques' in J P Sommerville (ed), *Filmer: Patriarcha and Other Writings* (Cambridge, Cambridge University Press, 1991) The Preface, 236.

[121] T Hobbes, *A Dialogue between a Philosopher and a Student of the Common Laws of England*, (ed) J Cropsey (London, University of Chicago Press, 1971) 73.

[122] Freud argued that in 'the psychoanalysis of individual human beings... the god of each of them is formed in the likeness of his father'; therefore 'God is nothing other than an exalted father': S Freud, 'Totem and Taboo' in *The Origins of Religion*, (tr) J Strachey, (ed) A Dickson (London, Penguin, 1990) 209.

[123] See respectively Coke, *Postnati. Calvin's Case*, 7 *Reports* (1608) 4: 12b; Coke, 3 *Reports* (1602) 2: Preface, viiia, viiib; Coke, 9 *Reports* (1613) 5: Preface, ia. On the iconic function of the archetypal lawgivers cited above, see Goodrich, above n 28, at 10–11.

Patriarchal Symbolism and the Common Law

The intention was to locate the ultimate source of legitimate constitutional authority; an issue of immense practical significance as successive Tudor monarchs sought, through increased use of the Royal Prerogative, to wrest jurisdiction from the courts of common law and relocate it in the person of the monarch.

In strict, Roman legal terminology, the image or *imago* was the social representation of the Father, in symbolic terms the ultimate lawgiver. As *paterfamilias*, the Roman father had power that mirrored that of the emperor.[124] His authority was absolute; he was *lex loquens*—the living, speaking law. In historical terms, the decision of Henry IV to govern in accordance with the power inherent in his personal, royal authority as *parens patriae* was the cause of much of the civil unrest that Shakespeare dramatised in the two plays. There were several instances of rebellion in the early years of Henry IV's reign, when local populaces rebelled against the authority of the King; not on the basis of his questionable dynastic right to the crown, but rather because they resented the assertion of a monarchic power that quashed their 'communal preference for self-regulation'.[125] It is the conflict between the *Imperium* of the monarch and the desire for communal self-regulation that Elyot addresses tangentially and allegorically in *The Book Named the Governor*, and that Shakespeare confronts more directly in the two parts of *Henry IV*. I have attempted to demonstrate that the Gloucestershire scenes of *2 Henry IV* offer a dramatic representation of a community governed by customary law, in accordance with the rights guaranteed English subjects by the ancient constitution. The Lord Chief Justice also upholds the law at a local, communal level, making his authoritative presence felt on the streets of London and in the Boar's Head Tavern, tempering the rigour of law with humanity, humour and equable judgment. Of the three paternal relationships that Hal experiences (with King Henry, Falstaff, and the Lord Chief Justice), his association with the Lord Chief Justice is the only one to survive until the end of *2 Henry IV*, by which time Henry IV is dead and Falstaff banished. It should be noted that in different ways both Falstaff and King Henry are kings of misrule: the former, for contriving to corrupt the heir to the throne, 'like his ill angel' (1.2.162–63); the latter for usurping the throne. Both must be sacrificed before the moral and legal order can be restored.[126] In their dealings with Hal throughout the two plays, Falstaff and King

---

[124] On the paternal source of law and the Roman origins of the Western legal tradition, see P Legendre, *Law and the Unconscious: a Legendre Reader*, (tr) P Goodrich, with A Pottage and A Schütz, (ed) P Goodrich (Basingstoke, Macmillan, 1997) Introduction, 8–12. On the classical law of images, see P Legendre, *Le Désir politique de dieu: Etude sur les montages de l'état et du droit* (Paris, Fayard, 1989); the title of Legendre's work derives from an essay by Lacan, in which he discusses the iconic image and its capacity to 'arouse the desire of God', J Lacan, *The Four Fundamental Concepts of Psycho-analysis*, (ed) J-A Miller, (tr) A Sheridan (Harmondsworth, Penguin, 1979) 113.

[125] S Walker, 'Rumour, Sedition and Popular Protest in the Reign of Henry IV' (2000) 166 *Past & Present* 31, 50.

[126] See N Sanders, 'The True Prince and the False Thief: Prince Hal and the Shift of Identity' (1977) 30 *Shakespeare Survey* 29, 30. The killing of the 'father' evokes the legend of Oedipus: on Freud's re-conceptualisation of the story as 'a myth of origin in the guise of a killing of the father that the primordial law is supposed to have perpetuated', see J Lacan, 'Psychoanalysis and its Teaching' in *Écrits*, (tr) B Fink (New York, W W Norton & Co, 2006) 375.

Henry appear as distorted representations of the same image of decay: the aged father, vying for the attention of an errant son.[127] In the end, Hal chooses to bind the body politic of the king to the only legitimate paternal model: the symbolic Father of law, the Lord Chief Justice.

Greenblatt has observed that the emphatic character trait of Hal in *1 Henry IV* is his skill at improvised role-playing.[128] Hal loves to act and he plays numerous roles, for his own and others' enjoyment. He continues to improvise in *2 Henry IV*, disguising himself again in order to entrap Falstaff and prove him 'a globe of sinful continents' (2.4.282). If the playacting of *2 Henry IV* is less spontaneous and exuberant than that of *1 Henry IV*, it has greater emotional impact for the serious intent with which Hal invests it. Hal's impersonation of the taproom 'drawer' in *2 Henry IV* (2.4.231–87) lacks the comic vitality (and the inventive dialogue) of his impressions of Hotspur, Lady Percy and the King in *1 Henry IV* (2.4.100–107, 2.4.429–66); but his purpose in the Boar's Head tavern of *2 Henry IV* is to draw Falstaff 'out by the ears' (2.4.286–87), thereby to incriminate him as a defamer of royalty. The Star Chamber punishment for defamation of the Crown would have been to 'have his ears cut off' (2.4.253–54), in light of which Falstaff's eventual (and temporary) banishment by the King, '[n]ot to come near our person by ten mile' (5.5.65), is an unusually lenient sentence.[129]

As Greenblatt notes of *1 Henry IV*, theatricality is the essential means through which power is expressed.[130] This is no less true of *2 Henry IV*, particularly when Hal is playing his most challenging role to date, that of King Henry V. The theatre of kingship is expressed by Hal in his first line as monarch, when he compares his regal status to a costume: 'This new and gorgeous garment, majesty, / Sits not so easy on me as you think'. (5.2.44–45) Despite his initial nervousness, Hal immediately demonstrates that his aptitude for and experience of improvised theatricality have prepared him for the royal stage, which he must now inhabit as king. He is astutely aware that the power of the king is dependent upon belief by

---

[127] Stewart makes the observation that in heroic myth the heroes often had two fathers: one divine and one human. He compares Falstaff to Chiron the Centaur, providing the young hero with an alternative 'father-model', offering an experience of humanity which his actual father could never provide. Like Silenus, the centaurs were renowned for their self-indulgence, but also for their wisdom and 'near-divine' powers; see D J Stewart, 'Falstaff the Centaur' (1977) 28 *Shakespeare Quarterly* 5.

[128] Greenblatt, above n 23, at 33.

[129] The lawyer and polemicist, William Prynne, was twice sentenced to 'ear-cropping' for the offence of seditious libel. The *Black Books* of Lincoln's Inn (of which Prynne was a member) record that in 1634, Prynne 'was censured in his Majesty's High Court of Starr Chamber for the contriveing, frameing, writing, and publishing of an infamous, scurrilous, and seditious booke and libel, by him intitled "Histrio Mastix, the Player's Scourge and Actor's Tragedie" . . . it was by the said Honoble Court ordered and decreed that the said William Prynne (being first expelled out of the Societie of Lincolne's Inne) should, beside his fine and ymprisonmt, suffer and undergoe such corporall punishment as in the said sentence is expressed', J D Walker (ed), *Black Books of Lincoln's Inn*, 5 vols (London, Lincoln's Inn, 1897) 2: 317. Following the publication in 1637 of his *News from Ipswich*, Prynne again suffered the same punishment; in addition, his cheek was branded with the initials, 'SL': 'Seditious Libeller'; on Prynne, see Raffield, above n 12, at 190–99; also, ch 2, n 53, above.

[130] Greenblatt, above n 23, at 33.

his subjects in the particular image of kingship that he reflects.[131] Without hesitation, he modestly presents himself as a king, not only under God but under law. No absolute monarch this: 'Not Amurath an Amurath succeeds, / But Harry Harry'. (5.2.48–49) Twice in the last act, we are reminded that Henry V will govern as King in Parliament (5.2.134, 5.5.103) and not, like Richard II, as '[t]he deputy elected by the Lord'. (*Richard II*, 3.2.57)[132]

Promises of symbolic Fatherhood abound: after announcing to his brothers that 'I'll be your father and your brother too' (5.2.57), he offers his hand to the Lord Chief Justice, proclaiming that 'You shall be as a father to my youth' (5.2.118): the new King casts himself as both symbolic Father and Son of the law. Falstaff, 'that reverend Vice, that grey Iniquity, that father Ruffian' (*1 Henry IV*, 2.4.441–42), has been exposed as an idol: in classical terms, he is nothing more than the reflection of a lie. In binding himself to the icon and Father of English law, the Lord Chief Justice, Henry V embraces truth and rejects falsehood. He is the true image of majesty; a model of accountable kingship and limited monarchy, as proposed across the centuries by Bracton, Fortescue and Coke:

> [T]he King is under no man, but only God and the law, for the law makes the King: therefore let the King attribute *that* to the law, which from the law he hath received, to wit, power and dominion: for where will, and not law doth sway, there is no King.[133]

---

[131] Marin argues that the king exists only in images; belief in his iconic status is a condition of his effectiveness as monarch: '[t]he king is only truly king, that is, monarch, in images. They are his real presence', L Marin, *Portrait of the King*, (tr) M M Houle (Basingstoke, Macmillan, 1988) 9.

[132] Henry V's immediate decision to 'call we our high court of parliament' (5.2.134) demonstrates respect for ancient custom and the sovereignty of common law, as approved by Christopher St German in *Doctor and Student*; see ch 2, n 81, above.

[133] Coke, 4 *Reports* (1604) 2: Preface, xixa.

6

The Congregation of the Mighty: the Juridical State and the Measure of Justice

I. Prerogative Power and the Impression of Legitimacy

THE CONCLUSIONS TO all of the plays considered so far have witnessed a level of transformation—the ambivalence, incompleteness and uncertainty of any change notwithstanding. In *Titus Andronicus*, the new imperial order promises '[t]o heal Rome's harms and wipe away her woe'. (5.3.147) In *The Comedy of Errors*, a draconian law is repealed by an equable magistrate, facilitating the emergence of a fairer society in which citizens 'go hand in hand, not one before another'. (5.1.426) In *Richard II*, change is instanced in the form of usurpation of the crown and the murder of a king, presaging a period of prolonged unrest and rebellion. *A Midsummer Night's Dream* incorporates throughout the play fantastical transformations of an Ovidian nature, overseen and controlled by a benevolent spirit world. In the coronation of Henry V, *Henry IV, Part 2* provides a unifying symbol and temporary respite from the discordant civil clamour initiated by Bolingbroke's seizure of the crown in *Richard II*. No such change is evident at the end of *Measure for Measure*, the conclusion of which has been described as 'anti-Ovidian' in its stark and uncompromising portrayal of inherently immutable government.[1] The Duke returns from his sabbatical, having observed at close quarters the inadequacies and injustices of the legal system over which he presides, and proceeds to exercise the Royal Prerogative in order to rectify particular grievances, while failing completely to address the flawed constitutional, political and social arrangements of his dukedom. He governs a Vienna that is predicated on a juridical (rather than a parliamentary) model,[2] in which the supreme magistrate is a highly proactive head of the judiciary as well as Head of State. The power of the State is transmitted exclusively through the courts,

---

[1] Hadfield describes *Measure for Measure* as 'an anti-Ovidian play, tantalizing the audience with exciting possibilities of change, only to frustrate and thwart such desires', A Hadfield, *Shakespeare and Renaissance Politics* (London, Arden Shakespeare, 2004) 198.

[2] Shuger refers to the 'juridic conception of the state' and its relevance to *Measure for Measure* in D K Shuger, *Political Theologies in Shakespeare's England: The Sacred and the State in 'Measure for Measure'* (Basingstoke, Palgrave, 2001) 72.

whether in the ordinary courts of law (as, for example, in the trials of Froth and Pompey in Act 2, scene 1, and the offstage trial of Claudio before Act 1, scene 2) or the prerogative court of the Duke (as in Act 5, scene 1).

Elizabeth I died on 24 March 1603. The playhouses were closed between March 1603 and April 1604, due to a severe outbreak of plague.[3] The earliest recorded reference to a performance of *Measure for Measure* is contained in the revels accounts for entertainment at the royal court during the Christmas festivities of 1604: 'By his Matis plaiers: On St Stivens night Mister Shaxberd . . . A play Caled Mesur for Mesur'.[4] The performance, attended by James I, took place at the Banqueting House in Whitehall. At the end of chapter one, I asked whether the death of England's Astraea, Elizabeth I, would portend an Ovidian age of iron, characterised by violence and social discord; or whether her demise promised a new golden age, in which subjects were governed not by statute or *Imperium* but by the institutional representation of their natural propensity for justice. The succession of James I and the consequent form of Jacobean government would go a long way towards answering that question.

Prior to his accession to the throne of England, James VI of Scotland demonstrated interest in theories of kingship and attracted considerable public attention through the publication of his opinions on the subject. *Basilicon Doron* (ostensibly intended as a practical guide to kingship for his eldest son, Henry) was written in 1598 and published in 1599.[5] In 1603, revised editions of *Basilicon Doron* were published in Edinburgh and London. *The Trew Law of Free Monarchies* was first published in 1598.[6] It is partly because of their dates of publication that I include *Measure for Measure* in a book that is subtitled *Late-Elizabethan Politics and the Theatre of Law*. Despite its post-Elizabethan period of composition, it appears that *Measure for Measure* was influenced by the above works of James VI, which were produced during the last five years of Elizabethan rule. The major political themes developed by James in *Basilicon Doron* and *The Trew Law* are reflected in *Measure for Measure*, most notably the conjunction of spiritual and secular authority in the person of the supreme civil magistrate. Arguably the two most striking themes of James's political writing are the continuous appeal to scripture as the source of legitimate monarchic authority and the sacrosanct nature of the Royal Prerogative:

---

[3] On plague and the playhouses, see A Gurr, *The Shakespearean Stage, 1574–1642* (Cambridge, Cambridge University Press, 1992) 78; E K Chambers, *The Elizabethan Stage*, 4 vols (Oxford, Clarendon, 1923) 4: 345–51.

[4] PRO AO3/908/13 in W R Streitberger (ed), *Collections Volume XIII: Jacobean and Caroline Revels Accounts, 1603–1642* (Oxford, The Malone Society, 1986) 8. On The King's Men and the St Stephen's Day performance of *Measure for Measure*, see J H Astington, 'The Globe, The Court and *Measure for Measure*' (1999) 52 *Shakespeare Survey* 133.

[5] Prince Henry was aged 4 when *Basilicon Doron* was written; he died aged 18 in 1612. The subtitle of *Basilicon Doron* is *His Maiesties Instructions To His Dearest Sonne, Henry The Prince*. The book is prefaced by a sonnet, the last lines of which read: 'Your father bids you studie here and reede. / How to become a perfite King indeed', 'Basilicon Doron' in J P Sommerville (ed), *King James VI and I: Political Writings* (Cambridge, Cambridge University Press, 1994) 1.

[6] The subtitle of *The Trew Law of Free Monarchies* is *The Reciprock and mutuall duetie betwixt a free King and his naturall Subiects*; see Sommerville (ed), above n 5, at 62.

The Congregation of the Mighty: the Juridicial State and the Measure of Justice

> The duetie, and alleageance of the people to their lawfull king, their obedience, I say, ought to be to him, as to Gods lieutenant in earth, obeying his commands in all things, except directly against God, as the commands of Gods Minister, acknowledging him a Iudge set by GOD over them, having power to iudge them, but to be iudged only by God, whom to only hee must give count of his judgment.[7]

As I discuss later in this chapter, the conviction held by James that his kingly office entitled him to sit in judgment in the king's courts was the cause of constitutional controversy and debate during his reign, and led directly to the intensification of jurisdictional conflict between the courts of common law and the prerogative courts of the king. Equally contentious was his stated belief in the inviolable status of the Royal Prerogative, on the subject of which he addressed the judges of common law in the court of Star Chamber in June 1616, instructing them to '[i]ncroach not upon the Prerogative of the Crowne... for they are transcendent matters'.[8]

In subsequent discrete sections I address the related themes of the king as supreme judge and divine lawgiver; law and the religious State; and the rivalry between different jurisdictions within the English legal system. I start here with an examination of the Royal Prerogative in its juridical context, as interpreted by the courts of common law. The salient image of absolute monarchic authority which I consider is one that recurs throughout *Measure for Measure*; it is that of incorruptible precious metal, whose unique stamp betokens impregnable and incontrovertible power.[9] The image of the royal stamp that bestows authenticity upon coinage is introduced in the first scene of the play when the Duke asks Escalus 'What figure of us think you he will bear?' (1.1.16), referring to Angelo and his capacity to deputise adequately and authentically for the Duke during his absence. Angelo uses the same image a few lines later when he protests to the Duke: 'Let there be some more test made of my metal / Before so noble and so great a figure / Be stamped upon it'. (1.1.48–50)[10] Simultaneously, Shakespeare has introduced two complementary images: substitution in the form of role-play and the authen-

---

[7] James I, 'The Trew Law', *ibid* at 72. The purpose of 'The Trew Law' was partly to 'set downe the trew grounds, whereupon I am to build, out of the Scriptures, since *Monarchie* is the trewe paterne of Divinitie', *ibid* at 64.

[8] James I, 'A Speech In The Starre-Chamber, The XX. Of June. Anno 1616' in Sommerville (ed), above n 5, at 212–13. On sovereignty and the distinction between 'immanence' and 'transcendence' in political and constitutional theory, see L Barshack, 'Time and the constitution' (2009) 7 *International Journal of Constitutional Law* 553.

[9] Dollimore argues 'that in the play the stamp metaphor signifies the formative and coercive power of authority', J Dollimore, 'Transgression and surveillance in *Measure for Measure*' in J Dollimore and A Sinfield (eds), *Political Shakespeare: Essays in Cultural Materialism* (Manchester, Manchester University Press, 1994) 82.

[10] Regarding the character's fall from grace, the name 'Angelo' has several ironic connotations in the play: in the context of coinage and the stamp metaphor, it is significant that the use of the word 'noble' by Angelo would suggest to an early modern audience the English gold coin, the 'Angel-noble'; see B Gibbons (ed), *Measure for Measure* (Cambridge, Cambridge University Press, 2006) 91, note to 1.1.49–50. All references to the text of the play are from this edition. In October 1604, James I proclaimed himself King of Great Britain (the title was not recognised by Parliament); in November 1604, the King announced the issue of a new coin that symbolised the union of England and Scotland—the 'unite', worth 20 shillings.

tic sign of legitimate authority. The theme of substitution is one to which I shall return in relation to the role of the judiciary as delegates or representatives of the king, an issue of considerable constitutional importance during the reign of James I. For now, I wish only to note the play's peculiar emphasis on the theatricality of substitution and the particular resonance of deputisation and disguise with the rule of James I.

The language of substitution was not unfamiliar to James, who referred to the common law judiciary as his 'subordinate Magistrates' and stated that the judges of the Old Testament 'were deputed for easier questions, and the greater and more profound were left to *Moses*'.[11] Indeed, he explicitly described the itinerant judges of the common law as 'my Substitutes in the Circuits'.[12] In the sense that the courts of common law were *curiae regis* then of course the judges were substitutes for the King; but it is apparent from various of his pronouncements on the role of the judiciary that James envisaged himself as the supreme judge, with the judiciary playing the subordinate parts of puisne judges. James shared with Shakespeare's Duke an astute awareness of the theatre of kingship, famously declaring before he ascended the throne of England, '[t]hat a King is as one set upon a stage'.[13] In March 1610, James again referred to the correlation between kingship and theatre, when he told the Members of the two Houses of Parliament, assembled at the Palace of Whitehall, that '[a]s I have already said, Kings Actions (even in the secretest places) are as the actions of those that are set upon the Stages'.[14] It is noteworthy in connection with *Measure for Measure* and the Duke's chosen disguise as 'a true friar' (1.3.49) that, towards the end of the same speech, James informed his audience that 'I must conclude like a Grey Frier, in speaking for my selfe at last'.[15] It is intriguing also that he should have considered it necessary to adopt an alternative identity in order to speak 'for my selfe'. The issue of disguise 'in the secretest places' operating as the means whereby the State may effectively exercise surveillance over its subjects is one that I consider later in this chapter, when I analyse the sacral and juridical importance of 'the eye of the law' and its relevance to the policing of the early modern State.[16]

When Isabella intercedes with Angelo on behalf of her brother, Claudio, who has been sentenced to death for the offence of fornication, Angelo rejects her plea, telling her that it were as good to pardon a murderer, 'as to remit / Their saucy sweetness, that do coin heaven's image / In stamps that are forbid'. (2.4.43–45) In the context of Angelo's argument, 'heaven's image' is of course the child with whom

---

[11] James I, 'Speech In The Starre-Chamber', above n 8, at 205.
[12] *Ibid* at 219.
[13] James I, 'Basilicon Doron' in Somerville (ed), above n 5, at 49.
[14] James I, 'A Speach To The Lords And Commons Of The Parliament At White-Hall, On Wednesday The XXI. Of March. Anno 1609' (1610), *ibid* at 184.
[15] *Ibid* at 203.
[16] On the history and development of 'the eye of the law' metaphor, from classical antiquity to the present, see M Stolleis, *The Eye of the Law: Two Essays on Legal History* (Abingdon, Birkbeck Law Press, 2009). In his collection of adages of the ancients, Erasmus quotes a proverbial hexameter: '*Est oculus aequitatis omnia intuens*' ('It is the eye of justice that notices all things'), *ibid* at 16.

Juliet is pregnant by Claudio[17]; but with reference to the stamp metaphor that Angelo incorporates into his speech, it is the image also of the king, God's lieutenant on earth or 'heaven's image'. By virtue of the Royal Prerogative, only the king had the power and authority to stamp and issue coinage. In *De Republica Anglorum*, Sir Thomas Smith used the identical language of stamps, coins and images with which to impart the mysterious and supreme power of the Royal Prerogative:

> The prince useth also absolute power in crying and decreeing the monies of the realme by his proclamation onely. The monies be always stamped with the princes image and title. The forme, fashion, maner, weight, finenesse, and basenesse thereof, is at the discretion of the prince. For whom should the people trust more in that matter than their prince, for the coine is only to certifie the goodnes of the mettall and the weight, which is affirmed by the princes image and marke?[18]

The increased use of Proclamations (to which Smith refers in the above passage), by which to legislate, was one of the factors that led in the first few years of James's reign to conflict between the Crown and the courts of common law. Coke records that in September 1610, as Chief Justice of the Common Pleas, he was summoned to appear before the Lord Chancellor (Lord Ellesmere), the Lord Treasurer, the Lord Privy Seal, the Chancellor of the Duchy of Lancaster, the Attorney-General, and the Solicitor General to give his opinion as to whether by Proclamation the king 'may prohibit new buildings in and about London, &c the other, if the king may prohibit the making of starch of wheat'. According to the Lord Treasurer, James I had decided to 'confer with his Privy Council, and his Judges', before making a decision on the matter. Unusually for Coke, who normally claimed for the courts of common law the status of ultimate arbiter of constitutional probity, he affirmed the primacy of Parliament in the law-making process, replying to the Lord Treasurer '[t]hat they concerned the answer of the King to the body, viz to the Commons of the house of Parliament'. Given the loyalty consistently displayed by Lord Ellesmere towards the King, it is not surprising that the Lord Chancellor should have declared in favour of the exercise of the Royal Prerogative in this instance:

> He would advise the Judges to maintain the power and prerogative of the King; and in cases in which there is no authority and precedent, to leave it to the King to order in it, according to his wisdom, and for the good of his subjects, or otherwise the King would be no more than the Duke of Venice.[19]

Despite the professional antipathy and personal animosity which over the course of many years characterised the fractious relationship between Ellesmere and

---

[17] Claudio informs Lucio that '[u]pon a true contract / I got possession of Julietta's bed—/ You know the lady, she is fast my wife, / Save that we do the denunciation lack / Of outward order'. (1.2.126–30) If this is true then, according to English law of the period, neither he nor Juliet had committed any offence, since they were already legally obligated to each other at the time sexual intercourse between them took place; see text to nn 106–13, below.

[18] Sir Thomas Smith, *De Republica Anglorum*, (ed) M Dewar (Cambridge, Cambridge University Press, 1982) 86.

[19] *Proclamations* in Part 12 (1655) of *The Reports of Sir Edward Coke, Knt. In English*, (ed) G Wilson, 7 vols (London, Rivington, 1777) 7: 74b.

Prerogative Power and the Impression of Legitimacy

Coke (and that led eventually to the dismissal in November 1616 of Coke as Chief Justice of the King's Bench), it is reasonable to assume that Coke was probably correct in his recollection that Ellesmere

> told the king that he as chancellor was keeper of the king's conscience and therefore whatsoever the king directed in any case he would decree accordingly.[20]

In response to the questions put to him regarding the Proclamations of the King, Coke was adamant that neither by Proclamation nor any 'other ways' may the King 'change any part of the common law, or statute law, or the customs of the realm'.[21] It is indicative of the lack of respect shown the courts of common law by James I that Coke was apparently summoned to appear before the assembled officers of the king with minimal notice: he records that 'I did not hear of these questions until this morning [20 September 1610] at nine of the clock'.[22] With some reluctance on the part of Lord Ellesmere and the other representatives of the King, Coke was granted his request to confer on the matter with the Chief Justice of the King's Bench (Sir Thomas Fleming), the Chief Baron of the Exchequer and his fellow Baron, Sir James Altham. They unanimously concluded that 'the King hath no prerogative, but that which the law of the land allows him'.[23] Their decision would continue to confound relations between James and the courts of common law, at least until the dismissal of Coke in 1616. More ominously, it would have far-reaching and catastrophic consequences for the reign of James's successor, Charles I.[24]

As Smith suggested in *De Republica Anglorum*, the imprint of the king's image on coinage is, like the use of Proclamations, affirmation of both the pervasive force of the Royal Prerogative and the omnipresence of the monarch. Hence, as

---

[20] CUL, MS Ii.5.21 fo 47.v. On the personalisation by Coke and Ellesmere of the dispute over the respective jurisdictions of common law and Chancery, culminating in Coke's dismissal as Chief Justice, see J H Baker, 'The Common Lawyers and the Chancery: 1616' in J H Baker, *The Legal Profession and the Common Law: Historical Essays* (London, Hambledon, 1986) 205.

[21] Coke, *Proclamations*, 12 *Reports* (1655) 7: 75a. In *Measure for Measure*, the First Gentleman refers to 'the proclamation' (1.2.65), regarding the criminal offence of fornication, of which Claudio stands convicted and sentenced to death. A few lines later, Pompey asks Mistress Overdone if she has 'not heard of the proclamation', that '[a]ll houses in the suburbs of Vienna must be plucked down'. (1.2.77–80) The suburbs, in the Liberties beyond the jurisdiction of the City of London, housed the brothels (on which Mistress Overdone's is clearly modelled). In September 1603, a Proclamation was made by James I, which prohibited people from lodging in houses afflicted with plague and called for the demolition of houses likely to be breeding grounds for disorder and disease. The Proclamation of 1603 followed one made by Elizabeth I in June 1602, which sought to prevent the further development of London by prohibiting the erection of new buildings, unless they were built on the foundations of old ones; see N W Bawcutt (ed), *Measure for Measure* (Oxford, Oxford University Press, 1994) Introduction, 2–3. Coke notes that in '37 H.8. the whorehouses, called the stews, were suppressed by proclamation and sound of trumpet, &c', Coke, *Proclamations*, 12 *Reports* (1655) 7: 76a.

[22] Coke, Proclamations, 12 *Reports* (1655) 7: 74b.

[23] *Ibid* at 76b.

[24] On Charles I and the actions taken by common lawyers and Parliament to restrict the prerogative powers of the Crown, see P Raffield, *Images and Cultures of Law in Early Modern England: Justice and Political Power, 1558–1660* (Cambridge, Cambridge University Press, 2004) 194–208; more generally, see also C Russell, *The Causes of the English Civil War* (Oxford, Clarendon, 1990); J Morrill, *The Nature of the English Revolution* (London, Longman, 1993).

Plowden observed in his report of *The Case of Mines* (*Attorney General v Earl of Northumberland*),

> it belongs to the king only to fix the value of coin, and to ascertain the price of the quantity, and to put a print upon it, which being done, the coin becomes current for so much as the king has limited.[25]

The counterfeiting of the king's money was, according to the Statute of Treasons 1352 (*25 Ed.3. cap. 2*), an act of High Treason,[26] as was the counterfeiting of the Great and Privy Seals. Like the coinage of the realm, the Great Seal (of which the Lord Chancellor was custodian) was a sign of both the legitimacy and coercive authority of the Crown, and, as Lord Ellesmere reported, 'the print whereof is directed by the pleasure of the Prince, the validity thereof I dare not to dispute'.[27] The validity of law and the counterfeiting of legitimate authority are central themes of *Measure for Measure*, in which the image of uncorrupted metal serves not only as an 'assay' of virtue but as the symbol also of penetrative State power. The same may be argued in relation to the contentious subject-matter of *The Case of Mines*. The case concerned the right of the Crown to ownership of gold and silver ore on land belonging to a private individual. Put simply,

> the common law, which is no other than pure and tried reason, has appropriated the ore of gold and silver to the king, in whatever land it be found.[28]

The disputed veins of gold and silver ore were located in land belonging to the Earl of Northumberland, and had been granted to him by letters patent of the late Queen Mary in 1557.[29] As in *The Case of the Dutchy of Lancaster*, heard seven years before *The Case of Mines*, the mystical quality of the Royal Prerogative became the principal tenet of the Crown's argument:

> This royal metal is given to him by reason of his dignity-royal, and is appropriated to the crown by prerogative, so that the king shall have it in his own land, and in the land of others in one same degree, for he has it not in his own land in respect that he is the

---

[25] *The Case of Mines* (1568), *The Commentaries or Reports of Edmund Plowden*, 2 vols (Dublin, H Watts, 1792) 1: 310, at 316. For the argument that Shakespeare engaged with the legal issues of *The Case of Mines* in *Hamlet*, see C Sale, ' "The King is a Thing": the King's Prerogative and the Treasure of the Realm in Plowden's Report of the Case of Mines and Shakespeare's *Hamlet*' in P Raffield and G Watt (eds), *Shakespeare and the Law* (Oxford, Hart Publishing, 2008) 137.

[26] Dugdale records that a 'Charter of Confirmation' in the reign of Henry I included a clause to the effect 'that Counterfeiters of money should have their Eyes pulled out, be gelt, and lose their right hands', Sir William Dugdale, *Origines Juridiciales or Historical Memorials of the English Laws* (London, F & T Warren, 1666) 7–8. In *Basilicon Doron*, the future king of England argues that there are 'some horrible crimes that yee are bound in conscience never to forgive'; these include witchcraft, murder, incest, sodomy, poisoning, 'and false coine', James I, 'Basilicon Doron' in Somerville (ed), above n 5, at 23.

[27] Lord Ellesmere, *Certaine Observations Concerning the Office of the Lord Chancellor* (London, Henry Twyford and Iohn Place, 1651) 33. The seal is the legitimate substitute of the king himself, the sign of absolute authority. Unquestioning faith in the validity of the sign is an important theme in *Measure for Measure*, as when the disguised Duke reveals the seal of ducal authority to the Provost: '[H]ere is the hand and seal of the Duke. You know the character I doubt not, and the signet is not strange to you'; to which the Provost immediately replies: 'I know them both'. (4.2.168–71)

[28] Plowden, *The Case of Mines*, above n 25, at 316.

[29] *Ibid* at 312.

possessor of the land, but in respect that he is possessor of the crown, and in that respect he has it alike in his own soil, and in the soil of others.[30]

The grant to the Earl by letters patent notwithstanding, the arguments of the Attorney-General (Gilbert Gerard) prevailed and the Earl was found to have unlawfully 'hindered and disturbed . . . to the damage of the said lady the queen', while her agents excavated and appropriated 'six hundred thousand pounds weight of ore and metal of copper' from his own land.[31] Counsel for the Queen successfully argued that the symbolic qualities of gold and silver warranted their appropriation by the Crown. Of

> all things which the soil within this realm produces or yield, gold and silver is the most excellent; and of all persons in the realm, the king is in the eye of the law most excellent.[32]

Like gold itself, the king is pure, virtuous and excellent in all things[33]; consequently, he draws the precious metal towards himself, claiming it as of right by virtue of his greatness: '. . . the excellency of the king's person draws to it things of an excellent nature'.[34]

The absolute and perpetual power of the prerogative appears from the judgment in *The Case of Mines* to be coterminous with the scope of Roman imperial power: *quod principi placuit legis habet vigorem*.[35] Indeed, in 1607 John Cowell sought to equate the absolute powers of the English Crown with those of its Continental counterparts when he argued in *The Interpreter* that

> our lawyers (*sub prærogativa regis*) doe comprise also, all that absolute height of power that the Civilians call (*maiestatem, vel potestatem, vel ius imperii,*) subject only to god . . .[36]

---

[30] *Ibid* at 332.

[31] *Ibid* at 310. The court declared that the grant of mines by letters patent did not extend to 'the ores-royal nor the mines-royal', *ibid* at 337.

[32] *Ibid* at 315.

[33] Noting the emblematic quality of gold, Gerard Legh remarks that 'Plato, telleth of it to be pliant, pure, & temperate, and to have virtue to clense superfluities gathered in bodies . . . For looke how muche thys mettall, excelleth all others in the kynde thereof, as in fynes and puritie: So much should the bearer thereof, excel all other, in prowes and virtue', G Legh, *The Accedens of Armory* (London, Richard Tottill, 1562) A.iii.*v*–A.iiii.*r*.

[34] Plowden, *The Case of Mines*, above n 25, at 315.

[35] The unrestricted power of the Crown is claimed in *Fleta*, as quoted by Dugdale: 'It is not incongruous to call our English Constitutions, Laws, though they be not committed to writing; forasmuch as the Law it self is, that what the King appointeth hath the strength of Law', above n 26, at 3.

[36] J Cowell, *The Interpreter: or Booke containing the signification of words wherein is set foorth the true meaning of all, or the most part of such words and termes, as are mentioned in the law writers* (Cambridge, Iohn Legate, 1607) Ddd3.*v*. A statute of uncertain date, but probably of 1322, *Prerogativa Regis* (15 or 17 Ed.2. cap. 13), listed some prerogative powers, including the following, cited by Plowden: 'the king shall have whales and sturgeons taken in the sea, or elsewhere within the realm', Plowden, *The Case of Mines*, above n 25, at 315. Cowell was adamant that *Prerogativa Regis* was not a comprehensive or exhaustive list of prerogative powers, 'but onely so much thereof, as concernes the profit of his cofers growing by virtue of his regall power and crowne. For it is more then manifest, that his prerogative reacheth much farder', Cowell, *Interpreter*, Ddd3.*v*. In another work, *The Institutes of the Lawes of England*, Cowell claimed that regarding the grant of monopolies, the king was above the law: 'And in one particuler the supream power wheresoever it rest . . . is above the Lawes for that it may grant priviledges at pleasure as to single persons, as to Corporations and Colledges', J Cowell, *The Institutes of the Lawes of England, Digested into the Method of the Civill or Imperiall Institutions*, (tr) W G Esquire (London, Jo Ridley, 1651) 5.

The Congregation of the Mighty: the Juridicial State and the Measure of Justice

Remarks such as this, along with the assertion that 'the king of England is an absolute king', antagonised Parliament, whose members complained that Cowell's intention 'was to take away the power and authority of the parliament'.[37] When *The Interpreter* was published in 1607, Cowell held the influential post of Regius Professor of Civil Law at Cambridge, and his pronouncements on the absolute power of the king were perceived by common lawyers (notably Coke, who referred to him as Dr Cowheel) and Parliamentarians as a threat to the jurisdictional sovereignty of the common law itself. Accused by Parliament of betraying the liberties of the people, Cowell was saved from imprisonment only by the intervention of James I, who suppressed *The Interpreter* by Proclamation and attempted to appease Parliament by informing its members that '[t]here was never any reason to move men to thinke, that I could like of such grounds'.[38] Suspicion lingered as to which form of legal system was favoured by James: it was suggested that he 'contemned' the common law 'and preferred the Civil Law thereunto'. The King assured Parliament that 'I have least cause of any man to dislike the Common Law', on the singular and debatable grounds that 'no Law can bee more favourable and advantagious for a King, and extendeth further his Prerogative, then it doeth'.[39]

It is unsatisfactory to describe *Measure for Measure* as a play 'about' law.[40] Insofar as it engages with juristic themes, it is a play about different forms of law, the most effective of which is that exercised by the Duke. The actions of the Duke as supreme magistrate conform to a recognisable and specific legal norm: the extraordinary and absolute power of the prerogative to interfere with due process and supersede the jurisdiction of the ordinary national tribunals. Shakespeare's Duke is not James I, but extensive use by the former of prerogative powers with which to attempt the resolution of grievances within the Viennese commonwealth is consonant with the explicit claim of James 'that the King is above the law'.[41] I turn now to the putative sources of the Royal Prerogative and the conflict that its exercise inevitably caused between the Crown and the courts of common law.

---

[37] E R Foster (ed), *Proceedings in Parliament, 1610*, 2 vols (New Haven, Conn, Yale University Press, 1966) 1: 18. On Cowell and 17th-century civil lawyers, see B P Levack, *The Civil Lawyers in England, 1603–1641: a Political Study* (Oxford, Clarendon, 1973); also, D R Coquillette, 'Legal Ideology and Incorporations I: the English Civilian Writers, 1523–1607' (1981) 61 *Boston University Law Review* 1.

[38] James I, 'Speech To The Lords And Commons', above n 14, at 180; see also, J F Larkin and P L Hughes (eds), *Stuart Royal Proclamations*, 2 vols (Oxford, Clarendon, 1973) 1: 244.

[39] James I, 'Speech To The Lords And Commons', above n 14, at 184.

[40] Bawcutt argues that 'it seems a little too easy to say, as so many critics do, that Angelo stands for the Law, rigidly applied, while the Duke represents Mercy. It is not false, but it is an over-simplification', N W Bawcutt, ' "He Who The Sword Of Heaven Will Bear": The Duke Versus Angelo In *Measure for Measure*' (1984) 37 *Shakespeare Survey* 89, 90.

[41] James I, 'The Trew Law' in Somerville (ed), above n 5, at 75; for the argument that the Duke was modelled on the providential kingship of James I, see D L Stevenson, *The Achievement of Shakespeare's 'Measure for Measure'* (New York, Cornell University Press, 1966).

II. The Divine Lawgiver and the Eye of the Law

Confiding in Friar Thomas prior to disguising himself as a friar, the Duke compares his inaction as supreme magistrate of Vienna to that of 'fond fathers' (1.3.24), who threaten but never punish their wayward children. The equation of the ruler with the image of an omnipotent father was a device with which renaissance audiences were familiar, and although the Duke is a character rather than an allegorical cipher, he embodies certain recognisable qualities of providential kingship.[42] Not least of these is the metaphysical capacity for omnipresence: he appears to be among his subjects at all times, watching, listening and judging.[43] As I noted in chapter two, regarding *The Case of Monopolies*, Coke described Elizabeth I as '*parens patriae, & paterfamilias totius regni*'.[44] For James I, the image of the king as *parens patriae* was complex and replete with religious overtones. He regarded himself not only as father of the nation, but also as its husband, head and shepherd. In a speech given in the House of Lords at the opening of Parliament in March 1604, he insisted that

> [w]hat God hath conioyned then, let no man separate. I am the Husband, and all the whole Isle is my lawfull Wife; I am the Head, and it is my Body; I am the Shepherd, and it is my flocke . . .[45]

The principal source of Biblical authority for the claim by James to incontrovertible and supreme authority was predicated upon two extracts from the Old Testament: 'Thou shalt not revile the gods, nor curse the ruler of thy people' (*Exodus* 22.28); and 'I have said, Ye are gods; and all of you are children of the most High'. (*Psalms* 82.6)[46] In *The Trew Law*, James interprets the first of these

---

[42] Pope notes that 'the Duke moves through so much of the action of *Measure for Measure* like an embodied Providence . . . his character has such curiously allegorical overtones, yet never quite slips over the edge into actual allegory', E M Pope, 'The Renaissance Background of *Measure for Measure*' (1949) 2 *Shakespeare Survey* 66, 71. When the Duke remarks to the Provost on the imminence of dawn, with the line 'Look, th'unfolding star calls up the shepherd' (4.2.177–78), the association with Christian allegory is unavoidable. Pope comments on this line of the Duke: 'one wonders if he may not be thinking of himself and his office', *ibid.*

[43] The theme of omnipresence, State surveillance and the eye of the law has obvious parallels with Foucault's analysis of Bentham's *Panopticon*, the effect of which was 'to induce in the inmate a state of conscious and permanent visibility that assures the automatic functioning of power', M Foucault, *Discipline and Punish: The Birth of the Prison*, (tr) A Sheridan (London, Penguin, 1991) 201.

[44] Coke, *The Case of Monopolies*, 11 *Reports* (1615) 6: 84b, at 85b; see ch 2, text to n 105, above.

[45] James I, 'A Speach, As It Was Delivered In The Upper House Of The Parliament . . . On Munday The XIX. Day Of March 1603 [1604]' in Sommerville (ed), above n 5, at 136; the references to the wife and the head derive from *The Epistle of Paul to the Ephesians*: 'For the husband is the head of the wife, even as Christ is the head of the church: and he is the saviour of the body', *Ephesians* 5.23. In *Measure for Measure* Pompey alludes to the same verse, when asked if he can 'cut off a man's head': 'If the man be a bachelor, sir, I can; but if he be a married man, he's his wife's head, and I can never cut off a woman's head'. (4.2.1–4) On the reference by James I to the shepherd, and its allegorical associations in *Measure for Measure*, see above n 42.

[46] Unless otherwise stated, references to The Bible are from the *Authorised King James Version*; this translation was proposed at the Hampton Court Conference of 1604, convened by James I. The translation was completed in 1611; see D Norton, *A Textual History of The King James Bible* (Cambridge,

quotations as a divine injunction to unquestioning obedience, owed by subjects to their king. It is interesting that in the version of *Exodus* 22.28 from which James I quotes in *The Trew Law*, 'Elohim' is translated as 'judges' rather than 'gods' or 'rulers'.[47] Although in *The Torah*, 'Elohim' is used to describe the God of the Hebrews and the Creator of mankind, the word 'Elohim' (אלהים) is the plural of the common Canaanite word for 'god': 'el' (אל). 'Elohim' was subsequently translated variously as 'judges', 'gods' or 'rulers'.[48] In *The Reverse or Back-Face of the English Janus*, John Selden stated emphatically (with explicit reference to *Exodus* 22 and *Psalms* 82) that 'the Eternal and sacred Scriptures themselves do more than once call Judges by that most holy name *Elohim*, that is, *Gods*', while James I claimed of the same verse in *Psalms* 82 that 'Kings are called Gods'.[49] James I referred to *Psalms* 82 again, in his speech to Parliament in 1610, where his description of the divine status with which he attributes kings is notable for its stridency: 'For Kings are not onely GODS Lieutenants upon earth, and sit upon GODS throne, but even by GOD himselfe they are called Gods'.[50] *Psalms* 82 refers to a celestial tribunal in which God almighty is the supreme judge: 'God standeth in the congregation of the mighty: he judgeth among the gods'. (*Psalms* 82.1)[51] Selden provides a succinct history of the origins of law and kingship in classical myth and Biblical tradition. It is a history of lawgivers as divine artefacts, in which the judiciary are puisne or subordinate judges in the supreme court of Heaven. In delineating the mythography on which it was believed the legal institution to be founded, Selden was providing a historical and cultural background to contemporary common law orthodoxy (traceable at least to Fortescue's description of the judiciary as *sacer-*

Cambridge University Press, 2005); D Danniell, *The Bible in English* (New Haven, Conn, Yale University Press, 2003) 427–60. On the Hampton Court Conference, see F Shriver, 'Hampton Court Re-Visited: James I and the Puritans' (1982) 33 *Journal of Ecclesiastical History* 48. For a transcript of proceedings at the Hampton Court Conference, see T B Howell (ed), *A Complete Collection of State Trials*, 21 vols (London, Longman, 1816) 2: 70–92.

[47] 'Thou shalt not rayle upon the Iudges, neither speake evill of the ruler of thy people', James I, 'The Trew Law' in Somerville (ed), above n 5, at 71.

[48] See J M Hoffmann, *In The Beginning: A Short History of the Hebrew Language* (New York, New York University Press, 2006).

[49] J Selden, *The Reverse or Back-Face of the English Janus*, (tr) R Westcot (London, Thomas Basset & Richard Chiswell, 1682) 4; James I, 'The Trew Law' in Somerville (ed), above n 5, at 64.

[50] James I, 'Speech To The Lords And Commons Of The Parliament', above n 14, at 181. Shuger notes that the language of divine right 'could serve different ends', and the claim 'that authority existed by divine right could simply mean that it was legitimate', Shuger, above n 2, at 58. While the proposition that monarchic authority derived from God was not controversial, the extent to which the king's powers purported to extend under the early Stuart monarchs was contentious; hence, the various attempts by the courts of common law (and later, Parliament) to impose limits on the legitimate scope of the king's authority. For the argument that institutional authority in early modern England was commonly accepted as divinely ordained, see C Russell, 'Divine Rights in the Early Seventeenth Century' in J Morrill, P Slack and D Woolf (eds), *Public Duty and Private Conscience in Seventeenth-Century England: Essays Presented to G E Aylmer* (Oxford, Clarendon, 1993) 101; Russell, above n 24, at 65–68, 145–49; for an alternative perspective to Russell's, see J P Sommerville, *Politics and Ideology in England, 1603–1640* (London, Longman, 1986) 3–4.

[51] In *The New English Bible*, the same verse reads: 'God takes his stand in the court of heaven to deliver judgement among the gods themselves'.

The Divine Lawgiver and the Eye of the Law

dotes),[52] according to which the judiciary perform a sacral role in articulating the Word of God to His people. At the level of textual interpretation or hermeneutics, the conflict during the reign of James I between the rival jurisdictions of Crown and common law can be read as a theological dispute, both as to the specific meaning of 'Elohim' and as to which organ of the body politic the word applies.

Similar problems of interpretation beset a central passage in *The Trew Law*, in which James quotes 12 verses from *The Book of Samuel*.[53] The relevant chapter (1 *Samuel* 8) concerns the request made by the elders of the Israelites to Samuel, that they no longer be ruled by judges but instead should have 'a king to judge us like all the nations'. (1 *Samuel* 8.5)[54] In chapter three, I discuss Fortescue's interpretation of 1 *Samuel* 8, in which he claimed that God was offended with the Israelites for choosing a king to reign over them when they already had a king, 'which was God, who reigned upon them politically and royally'.[55] Mindful at the time of writing *The Trew Law* (1598) that upon his accession to the English throne he would be likely to encounter suspicion and hostility from some of his new subjects,[56] James interprets 1 *Samuel* 8 as an endorsement of kingly rule, in which Samuel 'was to prepare their hearts' for the king 'which God was to give unto them'.[57] It is probable that James was influenced in his interpretation by the singular exegesis on 1 *Samuel* 8 provided by Jean Bodin. In *Les six livres de la république*, published in 1576, Bodin describes a divinely appointed monarchic order in which sovereign princes are God's 'lieutenants for commanding other men'.[58] Bodin's interpretation of 1 *Samuel* 8 goes even further than James in its exposition of the Biblical text as an *apologia* for sacral kingship:

---

[52] Sir John Fortescue, *De Laudibus Legum Angliae*, (ed) J Selden (London, R Gosling, 1737) 4–5; see ch 1, text to n 127, above.

[53] James I, 'The Trew Law' in Somerville (ed), above n 5, at 66.

[54] After the death of Joshua, God gave the Israelites judges as their leaders, but God remained their king. Samuel was the last of these judges. As an old man, he appointed his sons as judges. The elders sought to replace rule by judges with monarchy because 'his sons walked not in his ways, but turned aside after lucre, and took bribes, and perverted judgment'. (1 *Samuel* 8.3) The appointment of a king in 1 *Samuel* was prophesied in *Deuteronomy*: 'When thou art come unto the land which the Lord thy God giveth thee, and shalt possess it, and shalt dwell therein, and shalt say, I will set a king over me, like as all the nations that are about me' (*Deuteronomy* 17.14).

[55] Sir John Fortescue, 'The Governance of England' in S Lockwood (ed), *On the Laws and Governance of England* (Cambridge, Cambridge University Press, 1997) 84; see ch 3, text to n 32, above. It will be apparent from my analysis of kingship in ch 3 that I am sceptical of the claim made by Kantorowicz that, according to Fortescue, '[t]he body politic of kingship appears as a likeness of the "holy sprites and angels"', E H Kantorowicz, *The King's Two Bodies: A Study in Medieval Political Theology* (New Jersey, Princeton University Press, 1957) 8; on Fortescue, Kantorowicz and theories of sacred kingship, see Shuger, above n 2, at 54–61.

[56] As Fincham and Lake note of James's accession, '[t]his new epoch of Protestant virtue and Christian unity was threatened by two disaffected and aggressive minorities, the papists and the Puritans', K Fincham and P Lake, 'The Ecclesiastical Policy of James I' (1985) 24 *The Journal of British Studies* 169, 170. Shuger notes that as James VI of Scotland was not head of the Kirk, the references to sacral kingship in *Basilicon Doron* were probably written with accession to the English throne in mind: Shuger, above n 2, at 59.

[57] James I, 'The Trew Law' in Somerville (ed), above n 5, at 67.

[58] J Bodin, *On Sovereignty*, (ed) and (tr) J H Franklin (Cambridge, Cambridge University Press, 1992) 46, Bk I.10.

The Congregation of the Mighty: the Juridicial State and the Measure of Justice

> Contempt for one's sovereign prince is contempt towards God, of whom he is the earthly image. That is why God, speaking to Samuel, from whom the people had demanded a different prince, said 'It is me they have wronged'.[59]

The inherent contentiousness of Bodin's interpretation is firmly located in its description of Samuel as a 'sovereign prince', rather than as a judge. Even taking into account linguistic ambiguities and translational infelicities, *The Book of Samuel* describes Samuel in an exclusively judicial role:

> And Samuel judged Israel all the days of his life. And he went from year to year in circuit to Bethel, and Gilgal, and Mispeh, and judged Israel in all those places. (1 *Samuel* 7.15–16)

If (as the above interpretations of the Scriptures tend to suggest) James sought to conflate the judicial, executive and legislative functions of the State in the person of the king, it was because he envisaged for himself not only an omnipotent role—his various pronouncements on the irrefutable supremacy and unlimited authority of the king are incapable of any other interpretation—but an omniscient one, overseeing and directing his State and his subjects in whichever matters he considered appropriate. In this respect, his political theory was related not only to a singular interpretation of Judaeo-Christian scripture, but also to Platonic ideas of governance, especially as expressed by Plato in *The Laws*. There are definite parallels between the themes of this work and those expounded in *Basilicon Doron* and *The Trew Law* on the subject of providential and divinely ordained kingship. The spiritual emphasis of *The Laws* is established in its opening dialogue, in which the Athenian Stranger asks Cleinias whether he accredits to god or man the establishment of law. The immediate reply of Cleinias is: 'A god, sir, a god—and that's the honest truth.' The Cretans, he states, believe Zeus to have founded the law, while the Spartans attribute its foundation to Apollo.[60] For the Athenian Stranger, legislation 'is the task of a god, or a man of god-like stature',[61] and the best lawgiver is 'a man who combined human nature with some of the powers of a god'.[62] Given the religious tone of *The Laws*, the reader should not be surprised that the governance of the utopian State under discussion implies a level of omniscience by its ruler, in the form of delegated powers of surveillance. While probably better described as theocentric rather than theocratic, Plato's utopia (named Magnesia) recognises the importance of religion as a necessary fortification against immorality. As morality is enshrined in the Magnesian legal code, Magnesian citizens must

---

[59] *Ibid*; on Bodin's theory of sovereignty, see J H Franklin, *Jean Bodin and the Rise of Absolutist Theory* (Cambridge, Cambridge University Press, 1973); J H Franklin, *Jean Bodin and the Sixteenth-Century Revolution in the Methodology of Law and History* (Westport, Conn, Greenwood Press, 1977).

[60] Plato, *The Laws*, (tr) T J Saunders (London, Penguin, 2004) 3, Bk I.I.624a. Shuger makes a fundamental distinction between *The Laws* of Plato and *The Politics* of Aristotle, on the basis that the former is predominantly concerned with the divine status of the earthly ruler and the law 'as the bearer of the holy', Shuger, above n 2, at 40; *The Politics*, on the other hand, is concerned with the purely secular issue of the constitutional disposition of power, and the ethical and political consequences of these arrangements, *ibid* at 41.

[61] Plato, above n 60, at 48, Bk II.III.657a.

[62] *Ibid* at 95, Bk III.IV.691e.

The Divine Lawgiver and the Eye of the Law

subscribe to religious belief. Plato writes of the necessity of appointing officials with high moral standards to oversee the activities of those in positions of authority; these agents should act as 'scrutineers' or 'god-like "straighteners"'.[63] He writes also of the importance of 'observers', appointed to travel to neighbouring States in order that they should monitor the customs and laws of societies other than their own, and upon their return to report their findings to a Magnesian legislative council.[64] It is a role similar to that which the disguised Duke claims, as Friar Lodowick, to have played:

> ... my business in this state
> Made me a looker-on here in Vienna,
> Where I have seen corruption boil and bubble ... (5.1.312–14)

Of course, at the start of James's reign as King of England, the development of State surveillance found a precedent both more recent and of more direct practical relevance than Plato's *The Laws*. It is not my intention here to discuss in any detail the various plots against Queen Elizabeth herself, the threat of Spanish invasion, the Jesuit mission to England or the descent of late-Elizabethan domestic politics into factionalism, all of which were major factors in the creation of a systemised network of surveillance, initiated and overseen by the Queen's principal secretary, Sir Francis Walsingham.[65] At the start of his reign in 1603, James I was the intended victim of two conspiracies, the Main and Bye plots[66]; but the language of suspicion and surveillance was apparent in the writings of James long before he ascended the English throne. In *Basilicon Doron* he counselled his son to 'delite to haunt your Session, and spie carefully their proceedings' and to 'let it be your owne craft, to take a sharpe account of every man in his office'.[67] An incident recorded during the coronation celebrations of 1604 gives some indication of the new king's predilection for disguise and surveillance. *The Time Triumphant* notes that James secretly visited the Royal Exchange in the City of London prior to the celebrations,

---

[63] *Ibid* at 453, Bk XII.XXV.945c.

[64] *Ibid* at 461, Bk XII.XXV.951a–952d.

[65] The principal plots against Elizabeth I were: the Ridolfi Plot (1571); the Throckmorton Plot (1583); the Parry Plot (1585); and the Babington Plot (1586). On State surveillance (at home and abroad), see C Read, *Mr Secretary Walsingham and the Policy of Queen Elizabeth*, 3 vols (New York, A M S Press, 1978); A Haynes, *The Elizabethan Secret Services* (Stroud, Sutton, 2004); M Leimon and G Parker, 'Treason and Plot in Elizabethan Diplomacy: The "Fame of Sir Edward Stafford" Reconsidered' (1996) 111 *The English Historical Review* 1134.

[66] The Bye Plotters intended to kidnap the uncrowned James I and hold him hostage, thereby forcing him to repeal anti-Catholic legislation and remove anti-Catholic government advisers and ministers. The intention of the Main Plotters was to stage a coup d'état, in which James I would be deposed and replaced on the throne by his cousin, Lady Arabella Stuart. For a general outline of these plots, see S R Gardiner, *History of England from the Accession of James I to the Outbreak of the Civil War, 1603–1642*, 10 vols (London, Longmans, Green, 1883–84) I: 108–40; for a more detailed discussion of the resultant treason trials, see M Nicholls, 'Sir Walter Ralegh's Treason: A Prosecution Document' (1995) 110 *The English Historical Review* 902; M Nicholls, 'Two Winchester Trials: The Prosecution of Henry Brooke, Lord Cobham, and Thomas Lord Grey of Wilton, 1603' (1995) 68 *Historical Research* 26. For a transcript of the trial of Sir Walter Ralegh, see Howell (ed), above n 46, 2: 1.

[67] James I, 'Basilicon Doron' in Somerville (ed), above n 5, at 45, 46.

hearing of the preparation to be great, aswell to note the other things as that was desirous privately at his owne pleasure . . . thinkeing to passe unknowne . . .

He was spotted by 'the wylie Multitude' and the doors of the Exchange had to be shut in order to keep out the crowd. James contented himself instead with spying on 'the Marchantes from a Windowe all below in the walkes not thinking of his comming'.[68] Shakespeare's Duke spends most of *Measure for Measure* disguised in order that he may remain undetected while spying on his subjects. His intention, so he tells Friar Thomas, is to observe Angelo—his deputy and chief judge:

> . . . And to behold his sway
> I will, as 'twere a brother of your order,
> Visit both prince and people. (1.3.44–46)

The idea of a magistrate disguising himself in order that he might more effectively operate as the eye of the law was not invented by Shakespeare. In 1604, the year of the first performance of *Measure for Measure*, William Willymat wrote *A Loyal Subiects Looking-Glasse*. This treatise on good magistracy was dedicated by its author to Prince Henry, the Prince of Wales. In the dedication, Willymat refers to his earlier translation 'into Latin and English verse' of *Basilicon Doron*, which he described as 'that Princes Looking-glasse, or Princes direction'.[69] So it is reasonable to suggest that Willymat had James I in mind when he wrote that good magistrates

> do use oftentimes for diverse causes to disguise their purposes with pretenses and colours of other matters, so that the end of their drifts and secret purposes are not right seene into nor understood at the first, this to be lawful the word of God doth not deny.[70]

A magistrate such as Willymat's is no scheming Machiavellian but rather a benevolent paternalist, acting in accordance with divine will. Indeed, Willymat describes Machiavelli as 'that Italian hellhound', mentioning him in the same breath as 'desperate careless Atheists' and 'obstinate dissembling corner-creeping Papists'.[71] The closest Machiavellian analogue to the plot of *Measure for Measure* occurs in chapter seven of *The Prince*, in which Cesare Borgia, having conquered the Romagna, attempts to rid the region of corruption by appointing as governor 'a cruel, efficient man', Remirro de Orco. The new governor restored order through

---

[68] G Dugdale, *The Time Triumphant* (London, R B, 1604) B.*v*; Gibbons notes that Robert Armin, of Shakespeare's company, claimed to have written *The Time Triumphant* and that he based it on Dugdale's observations, Gibbons (ed), above n 10, Introduction, 22. In Shakespeare's play, there is a possible allusion to the events recorded in *The Time Triumphant*, when the Duke declares: 'I love the people, / But do not like to stage me to their eyes: / Though it do well I do not relish well / Their loud applause and aves vehement' (1.1.67–70).

[69] W Willymat, *A Loyal Subiects Looking-Glasse, Or A good subiects Direction, necessary and requisite for every good Christian* (London, Robert Boulton, 1604) A2.*r*; Willymat claimed in his dedication to Prince Henry that the work was 'an instrument of mine inward good affection, and a faithfull witnessing messenger before both God and man, of my well-willing and well-meaning heart', A2.*v*.

[70] *Ibid* at K.*v*.
[71] *Ibid* at A3.*r*.

The Divine Lawgiver and the Eye of the Law

his rigorous enforcement of law, at a cost to Cesare of his popularity with the citizens of the Romagna. He therefore arranged to have de Orco put to death: his body was discovered

> cut in two pieces on the piazza at Cesena, with a block of wood and a bloody knife beside it. The brutality of this spectacle kept the people of the Romagna at once appeased and stupefied.[72]

The Duke in *Measure for Measure* takes no such retributive action against Angelo; indeed the injunction to Christian forgiveness rather than the imposition of *lex talionis*, and the centrality of mercy to a humane sentencing process, are crucial thematic features of the play's final act.[73] It is the only one of Shakespeare's plays to incorporate a passage from The Bible into its title, and it is surely not coincidental that the particular passage in 'The Gospel According to St Matthew' from which it is taken is notable not only for its Christian message of tolerance and forgiveness, but also for its ocular imagery, through which the message is transmitted:

> Judge not, that ye be not judged. For with what judgment ye judge, ye shall be judged: and with what measure ye mete, it shall be measured to you again. And why beholdest thou the mote that is in thy brother's eye, but considerest not the beam that is in thine own eye?[74]

The eye of judgement, which in The Old Testament exercised surveillance on behalf of a stern and vengeful God,[75] is here criticised for failing to recognise and redress its own weaknesses, follies and misdemeanours. The ocular image of an omniscient power exerting oppressive and coercive authority is replaced by one of self-reflection and self-correction. It is a curious aspect of *Measure for Measure* that the only character to show any sense either of self-reflection or genuine remorse for his conduct should be the fallen angel himself, Angelo:

---

[72] N Machiavelli, *The Prince* (tr) G Bull (London, Penguin, 2003) 25.

[73] On the relevance of ch 7 of *The Prince* to *Measure for Measure*, Bawcutt notes the narrative similarities of a duke delegating authority to a cruel but efficient deputy; but she imputes a level of conscience to Shakespeare's Duke that is lacking in Machiavelli's Cesare Borgia. She adds that there is no evidence that Shakespeare either read or admired Machiavelli: Bawcutt, above n 40, at 96; see also Hadfield, above n 1, at 196. On the representation of Machiavellian political theory in the plays of Shakespeare, see J Roe, *Shakespeare and Machiavelli* (Cambridge, D S Brewer, 2002); on Elizabethan and Jacobean debate over the 'Machiavellian' interpretation of religion as an instrument of ideological control, see J Dollimore, *Radical Tragedy: Religion, Ideology and Power in the Drama of Shakespeare and his Contemporaries* (Basingstoke, Palgrave Macmillan, 2004) 9–17.

[74] *Matthew* 7.1–3. The 'measure for measure' passage recurs in *Luke* 6.37–38; this is followed by the same parable of the 'mote' and 'beam' blinding the hypocrite to his own faults, *Luke* 6.41–42. As Pope notes, Isabella's 'sheer, reckless forgiveness' of Angelo is 'of the kind Christ advocates in the Sermon on the Mount—the great pronouncement which in Luke immediately precedes and forms part of the measure-for-measure passage', Pope, above n 42, at 79. In *Basilicon Doron* James distorts the Biblical message of forgiveness, his advice being: 'above all, let the measure of your love to every one, be according to the measure of his virtue', James I, 'Basilicon Doron' in Somerville (ed), above n 5, at 60. At the start of *Basilicon Doron* James refers directly to *Matthew* 7.1–3, adapting the meaning of the verse to reflect the onerous responsibility of kingship: 'A moate in anothers eye, is a beame into yours: a blemish in another, is a leprous byle into you', *ibid* at 12.

[75] Old Testament examples include: '[T]hey are the eyes of the LORD, which run to and fro through the whole earth' (*Zechariah* 4.10); 'But the eye of their God was upon the elders of the Jews' (*Ezra* 5.5); 'Behold, the eye of the LORD is upon them that fear him' (*Psalms* 33.18).

The Congregation of the Mighty: the Juridicial State and the Measure of Justice

> I am sorry that such sorrow I procure,
> And so deep sticks it in my penitent heart
> That I crave death more willingly than mercy. (5.1.467–69)

That Isabella should plead for Angelo's life and the Duke eventually pardon him represents the rejection of *lex talionis*,[76] the enforcement of which provided the macabre denouement in one of the sources of the Angelo/Isabella story. Giovanni Baptista Giraldi Cinthio's *Hecatommithi* (1565), George Whetstone's *Promos and Cassandra* (1578) and Thomas Lupton's *The Second Part of Too Good to be True* (1581) contain variations on the story of a tyrannical, duplicitous and hypocritical magistrate, to whom a young woman pleads for the life of her brother (in Lupton's version the condemned man is the heroine's husband) who stands convicted of a capital offence. In each of these works the judge is accountable to a higher authority: a Platonic 'overseer', acting as an omniscient eye of the law, with discretion to temper justice with mercy in passing judgment on the corrupt deputy.[77] In *Hecatommithi*, the Emperor Maximilian pardons his deputy, Juriste, and the king pardons Promos in *Promos and Cassandra*. Lupton's *The Second Part of Too Good to be True* is a sequel to his *Siuqila: Too Good to be True* (1580), a dialogue between two characters from different countries, Omen (*Nemo* = 'Nobody') and Siuqila (*Aliquis* = 'Somebody'), in which the repressive laws of the utopian Mauqsun (*Nusquam* = 'Nowhere') are compared favourably with those of Ailgna (*Anglia*). The law of Mauqsun is predicated on a retributive model, so that when in *The Second Part of Too Good to be True*, the judge tricks the gentlewoman into having sex with him and subsequently orders the execution of her husband, the gentlewoman appeals to the 'Lords of the Counsel' for 'equitie, justice, and reason'.[78] Their sentence is that 'the wicked Judge' should marry the gentlewoman,

---

[76] The use of ocular imagery is a notable feature of the law of retributive justice, as stated in The Old Testament: 'Eye for eye, tooth for tooth, hand for hand, foot for foot. Burning for burning, wound for wound, stripe for stripe' (*Exodus* 21.24–25); '[b]reach for breach, eye for eye, tooth for tooth: as he hath caused a blemish to a man, so it shall be done to him again' (*Leviticus* 24.19–20); '[a]nd thine eye shall not pity; but life shall go for life, eye for eye, tooth for tooth, hand for hand, foot for foot'. (*Deuteronomy* 19.21) In the Sermon on the Mount, Christ rejects The Old Testament law: 'Ye have heard that it hath been said, An eye for an eye, and a tooth for a tooth: But I say to you, That ye resist not evil: but whosoever shall smite thee on thy right cheek, turn to him the other also'. (*Matthew* 5.38–39)

[77] Cinthio subsequently wrote a five-act play, based on *Hecatommithi*, entitled *Epitia*, published in 1583. Whetstone's drama is a morality play, concerned primarily with 'the insufferable abuse, of a lewde magistrate: the virtuous behaviours of a chaste ladye', G Whetstone, *The right excellent and famous historye, of Promos and Cassandra* (London, Richard Ihones, 1578) A.i.r. The play is dedicated to the Recorder of London, William Fleetwood, who believed that theatres caused much of the civil disorder in London. In 'The Epistle Dedicatorie', Whetstone sought to reassure him of the theatre's beneficial public role: 'The auncient *Romans*, heald these shows of such prise, that they not onely allowed the publike exercise of them, but the grave Senators themselves countenaunced the Actors with their presence: who from these trifles wonne morallytye, as the Bee suckes honny from weeds', *ibid* at A.ii.v. On the sources for *Measure for Measure*, see Gibbons (ed), above n 10, Introduction, 6–18; Bawcutt (ed), above n 21, Introduction, 12–25.

[78] T Lupton, *The second part and knitting up of the boke entitled Too good to be true* (London, Henry Binneman, 1581) O.iii.r.

and 'that immediately after you are married, you must be executed'.[79] The conclusion to Lupton's story is dependent for its reception on the perceived rectitude of *lex talionis*, but there is at least a logical consistency in both the appeal of the gentlewoman to a superior judicial tribunal and its consequent decision. The dramatic climax to *Measure for Measure* is provided by a *deus ex machina*—the unlikely intervention of a figure of supreme authority, by means of which the disparate strands of the plot are neatly resolved. The last-minute commutation by the Duke of the death sentences, which he has just passed on Angelo and Lucio, mirrors the dramatic intervention of James I on 9 December 1603, when he pardoned Baron Cobham, Lord Grey and Sir Griffin Markham on the scaffold at Winchester, moments before they were due to be beheaded for their various traitorous involvements in the Main and Bye Plots.[80] The events of 9 December 1603 and the theatrical nature of the reprieve were noted in a private letter, according to which each of the traitors had in turn knelt down to pray on the scaffold, 'while the axe was preparing',[81] only to be told that 'the strange and undeserved grace and mercie' of the King had spared their lives. The writer concedes that 'my relation may rather seem to be a description of some ancient History, expressed in a well-acted comedy'.[82] It is noteworthy in terms of the perception of the theatrical

---

[79] *Ibid* at O.iii.v, O.iv.r. Lambarde describes debased 'publike persons' such as these, as 'either racking Law too long, that it may overreach the one side; or shrinking it too short, that the benefit thereof shall not extend to the other side; or otherwise, indirectly abusing the course of the Courts, or leaping the Pale of integritie, and Iustice', W Lambard, *Archeion, Or, A Discourse Upon the High Courts of Iustice in England* (1591) (London, Henry Seile, 1635) 82–83. The familiar metaphor of precious metal is used by Fuller to describe the good judge: 'And surely Integrity is the proper portion of a Judge. Men have a touch-stone whereby to try gold, but gold is the touch-stone whereby to trie men', T Fuller, *The Holy State* (Cambridge, John Williams, 1642) 271. Angelo demonstrates himself to be flawed as a judge, even before his corruption becomes apparent; he leaves the trial of Pompey and Froth prematurely because he finds their evidence tedious: 'This will last a night in Russia / When nights are longest there'. (2.1.118–19) The good judge, according to Fuller, 'hearkens to the witnesses, though tedious. He may give a waking testimony who hath but a dreaming utterance; and many countrey people must be impertinent, before they can be pertinent, and cannot give evidence about an hen, but first they must begin with it in the egge. All which our judge is contented to hearken to', Fuller, *ibid* at 270.

[80] The trials of the accused were held in Winchester, as there was widespread plague in London during 1603. On the punishment of the convicted traitors in the Bye Plot, see M Nicholls, 'Treason's Reward: The Punishment of Conspirators in the Bye Plot of 1603' (1995) 38 *The Historical Journal* 821; also, n 66 above. Quoting the principle formulated by the 18th-century French philosopher, Gabriel Bonnot de Mably, that '[p]unishment, if I may so put it, should strike the soul rather than the body', Foucault notes the shift in penal policy from punishment of the body to 'a punishment that acts in depth on the heart, the thoughts, the will', Foucault, above n 43, at 16. Foucault was writing here of developments in the 18th century, but his discussion of punishment acting on the heart and soul (as opposed to the body) of the offender is relevant to a general discussion of the representation in the playhouse and the courtroom of conscience, mercy and juridical procedure: 'It was the end of a certain kind of tragedy; comedy began, with shadow play, faceless voices, impalpable entities. The apparatus of punitive justice must now bite into this bodiless reality', *ibid* at 17.

[81] Howell (ed), above n 46, 2: 67. In *Measure for Measure* warrants are issued for the execution of Claudio and Barnardine. Dramatic tension is heightened by the physical proximity of the executioner's axe; it appears that Barnardine is moments from death when Abhorson asks Pompey: 'Is the axe upon the block, sirrah?' (4.3.31)

[82] Howell (ed), above n 46, 2: 68. The report of the dramatic reprieve forms an addendum to a transcript of the trial of the Bye Plotters (Sir Griffin Markham, Sir Edward Parham, George Brooke, Bartholomew Brooksby, Anthony Copley, William Watson and William Clarke) at Winchester,

style of James's kingship that he should conclude: '[T]his blessed king hath not proceeded after the manner of men and kings, Sed cælestis Judicis, æternique Regis [But of divine Judges, and eternal Kings]'.[83]

The theatrical manner in which James commuted the death sentence passed on Cobham, Grey and Markham was indicative of his idiosyncratic style of government, and in particular of his self-portrayal as the supreme judge, endowed with divine attributes. He passes unseen but all-seeing among his subjects, dispensing 'grace and mercie' in 'strange' and unaccustomed fashion, recalling Angelo's awed response to the discovery of his guilt by the Duke:

> To think I can be undiscernible
> When I perceive your grace, like power divine,
> Hath looked upon my passes. (5.1.361–63)[84]

James's intervention on the Winchester scaffold, taken together with the theory of kingship he propounded in *Basilicon Doron* and *The Trew Law*, conveys the strong impression that he imagined himself to rule over an allegorised world in which divine justice was dispensed summarily by 'Gods Viceregent and Officer on Earth'.[85] Authoritative claims for this allegorical vision of kingship may be found not only in imaginative fiction of the period (as written by Cinthio, Lupton, Whetstone, *et al*), but also in works that purported to delineate and codify the constituent parts of the English legal institution, thereby identifying the salient features of the English constitution itself. For example, in *Archeion*, Lambarde states categorically that 'the Prince of this Realme is the immediate minister of Iustice under God' and claims further that 'hee is within his owne Kingdome the Vice-roy

---

15 November 1603, *ibid* at 61–65. The report states that it is '[t]he Copie of a LETTER written from master T.M. neere Salisbury, to Master H.A. at London'; it is signed, 'From my house, neere Salisbury, the 15th Dec. 1603. Your lovin cousin and friend, T.M.', *ibid* at 65, 69. With the exception of Markham, all the Bye Plotters were executed. Markham's penitent demeanour at his trial might have influenced the decision of James to commute the death sentence: an observer noted of him that he made 'many men sory for him, and my Lord Cecill weepe aboundantly', BL Egerton MS 2877 fo 175.*v*. Cobham was imprisoned in The Tower and released in 1618; he died impoverished in 1619; for an account of his death, see Sir Walter Scott, *Secret History of the Court of James I*, 2 vols (Edinburgh, John Ballantyne, 1811) 1: 156. Grey remained in The Tower until his death in 1614. Markham was exiled in 1604 after a brief period of imprisonment in The Fleet; the last sighting of him was in Vienna, in 1644.

[83] Howell (ed), above n 46, 2: 69.

[84] On the relevance of the trials of the Main and Bye Plotters to the trial scenes in *Measure for Measure*, see C A Bernthal, 'Staging Justice: James I and the Trial Scenes in *Measure for Measure*' (1992) 32 *Studies in English Literature* 247.

[85] H de Bracton, *De Legibus et Consuetudinibus Angliae*, Bk III.IX–X, quoted in Dugdale, above n 26, at 19. Diehl argues that in *Measure for Measure*, Shakespeare was attempting 'to write not an allegory but a play about living in an allegorised world', H Diehl, '"Infinite Space": Representation and Reformation in *Measure for Measure*' (1998) 49 *Shakespeare Quarterly* 393, 398. The allegorisation of justice in the realm over which James I governed demonstrates the validity of Foucault's thesis that discourse is not expressed exclusively through the medium of speech and writing; it can and often does take the form of visual symbols, A Hunt and G Wickham, *Foucault and Law: Towards a Sociology of Law as Governance* (London, Pluto Press, 1994) 8.

The Divine Lawgiver and the Eye of the Law

of God, (the supreme Iudge of the World)'.[86] In 1584, six years after the publication of *Promos and Cassandra*, Whetstone wrote his own allegorical book of advice for rulers, entitled *A Mirour For Magestrates Of Cyties*. The book is dedicated to the Lord Mayor and magistrates of London (included in the dedication is the Recorder of London, William Fleetwood, to whom Whetstone dedicated *Promos and Cassandra*), whom he describes as chastening offenders 'with the Scourdge of Lawe' and 'the Swoorde of Iustice'.[87] He repeats the familiar adage, derived from *Psalms* 82, that 'all principal Magestrates, have on Earth, the names and places of Goddes'.[88] But despite the deference expressed in the Epistle Dedicatory to the civic magistracy of London, the remainder of the book is a thinly veiled allegory in which imperial Rome stands for London, and the Roman emperor Alexander Severus corresponds to an omniscient and omnipresent king; one who has 'visible Lightes, in obscure Corners',[89] employing his absolute power to restore order and concord to a city whose prosperity is threatened by the immoral conduct of its inhabitants.[90]

Its thematic resemblance to (and possible influence over) *Measure for Measure* apart, Whetstone's *Mirour For Magestrates* was to become an apt metaphor for the personal style of government favoured by James I, and in particular for the subservient status of the judiciary within the constitutional settlement. Whetstone describes a hierarchical order of estates in which 'the Prince doth (iustly) commaunde: the Maiestrates (advisedly) direct: and inferior Subiectes (faithfully) obey'.[91] Implicit in such a hierarchy of governance is the deference of the judiciary to the authority of an imperial prince: judges exist in order to enforce the commands of the absolute ruler. Apologists for an imperial model of government did not envisage that the judiciary would be an independent organ within the body politic. In the notorious words of Sir Francis Bacon: '[L]et them be lions, but yet

---

[86] Lambard, above n 79, at 68, 97; Lambarde's description of the king as God's minister of justice illustrates the accuracy of Collinson's observation that during this period in English history, subjects believed themselves to be living within the pages of the Bible, P Collinson, *The Birthpangs of Protestant England: Religious and Cultural Change in the Sixteenth and Seventeenth Centuries* (Basingstoke, Macmillan, 1988) 7–10.
[87] G Whetstone, *A Mirour For Magestrates Of Cyties* (London, Richard Iones, 1584) A.iii.*r*.
[88] *Ibid* at A.iii.*v*.
[89] *Ibid*. Given the related subject-matter of Whetstone's *Mirour For Magestrates* and Shakespeare's *Measure for Measure*, the similarity between this line and Lucio's 'the old fantastical Duke of dark corners' (4.3.147–48) is striking. Compare also the Duke's: 'How may likeness made in crimes, / Making practice on the times, / To draw with idle spiders' strings / Most ponderous and substantial things?' (3.2.235–38) with Whetstone's: 'the severest laws, were (without execution) . . . Lyke unto Cobwebs, through which, the Hornets breake when the small Flies are intangled', Whetstone, above n 87, at F.ii.*r*.
[90] 'Dice, Drunkennesse and Harlots, had consumed the wealth of a great number of ancient Gentlemen, whose Purses were in the possession of vile persons, and their Landes at morgage with the Marchants', *ibid* at B4.*v*. Dollimore argues that Whetstone attributed to the gentry responsibility for the survival of England; therefore, it was necessary to save their wealth from the predatory 'low-life' who inhabited the brothels, taverns and gaming houses which the gentry frequented: Dollimore, 'Transgression and surveillance in *Measure for Measure*', above n 9, at 79.
[91] Whetstone, above n 87, at C3.*r*.

lions under the throne'.⁹² The boundaries of judicial commission were delineated by Bacon in the opening sentence of 'Of Judicature': 'Judges ought to remember that their office is *jus dicere*, and not *jus dare*; to interpret law, and not to make law'.⁹³ James quoted from the above passage in his speech to the judiciary in June 1616:

> And remember you are no makers of Law, but Interpretours of Law, according to the trew sence thereof; for your Office is *Ius dicere*, and not *Ius dare*.⁹⁴

Neither Bacon nor James I defined the meaning of 'interpreters' in this context, nor did either of them attempt to circumscribe the discretion available to judges when formulating their judgments. For Coke especially, the judicial function was to articulate law through the application of artificial reason. This was a role for which the King (for all his other gifts) was unqualified:

> God had endowed his Majesty with excellent science, and great endowments of nature; but his Majesty was not learned in the laws of his realm of England . . .⁹⁵

Coke took issue with the claim made on behalf of James I that he was entitled to determine cases in person, arguing that 'the King in his own person cannot adjudge any case'.⁹⁶ He conceded that the King was entitled to sit in the Court of Star Chamber, but then only 'to consult with the Justices, upon certain questions proposed to them, and not *in judicio*'.⁹⁷ That an imperial style of rule was favoured by James I may be inferred from his demand of the common law judiciary that they do not encroach upon the Royal Prerogative and that they consult with the King or the Privy Council over any issues arising in the courts relating to its exercise, thereby implying that prerogative powers were not subject to due process of

---

⁹² F Bacon, 'Of Judicature' in *The Major Works*, (ed) B Vickers (Oxford, Oxford University Press, 2002) 449. According to the Biblical source from which the image derives, the lions stood at the side of King Solomon's throne, rather than under it: 'And twelve lions stood there on the one side and on the other upon the six steps' (1 *Kings* 10.20).

⁹³ Bacon, above n 92, at 446. There is a peculiar resonance with *Measure for Measure* in the following passage from 'Of Judicature': 'Specially in case of laws penal, they ought to have care that that which was meant for terror be not turned into rigour; and that they bring not upon the people that shower whereof the Scripture speaketh, "Pluet super eos laqueos" ["He shall rain snares upon them", *Psalms* 11.6]; for penal laws pressed are "a shower of snares" upon the people. Therefore let penal laws, if they have been sleepers of long, or if they have grown unfit for the present time, be by wise judges confined in the execution', *ibid* at 447.

⁹⁴ James I, 'Speach In The Starre-Chamber' in Somerville (ed), above n 5, at 211. 'Of Judicature' was written in 1612; James did not attribute the quotation to Bacon.

⁹⁵ Coke, *Prohibitions del Roy*, 12 *Reports* (1655) 7: 64a, at 65a; on the 'artificial reason' of law, see ch 5, text to nn 52–59, above.

⁹⁶ *Ibid* at 64a.

⁹⁷ *Ibid* at 64b. Spedding notes that 'the proceedings of the Court [of Star Chamber] were public, formal, elaborate, and governed by precedent', J Spedding (ed), *The Letters and the Life of Francis Bacon*, 7 vols (London, Longmans, 1874) 7: 91. Despite its regard for the formalities of procedure, Star Chamber was a court in which the absolute power of the prerogative manifested itself and, as even Spedding concedes, 'a King [Charles I] who was *not* otherwise strong enough to defy his people attempted to do it by means of the Star Chamber, and so provoked them to take it away from him', *ibid* at 94.

law.[98] James's suspicion of common lawyers and the unwritten constitution which they purported to protect was expressed in his unfavourable comparison of English juridical procedure with the Danish model:

> [A]ll their State is governed onely by a written Law; there is no Advocate or Proctour admitted to plead, onely the parties themselves plead their own cause, and then a man stands up and reads the Law, and there is an end, for the very Law-booke itself is their onely Iudge. Happy were all kingdoms if they could be so: But here, curious wits, various conceits, different actions, and varietie of examples breed questions in Law.[99]

In the same speech James protested that he had never intended the common law to be replaced by the civil law (a point he stressed in his speech to Parliament in 1610, regarding the furore over the publication of Cowell's *The Interpreter*), but he continued to enunciate the paradox that while he respected the constitutional sanctity of the common law, its judges were not permitted even to question the exercise of the Royal Prerogative, on the grounds that '[t]hat which concernes the mysterie of the Kings power, is not lawfull to be disputed'.[100] His prohibition on discussion of the prerogative, his belief in the necessity to simplify legal procedure, and his antipathy towards judicial interpretation of law find a precedent in Justinian's prohibition on juristic commentary and judicial interpretation. *The Digest* is explicit in requiring judges to refer obscurities in the law to 'the very summit of the empire'; and further, that jurists were prohibited

> from producing any other interpretations, or rather perversions, of our laws: lest their verbosity should bring dishonour to our laws by its confusion . . .[101]

None of the above is intended to suggest that *Measure for Measure* is 'about' the use and misuse of the Royal Prerogative in late-Elizabethan and early-Jacobean England. But the issue of a king who continually refers to the mysterious power of kingship and to his role within the realm as supreme judge is relevant to Shakespeare's depiction of absolute authority in the character of the Duke. The definitive meaning of the substitute is a problematic theme of *Measure for Measure*, in which the sign is often mistaken for that which it signifies.[102] If, as Calvin claimed, the world itself is a form of substitution or theatrical representation, then what is the legitimate status of the actors within that world? According to Calvin, the works of God are 'paynted tables' and 'in the myrrour of his woorkes shewe by representation bothe hymselfe and his immortall kyngedome'.[103] In the closest

---

[98] James I, 'Speach In The Starre-Chamber' in Somerville (ed), above n 5, at 212.
[99] *Ibid.*
[100] *Ibid* at 213.
[101] Quoted in I Maclean, *Interpretation and Meaning in the Renaissance: The Case of Law* (Cambridge, Cambridge University Press, 1992) 51, 52.
[102] Diehl argues that in *Measure for Measure* Shakespeare explores the representational power of theatre, formulating 'an aesthetic of the stage that marks and preserves the gap between the sign and the thing signified', Diehl, above n 85, at 397.
[103] J Calvin, *The institution of Christian religion*, (tr) T Norton (London, Reinolde Wolfe & Richarde Harison, 1561) B.i.v.

analogue to the claim of James I that kings are set upon the stage for people to behold, Calvin asks: 'For what else is the world but an open stage wheron God will have his maiestie seene'?[104] The disputed substance of representation was the theological crux of the religious reformation in early modern Europe. A parallel dispute was emerging in England between those who believed the king to be the law itself—*lex loquens*—and those, like Coke, for whom representation was symbolic rather than transformative. The latter constituency sought to restrict the mysterious power of kingship by rendering it accountable to law: the king was not *lex loquens*, although his crown was 'an hieroglyphic of the laws'.[105]

III. Religion, Conscience and Conflicts of Jurisdiction

'From too much liberty, my Lucio, liberty' (1.2.107): Claudio has been sentenced to death 'for getting madam Julietta with child'. (1.2.59–60) In English law of the period in which *Measure for Measure* was written, if Claudio was guilty of fornication the offence would have been within the jurisdiction of the ecclesiastical courts rather than the courts of common law. Despite the spiritual nature of the offence, the juridical consequences of fornication were of a highly visible temporal nature, involving ritualised public humiliation, the performance of penance in a public place, and excommunication from the parish community.[106] In addition, secular authorities were complicit in the prosecution of offences under ecclesiastical law: for example, regarding the duties of constables, Lambarde notes

> that if information be given to any such officer, that a man and a woman bee in adulterie, or fornication together, then the officer may take companie with him, and that if he finde them so, hee may carry them to prison.[107]

It is evident from the text of *Measure for Measure* that according to English law Claudio would not have been guilty of fornication, as he contracted marriage with Juliet before sexual intercourse had taken place:

---

[104] J Calvin, *The sermons of M Iohn Calvin, upon the Epistle of S. Paule too the Ephesians*, (tr) A Golding (London, Lucas Harison and George Byshop, 1577) 87.r.

[105] Coke, *Calvin's Case*, 7 *Reports* (1608) 4: 1a, at 11b; see ch 2, text to n 54, above.

[106] Punishment usually involved performing penance in a white sheet before the congregation during the Sunday church service. The following is an example, from the records of the church court of Stratford-upon-Avon, for May 1606: 'Anne Browne alias Watton: upon suspicion of incontinence with John Sadler: she appeared: admitted that she was pregnant by John Sadler: ordered public penance in a white sheet in the parish church on two Sundays, and in the market place and to certify on the next court day after childbirth' in E R C Brinkworth, *Shakespeare and the Bawdy Court of Stratford* (Chichester, Phillimore, 1972) 131.

[107] W Lambard, *The Dueties of Constables, Borsholders, Tythingmen, and such other lowe and Lay Ministers of the Peace* (London, Thomas Wight, 1602) 18.

Religion, Conscience and Conflicts of Jurisdiction

> Upon a true contract
> I got possession of Julietta's bed—
> You know the lady, she is fast my wife,
> Save that we do the denunciation lack
> Of outward order. (1.2.126–30)[108]

The marriage contract that Claudio has made with Juliet is either *sponsalia per verba de praesenti* or *sponsalia per verba de futuro*, depending on the tense used in the words of the agreement. Here, the phrase 'she is fast my wife' strongly suggests that the contract is *de praesenti*; the 'outward order' to which Claudio refers is the public solemnisation in church of the marriage contract.[109] Marriage could be contracted by consent alone, without church ceremony, so long as consent was notified in the present tense: *sponsalia per verba de praesenti*. Despite the validity and binding authority of *de praesenti* agreements, parties who contracted marriage with each other privately were subject to the ecclesiastical charge of 'clandestine marriage' and liable to be excommunicated by the church courts, even though the marriage was recognised by common law.[110] The sentence of excommunication in ecclesiastical law was a powerful means of exerting institutional control over local communities, in cases of clandestine marriage as well as those involving sexual relations outside of marriage. Lesser excommunication deprived 'the offender of the use of the sacraments and divine worship', while greater excommunication

> is that whereby men are deprived, not only of the sacraments, and the benefit of divine offices, but of the society and conversation of the faithful. If a person be excommunicated, generally; as if the judge say, *I excommunicate such a person*; this shall be understood of the greater excommunication.[111]

A mutual promise to marry in the future created an executory contract: *sponsalia per verba de futuro*. This was a binding agreement to marry (at common law an action of *assumpsit* lay for breach of promise),[112] although prior to consummation or formal celebration, the engagement could be dissolved by mutual consent. Subsequent sexual intercourse between the betrothed couple would make the

---

[108] On the 'handfast' as a symbol of a legally binding agreement, see L Stone, *The Family, Sex and Marriage in England 1500–1800* (London, Penguin, 1979) 30.

[109] Regarding the often imprecise distinction between *de praesenti* and *de futuro* contracts, Pollock and Maitland noted that 'of all people in the world, lovers are the least likely to distinguish precisely between the present and the future tenses', F Pollock and F W Maitland, *The History of English Law*, 2 vols (Cambridge, Cambridge University Press, 1898) 2: 368–69.

[110] The following is a record of proceedings from the church court of Banbury: '*Against* Richard Welford: incontinence with his wife before marriage . . . being interrogated replied "that he was married in the church or Chapel of Claydon by Mr Saunderson, the curate there, about the 9th day of August last was twelvemonth, for the which he had no other licence than now doth appear by the note he now exhibiteth, and he did not enter into any bond for the obtaining of any licence": for clandestine marriage, excommunicated', ACTS in the Parish Church of Banbury, 3rd January, 1625/6 1.v, quoted in E R C Brinkworth, *The 'Bawdy Court' of Banbury: The Act Book of the Peculiar Court of Banbury, 1625–1638*, (ed) R K Gilkes (Banbury, The Banbury Historical Society, 1997) 62.

[111] R Burns, *Ecclesiastical Law*, 4 vols (London, A Millar, 1767) 2: 201.

[112] See J H Baker, *An Introduction to English Legal History* (London, Butterworths, 2002) 480.

legal bond indissoluble.[113] If the agreement was *de praesenti* then under common law the couple were regarded as legally bound in marriage; if it was *de futuro* then, having consummated their espousal, they would also be regarded as legally bound to each other. The subsequent public affirmation of the marriage in the form of a religious ceremony was conventional but did not affect the legal status of the marriage contract. Henry Swinburne, an eminent ecclesiastical lawyer, states that 'the Law doth forbid all Persons to make *Secret* Contracts of Spousals, or Matrimony',[114] but he fails to specify that he is referring to offences under ecclesiastical law. At common law, provided the existence of a *de futuro* contract could be proved, no distinction was made between private and publicly-witnessed agreements, and breach of the espousal was actionable through the common law writ of *assumpsit*.

The legal distinction between *de praesenti* and *de futuro* contracts is not, of course a central theme of *Measure for Measure*, but the several references to the marriage contracts between Claudio and Juliet, and Angelo and Mariana, draw attention to the contemporaneous existence of two rival jurisdictions, the temporal and the spiritual.[115] As far as Angelo is concerned, it appears that he had entered into an agreement with Mariana to marry her in the future (*de futuro*), but revoked the agreement when her dowry failed: 'Partly for that her promisèd proportions / Came short of composition' (5.1.217–18).[116] Mariana swears that 'I am affianced

---

[113] For a late-Elizabethan account of marriage contracts, see R Greenham, 'A Treatise Of A Contract before Mariage' in *The Works of the Reverend and Faithfull servant of Iesus Christ M Richard Greenham, minister and preacher of the word of God* (London, Robert Dexter, 1599) 288. See R B Outhwaite, *The Rise and Fall of the English Ecclesiastical Courts, 1500–1860* (Cambridge, Cambridge University Press, 2006) 1–22, 47–56; more generally, on marriage in the 16th and early 17th centuries, see Stone, above n 108, at 21–146; also, R B Outhwaite, *Clandestine Marriage in England, 1500–1850* (London, Hambledon, 1995). On the jurisdiction of the ecclesiastical courts in disputes over the validity of marriages, see ch 4, n 85, above. An example of the *de praesenti* formula is: 'I here take you as my wife, for better or worse, to have and to hold until the end of my life, and of this I give you my faith'. Nuttall cites an example of the *de futuro* formula, from 1522: 'I promytt to yow Begis Abirnethy that I sall marry yow and that I sall never haiff ane uther wiff and thereto I giff yow my fayth', *Liber Officialis Sancti Andree*, quoted in A D Nuttall, '"Measure for Measure": The Bed-Trick' (1975) 28 *Shakespeare Survey* 51, 53.

[114] H Swinburne, *A Treatise of spousals, or matrimonial contracts* (London, Robert Clavell, 1686) 194; the 1686 edition of *A Treatise of spousals* is based on a draft found in Lincoln's Inn after Swinburne's death in 1624.

[115] Nuttall argues that the play makes no explicit contrast between *de praesenti* and *de futuro* contracts, and that any distinction could be made only by the audience, Nuttall, above n 113, at 52. He cites the use of the phrase *per verba de praesenti* in John Webster's *The Duchess of Malfi*: 'I have heard lawyers say, a contract in a chamber, / Per verba de presenti, is absolute marriage' (1.2.394–95), *John Webster: Three Plays*, (ed) D Gunby (Harmondsworth, Penguin, 1972) 193.

[116] Failure to deliver the agreed dowry entitled the fiancé to revoke an espousal *per verba de futuro*: 'when as the Party doth promise to give so much in Marriage, as afterwards he is not able to perform; In which Case the other Party is not bound to perform the Contract', Swinburne, above n 114, at 237; on *de praesenti* and *de futuro* espousals, see *ibid* at 11–17. Angelo falsely claims that the main reason he revoked his engagement to Mariana was 'that her reputation was disvalued / In levity' (5.1.219–20); if the implication of infidelity had been true, then these would have been acceptable grounds for revoking the *de futuro* contract, Swinburne, above n 114, at 237. As the Duke informs Isabella, Angelo was 'pretending in her discoveries of dishonour' (3.1.215–16) in order to avoid marriage to Mariana, an unnecessary ploy when the failure of her dowry alone gave him lawful grounds for renouncing the engagement. On the status of the marriage contracts in the play, see E Schanzer, 'The Marriage-Contracts in *Measure for Measure*' (1960) 13 *Shakespeare Survey* 81; also K P Wentersdorf, 'The Marriage Contracts in "Measure for Measure": A Reconsideration' (1980) 32 *Shakespeare Survey* 129.

this man's wife, as strongly / As words could make up vows'. (5.1.225–26)[117] By means of the bed-trick, in which Mariana is substituted for Isabella, Angelo had sexual intercourse with his ex-fiancée, believing her to be Isabella.[118] It is for this 'offence', together with the breach of his promise to spare Claudio's life, that the Duke sentences Angelo to death: 'Being criminal in double violation / Of sacred chastity and of promise-breach' (5.1.397–98). The problem here for the criminal lawyer is that although Angelo may have the requisite *mens rea* for the actions of which he is accused, the *actus reus* is missing: he did not violate Isabella, and Claudio was not executed. As Isabella reminds the Duke when she pleads for Angelo's life: 'Thoughts are no subjects, / Intents are merely thoughts'. (5.1.446–47) By depicting a society in which 'thoughts' are criminalised, and in which moral issues that have traditionally been the exclusive concern of spiritual courts are now in the jurisdiction of the temporal courts, Shakespeare was dramatising a topical debate in late-Elizabethan England. In so doing he also raised important questions over the relative status of competing and conflicting jurisdictions within the same legal system. In this section I address first the contentious issue of the theocratic State and the demands of puritan writers that Biblical injunctions on morality and conscience should be incorporated directly into English law.[119] Following this, I examine a jurisdictional dispute that was peculiar to the reign of James I. It was a dispute in which, although religion was not at issue, the question of conscience and its relevance to juridical procedure was uppermost. The conflict was between the court of the king's conscience—the Chancery—and the courts of common law.

As I have indicated in relation to the regulation of marriage, at a local level the church courts exerted a high level of surveillance and coercive authority over citizens. In 'office causes', where a prosecution was brought following a complaint about an individual's behaviour, the *ex officio mero* procedure resembled that of the court of High Commission, as discussed in chapter one.[120] The defendant was placed under oath and required to give truthful answers to any accusations made.

---

[117] Prior to the execution of the bed-trick, the Duke reminds Mariana that '[h]e is your husband on a pre-contract' (4.1.69); before this, the Duke informs Isabella that Mariana 'should this Angelo have married—was affianced to her oath, and the nuptial appointed' (3.1.204–205).

[118] Regarding the fact that Angelo thinks that he has had sexual intercourse with Isabella rather than Mariana, Schanzer notes that '*error personae*, i.e. marriage contracted with a person mistaken for someone else, was one of the recognised grounds for annulment', Schanzer, above n 116, at 89, n 21.

[119] It is ironical in this context, given the puritanically 'precise' predisposition of Angelo—'[a] man of stricture and firm abstinence' (1.3.13)—that the word 'puritan' in late-Elizabethan England was notoriously imprecise. I use it here in the sense in which Collinson describes it: '*Puritan* was a term of stigmatisation, which in Shakespeare's England was bandied about freely and loosely as a weapon against a certain kind of excessive religiosity and scrupulous morality', P Collinson, 'William Shakespeare's Religious Inheritance and Environment' in P Collinson, *Elizabethans* (London, Hambledon and London, 2003) 236; see also P Lake, *Anglicans and Puritans? Presbyterianism and English Conformist Thought from Whitgift to Hooker* (London, Unwin Hyman, 1988); P Lake, 'Puritan Identities' (1984) 35 *The Journal of Ecclesiastical History* 112.

[120] See ch 1, text to nn 37–46, above. Office causes are to be distinguished from instance causes, involving private disputes between litigants, in which an ecclesiastical judge adjudicated; see Outhwaite, above n 113, at 9–10.

Punishment for such offences involved not only the ritualised public humiliation of 'penance',[121] but also exclusion from the quotidian rites of social community and the imposition of harsh economic sanctions.[122] For some commentators in late-Elizabethan England the punishments imposed by the church courts were inadequate and failed to reflect a stringent and desirable moral code, which they insisted was to be found in the pages of The Bible. In *Measure for Measure*, the sentence of death passed on Angelo for his 'intents' reflects the arguments of writers such as Philip Stubbes, who asserted that 'who so lusteth after a woman in his hart, hath committed the fact alredy, and therefore is guiltie of death for the same'.[123] Stubbes's emphasis on the draconian aspect of the Sermon on the Mount ignores completely Christ's conciliatory injunction a few lines later, to '[j]udge not, that ye be not judged'. In particular he ignores the adjoining warning, whence Shakespeare derived the title of *Measure for Measure*: 'with what measure ye mete, it shall be measured to you again'. (*Matthew* 7.1–2) The invocation of the death sentence for lustful thoughts is Stubbes's own addendum to the Sermon on the Mount. Christ refers to exclusion from the kingdom of heaven for those whose righteousness does not exceed that of the Pharisees (*Matthew* 5.20). He warns also that 'whosoever shall kill shall be in danger of the judgment' (*Matthew* 5.21) and that anyone who calls his brother a fool 'shall be in danger of hell fire'. (*Matthew* 5.22) But nowhere in his oration does he empower or sanction the taking of human life by another human. Stubbes castigates the church courts for their leniency with offenders:

> For what great thing is it, to go ii. or three dayes in a white sheete before the congregation, and that somtymes not past an howre or two in a day, having their usuall garments underneth...[124]

He was vehement in the belief that all whores, adulterers and fornicators:

> [S]hould drinke a full draught of Moyses cuppe, that is, tast of present death or els, if yt be thought too severe (for in evill, men will be more mercifull, than the Author of mercie him selfe, but in goodnesse, fare well mercy,) than wold GOD they might be cauterized, and seared with a hote yron on the cheeke, forehead, or some other parte of their bodye that might be seene, to the end the honest and chast Christians might be discerned from the adulterous Children of Sathan.[125]

---

[121] See above n 106.
[122] Hill notes that excommunicated persons were not permitted to buy and sell goods, they could not be employed, nor could they bring legal actions to recover debts: C Hill, *Society and Puritanism in Pre-Revolutionary England* (London, Mercury Books, 1966) 355–56; see also M Ingram, *Church Courts, Sex and Marriage in England, 1570–1640* (Cambridge, Cambridge University Press, 1987) 52–54.
[123] P Stubbes, 'The horrible vice of Whoredome in Ailgna' in *The Anatomie of Abuses* (London, Richard Iones, 1583) H2.r; Stubbes adapted the following passage from the Sermon on the Mount: 'But I say unto you, That whosoever looketh on a woman to lust after her hath committed adultery with her already in his heart'. (*Matthew* 5.28)
[124] Stubbes, *Anatomie of Abuses*, above n 123, at H5.v.
[125] Ibid at H6.r.

In his elegant, witty and humane response to *The Anatomie of Abuses*, entitled *The Anatomie of Absurditie*, Thomas Nashe suggests that the graphic and repetitive descriptions of sexual incontinence in Stubbes's work are indicative of the puritan writer's own salacious obsessions: '... the mucke of their mellancholicke imaginations, pretending forsooth to anatomise abuses, and stubbe up sin by the rootes'.[126] Nashe is astute in recognising the insidious power of the printed word, by which means the 'ignorant zeale' of religious extremism could infiltrate 'every corner of the Common Wealth', exerting a level of political influence and control over the populace, under 'a glose of godliness'.[127] In *Measure for Measure*, the sentencing to death of Claudio—'[c]ondemned upon the act of fornication / To lose his head' (5.1.70–71)—is an example of dramatic imagination. As I have noted, in English law punishment for such offences (which did not extend to the death penalty) was within the jurisdiction of the church courts, and it is likely anyway that Claudio was already legally married to Juliet at the time sexual intercourse between them took place.[128] To this extent, the juridical procedure depicted in the play is an example of '*story-book* law'[129]; but it is not far removed from (rather it is identical to) the theocratic vision of Stubbes, for whom retribution for sinful intent is a central tenet of the godly (and therefore ideal) State. Before his sudden change of judicial mind, the Duke pays homage to such theocratic (and talionic) ideologies by sentencing Angelo to death for committing crimes which have no apparent victim, unless Angelo's immortal soul can be accounted one: 'Haste still pays haste, and leisure answers leisure; / Like doth quit like, and measure still for measure'. (5.1.403–404) The stern retributive justice of Stubbes demands Angelo's death, and in a precise inversion of equitable principles the Duke declares that '[t]he very mercy of the law cries out / Most audible' (5.1.400–401).

The dubious conflation of law, politics and religion was an issue addressed in idiosyncratic but effective fashion by Robert Burton in *The Anatomy of Melancholy*. While Nashe attacked the puritan theocrats primarily for their rank moral hypocrisy—'the cloake of zeale' acting as 'a covert for all naughtiness'[130]—Burton identified in politicians a pragmatic Machiavellian intent, ineffectually concealed by the mask of religious fervour: 'They make religion pollicy; *nihil æque valet ad regendos vulgi animos ac superstitio*'.[131] Appeal to irrational fear and superstition is the reason given by Burton for the appropriation of religion by politicians. In the

---

[126] T Nashe, *The Anatomie of Absurditie* (London, Thomas Hacker, 1589) B.ii.r.
[127] *Ibid* at B.iii.r.
[128] In *Basilicon Doron*, James I described fornication as a 'breach of Gods law' and 'amongst other grievous sinnes, that debarre the committers amongst *dogs and swine, from entry in that spirituall and heavenly Ierusalem*', James I, 'Basilicon Doron' in Somerville (ed), above n 5, at 39.
[129] Nuttall, above n 113, at 53.
[130] Nashe, above n 126, at B.iii.r.
[131] R Burton, *The anatomy of melancholy what it is*, 2nd edn (Oxford, Henry Cripps, 1621) 723; in the 1651 edition of *The anatomy*, the phrase immediately preceding the above Latin quotation reads: 'They make religion meer policie, a cloak, a humane invention', implying a greater level of political deception than did the 1621 edition: *ibid*, 6th edn (1651) 645. Dollimore discusses this passage from *The anatomy of melancholy* and translates the Latin as follows: '[N]othing is so effective for keeping the masses under control as superstition', Dollimore, above n 73, at 13.

manipulative hands of the accomplished statesman, described by Burton as 'Captaine Machiavel', religion is nothing more than an instrument of oppression:

> No way better to curb then superstition, to terrifie mens consciences, and to keepe them in awe: they make new lawes, statuts, invent new Religions, ceremonies to their owne endes.[132]

Burton refined the text of *The Anatomy of Melancholy* during the course of six editions. In the 1621 edition, he wrote that '[j]ustice, Religion, Peace, are the three chiefe proppes of a well govern'd Commonwealth'.[133] The alteration that he made to the same passage in the 1651 edition is minimal, but it serves to illuminate the meaning of a line in *Measure for Measure*. The amended line reads: 'Justice and religion are the two chief props and supporters of a well governed commonwealth'.[134] 'Peace' has been excised from the list of props, lending a pleasing symmetry to the remaining 'justice' and 'religion'. Burton almost certainly did not intend the pun on 'props', but in the present analysis the obvious theatrical connotation of the word is unavoidable. The histrionic association is useful also in understanding the symbolic or metaphorical role played by justice and religion in the governance of the commonwealth. In *Measure for Measure*, justice of a type finds it personification in the inappropriate figure of Angelo, of whom Escalus tells the disguised Duke: 'my brother justice have I found so severe that he hath forced me to tell him he is indeed Justice'. (3.2.215–17) Burton's amended description of justice and religion as 'the two chief props and supporters of a well governed commonwealth' echoes the lines of the Duke, in which he refers to the 'outward courtesies' (5.1.15) or external symbols of the commonwealth. These include the two figures of justice—Angelo and Escalus—who constitute the Duke's 'good supporters' (5.1.18). The allusion to heraldic devices, inherent in the word 'supporters', reinforces the sense of justice itself being used as a device, masking the political purpose of the magistrate, 'counterfeits only for polliticall ends'.[135]

---

[132] Burton, above n 131, 2nd edn (1621) 723.

[133] *Ibid.*

[134] *Ibid*, 6th edn (1651) 645. Burton died in 1640, but the 1651 edition is based on a version on which he was working when he died. See A S Chapple, 'Robert Burton's Geography of Melancholy' (1993) 33 *Studies in English Literature* 99; R G Barlow, 'Infinite Worlds: Robert Burton's Cosmic Voyage' (1973) 34 *Journal of the History of Ideas* 291; D Renaker, 'Robert Burton and Ramist Method' (1971) 24 *Renaissance Quarterly* 210.

[135] Burton, above n 131, 6th edn (1651) 645. The tendency of some scholars to describe Escalus as a personification of equity is misleading and simplistic, as for example: 'Escalus' appeal here and in his conduct elsewhere in the play clearly illustrate, then, the principles of equity', J W Dickinson, 'Renaissance Equity and *Measure for Measure*' (1962) 13 *Shakespeare Quarterly* 287, 297; also: 'Escalus by position and experience appears to be representative of the concept that on occasion conditions require relief from the letter of the law', W Dunkel, 'Law and Equity in *Measure for Measure*' (1962) 13 *Shakespeare Quarterly* 275, 281. It is difficult to reconcile statements such as these with the misjudgement and misconduct of Escalus, examples of which include: his instruction to torture the supposed Friar Lodowick (5.1.307–308); the misplaced trust he places in Lucio as a reliable witness (5.1.258–59); the lie he tells Isabella that 'here's a gentlewoman denies all that you have said' (5.1.277–78); and the lie he tells the supposed Friar Lodowick that Mariana and Isabella have confessed to slandering Angelo (5.1.284–85). As Shuger notes, 'Escalus has been drawn into the vertiginous spiral of lies, betrayal, and calumny, and ends up howling for innocent blood', Shuger, above n 2, at 69.

Religion, Conscience and Conflicts of Jurisdiction

In Stubbes's puritanical diatribe against irreligious abuses of all sorts, he equates the idolatrous worship of false gods and the satanic power of the mask with the beguiling artifice of theatre. He warns actors of the eternal damnation that awaits them for their misuse of the image, describing them as 'masking Players', 'painted sepulchres' and 'doble dealing ambodexters'.[136] It is an irony that would have appalled Stubbes that in *Measure for Measure* the imagery of theatre is utilised to explore the form and substance of idolatry. Shakespeare employs the conceit of the 'masking player' with which to identify the deception perpetrated on his subjects by an absolute ruler. In a play concerned at so many levels with appearance, concealment and deception, it is those characters in positions of the greatest political power—the Duke and Angelo—who enact the most elaborate deceits, affecting the lives of their vulnerable and powerless subjects in the most profound and disturbing manner. Angelo, the 'painted sepulchre' of Shakespeare's Vienna, is tormented by his own duplicity, but maintains the mask of probity while acknowledging its idolatrous purpose and damnable effect:

> Oh place, oh form,
> How often dost thou with thy case, thy habit,
> Wrench awe from fools and tie the wiser souls
> To thy false seeming. Blood, thou art blood:
> Let's write 'Good Angel' on the devil's horn,
> 'Tis not the devil's crest. (2.4.12–17)

Late-Elizabethan orthodoxy, regarding the indivisibility of law and religion, was expressed categorically by William Fulbecke, who in his advice to students of the common law stated that 'where God is not, there is no truth, there is no light, there is no lawe'.[137] The conflation by Fulbecke of God, light and law recalls the beginning of St John's Gospel: 'In him was life: and the life was the light of men'. (*John* 1.4) The Gospel According to St John starts with an assertion of the primacy of the word: 'In the beginning was the Word, and the Word was with God, and the Word was God'. (*John* 1.1) Stubbes invokes this Biblical passage in his attack on theatre, arguing that 'who soever abuseth this word of our God on stages in playes and enterluds, abuseth the Maiesty of God'.[138] In an inversion of conventional puritan dogma on the abuse of words by inherently duplicitous playwrights, Shakespeare

---

[136] Stubbes, 'Of Stage-playes and Enterluds, with their wickednes' in *Anatomie of Abuses*, above n 123, at L.v.*v*. Shakespeare's home town of Stratford-upon-Avon was the subject of an attack by Lewis Bayly (Chaplain to James I before his appointment to the Bishopric of Bangor in 1616), who attributed two serious fires in the town to the irreligious conduct of its inhabitants: 'Stratford upon Avon was twice on the same day twelve-moneth (being the Lords Day) almost consumed with fire: chiefly for prophaning the Lords Sabbath, and for contemning his word in the mouth of his faithfull Ministers', L Bayly, *The Practice of Piety: Directing a Christian How to Walk that he may Please God* (*c* 1612) (London, Philip Chetwinde, 1654) 265. Collinson suggests that Stratford was slow to adopt Protestantism, and that [i]t is probable that most members of this community were church papists', Collinson, 'William Shakespeare's Religious Inheritance', above n 119, at 246.

[137] W Fulbecke, *A Direction or Preparative to the study of the Lawe* (London, T Wight, 1600) C2.*r*.

[138] Stubbes, *Anatomie of Abuses*, above n 123, at L.v.*v*.

employs the self-referential theatrical device of the soliloquy to locate the systematic abuse of words in the puritanical figure of Angelo:

> When I would pray and think, I think and pray
> To several subjects: heaven hath my empty words
> Whilst my invention, hearing not my tongue,
> Anchors on Isabel. Heaven in my mouth
> As if I did but only chew his name,
> And in my heart the strong and swelling evil
> Of my conception. (2.4.1–7)[139]

Of all late-Elizabethan jurists, Richard Hooker was perhaps the most astute in observing that although the union of justice and religion was a natural phenomenon and 'that pure and unstayned Religion ought to bee the highest of all cares appertaining to publike Regiment',[140] the authority of scripture in secular jurisprudence should be of limited influence. He agreed with Fulbecke that there is neither justice nor religion where either one of these is missing,[141] but he shares Burton's scepticism about the motives of magistrates who would discard the rational precepts of natural law for the politically motivated application of scripture. If God had intended this, Hooker argued, He

> [S]hould cleane have abrogated amongst them the law of nature; which is an infallible knowledge imprinted in the minds of all the children of men . . . Admit this, and what shal the Scripture be but a snare and a torment to weake Consciences, filling them with infinite perplexities, scrupulosities, doubts insoluble, and extreme despaires?[142]

He condemned rulers who use religion as a political device and through their zealous enforcement of law exact obedience from their subjects only by the instillation in them of fear: 'Such are the counsels of men godless, when they would shew themselves politike devisers, able to create God in man by Art.'[143]

The potential conflict between the law of God and the law of man was the theme of much juristic discourse in late-Elizabethan and early-Jacobean England. For example, in his treatise on the office of Lord Chancellor, Ellesmere referred to two distinct kinds of '*leges conscientiæ*'. The first of these Ellesmere described as '*lex conscientiae politicæ*, by which the Chancellor ordereth matters', alluding to the jurisdiction of Equity in the Chancery; the second he termed '*lex conscientiae Divinæ*', which was a matter between the individual and his God,

---

[139] The same theme is explored in *Hamlet*, in which Claudius soliloquises over the impossibility of effective prayer: 'My words fly up, my thoughts remain below. / Words without thoughts never to heaven go'. (3.3.97–98)

[140] R Hooker, *Of the Lawes of Ecclesiastical Politie* (London, William Stansbye, 1622) 184, Bk V.I.

[141] *Ibid* at 185, Bk V.I.

[142] *Ibid* at 79–80, Bk II.VIII.

[143] *Ibid* at 190, Bk V.II. Dollimore discusses the above passage from *Of the Lawes* in terms of the different objectives of secular law and religious belief, Dollimore, above n 9, at 81.

by which there is no compulsive relief in this world, but the offendor standeth at the judgment of God only, and this in times past was said to be examinable between the Offendor and the Confessor.[144]

This law of divine conscience was not subject to temporal judgment, raising questions of jurisdictional legitimacy regarding Shakespeare's Duke when, disguised as the friar, he acts as spiritual confessor to Juliet and the condemned Claudio and Barnardine.[145] The reference above to the Lord Chancellor and the exercise of conscience in Equity recalls the epigrammatic remark of John Selden that 'Equity is according to the Conscience of him that is Chancellor, and as that is larger or narrower, so is Equity', leading him to the memorable conclusion that the standard for the measure of Equity is the variable measure of 'a Chancellor's Foot'. The comical image has proved durable, but it should not detract from the seriousness of Selden's opening remark on the subject, that 'Equity in Law, is the same that the Spirit is in religion, what every one pleases to make it'. It is for this reason that, according to Selden, 'Equity is a Roguish Thing'.[146] The idea of the conscience 'of him that is Chancellor' determining whether or not the rigour of the law is tempered by mercy is mimetically instanced in Act 5 of *Measure for Measure*. In an extraordinary demonstration of judicial discretion, the Duke pardons Claudio and Barnardine and condemns Angelo and Lucio to death, before commuting their sentences to marriage: respectively to Mariana and Kate Keepdown.

The tribunal over which the Duke presides in Act 5 is held not in a courtroom but at the gates of the city, extensive reference to which is made prior to the Duke's reappearance there. 'And why meet him at the gates, and redeliver our authorities there?' (4.4.4–5)[147] asks Angelo; to which the answer is that the Duke has expressed the wish 'that if any crave redress of injustice they should exhibit their petitions in the street' (4.4.8–9).[148] The link between the city-gates and the public manifestation of equitable judgment is well-established. Dugdale records that the Israelites had their courts of justice 'in the Gates of their Cities'. He refers to a conflict of spiritual and temporal jurisdictions in the case of the prophet Jeremiah, who was condemned to death 'by the Consistory of Priests' but 'was by the Consistory of Princes secular, or *Judges sitting in the Gate*, absolved and dischardged'. He goes on to note, regarding the choice of the city-gate as the location of the court, that 'the reason thereof was

---

[144] Lord Ellesmere, above n 27, at 48.

[145] Shuger notes that although medieval kings were often described as God's vice-regents or God's viceroys, Thomist political theology restricted the rule of kings to temporal matters: God's ministry on earth was confined to priests rather than kings, Shuger, above n 2, at 55; see St Thomas Aquinas, *On Politics and Ethics*, (ed) P Sigmund (New York, Norton, 1988) 26–27.

[146] J Selden, *Table-talk* (London, Jacob Tonson, Awnsham and John Churchill, 1696) 54.

[147] Other references to the city-gates include: 'Already he hath carried / Notice to Escalus and Angelo, / Who do prepare to meet him at the gates' (4.3.121–23); 'And bid them bring the trumpets to the gate' (4.5.9); 'The generous and gravest citizens / Have hent the gates' (4.6.13–14).

[148] There is an echo here of ch 7 of Machiavelli's *The Prince*, in which the duke set up a civil tribunal because he was 'determined to show that if cruelties had been inflicted they were not his doing but prompted by the harsh nature of this minister', Machiavelli, above n 72, at 25; see text to nn 72–73, above. On the dispensation of justice by the Duke in *Measure for Measure*, see C Lewis, ' "Dark Deeds Darkly Answered": Duke Vincentio and Judgment In *Measure for Measure*' (1983) 34 *Shakespeare Quarterly* 271.

(as tis very probable) partly that the equity of their proceedings might be seen by all'.[149] Lambarde makes a similar observation about the Israelites, noting that they

> did pronounce their *Iudgements* in the Gates of every Citie, to the end, that both all men might behold the indifferencie of their proceedings, and that no man should need to goe out of his way to seeke Iustice.[150]

Of particular interest is the fact that, in a chapter entitled 'The Court of Equitie, or Chancerie', Lambarde states that a good Chancellor will

> provide, that the Gate of *Mercie* may bee opened in all Calamitie of Suit: to the end, (where need shall bee) the Rigour of *Law* may bee amended.[151]

In the historiography of law, the gate has attained peculiar symbolic importance as the site of entrance to justice, suggestive both of inclusion and exclusion, access and denial. Derrida, for example, has interpreted the encounter between subject of law and legal institution in terms of the discourse of law guarding the law, denying or deferring access to it.[152] In Act 5 of *Measure for Measure*, the problem is not that access to law is denied or deferred. Indeed, the particular form of proceedings has certain features in common with procedure in the early Chancery; notably its relative informality, the inquisitorial style and the absence of a jury.[153] The

---

[149] Dugdale, above n 26, at 22; the Biblical episode to which Dugdale refers is recorded in *Jeremiah* 26: 'When the princes of Judah heard these things, then they came up from the king's house unto the house of the LORD, and sat down in the entry of the new gate of the LORD'S house'. (*Jeremiah* 26.10)

[150] Lambard, above n 79, at 6. Lambarde's is the earlier work, completed in 1591; it appears that Dugdale consulted *Archeion* when writing *Origines Juridiciales*. Both writers refer to the Greeks and Romans holding courts of justice in their temples: 'of purpose to shew that *Iudgement* was a *Divine thing*; then afterward in *Curia & Foro*', Lambard, above n 79, at 6; '[t]he old *Romans*, as we read, had at first their Seats of Justice within their Temples; purposely to shew, that Justice was a Divine thing: afterwards in *Curià & Foro*', Dugdale, above n 26, at 22.

[151] Lambard, above n 79, at 73; the distinct jurisdiction of Chancery was established by statute in the reign of Richard II: *17 R.2. cap. 6*. On the early history of Chancery, see Baker, above n 112, at 103–108. For an extensive discussion of Equity in the 16th and 17th centuries, its rules, literature and authorities, and the equitable jurisdiction of the Lord Chancellor, see WS Holdsworth, *A History of English Law*, 17 vols (London, Methuen, 1924) 5: 215–338.

[152] J Derrida, 'Before the Law' in J Derrida, *Acts of Literature*, (ed) D Attridge (New York, Routledge, 1992) 192. See Kafka's *At the Door of the Law*, in which the gatekeeper to the law denies the subject of law access for the duration of his life: F Kafka, 'At the Door of the Law', *Franz Kafka: Stories, 1904–1924*, (tr) J A Underwood (London, Abacus, 1995) 194.

[153] See D R Klinck, *Conscience, Equity and the Court of Chancery in Early Modern England* (Farnham, Ashgate, 2010); also J L Barton, 'Equity in the Medieval Common Law' in R A Newman (ed), *Equity in the World's Legal Systems* (Brussels, Établissements Émile Bruylant, 1973) 139; W J Jones, *The Elizabethan Court of Chancery* (Oxford, Oxford University Press, 1967). The offence of slandering the supreme magistrate, for which the Duke punishes Lucio in Act 5, would have been tried in Star Chamber. On the functions of Star Chamber in the Elizabethan legal system, see Lambard, above n 79, at 78; also, n 97, above. On defamation of the Crown, see ch 5, text to n 129, above. James I was extremely sensitive to slander: in 1585, the Scottish Parliament enacted a statute, by which slander of the king became an act of treason. James wrote of 'the false and unreverent writing or speaking of malicious men against your Parents and Predecessors', 'Basilicon Doron' in Somerville (ed), above n 5, at 23. In 1586 a second Act was passed by the Scottish Parliament, extending liability for slander to remarks made about the king's parents and forebears; see Bawcutt (ed), above n 21, Introduction, 4–5; also E Schanzer, *The Problem Plays of Shakespeare: a Study of 'Julius Caesar', 'Measure for Measure' and 'Antony and Cleopatra'* (London, Routledge & Kegan Paul, 1963) 125.

problem with the 'justice' dispensed by Shakespeare's Duke is that it represents the irrational exercise of arbitrary and unrestricted power.

The assertion made by Coke that 'nothing that is contrarie to reason, is consonant to Law'[154] is a summation of his faith in the sanctity of common law. At the time of writing *The First Part of the Institutes*, from which the above quotation is taken, Coke's judicial career was many years behind him. The king who had dismissed him from office as Chief Justice of the King's Bench, following the tumultuous jurisdictional dispute over *The Earl of Oxford's Case*,[155] had died. In 1628, the year in which *The First Part of the Institutes* was published, Coke faced new and more ominous battles over the lawful exercise of the Royal Prerogative, as a Parliamentarian proposing the Petition of Right to the House of Commons. While writing *The First Part of the Institutes*, a treatise on the law of property and a tribute also to Thomas de Littleton (d 1481), Coke would have had ample cause to reflect on 'the artificial reason and judgment of law',[156] particularly given his belief in the jurisdictional sovereignty of common law. If the reason of the law was perfect then, in Coke's opinion, the judgments at common law were indisputably correct. Barring the commission of judicial error, the decisions of the courts of common law were final and, as Coke categorically stated,

> to this court of King's Bench belongs authority, not only to correct errors in judicial proceedings, but other errors and misdemeanours extra-judicial . . .[157]

As Baker has noted, the conflict between Coke and Ellesmere arose not over the issue of Equity and its suitability in particular cases, but rather over 'the finality of judgments at common law and the enlargement of Chancery jurisdiction at the expense of the law courts'.[158] Chancery was the supreme court of the king's prerogative, and it was the absolute power which this juridical status implied that caused Coke to fear for the rule of law. Ellesmere distinguished between two types of power, which he claimed pertained to the judicial role of Lord Chancellor as head of the Chancery. The first type was an 'ordinary power': '*Ordinata potentia*, is where a certain order is observed, and so it is used in positive law'.[159] The second type was an 'absolute power': '*Potentia absoluta*', which Ellesmere claimed to be '*lex naturae*',[160]

---

[154] Sir Edward Coke, *The first part of the Institutes of the laws of England* (London, Societie of Stationers, 1628) 56b.

[155] On the conflict of 1615–16 between Coke and Ellesmere, see L A Knafla, *Law and Politics in Jacobean England: The Tracts of Lord Chancellor Ellesmere* (Cambridge, Cambridge University Press, 1977) 155–81; J P Dawson, 'Coke and Ellesmere Disinterred: the Attack on the Chancery in 1616' (1942) 36 *Illinois Law Review* 127. There is a useful discussion of the 1616 conflict and its consequences for the Chancery of the 1620s in G W Thomas, 'Equity and Lord Keeper John Williams' (1976) 91 *The English Historical Review* 506.

[156] Coke, *Prohibitions del Roy*, 12 *Reports* (1655) 7: 65a.

[157] Coke, *James Bagg's Case*, 11 *Reports* (1615) 6: 93b, at 98a.

[158] Baker, 'The Common Lawyers And The Chancery: 1616', above n 20, at 207–208.

[159] Lord Ellesmere, above n 27, at 44.

[160] *Ibid*. In his discussion of the distinction between the 'absolute' and 'ordinary' power of Chancery, Cromartie notes that Coke 'had no objection to cases being removed to Chancery during their progress through the justice system; the stand he chose to take in 1616 was over the re-opening, as he saw it, of cases he had previously settled', A Cromartie, 'The Constitutionalist Revolution: The Transformation of Political Culture in Early Stuart England' (1999) 163 *Past & Present* 76, 92.

the scope of which was apparently unlimited.[161] In 1574 Plowden had argued (in support of Aristotle) that

> if there was a defect in the law, it should be reformed by equity, which is no part of the law, but a moral virtue which corrects the law.[162]

The interpretive conundrum posed by Plowden's definition of equity is the same as that posed by the dilemma of the Chancellor's foot: Whose moral virtue is to be applied, and will the morality be tainted by the predilections and prejudices of the particular Lord Chancellor then in office? The suggestion that equity was 'no part of the law' was alarming not only to common lawyers such as Coke, but also to those who supported the principle of the king in Parliament. For constitutionalists such as these, legislators rather than judges were the source of sovereign lawful authority. Threatened actions for *Praemunire*, brought by aggrieved parties when decisions in the courts of common law were reversed in the Chancery, were the inevitable consequence of the disputed jurisdiction.[163] The suggestion that such actions lay against the Chancery led James I to demand of the judges: 'How can the King grant a *Premunire* against himself?'[164] The jurisdictional conflict was illustrated in the 1614 case of *Heath v Rydley*, in which judgment was given in King's Bench against the defendant in an action of Debt, after which he obtained an injunction from the Chancery 'to stay Judgment and Execution'. The injunction notwithstanding, the court of King's Bench 'did grant Judgment and Execution'. As presiding judge in the case, Coke remarked of the *Praemunire* statutes of Edward III and Henry IV that

> it is much to be wondered, that none will inform upon these Laws in such cases against the party that procures such Injunctions after Judgments at common Law . . . after Judgment given, the party ought to be quiet, and to submit unto it; for that Judgments being once given, *in Curia domini Regis*, are not to be reversed nor avoided, but by a legal course, *per errorem*, or *per attinctam*.[165]

In the same speech in which he questioned the right to bring an action of *Praemunire* against the Chancery, James I claimed that

> where the rigour of the Law in many cases will undoe a Subiect, there the Chancerie tempers the Law with equitie, and so mixeth Mercy with Iustice, as it preserves men from destruction.[166]

---

[161] In *Rooke's Case* (1599), Coke argued that the exercise of judicial discretion 'ought to be limited and bound with the rule of reason and law', Coke, *Rooke's Case*, 5 *Reports* (1605) 3: 99b, at 100a; in *Keighley's Case* (1609), he again argued that discretion was 'to be intended and interpreted according to law and justice', Coke, *Keighley's Case*, 10 *Reports* (1614) 5: 139a, at 140a.

[162] Plowden, *Eyston v Studd*, *Commentaries* 2: 460, at 466.

[163] The relevant *Praemunire* statutes were *27 Ed.3. cap. 1* and *4 H.4. cap. 23*. In the original *Praemunire* statute, *16 R.2. cap. 5*, the offence of *Praemunire* was directly or indirectly to assert the supremacy of the Pope over the Crown of England. It was said of Coke that 'four P's have overthrown and put him down—that is, pride, prohibitions, praemunire, and prerogative', in J R Tanner (ed), *Constitutional Documents of the Reign of James I, AD 1603–1625* (Cambridge, Cambridge University Press, 1930) 176.

[164] James I, 'Speech In The Starre-Chamber', above n 8, at 215.

[165] *Heath v Rydley* (1614), *The second part of The reports of Edward Bulstrode* (London, Richard and Edward Atkins, 1688) 194.

[166] James I, 'Speech In The Starre-Chamber', above n 8, at 214.

Such is the equitable justice dispensed by the Duke, at the end of *Measure for Measure*. But what if the conscience of the king does not permit access to his merciful judgment? What if his conscience decrees that mercy should be withheld, or dispensed only partially? In Shakespeare's Vienna, '[m]ortality and mercy' live in the 'tongue and heart' of the ruler (1.1.44–45). In Jacobean England, murmurings were heard to the effect that the exercise of kingly conscience should be constrained by the authority of law. The last prophetic word goes to Timothy Tourneur, a barrister of Gray's Inn. Writing in 1616 of 'the high power of the Chancellors', he issued the following warning:

> And thus in a short time they will enthral the common law (which yields all due prerogative), and by consequence the liberty of the subjects of England will be taken away, and no law practised on them but prerogative, which will be such that no one will know the extent thereof. And thus the government in a little time will lie in the hands of a small number of favourites who will flatter the King to obtain their private ends, and notwithstanding the King shall be ever indigent. And if these breeding mischiefs are not redressed by Parliament the body will in a short time die in all the parts.[167]

---

[167] BL MS Add 35957 fo 55.*v*, translated and quoted in Baker, 'The Common Lawyers and the Chancery: 1616', above n 20, at 222.

Conclusion

THE TITLE PAGE of the 1551 edition of Thomas More's *Utopia* describes it thus: 'A fruteful and pleasaunt worke of the beste state of a publique weale, and of the new yle called Utopia'.[1] Although I have attempted to identify the nature of Shakespeare's imaginary constitution, I have not sought to locate an explicit statement of thematic intent such as the above in any of his works. In the last play that Shakespeare wrote, *The Tempest*, the utopian kingdom is discussed; but the model offered there by Gonzalo is treated with derision, closer as it is to the fantastical Land of Cockaigne than to More's idiosyncratic (but realistic) description of the ideal State. Gonzalo's is a land with no apparent need for laws or constitutions:

> Letters should not be known. Riches, poverty,
> And use of service, none. Contract, succession,
> Bourn, bound of land, tilth, vineyard, none.
> No use of metal, corn, or wine, or oil.
> No occupation: all men idle, all,
> And women too, but innocent and pure.
> No sovereignty—(2.1.153–59)[2]

Gonzalo's government would, he claims, 'excel the Golden Age'. (2.1.173) The Ovidian reference is ironic, given that the island in *The Tempest* is, as Jonathan Bate has noted, 'shot through with Iron Age characteristics'.[3] Gonzalo's exposition of a State with no sovereignty, of which he would be king, is mocked by Antonio and Sebastian.

---

[1] Sir Thomas More, *A fruteful and pleasaunt worke of the beste state of a publique weale, and of the new yle called Utopia*, (tr) R Robinson (London, Abraham Vele, 1551) title page.

[2] *The Tempest*, (ed) A Barton (London, Penguin, 1968). Trüstedt describes Gonzalo's utopia as 'the fictional establishment of a new lawless law', K Trüstedt, 'The Tragedy of Law in Shakespearean Romance' in P Raffield and G Watt (eds), *Shakespeare and the Law* (Oxford, Hart Publishing, 2008) 111. On the Land of Cockaigne, see H Pleij, *Dreaming of Cockaigne: Medieval Fantasies of the Perfect Life* (New York, Columbia University Press, 2001); on the correlation between Gonzalo's words and the Land of Cockaigne, see A Hadfield, *Shakespeare and Renaissance Politics* (London, Arden Shakespeare, 2004) 219–21.

[3] J Bate, *Shakespeare and Ovid* (Oxford, Clarendon, 1993) 257; Ward describes Gonzalo's as 'the kind of utopia born of desperation as much as idealism', I Ward, *Shakespeare and the Legal Imagination* (London, Butterworths, 1999) 216. The influence of Montaigne's 'On the Cannibals' is evident throughout *The Tempest*, and especially in the above lines of Gonzalo. Montaigne argues that 'the descriptions with which poetry has beautifully painted the Age of Gold . . . could not even imagine a state of nature so simple and so pure as the one we have learned about from experience, they could not even believe that societies of men could be maintained with so little artifice, so little in the way of human solder', M de Montaigne, 'On the Cannibals' in *The Complete Essays*, (tr) (ed) M A Screech (London, Penguin, 2003) 232–33.

Conclusion

In chapter four I refer to Bottom's dream in *A Midsummer Night's Dream*. The subject of his dream is not divulged, but the 'wonders' of which he cannot speak appear to be related not to the fantastical illusion of a realm without law, but rather to the creation of a fairer society of the type described by St Paul in 1 *Corinthians*.[4] The difference between Bottom's inexpressible insight and Gonzalo's lucid but preposterous manifesto is striking. For all its inarticulate sense of wonder and its garbled reference to 1 *Corinthians*, the audience recognises in Bottom's recounting of his dream the hopes and desires of real people. His is not the whimsical and self-indulgent stuff of utopian fantasy, whose detachment from reality is symptomatic of its proponents' delusions.[5] At no place in the canon does Shakespeare present utopia as a realistic or attainable alternative to extant political and social arrangements. Indeed, it is reasonable to argue that the primary precondition for the creation of any utopian State (be it More's *Utopia* or Gonzalo's 'plantation of this isle' (2.1.145)) is the elimination of existing political structures. There is no place for negotiation, collaboration or discussion of any sort in the achievement of utopia. Paradoxically, in describing the ideal community, the authors of utopian fantasies discard the political ideals of community (in the Aristotelian sense of *koinonia*).[6] The condition for the realisation of earthly paradise is that it is imposed unilaterally.

Of the plays considered here, *Titus Andronicus* offers the clearest vision of a dystopian body politic, in which the unilateral imposition of positive law acts as a destructive force, enslaving rather than liberating its subjects. The imperial Rome of Saturninus is the antithesis of utopia. Subjection to the tyranny of absolutism is a precondition of life under his malevolent rule; but equally, life under the benevolent absolutism of the Duke in *Measure for Measure* is subject to the arbitrary whim of Vienna's chief magistrate. I am not drawing an analogy between the régimes of Saturninus and the Duke; I note only the authorial interest in the failings of absolutism, the motives of individual rulers notwithstanding. The purpose of this book is not to suggest that the plays of Shakespeare present in dramatic form a systematic constitutional charter. I argue instead that the themes, plots and characters reflect not only the author's evident interest in law and the English legal institution, but also his fascination with models of governance and their impact on the autonomous subject of law. The plays are not utopian landscapes; they offer no escape from the imperfections of quotidian existence in the early modern English

---

[4] See ch 4, text to nn 131–36, above.

[5] The utopian vision of Jack Cade is expressed in prose rather than iambic pentameter, but it shares with Gonzalo's a level of egotistic self-delusion, as for example when he informs his followers that when he is king, '[t]here shall be no money, all shall eat and drink on my score, and I will apparel them all in one livery, that they may agree like brothers and worship me their lord'. (*2 Henry VI*, 4.2.67–70) Carroll describes Cade's utopianism as '[p]art of a long tradition of radical utopian impossibility, echoing the land of cockayne, naivety and cunning cynicism fused together', W C Carroll, 'Language, Politics, and Poverty in Shakespearian Drama' (1991) 44 *Shakespeare Survey* 17, 20.

[6] I refer to Aristotle's theory of friendship and the community, in particular that '[a]ll communities are like parts of the political community'. Aristotle implies a level of active participation by all eligible citizens in the creation of the political structures of the State, Aristotle, *The Nicomachean Ethics* (tr) J A K Thomson (London, Penguin, 2004) 215, Bk VIII.IX.1159b25–1160a30.

Conclusion

State. Shakespeare engages with existing political arrangements, transforming contemporary events and accommodating them within the aesthetic framework of poetic drama. He utilises the unique capacity of theatre to facilitate political discourse within a design predicated upon the synthesis of visual and aural imagery. But its uniqueness is not related exclusively to the coalescence of pictorial and verbal images. Theatre is a communal venture, whose creators seek to facilitate the emergence of an animate relationship; not only between actors, but also between audience members, and between audience and actors. The audience is an engaged participant in the creative process, shaping through its collective response the meaning of the play.

At a symbolic level, the narratives of the plays and the journeys on which their characters are embarked address the issue of political status within the citizenry. Shakespeare was to explore this theme more thoroughly in *Coriolanus*: 'We have power in ourselves to do it, but it is a power that we have no power to do' (2.3.4–5), says the Third Citizen to his fellow Romans, in response to the suggestion that collectively they may, if they wish, deny Coriolanus 'our voices' (2.3.1).[7] Are the citizens political objects, to be manipulated and oppressed in the interests of effective government? Or are they autonomous subjects of law, whose relationship with the legal institution is based upon reciprocal rights and obligations? These questions were asked more obliquely in Shakespeare's Elizabethan plays and in his first post-Elizabethan work for the theatre, *Measure for Measure*. In that play he articulates a pre-Hobbesian dilemma over the desired balance between the command of the sovereign and the force of law on the one hand, and the natural rights and liberties of the individual subject on the other. In the State governed by Leviathan, law was to be defined simply as the will of the ruler: the sovereign was not subject to the law. Having the exclusive power to make laws, he had the concomitant right to repeal them, and was 'free himself from that subjection'.[8] It is noteworthy that Hobbes should have used identical metaphors to those employed by Shakespeare in *Measure for Measure*, with which to describe the unrestricted power of law. For Hobbes, the laws of nature (which he listed as justice, equity, modesty and mercy) would not be observed 'without the terror of some power ... covenants, without the sword, are but words'.[9] The echoes of the Duke's 'sword of heaven' (3.2.223), of the 'terror' (1.1.19) lent to Angelo and the 'deputed sword' (2.2.61), are resounding.

---

[7] Arnold argues that in the idiom of early modern English electoral politics, 'voice' here is synonymous with 'vote': O Arnold, *The Third Citizen: Shakespeare's Theater and the Early Modern House of Commons* (Baltimore, Md, Johns Hopkins University Press, 2007) 9; see also, Kermode: 'Voice, in the English of the time, was the word for "vote". Shakespeare never uses the word "vote", and it would have suited his purposes much less well, for "voice" relates the suffrage of the people to their disgusting bodies', Frank Kermode, *Shakespeare's Language* (London, Penguin, 2000) 247.

[8] T Hobbes, *Leviathan*, (ed) J C A Gaskin (Oxford, Oxford University Press, 1998) 176. See G Burgess, 'Repacifying the Polity: the Responses of Hobbes and Harrington to the "Crisis of the Common Law"' in I Gentles, J Morrill and B Worden (eds), *Soldiers, Writers and Statesmen of the English Revolution* (Cambridge, Cambridge University Press, 1998) 202; on Hobbes and the origins of legal positivism, see I Ward, *An Introduction to Critical Legal Theory* (London, Cavendish, 1998) 79–86.

[9] Hobbes, above n 8, at 111.

Conclusion

The above examples from *Measure for Measure* and *Leviathan* illustrate the thesis that the text is another form of sign[10]: an aesthetic artefact directing the reader to an understanding of its true meaning, which lies beneath the written word and awaits exegesis. The text itself is not the literal truth, a statement that applies as much to the plays of Shakespeare as it does to the records of common law (contained in its reports, statutes and commentaries). The text is the trace of an absent presence, and the interpreter of the text—be he actor, lawyer, or jurist—exposes the embedded truth through the application of 'artificial reason'.[11] Emotional attachment and willing obedience to the legal institution are contingent upon the persuasive power of the sign. The images and narratives of English law have been continuously adapted to suit the circumstances of its immediate condition.[12] Just as the crown—the image of the king—is 'an hieroglyphic of the laws',[13] so the plays of Shakespeare are signs, unravelling in pictorial and aural images the complex emotional bond between the legal institution and the subject of law. In the words of Sir Philip Sidney, they provide 'a speaking picture—with this end: to teach and delight.'[14] It is through the imagination and expression of an indestructible social order that Shakespeare is identifiable not only as an author of exhaustive emotional range and unsurpassed technical brilliance, but also, in Shelley's terms, as an institutor of laws and a founder of civil society, a lawmaker for all time:

> Poets are the hierophants of an unapprehended inspiration; the mirrors of the gigantic shadows which futurity casts upon the present; the words which express what they understand not; the trumpets which sing to battle and feel not what they inspire; the influence which is moved not, but moves. Poets are the unacknowledged legislators of the world.[15]

---

[10] Goodrich makes a similar observation with reference to the history of reformist movements and their claims for the primacy of the written word: 'The text or word is no less a sign than the graven image or statue', P Goodrich, *Oedipus Lex: Psychoanalysis, History, Law* (Los Angeles, University of California Press, 1995) 42.

[11] *Prohibitions del Roy* in Part 12 (1655) of *The Reports of Sir Edward Coke, Knt. In English*, George Wilson (ed), 7 vols (London, Rivington, 1777) 7: 64a, at 65a.

[12] For a theoretical discussion of the adaptation of traditions to suit contemporary institutional circumstances, see H-G Gadamer, *Truth and Method*, (tr) W Glen-Doepel, (eds) J Cumming and G Barden (London, Sheed and Ward, 1979).

[13] Coke, *Postnati. Calvin's Case*, 7 *Reports* (1608) 4: 1a, at 11b.

[14] Sir Philip Sidney, 'The Defence of Poesy' in G Alexander (ed), *Sidney's 'The Defence of Poesy' and Selected Renaissance Literary Criticism* (Penguin, London 2004) 10.

[15] P B Shelley, *A Defence of Poetry* in H A Needham (ed), *Sidney, An Apology For Poetry; Shelley, A Defence of Poetry* (London, Ginn & Co, 1931) 109.

BIBLIOGRAPHY

Abel, L, *Metatheatre: a New View on Dramatic Form* (New York, Hill & Wang, 1963).
Abel, L, *Tragedy and Metatheatre: Essays on Dramatic Form* (New York, Holmes & Meier, 2003).
Alciatus, A, *Emblemata* (Lugudini, M Bonhomme, 1550).
Alexander, G (ed), *Sidney's 'The Defence of Poesy' and Selected Renaissance Literary Criticism* (London, Penguin, 2004).
Alexander, J and Binski, P (eds), *Age of Chivalry: Art in Plantagenet England, 1200–1400* (London, Royal Academy of Arts, in association with Weidenfeld & Nicolson, 1987).
Altick, R D, 'Symphonic Imagery in *Richard II*' (1947) 62 *Publication of the Modern Language Association of America* 341.
Anonymous, *A Complete Collection of State-Trials, and Proceedings for High Treason*, 11 vols (London, C Bathurst, J & F Rivington, 1776–81).
Anonymous, *The most strange and admirable discoverie of the three Witches of Warboys arraigned, convicted and executed at the last Assises at Huntington* (London, Thomas Man and Iohn Winnington, 1593).
Anonymous, *The Famous Victories of Henry the Fifth*, (ed) C Hanabusa (Manchester, Manchester University Press, 2007).
Apuleius, *The xi. Books of the Golden Asse conteininge the Metamorphosie of Lucius Apuleius*, (tr) W Adlington (London, Henry Wykes, 1566).
Aquinas, T, *On Politics and Ethics*, (ed) P Sigmund (New York, Norton, 1988).
Aquinas, T, *Summa Theologica (Pars Prima Secundae)* (Teddington, The Echo Library, 2007).
Archer, I W, *The Pursuit of Stability: Social Relations in Elizabethan London* (Cambridge, Cambridge University Press, 1991).
Archer, J, Goldring, E and Knight, S (eds), *The Intellectual and Cultural World of the Early Modern Inns of Court* (Manchester, Manchester University Press, Forthcoming).
Aristotle, *The Nicomachean Ethics*, (tr) J A K Thomson (London, Penguin, 2004).
Aristotle, *The Politics*, (tr) T A Sinclair, (rev) T R Saunders (London, Penguin, 1992).
Arlidge, A, *Shakespeare and the Prince of Love: The Feast of Misrule in the Middle Temple* (London, Giles de la Mere, 2000).
Arnold, O, *The Third Citizen: Shakespeare's Theater and the Early Modern House of Commons* (Baltimore, Md, Johns Hopkins University Press, 2007).
Artemidorus, D, *The iudgement, or exposition of dreames, written by Artimodorus, an auncient and famous author, first in Greek, then translated into Latin, after into French, and now into English*, (tr) R W (London, William Iones, 1606).
Ashelford, J, *Visual History of Costume: Sixteenth Centry* (London, Batsford, 1983).
Ashton, R, *Reformation and Revolution, 1558–1660* (London, Paladin, 1985).
Astington, J H, 'The Globe, The Court and *Measure for Measure*' (1999) 52 *Shakespeare Survey* 133.
Aubrey, J, *Brief Lives* (London, The Folio Society, 1975).
Bacon, F, *Letter to Coke from Sir Francis Bacon*, BL Sloane. 1775.

Bibliography

Bacon, F, *The Major Works*, (ed) B Vickers (Oxford, Oxford University Press, 2002).

Bacon, F and Davison, F et al, *Gesta Grayorum: Or, The History of the High and mighty Prince, Henry Prince of Purpoole* (London, William Canning, 1688).

Baker, J H, 'History of Gowns Worn at the English Bar' (1975) 9 *Costume: The Journal of the Costume Society* 15.

Baker, J H, *An Introduction to English Legal History* (London, Butterworths, 2002).

Baker, J H, *The Legal Profession and the Common Law: Historical Essays* (London, Hambledon, 1986).

Baker, J H, *Manual of law-French* (Amersham, Avebury, 1979).

Baker, J H, *The Order of Serjeants at Law* (London, Selden Society, 1984).

Baker, J H, 'The Three Languages of the Common Law' (1998) 43 *McGill Law Journal* 5.

Baker, J H and Milsom, S F C, *Sources of English Legal History: Private Law to 1750* (London, Butterworths, 1986).

Bakhtin, M, *Rabelais and His World*, (tr) H Iswolsky (Bloomington, Indiana University Press, 1984).

Barber, C L, *Shakespeare's Festive Comedy* (Cleveland, Ohio, World Publishing, 1968).

Barker, F, *The Culture of Violence: Essays on Tragedy and History* (Manchester, Manchester University Press, 1993).

Barlow, R G, 'Infinite Worlds: Robert Burton's Cosmic Voyage' (1973) 34 *Journal of the History of Ideas* 291.

Barroll, L, 'A New History for Shakespeare and His Time' (1988) 39 *Shakespeare Quarterly* 441.

Barshack, L, 'Time and the constitution' (2009) 7 *International Journal of Constitutional Law* 553.

Bataille, G, *Theory of Religion*, (tr) R Hurley (New York, Zone, 1989).

Bate, J, *Shakespeare and Ovid* (Oxford, Clarendon, 1993).

Bate, J, *Soul of the Age: the Life, Mind and World of William Shakespeare* (London, Penguin, 2008).

Bawcutt, N W, '"He Who The Sword Of Heaven Will Bear": The Duke Versus Angelo In *Measure for Measure*' (1984) 37 *Shakespeare Survey* 89.

Bayly, L, *The Practice of Piety: Directing a Christian How to Walk that he may Please God* (London, Philip Chetwinde, 1654).

Behrens, G, 'Equity in the Commentaries of Edmund Plowden' (1999) 20 *The Journal of Legal History* 25.

Beier, A L, *Masterless Men: The Vagrancy Problem in England, 1560–1640* (London, Methuen, 1985).

Bellamy, J G, *Criminal Law and Society in Late Medieval and Tudor England* (Gloucester, Alan Sutton, 1984).

Bellamy, J G, *The Law of Treason in England in the Later Middle Ages* (Cambridge, Cambridge University Press, 1970).

Bellamy, J G, *The Tudor Law of Treason: an Introduction* (London, Routledge & Kegan Paul, 1979).

Bennett, M, *Richard II and the Revolution of 1399* (Stroud, Sutton, 1999).

Bergeron, D M, *Elizabethan Civic Pageantry, 1558–1642* (London, Edward Arnold, 1971).

Bergeron, D M, '*Richard II* and Carnival Politics' (1991) 42 *Shakespeare Quarterly* 33.

Bernthal, C A, 'Staging Justice: James I and the Trial Scenes in *Measure for Measure*' (1992) 32 *Studies in English Literature* 247.

Berry, H, 'The First Public Playhouses, Especially the Red Lion' (1989) 40 *Shakespeare Quarterly* 133.

Bibliography

Betteridge, T, *Shakespearean Fantasy and Politics* (Hatfield, University of Hertfordshire Press, 2005).

Biancalana, J, *The Fee Tail and the Common Recovery in Medieval England* (Cambridge, Cambridge University Press, 2001).

Bland, D (ed), *Gesta Grayorum, or, the History of the High and Mighty Prince Henry Prince of Purpoole, Anno Domini, 1594* (Liverpool, Liverpool University Press, 1968).

Blatcher, M, *The Court of King's Bench, 1450–1550: a Study in Self-Help* (London, Athlone, 1978).

Bly, M, 'Playing the Tourist in Early Modern London: Selling the Liberties Onstage' (2007) 122 *Publication of the Modern Language Association of America* 61.

Bodin, J, *On Sovereignty*, (ed) and (tr) J H Franklin (Cambridge, Cambridge University Press, 1992).

Borch-Jacobson, M, *The Freudian Subject*, (tr) C Porter (Stanford, Conn, Stanford University Press, 1988).

Boris, E Z, *Shakespeare's English Kings, the People and the Law: a Study in the Relationship between the Tudor Constitution and the English History Plays* (New Jersey, Fairleigh Dickinson University Press, 1978).

Bossewell, J, *Workes of Armorie* (London, Richardi Totelli, 1572).

Boswell-Stone, W G, *Shakespeare's Holinshed: The Chronicle and the Historical Plays Compared* (London, Chatto & Windus, 1907).

Bowen, C D, *The Lion and the Throne: The Life and Times of Sir Edward Coke (1552–1634)* (London, Hamilton, 1957).

Boyer, A D, *Sir Edward Coke and the Elizabethan Age* (Stanford, Conn, Stanford University Press, 2003).

Bracton, H de, *De Legibus et Consuetudinibus Angliae*, (tr) SE Thorne, 4 vols (Cambridge, Massachusetts, Belknap Press, 1968-77).

Brand, P, *The Origins of the English Legal Profession* (Oxford, Blackwell, 1992).

Brathwaite, R, *Mercurius Britannicus, or the English Intelligencer: A Tragic-Comedy, at Paris* (London, Felix Kingston, 1641).

Braunmuller, A R and Hattaway, M (eds), *The Cambridge Companion to English Renaissance Drama* (Cambridge, Cambridge University Press, 2003).

Breitenberg, M, '". . . the hole matter opened": Iconic Representation and Interpretation in "The Quenes Majesties Passage"' (1986) 28 *Criticism* 1.

Briggs, K M, *The Anatomy of Puck: an Examination of Fairy Beliefs Among Shakespeare's Contemporaries* (New York, Arno, 1977).

Briggs, K M, *A Dictionary of Fairies: Hobgoblins, Brownies, Bogies, and Other Supernatural Creatures* (London, Lane, 1976).

Briggs, K M, *The Fairies in English Tradition and Literature* (Chicago, Ill, University of Chicago Press, 1967).

Briggs, K M, *Pale Hecate's Team: an Examination of the Beliefs on Witchcraft and Magic among Shakespeare's Contemporaries and his Immediate Successors* (London, Routledge & Kegan Paul, 1962).

Brinkworth, E R C, *The 'Bawdy Court' of Banbury: The Act Book of the Peculiar Court of Banbury, 1625–1638*, (ed) R K Gilkes (Banbury, The Banbury Historical Society, 1997).

Brinkworth, E R C, *Shakespeare and the Bawdy Court of Stratford* (Chichester, Phillimore, 1972).

Bristol, M D, *Carnival and Theater: Plebeian Culture and the Structure of Authority in Renaissance England* (New York, Methuen, 1985).

Bibliography

Brooks, C W, *Pettyfoggers and Vipers of the Commonwealth: the 'Lower Branch' of the Legal Profession in Early Modern England* (Cambridge, Cambridge University Press, 1986).

Browne, W, *Circe and Ulysses, The Inner Temple Masque, January 13, 1615*, (ed) G Jones (London, Golden Cockerel, 1954).

Bruster, D, *Drama and the Market in the Age of Shakespeare* (Cambridge, Cambridge University Press, 1992).

Bryson, W H (ed), *Cases Concerning Equity and the Courts of Equity, 1550–1660*, 2 vols (London, Selden Society, 2001–02).

Bulstrode, E, *The second part of The reports of Edward Bulstrode* (London, Richard and Edward Atkins, 1688).

Burnett, C, 'Justice, Myth and Symbol' (1987) 11 *Legal Studies Forum* 79.

Burns, J H, 'Fortescue and the Political Theory of *Dominium*' (1985) 28 *The Historical Journal* 777.

Burns, R, *Ecclesiastical Law*, 4 vols (London, A Millar, 1767).

Burrow, C, 'Reading Tudor Writing Politically: The Case of 2 *Henry IV*' (2008) 38 *The Yearbook of English Studies* 234.

Burton, R, *The anatomy of melancholy what it is, with all the kinds, causes, symptomes, prognostickes, & severall cures of it*, 2nd edn (Oxford, Henry Cripps, 1621).

Burton, R, *The anatomy of melancholy what it is, with all the kinds, causes, symptomes, prognostickes, & severall cures of it*, 6th edn (Oxford, Henry Cripps, 1651).

Calderwood, J L, *Shakespearian Metadrama: the Argument of the Play in 'Titus Andronicus', 'Love's Labours Lost', 'Romeo and Juliet', ' A Midsummer Night's Dream' and 'Richard II'* (Minneapolis, University of Minnesota Press, 1971).

Calvin, J, *The institution of Christian religion*, (tr) T Norton (London, Reinolde Wolfe & Richarde Harison, 1561).

Calvin, J, *The sermons of M. Iohn Calvin, upon the Epistle of S. Paule too the Ephesians*, (tr) A Golding (London, Lucas Harison and George Byshop, 1577).

Camden, W, *Remaines of a Greater Worke, Concerning Britaine, the inhabitants thereof, their Languages, Names, Surnames, Empreses, Wise speeches, Poesies, and Epitaphes* (London, Simon Waterson, 1605).

Campbell, L B (ed), *The Mirror for Magistrates* (Cambridge, Cambridge University Press, 1938).

Carlyle, A J, *The Influence of Christianity Upon Social and Political Ideas* (London, A R Mowbray, 1912).

Carlyle, R W and Carlyle, A J, *A History of Mediaeval Political Theory in the West*, 6 vols (Edinburgh, Blackwood, 1903–36).

Carroll, W C, 'Language, Politics, and Poverty in Shakespearian Drama' (1991) 44 *Shakespeare Survey* 17.

Cavell, S, *Disowning Knowledge in Seven Plays of Shakespeare* (Cambridge, Cambridge University Press, 2003).

Chambers, E K, *The Elizabethan Stage*, 4 vols (Oxford, Clarendon, 1923).

Chambers, E K, *William Shakespeare: a Study of Facts and Problems*, 2 vols (Oxford, Oxford University Press, 1930).

Chapple, A S, 'Robert Burton's Geography of Melancholy' (1993) 33 *Studies in English Literature* 99.

Chesterton, G K, *Chesterton on Shakespeare*, (ed) D Collins (Henley-on-Thames, Darwen Finlayson, 1971).

Bibliography

Cicero, M T, *Cicero's Brutus or History of Famous Orators*, (tr) G L Hendrickson (London, William Heinemann, 1962).

Cicero, M T, *De Re Publica, De Legibus*, (tr) C W Keyes (Cambridge, Mass, Harvard University Press, 2006).

Cicero, M T, *Laelius De Amicitia*, (ed) St G W J Stock (Oxford, Clarendon, 1930).

Clare, J, 'The Censorship of the Deposition Scene in *Richard II*' (1990) 41 *Review of English Studies* 89.

Clegg, C S, '"By the choise and Inuitation of al the realme": *Richard II* and Elizabethan Press Censorship' (1997) 48 *Shakespeare Quarterly* 432.

Clegg, C S, *Press Censorship in Elizabethan England* (Cambridge, Cambridge University Press, 1997).

Codrington, R, *Elegy on Sir Edward Coke* (1634), BL Add MS 37484.

Coke, E, *Exception to Coke's Reports, and examination of Coke by Ellesmere (Lord Chancellor)* (1616), BL Add MS 4107.

Coke, E, *The first part of the institutes of the laws of England. Or, a commentary upon Littleton, not the name of a lawyer onely, but of the law it selfe* (London, Societie of Stationers, 1628).

Coke, E, *The Fourth Part of the Institutes of the Laws of England, Concerning the Jurisdiction of the Courts* (London, E and R Brooke, 1797).

Coke, E, *The Lord Coke His Speech and Charge. With a Discoverie of the Abuses and Corruption of Officers* (London, Christopher Pursett, 1607).

Coke, E, *The Reports of Sir Edward Coke, Knt. In English*, G Wilson (ed), 7 vols (London, Rivington, 1777).

Coke, E, *The second part of the Institutes Of the lawes of England containing the exposition of many ancient, and other statutes* (London, E Dawson, R Meighen, W Lee and D Pakeham, 1642).

Coke, E, *The third part of the Institutes of the laws of England concerning high treason, and other pleas of the crown, and criminall causes* (London, W Lee and D Pakeman, 1644).

Coleridge, S T, *On the Constitution of the Church and State* (London, J M Dent, 1972).

Collinson, P, *The Birthpangs of Protestant England: Religious and Cultural Change in the Sixteenth and Seventeenth Centuries* (Basingstoke, Macmillan, 1988).

Collinson, P, *Elizabethans* (London, Hambledon and London, 2003).

Coperario, J, *The Maske of Flowers. Presented by the Gentlemen of Graies-Inne, at the Court of White-hall, in the Banquetting House, upon Twelfe night, 1613* (London, Robert Wilson, 1614).

Coquillette, D R, 'Legal Ideology and Incorporations I: the English Civilian Writers, 1523–1607' (1981) 61 *Boston University Law Review* 1.

Corbin, P and Sedge, D (eds), *Thomas of Woodstock, or King Richard the Second, Part One* (Manchester, Manchester University Press, 2002).

Coupe, C, 'An Old Picture' (1895) 84 *The Month* 229.

Cover, R M, 'The Supreme Court, 1982 Term—Foreword: *Nomos* and Narrative' (1983) 97 *Harvard Law Review* 4.

Cowell, J, *The Institutes of the Lawes of England, Digested into the Method of the Civill or Imperiall Institutions*, (tr) W G Esquire (London, Jo Ridley, 1651).

Cowell, J, *The Interpreter: or Booke containing the signification of words wherein is set foorth the true meaning of all, or the most part of such words and termes, as are mentioned in the law writers* (Cambridge, Iohn Legate, 1607).

Cox, L, *The Arte or Crafte of Rhetoryke* (London, R Redman, 1529).

Bibliography

Cromartie, A, *The Constitutionalist Revolution: An Essay on the History of England, 1450–1642* (Cambridge, Cambridge University Press, 2006).

Cromartie, A, 'The Constitutionalist Revolution: The Transformation of Political Culture in Early Stuart England' (1999) 163 *Past & Present* 76.

Cross, C, *The Royal Supremacy in the Elizabethan Church* (London, Allen & Unwin, 1969).

Crouch, D, *The Image of Aristocracy in Britain, 1000–1300* (London, Routledge, 1992).

Cruickshank, C G, *Elizabeth's Army* (Oxford, Oxford University Press, 1968).

Daniel, S, *The History of the Civil War* (London, R Gosling, 1718).

Danniell, D, *The Bible in English* (New Haven, Conn, Yale University Press, 2003).

Danto, A C, *Embodied Meanings: Critical Essays and Aesthetic Meditations* (New York, Farrar, Straus and Giroux, 1995).

Davidson, C, *Festivals and Plays in Late Medieval Britain* (Aldershot, Ashgate, 2007).

Dawson, A B and Yachnin, P, *The Culture of Playgoing in Shakespeare's England: a Collaborative Debate* (Cambridge, Cambridge University Press, 2001).

Dawson, J P, 'Coke and Ellesmere Disinterred: the Attack on the Chancery in 1616' (1942) 36 *Illinois Law Review* 127.

Day, J, *Law-Trickes or, Who Would Have Thought It. As it hath bene divers times Acted by the Children of the Revels* (London, R More, 1608).

Dekker, T, *The Dramatic Works of Thomas Dekker*, (ed) R H Shepherd, 4 vols (London, John Pearson, 1873).

Dekker, T, *The Guls Horne-booke* (London, RS, 1609).

Dekker, T, *The Pleasant Comedie of Old Fortunatus. As it was plaied before the Queenes Maiestie this Christmas, by the Right Honourable the Earle of Nottingham, Lord high Admirall of England his Servants* (London, William Aspley, 1600).

Denning, A T, *The Due Process of Law* (London, Butterworths, 1980).

Denning, A T, *The Family Story* (London, Butterworths, 1981).

Denning, A T, *Leaves from My Library* (London, Butterworths, 1986).

Derbyshire, H and Hodson, L, 'Performing Injustice: Human Rights and Verbatim Theatre' (2008) 2 *Law and Humanities* 191.

Derrida, J, *Acts of Literature*, (ed) D Attridge (New York, Routledge, 1992).

Derrida, J, 'Force of Law: The "Mystical Foundations of Authority"', (tr) M Quaintance (1990) 11 *Cardozo Law Review* 919.

Dicey, A V, *Introduction to the Study of the Law of the Constitution* (London, Macmillan, 1959).

Dickinson, J W, 'Renaissance Equity and *Measure for Measure*' (1962) 13 *Shakespeare Quarterly* 287.

Diehl, H, '"Infinite Space": Representation and Reformation in Measure for Measure' (1998) 49 *Shakespeare Quarterly* 393.

Doddridge, J, *Describing a Method for the managing of the Lawes of this Land* (London, I More, 1631).

Doddridge, J, *The Lawyers Light: or, A due direction for the study of the law for methode* (London, Benjamin Fisher, 1629).

Doe, N, 'Fifteenth-Century Concepts of Law: Fortescue and Pecock' (1989) 10 *History of Political Thought* 257.

Dollimore, J, *Radical Tragedy: Religion, Ideology and Power in the Drama of Shakespeare and his Contemporaries* (Basingstoke, Palgrave Macmillan, 2004).

Dollimore, J and Sinfield, A (eds), *Political Shakespeare: Essays in Cultural Materialism* (Manchester, Manchester University Press, 1994).

Bibliography

Douzinas, C, 'Whistler v Ruskin: Law's Fear of Images' (1996) 19 *Art History* 353.
Douzinas, C, and Nead, L (eds), *Law and the Image: The Authority of Art and the Aesthetics of Law* (Chicago, Ill, University of Chicago Press, 1999).
Douzinas, C, and Warrington, R, *Justice Miscarried: Ethics, Aesthetics and the Law* (London, Harvester Wheatsheaf, 1994).
Dugdale, G, *The Time Triumphant* (London, RB, 1604).
Dugdale, W, *Origines Juridiciales or Historical Memorials of the English Laws* (London, F & T Warren, 1666).
Dunkel, W, 'Law and Equity in *Measure for Measure*' (1962) 13 *Shakespeare Quarterly* 275.
Dutton, R, *Mastering the Revels: The Regulation and Censorship of English Renaissance Drama* (Iowa, University of Iowa Press, 1991).
Dworkin, R, *Law's Empire* (London, Fontana, 1986).
Eccles, C, *The Rose Theatre* (London, Nick Hern, 1990).
Egerton, T (Lord Ellesmere), *Certaine Observations Concerning the Office of the Lord Chancellor* (London, Henry Twyford and Iohn Place, 1651).
Eisenstein, E L, *The Printing Press as an Agent of Change*, 2 vols (Cambridge, Cambridge University Press, 1979).
Eliot, T S, *Selected Essays 1917–1932* (London, Faber, 1932).
Elliott, R C, *The Shape of Utopia: Studies in a Literary Genre* (Chicago, Ill, University of Chicago Press, 1970).
Elyot, T, *The Book Named the Governor* (London, J M Dent, 1962).
Emmison, F G, 'Morals and the Church Courts' in *Elizabethan Life*, 5 vols (Chelmsford, Essex Records Office, 1973) vol 2.
Erasmus, D, *The Praise of Folie*, (tr) T Chaloner (London, Thomas Berthelet, 1549).
Estienne, C, *De Dissectione partium corporis humani* (Paris, 1545).
Evans, D, 'The Inns of Court: Speculations on the Body of Law' (1993) 1 *Arch-Text* 5.
Evans, D, 'Theatre of Deferral: The Image of the Law and the Architecture of the Inns of Court' (1999) 10 *Law and Critique* 1.
Evans, M and Jack, R I (eds), *Sources of English Legal and Constitutional History* (Sydney, Butterworths, 1984).
Ferne, J, *The Blazon of Gentrie* (London, Toby Cooke, 1586).
Fincham, K and Lake, P, 'The Ecclesiastical Policy of James I' (1985) 24 *The Journal of British Studies* 169.
Finkelpearl, P J, *John Marston of the Middle Temple: An Elizabethan Dramatist in his Social Setting* (Cambridge, Mass, Harvard University Press, 1969).
Fischer Taylor, K, *In the Theater of Criminal Justice: Palais de Justice in Second Empire Paris* (New Jersey, Princeton University Press, 1993).
Foakes, R A (ed), *Henslowe's Diary* (Cambridge, Cambridge University Press, 2002).
Foakes, R A, *Shakespeare and Violence* (Cambridge, Cambridge University Press, 2003).
Fortescue, J, *De Laudibus Legum Angliae*, (ed) J Selden (London, R Gosling, 1737).
Fortescue, J, *On the Laws and Governance of England*, (ed) S Lockwood (Cambridge, Cambridge University Press, 1997).
Fortier, M, *The Culture of Equity in Early Modern England* (Aldershot, Ashgate, 2005).
Foster, E R (ed), *Proceedings in Parliament, 1610*, 2 vols (New Haven, Conn, Yale University Press, 1966).
Foucault, M, *Aesthetics, Method, and Epistemology*, (tr) R Hurley, (ed) J D Faubion (London, Penguin, 1998).

Bibliography

Foucault, M, *Discipline and Punish: The Birth of the Prison*, (tr) A Sheridan (London, Penguin, 1991).
Foucault, M, *The History of Sexuality: An Introduction*, (tr) R Hurley, 3 vols (New York, Random House, 1978).
Fox, A and Guy, J, *Reassessing the Henrician Age: Humanism, Politics and Reform, 1500–1550* (Oxford, Blackwell, 1986).
Franklin, J H, *Jean Bodin and the Rise of Absolutist Theory* (Cambridge, Cambridge University Press, 1973).
Franklin, J H, *Jean Bodin and the Sixteenth-Century Revolution in the Methodology of Law and History* (Westport, Conn, Greenwood Press, 1977).
Fraunce, A, *The Lawiers Logike, exemplifying the precepts of Logike by the practise of the common Lawe* (London, T Gubbin and T Newman, 1588).
Frazer, J, *The Golden Bough: a Study in Magic and Religion* (Ware, Wordsworth, 1993).
Freedberg, D, *The Power of Images: Studies in the History and Theory of Response* (Chicago, Ill, University of Chicago Press, 1990).
Freeman, T F and Doran, S (eds), *The Myth of Elizabeth* (London, Palgrave Macmillan, 2003).
Freud, S, *The Interpretation of Dreams* (tr) J Crick (Oxford, Oxford University Press, 1999).
Freud, S, *The Origins of Religion*, (tr) J Strachey, (ed) A Dickson (London, Penguin, 1990).
Froissart, J, *Chronicles*, (tr) and (ed) G Brereton (London, Penguin, 1978).
Fulbecke, W, *A Direction or Preparative to the Study of the Lawe Wherein is showed, what things ought to be observed and used of them that are addicted to the study of the Law* (London, T Wight, 1600).
Fuller, T, *The Holy State* (Cambridge, John Williams, 1642).
G, H, *The Mirrour of Maiestie: or, the Badges of Honour Conceitedly Emblazoned: with Emblems Annexed, Poetically Unfolded* (London, W Jones, 1618).
Gadamer, H-G, *Truth and Method*, (tr) W Glen-Doepel, (eds) J Cumming and G Barden (London, Sheed and Ward, 1979).
Gardiner, S R, *History of England from the Accession of James I to the Outbreak of the Civil War, 1603–1642*, 10 vols (London, Longmans, Green, 1883–84).
Geckle, G L, *John Marston's Drama: Themes, Images, Sources* (New Jersey, Fairleigh Dickinson University Press, 1980).
Geminus, T, *Compendiosa totius anatomie delineation* (London, J Herfordie, 1545).
Gentles, I, Morrill, J and Worden, B (eds), *Soldiers, Writers and Statesmen of the English Revolution* (Cambridge, Cambridge University Press, 1998).
Geoffrey of Monmouth, *The History of the Kings of Britain*, (tr) L Thorpe (London, Penguin, 1966).
George, D, 'Plutarch, Insurrection, and Dearth in *Coriolanus*' (2000) 53 *Shakespeare Survey* 60.
Girard, R, *A Theater of Envy: William Shakespeare* (New York, Oxford University Press, 1991).
Girard, R, *Violence and the Sacred*, (tr) P Gregory (Baltimore, Md, Johns Hopkins University Press, 1977).
Gleason, J H, *The Justices of the Peace in England, 1558–1640: A Later Eirenarcha* (Oxford, Clarendon, 1969).
Goldsworthy, J, *The Sovereignty of Parliament: History and Philosophy* (Oxford, Clarendon, 1999).
Goodrich, P, 'Druids and Common Lawyers: Notes on the Pythagoras Complex and Legal Education' (2007) 1 *Law and Humanities* 1.

Bibliography

Goodrich, P, 'Eating Law: Commons, Common Land, Common Law' (1991) 12 *The Journal of Legal History* 246.

Goodrich, P, *Languages of Law: From Logics of Memory to Nomadic Masks* (London, Weidenfeld & Nicolson, 1990).

Goodrich, P, *The Laws of Love: a Brief Historical and Practical Manual* (Basingstoke, Palgrave Macmillan, 2006).

Goodrich, P, 'Legal Enigmas—Antonio de Nebrija, *The Da Vinci Code* and the Emendation of Law' (2010) 30 *Oxford Journal of Legal Studies* 71.

Goodrich, P, *Oedipus Lex: Psychoanalysis, History, Law* (Los Angeles, University of California Press, 1995).

Goodrich, P, 'Poor Illiterate Reason: History, Nationalism, Common Law' (1992) 1 *Social & Legal Studies* 7.

Goodrich, P, 'Signs Taken for Wonders: Community, Identity, and A History of Sumptuary Law' (1998) 23 *Law & Social Inquiry* 707.

Goodrich, P, 'Specula Laws: Image, Aesthetic and Common Law' (1991) 2 *Law and Critique* 233.

Goodrich, P and Carlson, D G (eds), *Law and the Postmodern Mind: Essays on Psychoanalysis and Jurisprudence* (Ann Arbor, University of Michigan Press, 1998).

Goodrich, P and Warrington, R, 'The Lost Temporality of Law: An Interview with Pierre Legendre', (tr) A Pottage (1990) 1 *Law and Critique* 3.

Gordon, D, 'A New Discovery in the Wilton Diptych' (1992) 134 *The Burlington Magazine* 662.

Gosson, S, *The Schoole of Abuse Conteining A Pleasaunt Invective Against Poets, Pipers, Plaiers, Iesters, and Such Like Caterpillers of a Comonwealth* (London, Thomas Woodcocke, 1579).

Graves, M A R, *Thomas Norton: The Parliament Man* (Oxford, Blackwell, 1994).

Greenblatt, S, *Hamlet in Purgatory* (New Jersey, Princeton University Press, 2001).

Greene, R, *Greenes Groatsworth of Wit, Bought with A Million of Repentance* (London, Henry and Moses Bell, 1637).

Greene, R, *Menaphon Camillas alarum to slumbering Euphues, in his melancholie cell at Silexedra* (London, Sampson Clarke, 1589).

Greene, R, *A Quip for an Upstart Courtier: Or, A quaint dispute between Velvet breeches and Cloth-breeches* (London, Iohn Wolfe, 1592).

Greenham, R, *The Works of the Reverend and Faithfull servant of Iesus Christ M. Richard Greenham, minister and preacher of the word of God* (London, Robert Dexter, 1599).

Griffin, B, *Playing the Past: Approaches to English Historical Drama, 1385–1600* (Woodbridge, D S Brewer, 2001).

Gurr, A, ' "Coriolanus" and the Body Politic' (1975) 28 *Shakespeare Survey* 63.

Gurr, A, *Playgoing in Shakespeare's London* (Cambridge, Cambridge University Press, 1987).

Gurr, A, *The Shakespearean Stage, 1574–1642* (Cambridge, Cambridge University Press, 1992).

Guy, J, *Christopher St German on Chancery and Statute* (London, Selden Society, 1985).

Guy, J (ed), *The Reign of Elizabeth I: Court and Culture in the Last Decade* (Cambridge, Cambridge University Press, 1995).

Guy, J, *Tudor England* (Oxford, Oxford University Press, 1990).

Guy, J (ed), *The Tudor Monarchy* (London, Arnold, 1997).

Hachamovitch, Y, 'The Ideal Object of Transmission: An essay on the faith which attaches to instruments (*de fide instrumentorum*)' (1991) 2 *Law and Critique* 85.

Hadfield, A, *Shakespeare and Renaissance Politics* (London, Arden Shakespeare, 2004).

Bibliography

Haigh, C (ed), *The Reign of Elizabeth I* (Basingstoke, Macmillan, 1984).
Haines, R M, *King Edward II: Edward of Caernarfon, His Life, His Reign, and its Aftermath, 1284–1330* (Montreal, McGill-Queen's University Press, 2003).
Hamilton, D B, 'The State of Law in *Richard II*' (1983) 34 *Shakespeare Quarterly* 5.
Hammer, P E J, 'Shakespeare's *Richard II*, the Play of 7 February 1601, and the Essex Rising' (2008) 59 *Shakespeare Quarterly* 1.
Hartley, T E (ed), *Proceedings in the Parliaments of Elizabeth 1*, 3 vols (Leicester, Leicester University Press, 1995).
Harvey, J H, 'The Wilton Diptych—A Re-examination' (1961) 98 *Archaeologia* 1.
Haynes, A, *The Elizabethan Secret Services* (Stroud, Sutton, 2004).
Hearne, T (ed), *A Collection of Curious Discourses, Written by Eminent Antiquaries Upon several Heads in our English Antiquities* (Oxford, Thomas Hearne, 1720).
Heinze, E, '"Were it not against our laws": Oppression and Resistance in Shakespeare's *Comedy of Errors*' (2009) 29 *Legal Studies* 230.
Henze, R, '*The Comedy of Errors*: A Freely Binding Chain' (1971) 22 *Shakespeare Quarterly* 35.
Hersey, G, *The Lost Meaning of Classical Architecture: Speculations on Ornament from Vitruvius to Venturi* (Cambridge, Mass, MIT Press, 1988).
Heywood, T, *An Apology for Actors* (London, Nicholas Okes, 1612).
Hibbitts, B J, 'Making Sense of Metaphors: Visuality, Aurality and the Reconfiguration of American Legal Discourse' (1994) 16 *Cardozo Law Review* 229.
Hill, C, *Society and Puritanism in Pre-Revolutionary England* (London, Mercury Books, 1966).
Hill, R F, 'The Composition of *Titus Andronicus*' (1957) 10 *Shakespeare Survey* 60.
Hobbes, T, *A Dialogue between a Philosopher and a Student of the Common Laws of England*, (ed) J Cropsey (London, University of Chicago Press, 1971).
Hobbes, T, *Leviathan*, (ed) J C A Gaskin (Oxford, Oxford University Press, 1996).
Hobday, C, 'Clouted Shoon and Leather Aprons: Shakespeare and the Egalitarian Tradition' (1979) 23 *Renaissance and Modern Studies* 63.
Hodges, D L, *Renaissance Fictions of Anatomy* (Amherst, University of Massachusetts Press, 1985).
Hoffmann, J M, *In The Beginning: A Short History of the Hebrew Language* (New York, New York University Press, 2006).
Hogge, A, *God's Secret Agents: Queen Elizabeth's Forbidden Priests and the Hatching of the Gunpowder Plot* (London, Harper Perennial, 2005).
Holderness, G (ed), *The Politics of Theatre and Drama* (London, Macmillan, 1992).
Holdsworth, W S, *A History of English Law*, 17 vols (London, Methuen, 1924).
Holland, P, 'Theseus' Shadows in *A Midsummer Night's Dream*' (1994) 47 *Shakespeare Survey* 139.
Honigmann, E A J, *The Stability of Shakespeare's Text* (London, Arnold, 1965).
Hooker, R, *A Faithful Abridgment of the Works of that Learned and Judicious Divine, Mr Richard Hooker* (London, Benjamin Bragg, 1705).
Hooker, R, *A Learned Sermon of the Nature of Pride* (London, John Barnes, 1612).
Hooker, R, *Of the Lawes of Ecclesiastical Politie* (London, William Stansbye, 1622).
Hooker, R, *Of the Laws of Ecclesiastical Polity*, (ed) A S McGrade (Cambridge, Cambridge University Press, 1989).
Hopwood, C H (ed), *Calendar of the Middle Temple Records*, 4 vols (London, Butterworths, 1903).
Hotson, J L, *Shakespeare's Sonnets Dated* (London, R Hart-Davis, 1949).

Bibliography

Howell, T B (ed), *A Complete Collection of State Trials*, 21 vols (London, Longman, 1816).
Hoyle, R W (ed), *The Estates of the English Crown, 1558–1640* (Cambridge, Cambridge University Press, 1992).
Hughes, T, *Certaine Devises and shewes presented to her Maiestie by the Gentlemen of Grayes-Inne at her Highnesse Court in Greenwich, the twenty eighth day of Februarie in the thirtieth yeare of her Maiesties most happy Raigne* (London, Robert Robinson, 1587).
Hunt, A, *Governance of the Consuming Passions: A History of Sumptuary Law* (Basingstoke, Macmillan, 1996).
Hunt, A and Wickham, G, *Foucault and Law: Towards a Sociology of Law as Governance* (London, Pluto Press, 1994).
Hunt, M, 'Slavery, English Servitude, and *The Comedy of Errors*' (1997) 27 *English Literary Renaissance* 31.
Hunter, W B, 'The First Performance of *A Midsummer Night's Dream*' (1985) 32 *Notes and Queries* 45.
Hutson, L, *The Invention of Suspicion: Law and Mimesis in Shakespeare and Renaissance Drama* (Oxford, Oxford University Press, 2007).
Hutton, R, *Blood and Mistletoe: the History of the Druids in Britain* (New Haven, Conn, Yale University Press, 2009).
Hutton, R, *The Rise and Fall of Merry England: the Ritual Year, 1400–1700* (Oxford, Oxford University Press, 1994).
Ibbetson, D, 'Sixteenth Century Contract Law: *Slade's Case* In Context' (1984) 4 *Oxford Journal of Legal Studies* 295.
Ingram, M, *Church Courts, Sex and Marriage in England, 1570–1640* (Cambridge, Cambridge University Press, 1987).
Jackson, B S, *Law, Fact and Narrative Coherence* (Roby, Deborah Charles, 1988).
James, H, *Shakespeare's Troy: Drama, Politics and the Translation of Empire* (Cambridge, Cambridge University Press, 1997).
Jardine, L and Stewart, A, *Hostage to Fortune: The Troubled Life of Francis Bacon* (London, Gollancz, 1998).
Johnson, R C, Keeler, M F, Jansson Cole, M and Bidwell, W B (eds), *Proceedings in Parliament 1628*, 6 vols (New Haven, Conn, Yale University Press, 1977).
Johnson, S (ed), *The Plays of William Shakespeare*, 8 vols (London, J and R Tonson, 1765).
Jones, W J, *The Elizabethan Court of Chancery* (Oxford, Oxford University Press, 1967).
Jonson, B, 'A Particular Entertainment of the Queen and Prince at Althorpe: A Satyr' in *The Works of Ben Jonson. In six volumes. Adorn'd with cuts*, 6 vols (London, J Walthoe, M Wotton, 1716–17) vol 3.
Jordan, C and Cunningham, K (eds), *The Law in Shakespeare* (Basingstoke, Palgrave Macmillan, 2007).
Jung, C G, *Memories, Dreams, Reflections*, (tr) R and C Winston, (ed) A Jaffé (London, Fontana, 1983).
Kafka, F, *Franz Kafka: Stories, 1904–1924*, (tr) J A Underwood (London, Abacus, 1995).
Kahn, V and Hutson, L (eds), *Rhetoric and Law in Early Modern Europe* (New Haven, Conn, Yale University Press, 2001).
Kantorowicz, E H, *The King's Two Bodies: A Study in Medieval Political Theology* (New Jersey, Princeton University Press, 1957).
Kantorowicz, E H, *Selected Studies* (New York, J J Augustin, 1965).
Kastan, D S, 'Proud Majesty Made a Subject: Shakespeare and the Spectacle of Rule' (1986) 37 *Shakespeare Quarterly* 459.

Bibliography

Kastan, D S and Stallybrass, P (eds), *Staging the Renaissance: Reinterpretations of Elizabethan and Jacobean Drama* (London, Routledge, 1991).

Keeton, G, *Shakespeare's Legal and Political Background* (London, Sir Isaac Pitman & Sons, 1917).

Kermode, F, *Shakespeare's Language* (London, Penguin, 2000).

Kliger, S, *The Goths in England: a Study in Seventeenth and Eighteenth Century Thought* (Cambridge, Mass, Harvard University Press, 1952).

Klinck, D R, *Conscience, Equity and the Court of Chancery in Early Modern England* (Farnham, Ashgate, 2010).

Klinck, D R, 'Shakespeare's *Richard II* as Landlord and Wasting Tenant' (1998) 25 *College Literature* 21.

Klinck, D R, '"This Other Eden": Lord Denning's Pastoral Vision' (1994) 14 *Oxford Journal of Legal Studies* 25.

Knafla, L A, *Law and Politics in Jacobean England: The Tracts of Lord Chancellor Ellesmere* (Cambridge, Cambridge University Press, 1977).

Kornstein, D J, *Kill All The Lawyers? Shakespeare's Legal Appeal* (Lincoln, University of Nebraska Press, 2005).

Kott, J, *Shakespeare Our Contemporary* (New York, W W Norton & Co, 1974).

Kraye, J (ed), *The Cambridge Companion to Renaissance Humanism* (Cambridge, Cambridge University Press, 1996).

L, F, 'Queen Elizabeth and Richard II' (1913) 7 *Notes and Queries* 6.

Lacan, J, *Écrits*, (tr) B Fink (New York, W W Norton & Co, 2006).

Lacan, J, The Ethics of Psychoanalysis 1959–1960: the Seminar of Jacques Lacan. Book 7, (tr) D Porter, (ed) J-A Miller (London, Routledge, 1992).

Lacan, J, The Four Fundamental Concepts of Psycho-analysis, (ed) J-A Miller, (tr) A Sheridan (Harmondsworth, Penguin, 1979).

Lacan, J, *The Seminar of Jacques Lacan. Book 2*, (tr) S Tomaselli, (ed) J-A Miller (Cambridge, Cambridge University Press, 1988).

Lake, P, *Anglicans and Puritans? Presbyterianism and English Conformist Thought from Whitgift to Hooker* (London, Unwin Hymen, 1988).

Lake, P, 'Puritan Identities' (1984) 35 *The Journal of Ecclesiastical History* 112.

Lambard, W, *Archeion, Or, A Discourse Upon the High Courts of Iustice in England* (London, Henry Seile, 1635).

Lambard, W, *The Dueties of Constables, Borsholders, Tythingmen, and such other lowe and Lay Ministers of the Peace* (London, Thomas Wight, 1602).

Lambard, W, *Eirenarcha: or of The office of the Iustices of the peace, in two Bookes: Gathered 1579, and now revised, and first published, in the 24. yeere of the peaceable reigne of our gratious Queene Elizabeth* (London, Assigns of Richard Tottell and Chr Barker, 1582).

Larkin, J F and Hughes, P L (eds), *Stuart Royal Proclamations*, 2 vols (Oxford, Clarendon, 1973).

Larner, C, *Witchcraft and Religion: the Politics of Popular Belief*, (ed) A Macfarlane (Oxford, Blackwell, 1984).

Lawrence, W J, *The Elizabethan Playhouse and Other Studies* (Stratford-upon-Avon, Shakespeare Head Press, 1912).

Legendre, P, *Le Désir politique de dieu: Etude sur les montages de l'état et du droit* (Paris, Fayard, 1989).

Legendre, P, *L'Inestimable Objet de la Transmission: Etude sur le principe généalogique en Occident* (Paris, Fayard, 1985).

Bibliography

Legendre, P, *Law and the Unconscious: a Legendre Reader*, (tr) P Goodrich, with A Pottage and A Schütz, (ed) P Goodrich, (Basingstoke, Macmillan, 1997).

Legh, G, *The Accedens of Armory* (London, Richard Tottill, 1562).

Leimon, M and Parker, G, 'Treason and Plot in Elizabethan Diplomacy: The "Fame of Sir Edward Stafford" Reconsidered' (1996) 111 *The English Historical Review* 1134.

Levack, B P, *The Civil Lawyers in England, 1603–1641: a Political Study* (Oxford, Clarendon, 1973).

Levack, B P, *The Witch-Hunt in Early Modern Europe* (Harlow, Pearson Longman, 2006).

Levine, L, 'Men in Women's Clothing: Anti-theatricality and Effeminization from 1579 to 1642' (1986) 28 *Criticism* 121.

Lewis, C, '"Dark Deeds Darkly Answered": Duke Vincentio and Judgment in *Measure for Measure*' (1983) 34 *Shakespeare Quarterly* 271.

Lewis, E, 'King Above Law? "Quod Principi Placuit" in Bracton' (1964) 39 *Speculum* 240.

Lindley, L (ed), *The Court Masque* (Manchester, Manchester University Press, 1984).

Loengard, J S, 'An Elizabethan Lawsuit: John Brayne, his Carpenter, and the Building of the Red Lion Theatre' (1983) 34 *Shakespeare Quarterly* 298.

Lupton, T, *The second part and knitting up of the boke entitled Too good to be true* (London, Henry Binneman, 1581).

Macfarlane, A, *Witchcraft in Tudor and Stuart England: a Regional and Comparative Study* (London, Routledge & Kegan Paul, 1970).

Machiavelli, N, *The Prince* (tr) G Bull (London, Penguin, 2003).

Macintyre, A, *After Virtue: a Study in Moral Theory* (London, Duckworth, 1981).

Mack, P, *Elizabethan Rhetoric: Theory and Practice* (Cambridge, Cambridge University Press, 2002).

Maclean, I, *Interpretation and Meaning in the Renaissance: The Case of Law* (Cambridge, Cambridge University Press, 1992).

Madden, D H, *The Diary of Master William Silence, a Study of Shakespeare and of Elizabethan Sport* (New York, Longmans, Green & Co, 1907).

Maine, H, *Ancient Law* (London, Dent, 1917).

Maitland, F W, *English Law and the Renaissance* (Cambridge, Cambridge University Press, 1901).

Manning, R B, *Village Revolts: Social Protest and Popular Disturbances in England, 1509–1640* (Oxford, Clarendon, 1988).

Manningham, J, *The Diary of John Manningham of the Middle Temple* (London, Camden Society, 1885).

Manuel, F E and Manuel, F P, *Utopian Thought in the Western World* (Oxford, Blackwell, 1979).

Marin, L, *Portrait of the King*, (tr) M M Houle (Basingstoke, Macmillan, 1988).

Marston, J, *Histrio-Mastix Or, The Player Whipt!* (London, T Thorp, 1610).

Matthews, W H, *Mazes and Labyrinths: their History and Development* (New York, Dover Publications, 1970).

McAlindon, T, *Shakespeare's Tudor History: A Study of Henry IV, Parts 1 and 2* (Aldershot, Ashgate, 2001).

McGrade, A S (ed), *Richard Hooker and the Construction of Christian Community* (Binghampton, Medieval & Renaissance Texts & Studies, 1997).

McMillan, S and MacLean, S-B, *The Queen's Men and their Plays* (Cambridge, Cambridge University Press, 1998).

Mertes, K, *The English Noble Household, 1250–1600: Good Governance and Political Rule* (Oxford, Blackwell, 1988).
Miles, C A, *Christmas in Ritual and Tradition, Christian and Pagan* (London, T F Unwin, 1912).
Mill, J S and Bentham, J, *Utilitarianism and Other Essays*, (ed) A Ryan (London, Penguin, 2004).
Milton, J, *The Readie & Easie Way To Establish a Free Commonwealth*, 1659 (Thomason Tracts E 1016 [11]).
Montaigne, M de, *The Complete Essays*, (tr) and (ed) M A Screech (London, Penguin, 2003).
Montrose, L A, '"Shaping Fantasies": Figurations of Gender and Power in Elizabethan Culture' (1983) 2 *Representations* 61.
Moore, T, 'Recycling Aristotle: The Sovereignty Theory of Richard Hooker' (1993) 19 *History of Political Thought* 345.
More, T, *A fruteful and pleasant worke of the beste state of a publique weale, and of the new yle called Utopia*, (tr) R Robinson (London, Abraham Vele, 1551).
Morrill, J, *The Nature of the English Revolution* (London, Longman, 1993).
Morrill, J, Slack, P, and Woolf, D (eds), *Public Duty and Private Conscience in Seventeenth-Century England: Essays Presented to GE Aylmer* (Oxford, Clarendon, 1993).
Mortimer, I, 'The Death of Edward II in Berkeley Castle' (2005) 120 *The English Historical Review* 1175.
Morton, A L, *The English Utopia* (London, Lawrence & Wishart, 1952).
Mukherji, S, *Law and Representation in Early Modern Drama* (Cambridge, Cambridge University Press, 2006).
Muldrew, C, *The Economy of Obligation: the Culture of Credit and Social Relations in Early Modern England* (Basingstoke, Macmillan, 1998).
Mundy, A, *The Triumphes of re-united Britania* (London, W Jaggard, 1605).
Myers, A R, *Crown, Household and Parliament in Fifteenth-Century England* (London, Hambledon, 1985).
Nalson, J (ed), *The Trial of Charles the First, King of England, before the High Court of Justice* (Oxford, R Walker and W Jackson, 1746).
Nashe, T, *The Anatomie of Absurditie* (London, Thomas Hacker, 1589).
Nashe, T, *The Terrors of the night Or, A Discourse of Apparitions* (London, William Iones, 1594).
Neale, J E, *Elizabeth I and her Parliaments, 1584–1601*, 2 vols (London, Cape, 1965).
Needham, H A (ed), Sidney, *An Apology For Poetry*; Shelley, *A Defence of Poetry* (London, Ginn & Co, 1931).
Newlands, C E, *Statius' Silvae and the Poetics of Empire* (Cambridge, Cambridge University Press, 2010).
Newman, R A (ed), *Equity in the World's Legal Systems* (Brussels, Établissements Émile Bruylant, 1973).
Nicholl, C, *The Lodger: Shakespeare on Silver Street* (London, Allen Lane, 2007).
Nicholls, M, 'Sir Walter Ralegh's Treason: A Prosecution Document' (1995) 110 *The English Historical Review* 902.
Nicholls, M, 'Treason's Reward: The Punishment of Conspirators in the Bye Plot of 1603' (1995) 38 *The Historical Journal* 821.
Nicholls, M, 'Two Winchester Trials: The Prosecution of Henry Brooke, Lord Cobham, and Thomas Lord Grey of Wilton, 1603' (1995) 68 *Historical Research* 26.

Bibliography

Nichols, J G (ed), 'Two Sermons Preached by the Boy-Bishop, One at at St Paul's, Temp. Henry VIII., the Other at Gloucester, Temp. Mary', 7 [New Series XIV] *The Camden Miscellany* (London, The Camden Society, 1875) 1.

Nietzsche, F, *The Birth of Tragedy*, (tr) W A Haussmann (Edinburgh, Foulis, 1909).

Nietzsche, F, *The Genealogy of Morals*, (tr) HB Samuel (New York, Boni and Liveright, 1913).

Norbrook, D, 'The Emperor's New Body? *Richard II*, Ernst Kantorowicz, and the Politics of Shakespeare Criticism' (1996) 10 *Textual Practice* 329.

Norton, D, *A Textual History of The King James Bible* (Cambridge, Cambridge University Press, 2005).

Norton, T and Sackville, T, *The Tragidie of Ferrex and Porrex, set forth without addition or alteration but altogether as the same was shewed on stage before the Queenes Maiestie, about nine years past, vz. the xviii day of Ianuarie. 1561. by the gentlemen of the Inner Temple* (London, Iohn Daye, 1570).

Nussbaum, M, *Poetic Justice: the Literary Imagination and Public Life* (Boston, Mass, Beacon Press, 1995).

Nuttall, A D, ' "Measure for Measure": The Bed-Trick' (1975) 28 *Shakespeare Survey* 51.

Nuttall, A D, '*A Midsummer Night's Dream*: Comedy as *Apotrope* of Myth' (2000) 53 *Shakespeare Survey* 49.

Nuttall, A D, *Shakespeare the Thinker* (New Haven, Conn, Yale University Press, 2007).

Nuttall, J, *The Creation of Lancastrian Kingship: Literature, Language and Politics in Late Medieval England* (Cambridge, Cambridge University Press, 2007).

Orgel, S, *The Illusion of Power* (Berkeley, University of California Press, 1975).

Outhwaite, R B, *Clandestine Marriage in England, 1500–1850* (London, Hambledon, 1995).

Outhwaite, R B, *The Rise and Fall of the English Ecclesiastical Courts, 1500–1860* (Cambridge, Cambridge University Press, 2006).

Ovid, *Metamorphoses*, (tr) D Raeburn (London, Penguin, 2004).

Palmer, D W, *Writing Russia in the Age of Shakespeare* (Aldershot, Ashgate, 2004).

Patterson, A, *Censorship and Interpretation: The Conditions of Writing and Reading in Early Modern England* (Madison, University of Wisconsin Press, 1984).

Patterson, A, *Shakespeare and the Popular Voice* (Cambridge, Basil Blackwell, 1989).

Peacham, H, *The Garden of Eloquence, Conteining the Most Excellent Ornaments, Exornations, Lightes, flowers and formes of speech, commonly called the Figures of Rhetorike* (London, H Iackson, 1593).

Petrasancta, S, *Tesserae Gentilitiae* (Rome, 1638).

Pettet, E C, '*Coriolanus* and the Midlands Insurrection of 1607' (1950) 3 *Shakespeare Survey* 34.

Pettitt, T, ' "Here comes I, Jack Straw": English Folk Drama and Social Revolt' (1984) 95 *Folklore* 3.

Pinciss, G M, 'The Queen's Men, 1583–1592' (1970) 11 *Theatre Survey* 50.

Plato, *Gorgias, Menexenus, Protagoras*, (tr) T Griffith, (ed) M Schofield (Cambridge, Cambridge University Press, 2010).

Plato, *The Laws*, (tr) T J Saunders (London, Penguin, 2004).

Plato, *The Republic* (tr) D Lee (London, Penguin, 1987).

Pleij, H, *Dreaming of Cockaigne: Medieval Fantasies of the Perfect Life* (New York, Columbia University Press, 2001).

Plowden, E, *The Commentaries or Reports of Edmund Plowden*, 2 vols (Dublin, H Watts, 1792).

Bibliography

Plutarch, *The Lives of the Noble Grecians and Romanes, Compared together by that grave learned Philosopher and Historiographer, Plutarke of Chaeronea: Translated out of Greeke into French by IAMES AMYOT, Abbot of Bellozane, Bishop of Auxerre, one of the Kings privy counsel, and great Amner of Fraunce, and out of French into Englishe, by Thomas North* (London, Thomas Vautroullier, 1579).

Plutarch, *Lives I: Theseus and Romulus; Lycurgus and Numa; Solon and Publicola*, (tr) B Perrin (Cambridge, Mass, Harvard University Press, 1914).

Pocock, J G A, *The Ancient Constitution and the Feudal Law: A Study of English Historical Thought in the Seventeenth Century* (Cambridge, Cambridge University Press, 1987).

Pocock, J G A, *The Machiavellian Moment: Florentine Political Thought and the Atlantic Republican Tradition* (New Jersey, Princeton University Press, 2003).

Pollock, F and Maitland, F W, *The History of English Law Before the Time of Edward I*, 2 vols (Cambridge, Cambridge University Press, 1898).

Pope, E M, 'The Renaissance Background of *Measure for Measure*' (1949) 2 *Shakespeare Survey* 66.

Powell, D, 'Coke in Context: Early Modern Legal Observation and Sir Edward Coke's Reports' (2000) 21 *The Journal of Legal History* 33.

Prest, W R, *The Inns of Court Under Elizabeth I and the Early Stuarts, 1590–1640* (London, Longman, 1972).

Prest, W R, *The Rise of the Barristers: A Social History of the English Bar, 1590–1640* (Oxford, Clarendon, 1986).

Prynne, W, *Histrio-Mastix: The Players Scourge, or, Actors Tragedie* (London, Michael Sparke, 1633).

Puttenham, G, *The Arte of English Poesie. Contrived into three Bookes: The first of Poets and Poesie, the second of Proportion, the third of Ornament* (London, Richard Field, 1589).

Raffield, P, 'Contract, Classicism, and the Common-Weal: Coke's *Reports* and the Foundations of the Modern English Constitution' (2005) 17 *Law & Literature* 69.

Raffield, P, 'A Discredited Priesthood: The Failings of Common Lawyers and Their Representation in Seventeenth Century Satirical Drama' (2005) 17 *Law & Literature* 365.

Raffield, P, *Images and Cultures of Law in Early Modern England: Justice and Political Power, 1558–1660* (Cambridge, Cambridge University Press, 2004).

Raffield, P, '*Lex facit regem v Quod principi placuit*: Dramatic Symbols of Crown and Common Law' (1999) 20 *The Journal of Legal History* 45.

Raffield, P, 'Reformation, Regulation and the Image: Sumptuary Legislation and the Subject of Law' (2002) 13 *Law & Critique* 127.

Raffield, P, 'The Separate Art Worlds of Dreamland and Drunkenness: Elizabethan Revels at the Inns of Court' (1997) 8 *Law and Critique* 163.

Raffield, P and Watt, G (eds), *Shakespeare and the Law* (Oxford, Hart Publishing, 2008).

Rappaport, S, *Worlds Within Worlds: Structures of Life in Sixteenth-Century London* (Cambridge, Cambridge University Press, 1989).

Rastall, W, *Collection in English of the Statutes now in force* (London, Deputies of C Barker, 1594).

Ravenscroft, E, *The English Lawyer; a Comedy* (London, James Vade, 1678).

Read, C, *Mr Secretary Walsingham and the Policy of Queen Elizabeth*, 3 vols (New York, AMS Press, 1978).

Renaker, D, 'Robert Burton and Ramist Method' (1971) 24 *Renaissance Quarterly* 210.

Rice, D W, *The Life and Achievements of Sir John Popham, 1531–1607* (New Jersey, Fairleigh Dickinson University Press, 2005).

Bibliography

Riess, A J and Williams, G W, '"Tragical Mirth": From *Romeo* to *Dream*' (1992) 43 *Shakespeare Quarterly* 214.
Roe, J, *Shakespeare and Machiavelli* (Cambridge, D S Brewer, 2002).
Ross, C D, 'Forfeiture for Treason in the Reign of Richard II' (1956) 71 *The English Historical Review* 560.
Russell, C, *The Causes of the English Civil War* (Oxford, Clarendon, 1990).
Russell, M J, 'Trial by Battle in the Court of Chivalry' (2008) 29 *The Journal of Legal History* 335.
Rust, J R, 'Political Theology and Shakespeare Studies' (2009) 6 *Literature Compass* 175.
Sales, R, *English Literature in History 1780–1830: Pastoral and Politics* (New York, St Martin's Press, 1983).
St German, C, *Dialogues Between a Doctor of Divinity and a Student in the Laws of England*, (ed) W Muchall (Cincinnati, Ohio, Robert Clarke, 1874).
Salmon, T (ed), *A Collection of Proceedings and Trials against State Prisoners* (London, J Wilcox, 1741).
Sanders, N, 'The True Prince and the False Thief: Prince Hal and the Shift of Identity' (1977) 30 *Shakespeare Survey* 29.
Saul, N, *Richard II* (New Haven, Conn, Yale University Press, 1999).
Saul, N, 'Richard II and the Vocabulary of Kingship' (1995) 110 *The English Historical Review* 854.
Sawday, J, *The Body Emblazoned: Dissection and the Human Body in Renaissance Culture* (London, Routledge, 1995).
Schanzer, E, 'The Marriage-Contracts in *Measure for Measure*' (1960) 13 *Shakespeare Survey* 81.
Schanzer, E, *The Problem Plays of Shakespeare: a Study of 'Julius Caesar', 'Measure for Measure' and 'Antony and Cleopatra'* (London, Routledge & Kegan Paul, 1963).
Schleiner, W, 'Imaginative Sources for Shakespeare's Puck' (1985) 36 *Shakespeare Quarterly* 65.
Schuster, L A (ed), *The Yale Edition of the Complete Works of St Thomas More*, 15 vols (New Haven, Conn, Yale University Press, 1973).
Scot, R, *The discoverie of witchcraft wherein the lewd dealing of witches and witchmongers is notablie detected* (London, William Brome, 1584).
Scott, W, *Secret History of the Court of James I*, 2 vols (Edinburgh, John Ballantyne, 1811).
Selden, J, *The Reverse or Back-Face of the English Janus*, (tr) R Westcot (London, Thomas Basset & Richard Chiswell, 1682).
Selden, J, *Table-talk* (London, Jacob Tonson, Awnsham and John Churchill, 1696).
Selden, J, *Titles of Honor* (London, Iohn Helme, 1614).
Shakespeare, W, *As You Like It*, (ed) H J Oliver (Harmondsworth, Penguin, 1968).
Shakespeare, W, *The Comedy of Errors*, (ed) R A Foakes (London, Arden Shakespeare, 1962).
Shakespeare, W, *The Comedy of Errors*, (ed) C Whitworth (Oxford, Oxford University Press, 2002).
Shakespeare, W, *The Comedy of Errors*, (ed) S Wells (Harmondsworth, Penguin, 1972).
Shakespeare, W, *Hamlet*, (ed) H Jenkins (London, Arden Shakespeare, 1982).
Shakespeare, W, *King Henry IV, Part 2*, (ed) A R Humphreys (London, Arden Shakespeare, 1981).
Shakespeare, W, *King Richard II*, (ed) C R Forker (London, Arden Shakespeare, 2002).
Shakespeare, W, *King Richard II*, (ed) A Gurr (Cambridge, Cambridge University Press, 2003).

Bibliography

Shakespeare, W, *Measure for Measure*, (ed) N W Bawcutt (Oxford, Oxford University Press, 1994).
Shakespeare, W, *Measure for Measure*, (ed) B Gibbons (Cambridge, Cambridge University Press, 2006).
Shakespeare, W, *The Merchant of Venice*, (ed) J R Brown (London, Arden Shakespeare, 2006).
Shakespeare, W, *A Midsummer Night's Dream*, (ed) R A Foakes (Cambridge, Cambridge University Press, 2003).
Shakespeare, W, *A Midsummer Night's Dream* (ed) P Holland (Oxford, Oxford University Press, 2008).
Shakespeare, W, *A Midsummer Night's Dream*, (ed) S Wells (Harmondsworth, Penguin, 1967).
Shakespeare, W, *The Most Lamentable Romaine Tragedie of Titus Andronicus* (London, Edward White & Thomas Millington, 1594).
Shakespeare, W, *The Tempest*, (ed) A Barton (London, Penguin, 1968).
Shakespeare, W, *Titus Andronicus*, (ed) J Bate (London, Arden Shakespeare, 1995).
Shakespeare, W, *William Shakespeare: The Complete Works*, (eds) S Wells and G Taylor (Oxford, Clarendon, 2005).
Shakespeare, W, *The Winter's Tale*, (ed) J H P Pafford (London, Arden, 1963).
Shapiro, B, 'Codification of the Laws in Seventeenth Century England' (1974) *Wisconsin Law Review* 428.
Shapiro, J, *Contested Will: Who Wrote Shakespeare?* (London, Faber, 2010).
Sharpe, J A, *Crime in Early Modern England, 1550–1750* (London, Longman, 1999).
Sharpe, J A, *Early Modern England: A Social History 1550–1760* (London, Arnold, 1987).
Sharpe, K, *Politics and Ideas in Early Stuart England* (London, Pinter Publishing, 1989).
Sharpe, K, *Selling the Tudor Monarchy: Authority and Image in 16th-Century England* (New Haven, Conn, Yale University Press, 2009).
Shaughnessy, R (ed), *The Cambridge Companion to Shakespeare and Popular Culture* (Cambridge, Cambridge University Press, 2007).
Shelley, P B, *Selected Poems: Percy Bysshe Shelley*, (ed) E Blunden (London, Collins, 1954).
Shriver, F, 'Hampton Court Re-Visited: James I and the Puritans' (1982) 33 *The Journal of Ecclesiastical History* 48.
Shuger, D K, *Political Theologies in Shakespeare's England: The Sacred and the State in 'Measure for Measure'* (Basingstoke, Palgrave, 2001).
Simpson, A W B, *A History of the Common Law of Contract: the Rise of the Action of Assumpsit* (Oxford, Clarendon, 1975).
Skyrme, T, *A History of the Justices of the Peace* (Chichester, Barry Rose, 1991).
Slack, P (ed), *Rebellion, Popular Protest and the Social Order in Early Modern England* (Cambridge, Cambridge University Press, 1984).
Smith, C S, *The National Portrait Gallery* (London, National Portrait Gallery, 2000).
Smith, E, 'The Shakespeare Authorship Debate Revisited' (2008) 5 *Literature Compass* 618.
Smith, T, *De Republica Anglorum*, (ed) M Dewar (Cambridge, Cambridge University Press, 1982).
Sokol, B J and Sokol, M, *Shakespeare's Legal Language: A Dictionary* (London, Athlone, 2000).
Solly-Flood, F, 'The Story of Prince Henry of Monmouth and Chief-Justice Gascoign', (1886) 3 *Transactions of the Royal Historical Society* 47.
Sommerville, J P (ed), *Filmer: Patriarcha and Other Writings* (Cambridge, Cambridge University Press, 1991).

Bibliography

Sommerville, J P (ed), *James VI and I: Political Writings* (Cambridge, Cambridge University Press, 1994).
Sommerville, J P, *Politics and Ideology in England, 1603–1640* (London, Longman, 1986).
Sophocles, *The Theban Plays*, (tr) E F Watling (Harmondsworth, Penguin, 1947).
Spedding, J (ed), *The Letters and Life of Francis Bacon*, 7 vols (London, Longman, 1869–74).
Spedding, J, Ellis, R L and Heath, D D (eds), *The Works of Francis Bacon*, 14 vols (London, Longmans, 1857-74).
Spelman, H, *The English Works of Sir Henry Spelman, Kt. Published in his life-time; together with his posthumous works, Relating to the Laws and Antiquity of England*, 2 vols (London, D Browne, 1723).
Spelman, H, *Of the Law Terms: A Discourse* (London, Gillyflower, 1684).
Spencer, B T, '2 *Henry IV* and the Theme of Time' (1944) 13 *University of Toronto Quarterly* 397.
Spenser, E, *The Faerie Queene*, (ed) T P Roche, Jr (London, Penguin, 1987).
Stevenson, D L, *The Achievement of Shakespeare's 'Measure for Measure'* (New York, Cornell University Press, 1966).
Stewart, D J, 'Falstaff the Centaur' (1977) 28 *Shakespeare Quarterly* 5.
Stolleis, M, *The Eye of the Law: Two Essays on Legal History* (Abingdon, Birkbeck Law Press, 2009).
Stone, L, *Road to Divorce, 1530–1987* (Oxford, Oxford University Press, 1990).
Stone, L, *The Family, Sex and Marriage in England 1500–1800* (London, Penguin, 1979).
Stow, J, *The Annales or Generall Chronicle of England* (London, Thomas Adams, 1615).
Stow, J, *A Survey of London, Written in the Year 1598* (Stroud, Sutton, 2005).
Streitberger, W R (ed), *Collections Volume XIII: Jacobean and Caroline Revels Accounts, 1603–1642* (Oxford, The Malone Society, 1986).
Strong, R, *Art and Power: Renaissance Festivals 1450–1650* (Berkeley, University of California Press, 1984).
Strong, R, *Gloriana: The Portraits of Queen Elizabeth I* (London, Pimlico, 2003).
Stubbes, P, *The Anatomie of Abuses* (London, Richard Iones, 1583).
Swinburne, H, *A Treatise of spousals, or matrimonial contracts* (London, Robert Clavell, 1686).
Tacitus, C, *Dialogus de Oratoribus* (tr) W Peterson (Cambridge, Mass, Harvard University Press, 1970).
Tanner, J R (ed), *Constitutional Documents of the Reign of James I, AD 1603–1625* (Cambridge, Cambridge University Press, 1930).
Tarver, A, *Church Court Records: An Introduction for Family and Local Historians* (Chichester, Phillimore, 1995).
Tawney, R H, *Religion and the Rise of Capitalism* (Harmondsworth, Penguin, 1984).
Taylor, A B, 'Golding's Ovid, Shakespeare's "Small Latin", and the Real Object of Mockery in "Pyramus and Thisbe"' (1990) 42 *Shakespeare Survey* 53.
The Holy Bible: Authorised King James Version (London, Lutterworth Press, 1949).
The Holy Bible: Revised Standard Version (London, Catholic Truth Society, 1966).
The New English Bible: With The Apocrypha (Oxford, Oxford University Press, 1970).
Thomas, G W, 'Equity and Lord Keeper John Williams' (1976) 91 *The English Historical Review* 506.
Thompson, E P, *Customs in Common* (London, Merlin, 1991).
Thompson, E P, *The Making of the English Working Class* (London, Victor Gollancz, 1980).
Tillyard, E M W, *Shakespeare's History Plays* (London, Chatto & Windus, 1944).

Bibliography

Trevelyan, G M, *English Social History: A Survey of Six Centuries from Chaucer to Queen Victoria* (London, Longman's, Green & Co, 1942).
Tubbs, J W, *The Common Law Mind: Medieval and Early Modern Conceptions* (Baltimore, Md, Johns Hopkins University Press, 2000).
Tucker, E F J, *Intruder into Eden: Representations of the Common Lawyer in English Literature 1350–1750* (Columbia, SC, Camden House, 1984).
Vesalius, A, *De humani corporis fabrica librorum epitome* (Basle, 1543).
Vickers, B, *Shakespeare, Co-Author: A Historical Study of Five Collaborative Plays* (Oxford, Oxford University Press, 2002).
Walker, D P, *Unclean Spirits: Possession and Exorcism in the Late Sixteenth and Early Seventeenth Centuries* (London, Scolar Press, 1981).
Walker, J D (ed), *Black Books of Lincoln's Inn*, 5 vols (London, Lincoln's Inn, 1897).
Walker, S, 'Rumour, Sedition and Popular Protest in the Reign of Henry IV', (2000) 166 *Past & Present* 31.
Walter, J, 'A "Rising of the People"? The Oxfordshire Rising of 1596' (1985) 107 *Past & Present* 90.
Walters, M D, 'St German on Reason and Parliamentary Sovereignty' (2003) 62 *Cambridge Law Journal* 335.
Walton, I, 'The Life of Mr Richard Hooker' in *The Works of that Learned and Judicious Divine, Mr Richard Hooker* (London, R Scot, 1670).
Ward, I, *An Introduction to Critical Legal Theory* (London, Cavendish, 1998).
Ward, I, *Shakespeare and the Legal Imagination* (London, Butterworths, 1999).
Ward, I, *A State of Mind? The English Constitution and the Popular Imagination* (Stroud, Sutton, 2000).
Waterhous, E, *Fortescutus Illustratus, Or A Commentary On That Nervous Treatise De Laudibus Legum Angliae* (London, Thomas Dicas, 1663).
Watt, G, *Equity Stirring: the Story of Justice Beyond Law* (Oxford, Hart Publishing, 2009).
Weber, M, *The Protestant Ethic and the Spirit of Capitalism*, (tr) T Parsons (London, Routledge, 1992).
Webster, J, *John Webster: Three Plays*, (ed) D Gunby (Harmondsworth, Penguin, 1972).
Weimann, R, *Shakespeare and the Popular Tradition in the Theater: Studies in the Social Dimension of Dramatic Form and Function*, (tr) & (ed) R Schwartz (Baltimore, Md, Johns Hopkins University Press, 1978).
Weisberg, R, *Poethics: And Other Strategies Of Law And Literature* (New York, Columbia University Press, 1992).
Welsford, E, *The Court Masque: a Study in the Relationship between Poetry and the Revels* (Cambridge, Cambridge University Press, 1927).
Wentersdorf, K P, 'The Marriage Contracts in "Measure for Measure": A Reconsideration' (1980) 32 *Shakespeare Survey* 129.
West, W N, '"But this will be a mere confusion": Real and Represented Confusions on the Elizabethan Stage' (2008) 60 *Theatre Journal* 217.
Wharton, T F (ed), *The Drama of John Marston: Critical Re-Visions* (Cambridge, Cambridge University Press, 2000).
Whetstone, G, *A Mirour For Magestrates Of Cyties* (London, Richard Iones, 1584).
Whetstone, G, *The right excellent and famous historye, of Promos and Cassandra* (London, Richard Ihones, 1578).
White, J B, *Heracles' Bow: Essays on the Rhetoric and Poetics of the Law* (Madison, University of Wisconsin Press, 1985).

Bibliography

White, S D, *Sir Edward Coke and the Grievances of the Commonwealth* (Manchester, Manchester University Press, 1979).

Whitgift, J, *The defense of the aunswere to the Admonition, against the replie of T.C.* (London, Henry Binneman, 1574).

Whitman, W, *Leaves of Grass*, (ed) J Loving (Oxford, Oxford University Press, 2009).

Williams, I, '*Dr Bonham's Case* and "void" statutes' (2006) 27 *The Journal of Legal History* 111.

Williams, P, *The Later Tudors: England 1547–1603* (Oxford, Oxford University Press, 1998).

Willymat, W, *A Loyal Subiects Looking-Glasse, Or A good subiects Direction, necessary and requisite for every good Christian* (London, Robert Boulton, 1604).

Wilson, L, 'Ben Jonson and the Law of Contract' (1993) 5 *Cardozo Studies in Law and Literature* 281.

Wilson, R, *Secret Shakespeare: Studies in Theatre, Religion and Resistance* (Manchester, Manchester University Press, 2004).

Wilson, T, *The Arte of Rhetorique* (London, George Robinson, 1585).

Wilson, T, 'The State of England, Anno Dom. 1600' in F J Fisher (ed), 16 *The Camden Miscellany* (London, Offices of the Society, 1936) 1.

Wood, M, *In Search of Shakespeare* (London, BBC Worldwide, 2003).

Worden, B, 'Which Play Was Performed at the Globe Theatre on 7 February 1601?' (10 July 2003) 25 *London Review of Books* 22.

Wormald, F, 'The Wilton Diptych' (1954) 17 *Journal of the Warburg and Courtauld Institutes* 191.

Yates, F A, *Astraea: The Imperial Theme in the Sixteenth Century* (London, Routledge & Kegan Paul, 1975).

Žižek, S, *The Plague of Fantasies* (London, Verso, 1997).

Zurcher, A, *Shakespeare and Law* (London, Arden Shakespeare, Forthcoming).

INDEX

absolutism:
    Acts of Supremacy, 20, 25, 26
    France, 163–4
    James I, 17, 190
    Measure for Measure, 17, 203–4, 219
    Richard II, 10, 86
    thematic focus on, 13–14
    Titus Andronicus, 18–29
    trend, 9, 10, 91
actors:
    Coke on, 28
    lawyers as, 11
    puritanism and, 211
Adlington, William, 136
adultery, 204, 208–9
Aegeus, 138
Aeneas, 34, 36
Aethra, 138
allegory, 19–20
Altham, James, 187
angels, 140–2
Anne of Bohemia, 82, 83, 85
Anne of Denmark, 126–7, 130–1
antirrhesis, 39
Apollo, 118
Apuleius, 136, 137
Aquinas, Thomas, 34, 46, 91
Arcadia, 118, 126, 129
Ariadne, 137
Aristotle:
    amici principis, 34
    city-state, 31
    civic republicanism, 25
    Coke and, 133
    community, 6, 9, 31, 34, 108, 112, 121, 171–2, 219
    equity, 216
    humanism and, 177, 178
    ideal state, 6, 14, 101
    judges as poets, 100
    justice, 121, 133, 171
    koinonia, 219
    natural law, 173
Artemidorus of Daldis, 127–8
Arthur, King, 40, 178
As You Like it, 1
assumpsit, 53, 55–8, 205
Astrea (goddess of justice), 23–4, 29, 36, 50, 111, 152, 183

Athens, 6, 10, 15, 30, 74, 126, 131, 134, 137, 138, 146, 178
Augustine of Hippo, Saint, 34
Aylmer, Bishop, 25

Bacon, Francis, 8, 80, 81, 132–3, 171, 201–2
Baker, JH, 54, 55, 56–7, 84, 170, 215
Bakhtin, Mikhail, 15, 120
Ball, John, 84
Barber, CL, 120
Barker, Francis, 20–1, 39
Basle Council (1435), 122
Bate, Jonathan, 21, 28, 29, 34, 42, 87, 218
Baxter, Richard, 78
blank charters, 106–7
Bodin, Jean, 193–4
bondsmen, 108
Borgia, Cesare, 196–7
Bossewell, John, 141–2
Boyer, Allen, 27–8
Bracton, Henry de:
    lex facit regem, 20, 25, 99
    limited monarchy, 86, 98, 101, 133, 181
    on princely education, 174
Brown J, Anthony, 97, 99–100
Browne, W, 40
Brutus, 34–6, 37, 38, 178
Buc, George, 156, 157
Burrow, Colin, 169
Burton, Robert, 144, 209–10, 212
Bye Plot, 195, 199

Caesar, Julius, 44
Calvin, John, 203–4
Canning, William, 51
canon law, 25
Carnival, 117–26
Catholicism:
    execution of Catholics, 42, 142
    Shakespeare's allusions to, 42
    torture of Jesuits, 42
Cavell, Stanley, 48
Cecil, Robert, 75–6
censorship, 10, 87, 113–15
certiorari, 88
chain, metaphor, 53–4, 59–64
Chaloner, Thomas, 149
Chamberlain, Lord, 10, 122
Chambers, EK, 126

Index

Chancery Court, 4, 215–16
Charles I, 17, 37, 86, 112, 187
Charles VI (King of France), 82
children, engagement, 138–9
Cicero, Marcus Tullius, 22, 34, 125, 139, 177, 178
Cinthio, Giovanni Baptista Giraldi, 198, 200
Cleinias, 194
Clement's Inn, 166–7, 168
Cobham, Baron, 199, 200
Codrington, Robert, 46
coins, 187–8
Coke, Edward:
   alternative constitution, 80–1
   artificial reason of law, 13, 38, 202, 215
   Bacon and, 80–1, 132–3
   on Brutus, 34–6, 38
   career, 171, 186–7, 215
   Cicero and, 22
   Codrington Elegy, 46
   common law and, 40, 50
      common pleas, 56
      custom, 45, 104
      property law, 97
      sovereignty, 215
   conservatism, 56, 79
   Court of High Commission and, 26–7
   on Cowell, 190
   Crown monopolies, 75, 76, 78
   on *de donis conditionalibus*, 97
   Dr Bonham's Case (1611), 38
   Ellesmere and, 186–7
   foundation of English law, 5, 16–17, 132–3, 178
   freedom of trade, 54
   James I's Proclamations and, 186
   on King's Bench, 57
   on kingship, 204
   lex terrae, 106
   limited monarchy, 181
   natural law, 5, 22, 33, 38, 46, 80, 133, 164
   Nicholas Fuller's Case (1607), 26
   poetic imagination, 132–3
   Postnati. Calvin's Case, 64, 99, 133, 161
   on *Premunire* statutes, 216
   primacy of Parliament, 186
   principles, 30
   religion and law, 44, 45, 62, 73, 78, 92
   Reports, royal examination, 80
   rhetoric, 64, 161
   on royal crown, 103
   Royal Prerogative and, 9, 36, 79
   Sir Anthony Roper's Case, 27
   Slade's Case, 61–2, 63, 64, 75
   Taylors of Ipswich, 79–80
   theatre and, 27–8, 36
   on treason, 108, 109–10, 112
   wager of law v jury trial, 61–2

Coleridge, Samuel Taylor, 6, 8, 13
Collinson, Patrick, 41
Comedy of Errors:
   assumpsit jurisdiction, 55–9
   breaking bonds, 73–81
   chain metaphor, 53–4, 59–64
   classical unities, 65
   commercial values, 53–4, 65–73
   conclusion, 182
   contract, 14–15, 53
      consideration, 67–9
      promise, 55–9, 67–8
   Ephesus location, 60, 65
   farce, 58, 61
   freedom of contract, 54
   laissez-faire market forces, 59
   lawyers and, 14
   mirrors, 70, 101–2
   performances, 8, 14, 51–2
   revels, 51–3, 69–73
   sorcery, 60
   sources, 51, 58–9, 64
commerce, *Comedy of Errors* and, 53–4, 65–73
common land, 151
common law:
   absolutism and, *Titus Andronicus*, 21–9
   artificial reason, 13
   authority, 50
   custom and, 45, 104, 170
   equity and, 4
   fiction of antiquity, 17, 160–2
   foundation, 5, 13, 16–17, 132–3, 178
   James I and, 190, 202–3
   landowners' knowledge of, 168
   legitimacy, 40
   'let's kill all the lawyers,' 152, 153–9
   lex terrae, 22, 85, 106, 120
   natural law and, 5, 22, 38, 80, 164
   pastoral idyll, *Henry IV, Part 2*, 159–73
   religion and, 92, 211–13
   royal powers and, 78
   sacerdotal role, 44–5, 154–5
   sovereignty, 29, 44, 215
   statute law or, 216
   Thomas of Woodstock, 88–9
Common Pleas, Court of, 53, 55–8, 59, 121
community:
   Aristotle, 6, 9, 31, 34, 108, 112, 121, 171–2, 219
   equitable commonwealth, 34
   Henry IV, Part 2, 179
   law and, 5–7, 10
   musical metaphor, 31
   Richard II, 108
conscience, 212–13
contract:
   assumpsit, 53, 55–8

Index

Comedy of Errors and, 14–15, 53
   chain symbol, 59–64
   consideration, 67–9
   deeds, 55
   freedom of contract, 54
   jurisdiction, 53, 55–8
   marriage, 204–10
   promise, 55–9, 65, 67–8, 75
   remedies, 55–7
   social contract, 81
Coriolanus, 28, 48, 148, 220
counterfeiting, 188
Cowell, John, 45, 169–70, 189–90, 203
Cromartie, Alan, 29
Curtain Theatre, 7, 113
custom:
   common law and, 45, 104, 170
   Fortescue, 164–5, 172–3
   lex terrae, 22, 85, 106, 120
   Midsummer Night's Dream, folkloric rites, 120–4
   natural law and, 172–3
   pastoralism, *Henry IV*, 162, 171, 179
   perfect justice and, 164–5
   Titus Andronicus, 49

Davison, Francis, 52
Day, John, 64, 155, 157, 158
de donis conditionalibus, 96–100
de presenti marriage, 205–6
Dekker, Thomas, 7, 112–13
Demetrius, 33
Denmark, judicial model, 203
Denning, Lord, 159–61, 171
Derrida, Jacques, 214
Diana, 111
Dido, 36
Dionysus, 118
Doddridge, John, 155
Draco, 74
dreams, 126–33, 219
Druids, 44–5, 47, 178
Dudley, Robert, 117–18
Dugdale, William:
   exercises for law students, 155
   Inner Temple revels (1561), 117, 118–19, 120
   on Inns of Court, 168
   on jurisdictional conflicts, 213–14
   patriarchy, 139
   sacerdotal role of judges, 44
Dyer CJ, James, 59, 93–4, 97, 98–9

Ebrington, 159, 160, 161–2
ecclesiastical causes, 25–7, 204–5, 208
Edmund the Martyr, Saint, 82, 83
Edward II, 108–9
Edward the Confessor, 82, 83
Egypt, 29

Elizabeth I:
   abolition of Feast of the Boy Bishop, 122
   censorship of theatre, 113
   death, 50, 183
   early poetic drama and, 7
   iconography, 111, 152
   imperialism and common law, 21–2, 23–9
   masks, 111
   poetic descriptions, 34
   portraits, 2
   Richard II and, 86
   succession issue, 17, 21, 24, 25, 173, 183
   surveillance, 195
   theatricality, 87, 115
   Virgin Queen, 42, 111
Ellesmere, Lord, 13, 40, 186–7, 188, 212–13, 215–16
Elyot, Thomas, 25, 34, 39, 171–2, 175–6, 179
entails, 96–100
Ephesus, 60, 65
equity, common law and, 4
escheat, 105
Essex, Earl of:
   rebellion (1601), 10, 86–7
   treason trial, 109–10, 112
ethics, aesthetics and, 3–4
Euripides, 133
Exchequer Court, 58
excommunication, 205

The Famous Victories of Henry V, 177
fatherhood:
   children's engagement, 138–9
   Henry IV, Part 2, 159, 162, 173–8
   kingship and, 178–81
   Measure for Measure, kingship and, 191
   symbolism, 178–81
Feast of Fools, 122
Feast of Saint Nicholas, 122
Feast of the Ass, 122, 131
Feast of the Boy Bishop, 122
Ferne, John, 77–8, 156–7
festivals, 117–26
Filmer, Robert, 177–8
Fleetwood, William, 201
Fleming, Thomas, 187
Foakes, RA, 20, 43
fools, 122, 130, 149–50
forfeiture, 105
fornication, 204–10
Fortescue, Denzil George, Lord, 162
Fortescue, John:
   ancient constitution thesis, 163–5
   career, 29, 161, 161–2
   custom, 164–5, 172–3
   De Laudibus Legum Angliae, 161–2
   English law and natural law, 4–5
   foundations of English law, 5, 131

Index

Fortescue, John (*cont.*):
  Henry IV and, 159, 161–2, 174
  influence on judiciary, 90–1
  on Inns of Court, 166, 167
  on kingship, 193
  on legal education, 156, 167
  limited monarchy, 89–90, 90–1, 133, 181
  mixed polity, 9, 25, 164
  natural law, 165, 172–3
  nostalgic values, 16, 156
  pastoralism, 165
  perfect justice, 164–5
  praecipe writs, 172
  on princely education, 174
  principles, 30
  sacerdotal role of judges, 44, 154
  superiority of English law, 164
  supremacy of common law, 29
Foucault, Michel, 81, 112
France:
  absolutism, 163–4
  Druids, 44
Fraunce, Abraham, 155, 156
free trade, 54, 72, 75–81
French, 176
Froissart, Jean, 84, 176
Fulbecke, William, 39, 40, 50, 145, 154–5, 211, 212

Gascoigne, William, 176, 178
gates of law, 214
Gerard, Gilbert, 189
Gesta Grayorum, 53, 71
Gheeraerts the Younger, Marcus, 2n7
Girard, René, 43, 48
Gleason, JH, 166, 168
Globe Theatre, 7, 113–14
Gloriana, 111
Gloucestershire, 159, 161, 162, 165, 169, 172–3, 179
gold, 188–9
Golding, Arthur, 73
good governance:
  Aristotle, 101, 171–2
  body politic, 95
  patriarchy and, 139
  Shakespeare's vision, 9
  Titus Andronicus, 29–33
  utopias, 8, 36, 37, 147, 194–5, 218–9
Goodrich, P, 48
Gordon, Dillian, 83
Gosson, Stephen, 116
Grand Vacation moots, 155–6
Gray's Inn:
  Feast of the Ass, 122, 131
  performance of *Comedy of Errors* (1594), 14, 51
  revels (1594), 52–3, 69–73

Great Seal, 188
Greece, ancient Greece, 6, 30, 132–3
  see also Athens
Greenblatt, Stephen, 1, 43n121, 115, 158, 180
Greene, Robert, 128–30, 133
Grey, Lord, 199, 200
Guy, John, 25, 34, 177

habeas corpus, 27, 88
Hall, Edward, 177
Hamlet, 92–3
Haringtom, John, 2n7
Hatton, Christopher, 118
Hector, 36
Hecuba, 36
Helen of Troy, 134, 135
Helmes, Henry, 52
Henry II, 44
Henry IV, Part 2:
  civil rebellion, 150
  conclusion, 182
  drama in two parts, 158
  Falstaff, 159, 162, 170–1, 172, 174, 179–80
  fatherhood, 159, 162, 173–78
    kingship and, 178–81
  Gloucestershire, 162, 165, 166, 169, 172–3, 179
  Justice Shallow, 16, 159, 161, 165–73
  'let's kill all the lawyers,' 129, 152, 153–9
  Lord Chief Justice, 159, 161, 162, 170–1, 174–81
  pastoral idyll of the common law, 159–73
  princely education, 159, 173–8
Henry IV, rebellion against, 150, 174, 177, 179
Henry VI, 29
Henry VIII, 25, 34, 122
Henry, Prince of Wales, 126, 127, 130–1, 196
Henslowe, Philip, 7, 18n1, 18n2, 51
heraldry, 104, 210
Hersey, George, 31
Heywood, Thomas, 1, 19, 20
High Commission, Court of, 25–7
Hippolytus, 135–6
Hobbes, Thomas, 177–8, 220
Holdsworth, WS, 168
Holinshed, Raphael, 175, 177
Holland, Peter, 136, 137
Homer, 36
Hooker, Richard:
  Church and State, 31
  justice and religion, 212
  limited monarchy, 25, 34, 86
  Of the Laws of Ecclesiastical Polity, 41
  reason and law, 139–40
  on religious ritual, 16, 42
Howard Carr, Frances, 122
Hoyle, Richard, 107
Hughes, Thomas, 40n108

Index

Humphreys, AR, 169, 173
Hunt, Maurice, 74, 75
Hutson, Lorna, 60, 85n13

Ibbetson, David, 61
Ìïžek, Slavoj, 149–50
Inner Temple, 7, 24, 117–19, 120, 141
Inns of Court:
   early poetic drama and, 7
   honour and virtue, 142, 156–7
   legal education, 156, 167, 168
   revels, 51–2, 117, 121, 141
Isabella of France, 82

James I:
   absolutism, 17, 190
   accession, 17
   as Brutus, 2n10
   Feast of the Ass, 122
   judiciary and, 185, 201–3, 216
   on kingship, 17, 183–4
      divine right, 191–2, 194
   Measure for Measure and, 183
   plots against, 195, 199
   Proclamations, 186–7, 190
   Royal Prerogative, 17
   sovereignty, 133
   surveillance, 195–6
   theatre of kingship, 185, 199–200
Jesuits, 42
John the Baptist, Saint, 82, 83
John's Gospel, 211
Jones, William, 45
Jonson, Ben, 127, 130–1, 133
judicial review, Rose Playhouse case, 18, 21
judiciary:
   Aristotle on, 100
   common law and religion, 92
   conservatism, 56
   Fortescue's influence, 90–1
   imperial governance and, 201–2
   James I and, 185, 201–3, 216
   kingship and, 100–1
   delegates, 185
   limitation of monarchy, 15
   pastoral idyll of the common law, 159–73
   poetic imagination, 4, 12, 100, 132–3, 138, 145–6, 221
   pragmatism, 85
   Royal Prerogative and, 203
   sacerdotal role, 44–5, 154–5
jury trial, 61
justice:
   Aristotle, 121, 133, 171
   goddesses, 29–30
   Henry IV, Part 2, 171–3
   Measure for Measure, 204–17
   Titus Andronicus

absolutism and, 18–23
anatomical image, 39
executive power and, 18–23
order, harmony and musicality, 22, 29–33
religion and, 40
justices of the peace, 162–3, 166, 168, 173
Justinian, 20, 29, 203

Kantorowicz, Ernst, 15, 85–6, 89–90, 94–5, 97–101
Keeton, George, 175
King's Bench:
   appeals from, 58
   assumpsit jurisdiction, 53, 55–8
   contract promise, 59, 65
   function, 57n25
   use, 121
kingship
   see also absolutism; Royal Prerogative
   anointment, 91
   coins and, 187–8
   common law and royal powers, 78
   divine right, 92
      Measure for Measure, 191–204
   fatherhood and
      Henry IV, Part 2, 159, 178–81
      James I, 191
   forfeiture, 108–9
   Henry IV, Part 2
      fatherhood and, 159, 178–81
      princely education, 159, 173–8
   Hooker on, 31
   James I on, 17, 183–4
   king's two bodies, 15, 39, 85, 94, 95, 98–9, 101, 103, 112
   lex facit regem, 20, 25, 99
   lex loquens, 204
   limited monarchy, 15
      Bracton, 86, 98, 101
      Elizabethan judiciary and, 100–1
      Fortescue, 89–90, 90–1, 133, 181
      property law, 88–101
   portraiture and, 2
   quod principi placuit legis habet vigorem, 20
   Richard II, 15, 82–8, 89, 98, 100, 181
      counterfeiting, 112–16
   theatre of kingship, 87–8, 115–16, 180–1, 185, 199–200
koinonia, 219
Kott, Jan, 136–7

Lambarde, William, 86, 163, 166, 169, 173, 200–1, 204, 214
language, legal language, 176
Latin, 176
law:
   artificial reason, 13, 38, 202, 215
   Athenian law, 15, 126, 137, 138

249

Index

law (*cont.*):
  chain metaphor, 53–4
  community and, 5–7, 10
  embodiment in plays, 9–10
  gates, 214
  imaginative application, 132–3, 137–8
  mirrors of the law, 104
  poetic imagination, 4, 12, 100, 132–3, 138, 145–6, 221
  reason and, 139–40, 146
  religion and, 44, 45, 62, 73, 78, 92, 211–13
  theatre of law, 16, 109
lawyers
  see also judiciary
  16th century expansion, 154
  as actors, 11
  Comedy of Errors and, 14, 69–73
  early poetic drama and, 7–8
  Henry IV, Part 2, 129, 152, 153–9
  pastoralism, 159–73
  popular perception, 155, 156–8
  traditional values, 16, 142, 156–7
  training, 155–6, 167–8
  venality, 64, 158
leases, 94–6, 98
Legh, Gerard, 118, 141, 142
lex facit regem, 20, 25, 99
lex loquens, 204
lex talionis, 198, 209
lex terrae, 22, 85, 106, 120
Littleton, Thomas de, 215
Livy, 22, 48
Lupton, Thomas, 198–9, 200
Lyon's Inn, 117

Ma'at, 29
Machiavelli, Niccolò, 196–7, 209, 210
Macintyre, Alasdair, 6
magic, 60
Magna Carta, 36, 56, 107
Main Plot, 195, 199
Manning, Roger, 150–1
Markham, Griffin, 199, 200
marriage:
  contractual forms, 204–10
  parental power, 138–9
Marston, John, 7, 151–2, 157–8
Mary I, 122, 188
Master of the Revels, 10
Matthew's Gospel, 197
Mayday festivities, 124
Mearns, Hugh, 137
Measure for Measure:
  1st performance, 17, 183
  absolutism, 17, 203–4, 219
  conclusion, 182–3
  conscience, 212–13
  departed law-maker, 36

  deus ex machina, 199–200
  divine lawgiver, 191–204
  jurisdictional conflicts, 204–17
  justice, 210
  lawyers, 154
  obliqueness, 220
  prerogative powers, 182–90
  puritanism, 207–12
  religion and politics, 204–17
  stamp metaphor, 186
  substitution, 184–5
  surveillance, 185, 195–7, 207
  theatre imagery, 211
mens rea, 207
mercantilism, 72
Merchant of Venice, 138
metadrama, 13, 126
metaphors, 1–2
middle class, ascendancy, 14–15
Middle Temple, 110–11, 117, 157–8
Midsummer Night's Dream:
  1st performance, 132
  Arcadia, 118, 126, 129
  conclusion, 182
  dreams, 126–33, 219
  festival and subversion, 117–26
  metadrama, 126
  rare vision, 145–52
  reality and illusion, 119, 120, 127
  rituals, 15–16, 120
  satyrs and fairies, 126–33, 140–1
  sources, 146, 149
  violence on the edge, 133–45, 152
Mill, John Stuart, 6, 8
mines, 188–9
Minos, 136
Minotaur, 136, 137
mirrors, 70, 101–4, 115
The Mirror for Magistrates, 104–5
Misrule, Lord of, 118–23, 179
monopolies, Crown monopolies, 54, 70, 75–81
Montaigne, Michel de, 2n9
More, Thomas, 8, 36, 40, 147, 218, 219
Moses, 178
Mulcaster, Robert, 162

Nashe, Thomas, 7, 128, 130, 142, 209
natural law:
  Aristotle, 100
  Coke, 5, 22, 33, 38, 46, 80, 133, 164
  common law and, 5, 8, 22, 80, 164
  custom and, 172–3
  Fortescue, 165, 172–3
  Hobbes, 220
  scripture and, 212
  Titus Andronicus, 38
Neoplatonism, 34
Nietzsche, Friedrich, 52, 81

Index

North, Thomas, 134, 146
Norton, Thomas, 7, 24, 42
Nussbaum, Martha, 4, 12
Nuttall, AD, 49, 59, 132

Orco, Remirro de, 196–7
Orpheus, 30, 31, 32–3
Ovid, 23, 36, 41, 50, 111–12, 137, 165, 218

Pasiphae, 136
pastoralism:
    ancient constitution thesis, 163–4
    common law and, 159–73
    English agrarianism, 164
    justices of the peace and, 162–3
patriarchy *see* fatherhood
Paul, Saint, 60, 63, 73, 147–8, 149, 219
Peacham, Henry, 39
Peasants' Revolt (1381), 84, 176
Petition of Right (1628), 17, 215
Phaedra, 135
Philomela, 36, 41
Pittheus, 138
plague, 17, 51, 183
Plato:
    chain metaphor, 64
    communitarianism and, 34
    dikaiosuné, 101
    good governance, 148, 194–5
    humanism and, 177, 178
    justice, 30, 39
    kosmos, 22
    nomos, 30
    on poets, 146
    Republic, 147
    utopia, 194–5
Plautus, 51, 58, 59, 64
playhouses:
    audiences, 112–13
    censorship, 113–15
    Elizabethan England, 2–3, 7
    liminal status, 88, 114
playing companies, patrons, 114
Plowden, Edmund:
    on coins, 188
    Comedy of Errors and, 54
    consideration, 68–9
    on equity, 216
    King's two bodies, 39
    law reports, 5
    property law, 15, 84, 88–101
    Sharington v Strotton, 68–9
Plutarch, 22, 73–4, 134–5, 146, 172
Pocock, JGA, 164
poetic drama:
    as microcosm, 1
    Elizabethan community and, 7
    ethics and aesthetics, 3–4

    origins, 7–8, 24
    textual ambivalence, 3
poetic imagination, 4, 12, 100, 132–3, 138, 145–6, 221
Polybius, 178
Popham, John, 56, 174–5
portraits, royal portraiture, 2
positive law, 138
praecipe writs, 75, 169–70, 172
precedents, 9, 11–12, 28–9, 43, 48, 173
Premunire, 216
prerogative powers *see* Royal Prerogative
printing, 34
Proclamations, 186–7, 190
property law:
    Crown forfeiture of land, 84, 88–101
    earth regulation, 123
    lex terrae, 106–7
    Plowden *Reports*, 15, 84, 88–101
    Richard II, 15, 84, 94, 95–6
    sale of Crown land, 107
    succession, 94–5
puritanism, 8, 207–12
Puttenham, George, 145, 146, 147

quod principi placuit legis habet vigorem, 20, 189

rebellion, 75, 150–2, 153, 165, 174, 179
religion:
    anointing kings, 91
    conscience and, 212–13
    corpus mysticum of the Church, 94
    executions of Catholics, 42
    law and, 44, 45, 62, 73, 78, 92, 211–13
    politics and, *Measure for Measure*, 204–17
    puritanism, 207–12
    rites, 140
    state supremacy, 48–9
    Titus Andronicus
        religious rites, 23, 37–42
        sacrifice, 42–50
revels, 51–3, 65–73, 110–11, 114, 117–18, 121, 141
rhetoric manuals, 12
Rice, Douglas, 175
Rich, Nathaniel, 17
Richard II:
    abdication, 109
    Wilton Diptych, 82–5
Richard II:
    absolutism, 10, 86
    conclusion, 182
    deposition scene, 87, 109, 115
    dominium, 90
    Essex Rebellion and, 10, 86–7
    image and mirrors, 101–5, 115
    John of Gaunt speech, 83, 107, 108
    kingship, 15, 82–8, 89, 91–2, 98, 100, 181

Index

Richard II (cont.):
 lex terrae, 106–7
 love of English earth, 105–6
 property law, 15, 84, 88–101
 Royal Prerogative, 85
 sale of Crown land, 107
 sources, 88, 104
 theatrical representation of monarchy, 112–16
 treason, 85–6, 105–6, 108–12
riots, 75, 150–2
rituals, Carnival, 117–26
Roman law, 5
Rome:
 allegory for London, 201
 bondsmen, 108
 lawyers as actors, 11
 liberty, 178
 paterfamilias, 179
 quod principi placuit legis habet vigorem, 189
 Shakespeare and, 22
 Titus Andronicus, 34–5
Romeo and Juliet, 127
Romulus, 133–4, 146
Rose Theatre, 7, 18, 21, 51, 113–14
Rose Theatre Trust, 18
Royal Prerogative
 see also absolutism
 Charles I and, 37
 Coke and, 36
 Cowdrey's Case (1591), 26
 Crown monopolies, 75–81
 Elizabethan emphasis, 25, 86
 increasing use, 9
 James I, 17, 202–3
 Measure for Measure, 182–90
 Petition of Right and, 215
 property law and, 97–9
 Richard II, 85, 91

Sacks, David Harris, 61
Sacks, DH, 57n25
Sackville, Thomas, 7, 24
St Germain, Christopher, 9, 25, 30, 69, 71, 100, 101, 133
Samuel, 193–4
Samuell, John, Alice and Agnes, 142–5
Saul, Nigel, 84
Saunders. Trevor, 30
scapegoats, 43
Selden, John, 37–8, 44–5, 50, 111–12, 161–2, 165, 192–3, 213
Seneca, 137
Serjeants at Law, 11
Sermon on the Mount, 208
Severus Alexander, Emperor, 201
Shakespeare, William:
 'The Phoenix and the Turtle,' 103
 plays *see* specific titles

Sharpe, JA, 167
Sharpe, Kevin, 28–9
Shelley, Percy Bysshe, 3–4, 221
Sidney, Philip, 1, 3–4, 24, 221
silver, 188–9
slavery, 54, 74–5
Smith, Thomas, 34, 108, 186
social contract, 9
Solly-Flood, Frederick, 176
Solon, 73–4
Somerset, Earl of, 122
Somerville, John, 174
Sophocles, 131–2, 133
Spain, war with, 107
Spelman, Henry, 44, 124–5
Spencer of Wormleighton, Lord, 126
Spenser, Edmund, 34, 36
sponsolia per verba de futuro, 138–9, 205–6
sponsolia per verba de praesenti, 205
standing, judicial review, 18
Star Chamber, 184, 202
Statius, Publius Papinius, 125
Straw, Jack, 84
Stubbes, Philip, 121, 124, 130, 208, 209, 211
suicide, 92–4
sumptuary laws, 79
surveillance, 185, 195–7
Swan Playhouse, 7, 113–14

Tacitus, 4
tailors, 79–80
Tawney, RH, 46
Tempest, 65, 218
Theatre Playhouse, 7, 113
Themis, 30
theocracy, 207–9
Theopompus, 172
Theseus, 133–8, 146
Thomas of Canterbury, Saint, 91
Thomas of Woodstock, 88–9
Thompson, EP, 121
Three Witches of Warboys, 144
Throgmorton, Joan, 144
Tillyard, EMW, 158, 159, 162, 168, 169, 170
tithes, 27
Titus Andronicus:
 1st performance (1594), 18, 51
 absolutism, 18–29
 allegory, 19–20
 central metaphor, 32
 Clown's execution, 20–1
 common law and Elizabethan imperialism, 23–9
 conclusion, 182
 images of body politic, 22–3
 law, justice and executive power, 18–23
 legal language, 28

252

Index

mutilation of Lavinia, 32–3, 36, 38–9, 48, 49, 135
order, harmony and musicality, 29–33
plot, 19, 29
religious rites, 23, 37–422
revenge tragedy, 23, 47
sacrifice, 42–50
triumph of unwritten law, 49
Troynovant, 33–7
violence, 42–50
virgin goddess of justice, 23–4
vision of dislocated body politic, 14, 32–3, 38–40, 219
Topcliffe, Richard, 42
torture, 42
Tourneur, Timothy, 217
treason, 85–6, 105–6, 108–12, 142, 188
Trevelyan, GM, 173
Trotte, Nicholas, 40n108
Troy, 22, 33–8
Troynovant, 22, 33–7
Twelfth Night, 8
Tyler, Wat, 84

Ulysses, 40
utopias, 8, 36, 37, 194–5, 218–9

utter barristers, 167

Venus, 111
Virgil, 22, 36
Virgin Mary, 42, 83–4

wager of law, 54, 60–2
Walsingham, Francis, 195
Warboys witchcraft trials, 142–5
Warwickshire, 159
Waterhouse, Edward, 11
Weston, J, 97, 98, 100, 101
Whetstone, George, 198, 200–1
White, James Boyd, 11
Whitman, Walt, 4
Willymat, William, 196
Wilson, Thomas, 12, 154
Wilton Diptych, 82–5
witchcraft trials, 142–5
women, transgressors, 40
Wray, Christopher, 174

Yates, Frances, 42
Yelverton, Serjeant, 110, 112

Zeus, 194